ACCA

PAPER P6

ADVANCED TAXATION (UK)
FA 2006

FOR THE EXAM IN DECEMBER 2007

BPP
LEARNING MEDIA

First edition 2007

ISBN 9780 7517 3373 0

British Library Cataloguing-in-Publication Data
A catalogue record for this book is available from the
British Library

Published by

BPP Learning Media ltd
BPP House, Aldine Place
London W12 8AA

www.bpp.com/learningmedia

Printed in Great Britain by
Page Bros
Mile Cross Lane
Norwich
NR6 6SA

Your learning materials, published by BPP Learning
Media Ltd, are printed on paper sourced from
sustainable, managed forests.

We are grateful to the Association of Chartered
Certified Accountants for permission to reproduce past
examination questions. The answers to past
examination questions have been prepared by BPP
Learning Media Ltd, except where otherwise stated.

Contents

Question index

The headings in this checklist/index indicate the main topics of questions, but questions often cover several different topics.

Preparation questions with helping hand provide you with a firm foundation for attempts at exam-standard questions and give tips on how to approach questions which will be helpful if you are unsure where to start.

Questions with answer plan offer a possible answer plan to give you a plan of attack for the question.

Questions with analysis show how to annotate questions to highlight key points, as you will need to do in the examination. The answers show the key points your answer should have contained.

Questions set under the old syllabus exam are included in this kit (labelled ATAX and the date of the exam) because their style and content are similar to those that will appear in the new syllabus exam. The questions have been amended as appropriate to reflect the new syllabus exam format.

BPP
LEARNING MEDIA

Mock exam 1

Questions 36-40

Mock exam 2

Questions 41-45

Mock exam 3 (Pilot paper)

Questions 46-50

Planning your question practice

Our guidance from page 27 shows you how to organise your question practice, either by attempting questions from each syllabus area or **by building your own exams** – tackling questions as a series of practice exams.

Topic index

Listed below are the key Paper P6 syllabus topics and the numbers of the questions in this Kit covering those topics.

If you need to concentrate your practice and revision on certain topics or if you want to attempt all available questions that refer to a particular subject, you will find this index useful.

Syllabus topic	Question numbers
Capital gains liabilities, exemptions and reliefs	2, 4, 6, 10, 11, 12, 14, 19, 22, 24, 25, 26, 27, 28, 29, 30, 32, 34, 35, 36, 37, 38, 39, 41, 46, 48, 49
Corporation tax liabilities, reliefs and planning including groups	5, 6, 14, 15, 16, 17, 18, 19, 20, 21, 22, 24, 25, 27, 30, 31, 34, 35, 36, 38, 42, 44, 46, 48, 49
Employment/sole trader/dividend planning	2, 3, 4, 5, 6, 7, 8, 9, 14, 23, 24, 28, 33, 35, 39, 45, 47, 48
Ethics	8, 16, 18, 22, 25, 30, 36, 39, 43, 47
Income tax liabilities and reliefs (including pensions)	1, 2, 5, 6, 7, 9, 10, 13, 14, 23, 24, 26, 28, 32, 33, 34, 35, 36, 37, 41, 43, 44, 45, 47, 48, 50
Inheritance tax liabilities and planning	10, 11, 12, 13, 14, 24, 27, 29, 32, 35, 36, 40, 43, 49, 50
NIC planning	5, 13, 33, 41, 45, 47
Personal and corporate financial planning	19, 21, 26, 30, 31, 32, 34, 42, 43, 47, 50
VAT liabilities and reliefs	6, 7, 15, 16, 17, 19, 22, 23, 24, 25, 33, 38, 41, 47

Using your BPP Practice and Revision Kit

Tackling revision and the exam

You can significantly improve your chances of passing by tackling revision and the exam in the right ways. Our advice is based on recent feedback from ACCA examiners.

- We look at the dos and don'ts of revising for, and taking, ACCA exams
- We focus on Paper P6; we discuss revising the syllabus, what to do (and what not to do) in the exam, how to approach different types of question and ways of obtaining easy marks

Selecting questions

We provide signposts to help you plan your revision.

- A full **question index**
- A **topic index** listing all the questions that cover key topics, so that you can locate the questions that provide practice on these topics, and see the different ways in which they might be examined
- **BPP's question plan** highlighting the most important questions and explaining why you should attempt them
- **Build your own exams**, showing how you can practise questions in a series of exams

Making the most of question practice

At BPP we realise that you need more than just questions and model answers to get the most from your question practice.

- Our **Top tips** provide essential advice on tackling questions, presenting answers and the key points that answers need to include
- We show you how you can pick up **Easy marks** on questions, as we know that picking up all readily available marks often can make the difference between passing and failing
- We summarise **Examiner's comments** to show you how students who sat the exam coped with the questions
- We include ACCA's **marking guides** to show you what the examiner rewards
- We refer to the **BPP Finance Act 2006 edition of the Study Text** for detailed coverage of the topics covered in each question
- A number of questions include **Analysis** and **Helping hands** attached to show you how to approach them if you are struggling

Attempting mock exams

There are three mock exams that provide practice at coping with the pressures of the exam day. We strongly recommend that you attempt them under exam conditions. **Mock exams 1 and 2** reflect the question styles and syllabus coverage of the exam; **Mock exam 3** is the actual Pilot Paper. To help you get the most out of doing these exams, we not only provide help with each answer, but also guidance on how you should have approached the whole exam.

Passing ACCA exams

Revising and taking ACCA exams

To maximise your chances of passing your ACCA exams, you must make best use of your time, both before the exam during your revision, and when you are actually doing the exam.

- Making the most of your revision time can make a big, big difference to how well-prepared you are for the exam

- Time management is a core skill in the exam hall; all the work you've done can be wasted if you don't make the most of the three hours you have to attempt the exam

In this section we simply show you what to do and what not to do during your revision, and how to increase and decrease your prospects of passing your exams when you take them. Our advice is grounded in feedback we've had from ACCA examiners. You may be surprised to know that much examiner advice is the same whatever the exam, and the reasons why many students fail don't vary much between subjects and exam levels. So if you follow the advice we give you over the next few pages, you will **significantly** enhance your chances of passing **all** your ACCA exams.

How to revise

☑ Plan your revision

At the start of your revision period, you should draw up a **timetable** to plan how long you will spend on each subject and how you will revise each area. You need to consider the total time you have available and also the time that will be required to revise for other exams you're taking.

☑ Practise Practise Practise

The **more exam-standard questions** you do, the **more likely you are to pass** the exam. Practising full questions will mean that you'll get used to the time pressure of the exam. When the time is up, you should note where you've got to and then try to complete the question, giving yourself practice at everything the question tests.

☑ Revise enough

Make sure that your revision covers the breadth of the syllabus, as in most papers most topics could be examined in a compulsory question. However it is true that some topics are **key** – they often appear in compulsory questions or are a particular interest of the examiner – and you need to spend sufficient time revising these. Make sure you also know the **basics** – the fundamental calculations, proformas and layouts.

☑ Deal with your difficulties

Difficult areas are topics you find dull and pointless, or subjects that you found problematic when you were studying them. You mustn't become negative about these topics; instead you should build up your knowledge by reading the **Passcards** and using the **Quick quiz** questions in the Study Text to test yourself. When practising questions in the Kit, go back to the Text if you're struggling.

☑ Learn from your mistakes

Having completed a question you must try to look at your answer critically. Always read the **Top tips guidance** in the answers; it's there to help you. Look at **Easy marks** to see how you could have quickly gained credit on the questions that you've done. As you go through the Kit, it's worth noting any traps you've fallen into, and key points in the **Top tips** or **Examiner's comments** sections, and referring to these notes in the days before the exam. Aim to learn at least one new point from each question you attempt, a technical point perhaps or a point on style or approach.

☑ Read the examiners' guidance

We refer at certain points throughout this Kit to **Examiner's comments**; these relate to old syllabus Paper 3.2 exams but will be equally valid for Paper P6. These are also available on ACCA's website. As well as highlighting weaknesses, examiners' reports as often provide clues to future questions, as many examiners will quickly test again areas where problems have arisen. ACCA's website also contains articles by examiners which you **must** read, as they may form the basis of questions on any paper after they've been published.

☑ Complete all three mock exams

You should attempt the **Mock exams** at the end of the Kit under **strict exam conditions**, to gain experience of selecting questions, managing your time and producing answers.

How NOT to revise

☒ Revise selectively

Examiners are well aware that some students try to forecast the contents of exams, and only revise those areas that they think will be examined. Examiners try to prevent this by doing the unexpected, for example setting the same topic in successive sittings or setting topics in compulsory questions that have previously only been examined in optional questions.

☒ Spend all the revision period reading

You cannot pass the exam just by learning the contents of Passcards, Course Notes or Study Texts. You have to develop your **application skills** by practising questions.

☒ Audit the answers

This means reading the answers and guidance without having attempted the questions. Auditing the answers gives you **false reassurance** that you would have tackled the questions in the best way and made the points that our answers do. The feedback we give in our answers will mean more to you if you've attempted the questions and thought through the issues.

☒ Practise some types of question, but not others

Paper P6 is predominately a written paper so you must focus your studies on **practising written question** parts. However, you will often need to provide supporting calculations for your written answers, usually in an appendix, so ensure that you **practise the numbers** element too.

☒ Get bogged down

Don't spend a lot of time worrying about all the minute detail of certain topic areas, and leave yourself insufficient time to cover the rest of the syllabus. Remember that a key skill in the exam is the ability to **concentrate on what's important** and this applies to your revision as well.

☒ Overdo studying

Studying for too long without interruption will mean your studying becomes less effective. A five minute break each hour will help. You should also make sure that you are leading a **healthy lifestyle** (proper meals, good sleep and some times when you're not studying).

How to PASS your exams

☑ Prepare for the day

Make sure you set at least one alarm (or get an alarm call), and allow plenty of time to get to the exam hall. You should have your route planned in advance and should listen on the radio for potential travel problems. You should check the night before to see that you have pens, pencils, erasers, watch, calculator with spare batteries, also exam documentation and evidence of identity.

☑ Select the right questions

You should select the optional questions you feel you can answer **best**, basing your selection on the topics covered, the requirements of the question, how easy it will be to apply the requirements and the availability of easy marks.

☑ Plan your three hours

You need to make sure that you will be answering the correct number of questions, and that you spend the right length of time on each question – this will be determined by the number of marks available. Each mark carries with it a **time allocation** of **1.8 minutes**. A 25 mark question therefore should be selected, completed and checked in 45 minutes. Unless you are extremely confident it is probably better to attempt the two optional question on Paper P6 first.

☑ Read the questions carefully

To score well, you must follow the requirements of the question, understanding what aspects of the subject area are being covered, and the tasks you will have to carry out. The requirements will also determine what information and examples you should provide. Reading the question scenarios carefully will help you decide what **issues** to discuss, **techniques** to use, **information** and **examples** to include and how to **organise** your answer.

☑ Plan your answers

You have fifteen minutes reading time for this paper. Use it wisely, selecting your optional questions and planning your answers. Consider when you're planning how your answer should be **structured, w**hat the **format** should be and **how long** each part should take.

Confirm before you start writing that your plan makes **sense,** covers **all relevant points** and does not include **irrelevant material.**

☑ Show evidence of application of knowledge

Remember that examiners aren't just looking for a display of knowledge; they want to see how well you can **apply** the knowledge you have. Evidence of application will include writing answers that only contain **relevant** material, using the facts to **support** what you say and stating any **assumptions** you make.

☑ Stay until the end of the exam

Use any spare time to **check and recheck** your script. This includes checking you have filled out the candidate details correctly, you have labelled question parts and workings clearly, you have used headers and underlining effectively and spelling, grammar and arithmetic are correct.

How to FAIL your exams

☒ Don't do the correct number of questions

If you don't attempt sufficient questions on the paper, you are making it harder for yourself to pass the questions that you do attempt. If for example you don't do a 20 mark question, then you will have to score 50 marks out of 80 marks on the rest of the paper, and therefore have to obtain 63% of the marks on the questions you do attempt. Failing to attempt all of the paper is symptomatic of poor time management or poor question selection.

Similarly, you only have to do two of the three optional questions. You will gain no credit for attempting a third optional question, but you will waste valuable time.

☒ Include irrelevant material

Markers are given detailed mark guides and will not give credit for irrelevant content. The markers will only give credit for what is **relevant**.

☒ Don't do what the question asks

Failing to provide all the examiner asks for will limit the marks you score.

☒ Present your work poorly

Markers will only be able to give you credit if they can read your writing. There are also plenty of other things that will make it more difficult for markers to reward you. Examples include:

- Not using black or blue ink
- Not showing clearly which question you're attempting
- Scattering question parts from the same question throughout your answer booklet
- Not showing clearly workings or the results of your calculations
- Crossing out your workings; never do this they may be right!

Using your BPP products

This Kit gives you the question practice and guidance you need in the exam. Our other products can also help you pass:

- **Learning to Learn Accountancy** gives further valuable advice on revision

- **Passcards** provide you with clear topic summaries and exam tips

- **Success CDs** help you revise on the move

- **i-Pass CDs** offer tests of knowledge against the clock

- **Learn Online** is an e-learning resource delivered via the Internet, offering comprehensive tutor support and featuring areas such as study, practice, email service, revision and useful resources

You can purchase these products by visiting www.bpp.com/mybpp.

Visit our website www.bpp.com/acca/learnonline to sample aspects of Learn Online free of charge.

Passing P6

Revising P6

The P6 syllabus covers a broad range of taxes for individuals and companies. The optional questions, ranging from 15 to 25 marks each, in Section B are similar in content to those set in the previous syllabus, although the style is different. The examiner is still Rory Fish. The two compulsory questions in Section A could now take up the majority of the marks, with 50 to 70 of the available marks allocated (probably unevenly) between them. All of the questions are scenario based, requiring the consideration of more than one tax and possibly the interaction of these taxes. The focus of the exam is now on written solutions with computations required in support of explanations or tax planning advice and not in isolation.

You will find it difficult to pass the exam if you do not attempt all four questions and you should therefore not attempt to 'question spot'. Instead ensure that you have covered the entire syllabus, even those areas that you find dull or uninteresting. It is better to have a broad knowledge for this exam to assist with useful all round tax planning advice than to be specialized in any one area.

Topics to revise

That said, you must have sound knowledge in the following fundamental areas if you are to stand a chance of passing the exam. You should therefore revise the following areas particularly well.

- Proformas for income tax (including capital allowances), capital gains, inheritance tax (IHT) and corporation tax computations so that you can calculate tax liabilities quickly. Make sure that you can also calculate NIC and VAT liabilities without difficulty.

- The calculation of benefits from employment so that you can make sensible comparisons between remuneration packages. Make sure you can advise on tax free benefits too.

- The reliefs available for the different taxes. For example, EIS relief for income tax and capital gains tax (CGT) and taper relief for both CGT and IHT (note the difference in the operation of the relief for these two different taxes). There are, of course, many more reliefs to consider; you must be familiar with them all to be able to provide sound tax advice. Reliefs are the foundation of any tax planning.

- All aspects of corporation tax groups including the impact of associated companies on corporation tax liabilities, loss relief, chargeable gains groups, the effect of group VAT registration and stamp duty groups. You should pay particular attention to the impact on corporate restructuring.

- The special VAT schemes available for small businesses so that you can advise if and when they might be appropriate.

- Overseas issues for income tax, CGT, IHT, corporation tax and VAT.

- Investment opportunities for clients, taking into account their objectives and attitude to risk.

Question practice

Question practice under timed conditions is essential, so that you can get used to the pressures of answering exam questions in **limited time** and practise not only the key techniques but allocating your time between different requirements in each question. Our list of recommended questions includes 23-39 mark Section A questions and Section B questions of various marks.

Passing the P6 exam

Displaying the right qualities

The examiner expects students to display the following qualities.

Qualities required	
Knowledge development	Basic knowledge of the core taxes from Paper F6 is key, extended to encompass further overseas aspects of taxation, capital taxes (IHT and trusts, stamp duty and stamp duty land tax), and additional exemptions and reliefs.
Knowledge application	You must be able to apply your knowledge to the issues commonly encountered by individuals and businesses. You will be expected to consider more than one tax at any one time and to identify planning issues and areas of interaction of the taxes.
Skill development	Paper P6 seeks to develop the skills of analysis and interpretation. You must be able to interpret and analyse the information provided in the question, keeping your answers focused and as accurate as possible, while avoiding waffle.
Communication skills	Paper P6 also seeks to develop the skill of communication. It is no good having the knowledge but not being able to communicate it effectively, so ensure you keep your communication appropriate to the intended audience. Practise using the appropriate terminology in your answers: you will need to be more technical when communicating with a tax manager (eg using section numbers where relevant for loss relief) and less so when speaking to a client (who may not understand 'Section 380 relief'!)
Keeping current	The examiner expects you to advise using established tax planning methods in the exam. Fortunately he does not expect you to invent new ones. However, you must be aware of current issues in taxation.
Computation skills	Computations are not the focus of the P6 exam. However they may be required in support of explanations. It is therefore essential that you can complete calculations of tax liabilities speedily and without difficulty to provide numerical evidence for your tax advice.

You will not always produce the exact same solution as we have in our answer section. This does not necessarily mean that you have failed the question, as marks are often available for any other relevant key points you make.

Avoiding weaknesses

We give details of the examiner's comments and criticisms (based on the previous syllabus, but still relevant to P6) at various points throughout this Kit. His reports always emphasised the need to demonstrate a fairly wide syllabus knowledge, but also to identify and justify the availability (or non-availability) of particular reliefs and exemptions. The emphasis remains the same for Paper P6. There are various things you can do on the day of the exam to enhance your chances. Although these all sound basic, the examiner has commented that scripts show:

- A failure to read the question and requirements properly and answer the question set, instead churning out irrelevant 'set pieces'

- Clear evidence of poor time management

- Tendency to confuse CGT and IHT and even personal and corporation tax issues

Make sure you attempt only four questions (as only four will be marked) and start each question on a new page, clearly labelled.

Finally, never ever cross your workings out. These may be correct and you will not be given credit if you have crossed the working out.

Reading time

You will have 15 minutes reading time for Paper P6. Here are some helpful tips on how to best utilise this time.

- Ignore the compulsory questions.

- Speed read through the optional questions, paying particular attention to the requirements, to enable you to decide which two questions to choose from the three. Jot down any ideas that come to you about either of them.

- Cross out the question that you have **not** decided to attempt.

- Decide the order in which you're likely to tackle the other two questions (probably easier question first, more difficult question last).

- Spend the remainder of the time reading the question you'll do first in detail, jotting down answer plans and proformas for supporting calculations (any plans or proformas written on the question paper should be reproduced in the answer booklet).

- When you can start writing, get straight on with the question(s) you've planned in detail.

The reason for attempting the optional questions first is, in the examiner's own words:

'The majority of...candidates appeared to attempt the compulsory questions first, and overrun the time allocation, which they may have regretted later when they reached some relatively straightforward areas in the Section B questions, but didn't have time to have a reasonable attempt at them.'

Doing these questions first should mean that you can manage your time more effectively and not run out of time answering the longer compulsory questions. Attempting the easier question first means that you will have been generating ideas and remembering facts for the more difficult question.

Choosing which questions to answer first

You will need to answer the two compulsory questions in Section A and two out of the three optional questions in Section B, with a larger number of marks awarded for the first two questions.

- The optional questions will be for equal marks. Answer the question on your most comfortable topic but be strict with timing. It is all too tempting to tell the examiner everything you know about your favourite topic. Don't!

- When answering the two compulsory questions, the marks may be allocated unevenly between them. Many students prefer to answer the question with the larger number of allocated marks first. Others again prefer to answer a question on their most comfortable topic.

- Whatever the order, make sure you leave yourself **sufficient time** to tackle all the questions. Don't get bogged down in the more difficult areas, or re-write your answer two or three times. Instead move on and try the rest of the question as there may be an easier part. You do not want to be in a position where you have to rush the rest of the paper.

- Allocate your time carefully between different question parts. If a question is split into a number of requirements, use the number of marks available for each to allocate your time effectively.

Tackling questions

You'll improve your chances by following a step-by-step approach along the following lines.

Step 1   Read the requirement

Identify the knowledge areas being tested and see precisely what the examiner wants you to do. This will help you focus on what's important in the question.

Step 2   Check the mark allocation

This helps you allocate time.

Step 3   Read the question actively

You will already know which knowledge area(s) are being tested from having read the requirement so whilst you read through the question underline or highlight key words and figures as you read. This will mean you are thinking about the question rather than just looking at the words blankly, and will allow you to identify relevant information for use in your advice and supporting calculations.

Step 4   Plan your answer

You may only spend five minutes planning your answer but it will be five minutes well spent. Identify the supporting calculations (and appropriate proformas) you will need to do, if any. Plan the structure of your written answer, even if it is only a series of bullet points, or maybe a spider diagram, using suitable headings and sub headings. Determine whether you can you use bullet points in your answer or if you need a more formal format.

Step 5   Write your answer

Stick carefully to the time allocation for each question, and for each part of each question.

Gaining the easy marks

There are two main ways to obtain easy marks in the P6 exam.

Supporting calculations

Although computations will not be required in isolation in Paper P6 as the focus is on written explanations and advice, there will always be marks available for calculating figures which will support your recommendations. Often you cannot provide any sensible advice until you know the tax cost of a course of action so make sure you can readily set out proformas and fill in the numbers from the question. Make it easy for yourself to pick up the easy marks.

Answer the question set

If you need to consider alternative planning strategies in a question and provide advice on which is the most suitable, do exactly that. If you do not advise on the most suitable plan you'll be losing easy marks. Similarly, if you are asked to consider CGT and IHT in a requirement, don't think that by including some income tax considerations you will pick up extra marks – you won't. Show the examiner you have read his question and requirements carefully and have attempted to answer them as expected – not how you would like to.

Exam information

Format of the exam

Time allowed: 3 hours (with 15 minutes reading time)

Tax rates and allowances and information on certain reliefs will be provided in the examination paper.

Paper P6 is split into sections A and B each comprising scenario based questions which will usually involve consideration of more than one tax, together with some elements of planning and the interaction of taxes. The focus is on explanations and advice rather than computations.

Section A contains two compulsory questions for a total of between 50 and 70 marks, which may be unevenly allocated between the two questions.

Section B consists of three questions, two of which must be answered, for the same number of marks.

Additional information

The Study Text provides more detailed guidance on the syllabus.

Pilot paper

Section A

Q1   Hutt plc – corporation tax losses; groups; purchase of subsidiary; VAT; chargeable gains

Q2   Pilar Mareno – comparing employing worker vs contractor; purchase vs lease of capital asset; VAT; employment status

Section B

Q3   Stanley Beech – incorporation; remuneration package advice

Q4   Mahia Ltd – company purchase of own shares; stamp duty; overseas aspects of CGT; IHT lifetime gifts

Q5   Vikram Bridge – CGT on sale of house; termination payments; IHT gift with reservation; employee share schemes; income tax on investment income; administration

The pilot paper is Mock Exam 3 in this Kit.

Useful websites

The websites below provide additional sources of information of relevance to your studies for *Advanced Taxation*.

- www.bpp.com

    Our website provides information about BPP products and services, with a link to the ACCA website.

- www.accaglobal.com

    ACCA's website. Includes student section. Read any articles in *Student Accountant* magazine.

Planning your question practice

Planning your question practice

We have already stressed that question practice should be right at the centre of your revision. Whilst you will spend some time looking at your notes and Paper P6 Passcards, you should spend the majority of your revision time practising questions.

We recommend two ways in which you can practise questions.

- Use **BPP's question plan** to work systematically through the syllabus and attempt key and other questions on a section-by-section basis

- **Build your own exams** – attempt questions as a series of practice exams

These ways are suggestions and simply following them is no guarantee of success. You or your college may prefer an alternative but equally valid approach.

BPP's question plan

The BPP plan below requires you to devote a **minimum of 87 hours** to revision of Paper P6. Any time you can spend over and above this should only increase your chances of success.

Step 1	For each section of the syllabus, **review your notes** and the relevant chapter summaries in the Paper P6 **Passcards**.
Step 2	Start by looking at any **preparation questions with helping hands** for some topics. These questions are designed to ease the transition from study to exam standard questions. If you are very confident you may wish just to look through the answers to these questions. However, if you are unsure about a topic attempt these questions properly.
Step 3	Then do the **key questions** for that section. These are shown in **white boxes** in the table below. Even if you are short of time you must attempt these questions if you want to pass the exam as these cover key topics or areas that often cause problems. Try to complete your answers without referring to our solutions. You will see that almost every question covers **more than one tax** and so may contain topics you have not revised yet. This follows the format of the real exam where only multi-tax questions will be set. Do not let this deter you from your revision plan. If you have not revised a topic, ignore it in the question then return to the question after you have studied the appropriate topic.
Step 4	For some questions we have suggested that you prepare **answer plans** rather than full solutions. This means that you should spend about 30% of the time allowance for the questions brainstorming the question and drawing up a list of points to be included in the answer.
Step 5	Once you have worked through all of the syllabus sections attempt **mock exam 1** under strict exam conditions. Then have a go at **mock exam 2**, again under strict exam conditions. Just before the exam, if you have time, attempt **mock exam 3**, again under strict exam conditions. This is the pilot paper.

Syllabus section	2007 Passcards chapters	Questions in this Kit	Comments	Done ☑
Revision period 1/2 Income tax computations, pensions and other investments Key question: income tax planning and pensions	1, 2, 3	1	This is a useful question. Make sure you plan your answer carefully. If short of time, work through alongside the answer, but remember pensions are topical, so are more likely to be examined.	☐
Revision periods 3/4 Employees & NIC Preparation question: benefits and share options	4, 5	3	You must be comfortable comparing the tax benefits of taking additional salary versus benefits. The new areas of termination payments and share remuneration are key. This is a useful preparation question which usefully analyses how you should be thinking when you approach a question.	
Key questions: employment	2, 4, 5, 6, 21, 22, 28, 30	2, 4, 5, 7	Useful questions. Answer Q2 and Q4 in full. Have a go at the corporate aspect of Q5 and answer the whole question. You should concentrate only on the termination payment in Q7 then return to the rest of the question after you have completed the next revision period.	☐
Revision periods 5/6 Trading profits and losses for individuals & NIC			These are key questions testing fundamental topics covered in 2.3 but with a planning focus.	
Question with helping hand	6, 28, 29, 30	6	A useful question with helping hand. Have a go at the income tax aspects of incorporation at this stage. Work through alongside the answer if your time is short. Ignore the VAT for now.	☐
Key questions: trading profits	4, 5, 6, 7, 8, 14, 21, 22, 28, 29	7	You can now return to Q7 and almost answer it in full (you still need to revise VAT – see how essential it is for your exam?). Come back to both of these questions after you have completed revision period 26/27.	☐
Revision period 7 Partnerships			Partnerships essentially revise the trading income rules again!	
Key question: partnerships	6, 7, 8, 9	8	You should find this question quite straightforward, although you may like to return to the ethics when you have completed revision period 28/29/30.	☐

Syllabus section	2007 Passcards chapters	Questions in this Kit	Comments	Done ☑
Revision period 8 Overseas aspects of income tax Key questions: overseas aspects	1, 4, 5, 6, 8, 10, 14, 15, 17, 18	9, 10	Overseas aspects is a new topic. Work through Q9 carefully making sure you understand the fundamentals of this area. Q10 deals with the overseas aspects of CGT and IHT too, so return to this question once you have completed revision period 13/14/15.	☐
Revision period 9/10/11 Capital gains, shares and securities, reliefs			It is unlikely that you will be examined only on capital gain tax. It is often tested alongside inheritance tax (IHT) for individuals and the questions in this section therefore contain both taxes. Focus **only** on the CGT aspects the first time you work through the questions, then return to the IHT aspects once you have completed the relevant revision period.	
Question with helping hand	11, 12, 13, 14, 15, 17, 18	11	A useful question with analysis. Work through alongside the answer if your time is short.	☐
Key questions: CGT	11, 12, 13, 14, 15, 17, 18,	12	This is a key question so return to it once you have completed the IHT revision periods. Try and follow through the analysis asking yourself whether you would have come up with the points.	☐
Revision period 12 Self assessment for individuals and partnerships			The administration rules will not be tested in isolation but will make up some of the marks on a number of questions. Whenever you are advising a client they must be aware of their responsibilities so giving submission and payment deadlines is always valid	
		16	There are no key questions for this revision period. Do however attempt to think of the administrative issues for all of your planning advice in the following questions.	☐ ☐
Revision period 13/14/ 15 IHT valuation, reliefs, death estate and additional aspects			This is a completely new topic so is fair game for the exam. Do you understand the interaction between CGT and IHT? You must be clear about this as the two taxes are often examined together.	
Preparation question	12, 14, 17, 18	11	Return to this question, this time working through the IHT issues. Again, you may work through alongside the answer if your time is short.	☐
Key questions: IHT	12, 14, 17, 18	12, 13	Return to 12 as this is a key question, this time answering the IHT elements. Then attempt Q13.	☐

Syllabus section	2007 Passcards chapters	Questions in this Kit	Comments	Done ☑
Revision period 17 Trusts and stamp duties			Remember the only trust you will see in the exam for CGT and IHT purposes is a discretionary trust but you may also see an interest in possession trust if income tax is being examined.	
Key question: trusts	5, 6, 7, 14, 20, 28	14	Q14 revisits topics you have seen earlier in your revision. Important question.	☐
Revision periods 18/19/ 20 Computing PCTCT and corporation tax, administration				
Key question: corporation tax computation & admin	21, 22, 23, 28, 29	15, 16	Important questions. Leave the VAT in both questions for now but return to them after you complete revision period 26/27. Also ignore the corporation tax group elements of Q15.	☐
Revision period 21/ 22 Corporation tax losses, close and investment companies				
Preparation question: close companies	4, 6, 7, 21, 22, 24, 25, 28, 29	17	Useful question. Work through alongside the answer if your time is limited.	☐
Key question: close companies	13,15, 21, 22, 25, 30	18	Important question. Work through carefully.	☐
Revision period 23/ 24 Groups and consortia				
Question with answer plan	11, 12, 14, 26, 28, 29,30	19	If you are short on time produce an answer plan and work through alongside the answer. This is a key area so make sure you are happy with the issues.	☐
Key questions: groups	11, 12, 14, 21, 22, 24, 26, 27, 28, 29	20, 21	Useful questions. Answer in full. Do you understand the topics tested?	☐

Syllabus section	2007 Passcards chapters	Questions in this Kit	Comments	Done ☑
Revision period 25 Overseas aspects of corporation tax				
Key question: overseas	7, 21, 22, 23, 24, 26, 27, 28	22	Useful question. Answer in full.	☐
Revision period 26/27 VAT				
Key questions: VAT	1, 6, 7, 11, 12, 17, 18, 19, 21, 22, 24, 26, 27, 28, 29	23, 24, 25	Important questions. Note that VAT can be tested for an individual or company.	☐
Revision period 28/29/30 Tax planning				
Questions with analysis	All	26, 27	If you are short on time work through alongside the answers.	☐
Key questions: planning	All	28, 29, 30, 31, 32	Essential questions. All questions in the exam will test more than one tax and possibly the interaction of those taxes. You have revised all of the topics now (apart from personal and corporate financial management) so if there are any areas you are unhappy with make sure you revisit them now.	☐
Revision period 31 Personal and corporate financial management				
Key questions: investments	All	33, 34, 35	Essential questions.	☐

Build your own exams

Having revised your notes and the BPP Passcards, you can attempt the questions in the Kit as a series of practice exams.

You can make up practice exams, either yourself or using the mock exams that we have listed below.

	Practice exams						
	1	2	3	4	5	6	7
1	7	30	19	24	20	33	14
2	18	8	35	3	32	9	15
3	5	2	4	1	21	26	28
4	23	29	27	22	13	25	10
5	31	34	12	6	17	11	16

Whichever practice exams you use, you must attempt **Mock exams 1, 2 and 3** at the end of your revision.

Questions

TAXATION OF INDIVIDUALS

Questions 1 to 10 cover the taxation of individuals. This is the subject of Chapters 1 to 10 in the BPP study text.

1 Question with answer plan: Styrax

38 mins

You have recently been approached to act as an accountant for Styrax, aged 32, who is self-employed.

The following information has been extracted from client files and from meetings with Styrax. You should assume that today's date is 15 March 2007.

Styrax:

- Annual trading profits have been fairly constant at approximately £20,000 for the last few years.

- Has building society savings amounting to around £6,000 which generate gross annual interest of approximately £300.

- Wife, Salvia, is aged 28, is expecting their first child and has recently given up employed work.

- The couple has no other sources of income.

- Disposable income is about £3,000 pa after paying their mortgage and living expenses.

Investment strategy:

- Neither Styrax nor his wife have made, and for the present do not wish to start making, any pension provision.

- Risk averse.

Stryax's brother, Taxus:

- Single.
- Prepared to take medium to high risk in his investments.
- Already has a portfolio of investments and wishes to shelter some of his gains.
- Considering investing in the Enterprise Investment Scheme (EIS) and in Venture Capital Trusts (VCTs).

Required

(a) (i) Prepare notes for a meeting with Styrax setting out any measures that could be undertaken by the couple in order to reduce their income tax and national insurance liabilities following Salvia leaving her employment.

You should assume that Styrax does not wish to incorporate his business and that Salvia does not wish to join him in partnership.

Detailed income tax computations are not required in this question part.   **(8 marks)**

(ii) Explain the options open to the couple regarding making future pension provision.   **(3 marks)**

You should assume that the tax rates and allowances for 2006/07 apply throughout.

(b) Write a memorandum to Taxus setting out the features of the EIS and VCTs. You should include details of the risk and taxation implications of each type of investment.   **(10 marks)**

(Total = 21 marks)

2 Charles Choice

40 mins

Charles Choice is aged 47. You should assume that today's date is 2 April 2007 and that the tax rates and allowances for 2006/07 apply throughout. You are *not* expected to take the time value of money into account in any of your answers.

The following information has been extracted from client files and from meetings with Charles.

Charles Choice:

- Assistant manager with Northwest Bank plc.
- Receives gross annual salary of £23,500.
- From 6 April 2007, Charles will be required to drive 8,000 miles each year for business purposes.
- Northwest Bank plc have offered him a choice of either a company car or a cash alternative.

Company car package:

- Diesel powered motor car with a list price of £15,400 and CO_2 emissions of 138 g/km.

- All running costs, including private fuel, will be paid for by the Northwest Bank plc.

- Charles will be required to contribute £50 per month towards the private use of the motor car, of which £15 will be partial reimbursement of private fuel.

- Under this alternative, Charles would not run a private motor car.

Additional salary package:

- Additional salary of £2,800 pa.

- Charles would use his private motor car for business mileage.

- The car is leased at a cost of £285 per month, and has a list price of £11,500.

- Annual running costs, including fuel, are £1,650.

- Will drive 12,000 miles per year.

- Northwest Bank plc pays a business mileage allowance of 23 pence per mile.

Pension provision:

- Has previously contributed £250 gross per month to his personal pension.

- Charles is considering joining the Northwest Bank plc occupational pension scheme.

- Under the company's scheme Charles would contribute 6% of his salary (assume this is £23,500).

- The company would contribute a further 6%.

Required

(a) Advise Charles as to which of the two alternatives will be the most beneficial from his point of view. Your answer should include calculations of the additional tax liabilities that will arise under each alternative, and a comparison of the total annual cost of each alternative. **(11 marks)**

(b) (i) Advise Charles of the maximum amount he can contribute to either pension scheme to obtain tax relief and comment on the likelihood of him making maximum contributions. **(4 marks)**

(ii) Explain the different methods by which Charles will be given tax relief for pension contributions to either a personal or occupational pension scheme. **(3 marks)**

(ii) How would your answer to (ii) above differ if Charles instead had a salary of £223,500 and wished to make maximum contributions to his personal pension. **(4 marks)**

(Total = 22 marks)

3 Question with analysis: Benny Fitt

41 mins

Your manager has had a meeting with Benny Fitt, the managing director of Usine Ltd, and has sent you a copy of the following memorandum.

To   The files
From   Tax manager
Date   20 December 2006
Subject   Usine Ltd

(a)   Provision of employment benefits to Benny Fitt (BF)

Petrol company car

Provided on 1 October 2006. Car has **list price of £28,400** and **CO2 emission figure of 227g/km**. **Sun-roof has been added costing £700**. BF made a **capital contribution of £2,500** towards the cost of the car.

> Value of car is the starting point to value the benefit

> Above base of 140g/km so need to calculate % to use

> Add this to value of car to calculate benefit

> Deduct from value of car to calculate benefit

Company credit card

During 2006/07 this will be used to pay for:

- motor repairs   £460
- business accommodation   £380
- customer entertaining   £720
- petrol   £425

Included in the figure for petrol is **£180 in respect of private mileage** which is not reimbursed to Usine Ltd.

> Need to calculate fuel benefit since private petrol provided

Lap top computer

Cost £3,000. Provided on 6 April 2006, for **private use** and occasional business use.

> Asset provided for private use is another benefit

(b)   Sales director changes

On 10 December 2006 Usine Ltd dismissed their sales director and paid him a lump sum redundancy payment of £45,000. This consisted of the following.

> Special rules

> Exempt

	£
Statutory redundancy pay	2,100
Payment in lieu of notice	**3,100**
Holiday pay	2,800
Ex gratia compensation for loss of office	**34,000**
Agreement not to work for a rival company	3,000
	45,000

> Both taxable as specific employment income

> Both *ex gratia* – £30,000 rule applies

A new sales director is to commence employment on 1 January 2007. She is to be paid a **lump sum payment of £10,000 upon the commencement of employment**. The new director currently lives 120 miles from Usine Ltd's head office, so the company has offered her two alternative arrangements.

> This is a 'golden hello' and is taxable as earnings

(i)   Usine Ltd will pay **£9,500 towards the cost of the director's relocation**, and will also provide an interest free loan of £50,000 in order for the director to purchase a property.

> Up to £8,000 of relocation is exempt

> **Benefit for this unless it is job related (unlikely)**

(ii)   Usine Ltd will **provide accommodation** for the director. The company owns a house which has an annual value of £4,400, is currently valued at £105,000, and has recently been **furnished at a cost of £10,400**. Usine Ltd will pay for the annual **running costs of £3,200**.

> **Furniture provided = benefit @ 20%**

(b)   Company Share Option Plan

The company is considering setting up a Company Share Option Plan for certain senior employees and directors.

Options will be granted to these individuals that will be exercisable between three and ten years after the grant.

An extract from an email from your manager is set out below.

Please prepare a letter to Benny Fitt setting out the following:

1   Employment benefits

Advise both Benny Fitt and Usine Ltd of the tax implications arising from the provision of the company car, the credit card and the laptop computer.

> **No private petrol provided = no taxable benefit**

Explain why it would be beneficial if Benny **paid Usine Ltd £180 for his private petrol**.

You can ignore the VAT implications.

2   Sales director changes

Explain the income tax implications of the lump sum payments of £45,000 and £10,000.

Explain the income tax implications of the two alternative arrangements offered to the new sales director.

You do not need to consider the tax implications for Usine Ltd and you should confine your statements to the implications for 2006/07.

3   Share option scheme

> **Need to know – hard to guess**

Outline the conditions required for the scheme to obtain HMRC approval.

You have extracted the following further information from client files.

- Usine Ltd is an unquoted trading company.

- It is a small company for the purposes of the Companies Acts.

- Benny Fitt is aged 39 and is paid a salary of £45,000 per annum.

> **Purchased for > £75,000 therefore additional benefit. Use MV as >6 yrs since purchase**

- Usine Ltd purchased the house available to the new sales director in **1994 for £86,000**. It was improved at a cost of £8,000 during 2003.

Required

Prepare the letter requested by your manager.

Marks are available for the components of the letter as follows:

1	Tax treatment of the employment benefits for Benny Fitt and Usine Ltd.	**(8 marks)**
2	Tax implications of the payments (and benefits) provided to the two sales director.	**(9 marks)**
3	The conditions for the share option scheme to be approved.	**(4 marks)**

Appropriateness of the format and presentation of the letter and the effectiveness with which its content is communicated.

(2 marks)

You may assume that the rates and allowances for the 2006/07 tax year and financial year 2006 continue to apply for the foreseeable future. The official rate of interest for 2006/07 is 5%.

(Total = 23 marks)

4 Benny Korere

Benny Korere has been employed as the sales director of Golden Tan plc since 1994.

The following information has been extracted from client files and from meetings with Benny.

Benny

- Age 42.
- Receives rental income of £4,000 (net of deductible expenses) each year.

Current remuneration package with Golden Tan plc:

- Annual salary of £32,000.

- Petrol company car with list price of £22,360, when first provided in August 2003, and CO_2 emission rate of 187g/km. Paid a £6,100 capital contribution towards the cost of the car. Pays £18 per month as a condition of being able to use the car for private purposes.

- Golden Tan plc does not pay for any of Benny's private petrol.

Redundancy package:

- Will be made redundant on 28 February 2007.

- Will be paid his final month's salary together with a payment of £8,000 in lieu of his six-month notice period in accordance with his employment contract.

- Will also be paid £17,500 in return for agreeing not to work for any of Golden Tan plc's competitors for the six-month period ending 31 August 2007.

New remuneration package with Summer Glow plc:

- Summer Glow plc is one of Golden Tan plc's competitors and one of the most innovative companies in the industry, although not all of its strategies have been successful.

- Has been offered a senior management position leading the company's expansion into Eastern Europe.

- Would join Summer Glow plc on 1 September 2007 for an annual salary of £39,000.

- Will be granted an option to purchase 10,000 ordinary shares in the company for £2.20 per share under an unapproved share option scheme.

- Can exercise the option once has been employed for six months but must hold the shares for at least a year before he sells them.

Relocation:

- Will be required to spend a considerable amount of time in London.

- Summer Glow plc has offered exclusive use of a flat, purchased by the company on 1 June 2003 for £165,000, which will be available from 1 September 2007.

- All utility bills, furnishing and maintenance costs will be paid by the company.

- Summer Glow plc has suggested that the company could sell the existing flat and buy a more centrally located one, of the same value, with the proceeds.

Capital transactions:

- Intends to sell 5,800 shares in Mahana plc, a quoted company, for £24,608 on 15 March 2007.

- Transactions in the company's shares have been as follows:

		£
June 1988	Purchased 8,400 shares	6,744
February 1996	Sale of rights nil paid	610
January 2005	Purchased 1,300 shares	2,281

- The sale of rights nil paid was not treated as a part disposal of Benny's holding in Mahana plc.

- Shareholding represents less than 1% of the company's issued ordinary share capital.

- Will not make any other capital disposals in 2006/07.

Required

(a)   Calculate Benny's employment income for 2006/07.   **(3 marks)**

(b)   (i)   Advise Benny of the income tax implications of the grant and exercise of the share options in Summer Glow plc on the assumption that the share price on 1 September 2007 and on the day he exercises the options is £3.35 per share. Explain why the share option scheme is not free from risk by reference to the rules of the scheme and the circumstances surrounding the company.   **(4 marks)**

(ii)   List the additional information required in order to calculate the employment income benefit in respect of the provision of the furnished flat for 2007/08 and advise Benny of the potential income tax implications of requesting a more centrally located flat in accordance with the company's offer.

(4 marks)

(c)   (i)   Calculate Benny's capital gains tax liability for 2006/07.   **(6 marks)**

(ii)   Advise Benny of the amount of tax he could save by delaying the sale of the shares by 30 days. For the purposes of this part, you may assume that the benefit in respect of the furnished flat is £11,800 per year.   **(3 marks)**

You should assume that the rates and allowances for the tax year 2006/07 apply throughout this question.

Relevant retail price index figures are:

June	1988	106.6
February	1996	150.9
April	1998	162.6

The official rate of interest is 5%.

(Total = 20 marks)

5 Nui Neu (BTX 6/05)   32 mins

For the purposes of this question you should assume that today's date is 1 March 2006.

Nui Neu is to commence in business on 6 April 2006 running a retail shop. She is unsure whether to run the new business as a sole trader or as a limited company.

The following information has been extracted from client files and from meetings with Nui.

Nui:

- Is not married.
- Has no other sources of income for 2006/07.
- Has a personal pension.

If she runs the retail shop as a sole trader:

- The tax adjusted trading profit for the year ended 5 April 2007 is expected to be £30,000.
- Nui will withdraw £25,000 of this profit as drawings.

If she runs the retail shop through a limited company:

- The company will make up accounts to 5 April.

- The company's trading profit for the year ended 5 April 2007 is also expected to be £30,000.

- This figure is before taking account of director's remuneration and employer's Class 1 national insurance contributions.
- Nui will personally withdraw £25,000 of the company's profits.

Nui's proposed extraction of profits from the company:

- This might be as gross director's remuneration of £25,000.
- Alternatively Nui might take net dividends of £25,000.

Required

(a)   Explain to Nui the income tax, national insurance and corporation tax implications if she runs her business:

(i)   as a sole trader
(ii)   as a limited company and she withdraws gross director's remuneration of £25,000, and
(iii)   as a limited company and withdraws net dividends of £25,000.

You should provide calculations in support of your explanations, stating the net spendable income available to Nui for each option.

You should assume that the corporation tax rates and limits for the financial year 2007 are the same as those for the financial year 2006.   **(14 marks)**

(b)   Based on your calculations, advise Nui whether it will be beneficial to run her business as a sole trader or whether she should run it as a limited company. In your conclusion, suggest one other simple remuneration planning strategy that will increase Nui's net spendable income.   **(4 marks)**

(Total = 18 marks)

6 Preparation question with helping hand: Alex Zong   38 mins

Alex Zong, aged 38, commenced self-employment as a builder on 1 October 2003.

The following information has been extracted from client files and from meetings with Alex.

Alex Zong:

- Has capital losses of £12,500 resulting from the sale of investments in 2006/07.
- Is registered for VAT; does not operate the cash accounting scheme.
- Drives 12,000 miles per year, of which 4,800 are for private purposes.
- Plans to incorporate the trade into a new limited company, Lexon Ltd, on 31 December 2006.

Tax adjusted trading profits (*before* capital allowances):

- Period ended 30.6.04 – £28,000
- Year ended 30.6.05 – £44,000
- Year ended 30.6.06 – £53,000
- Estimated profits for the period ended 31.12.06 – £29,000

Capital assets:

- *1 October 2003:*   Introduced his private motor car into the business at its market value of £4,000.

- *1 October 2003:*   Purchased freehold office premises for £32,000.

- *1 October 2003:*   Purchased lorry for £8,800.

- *15 March 2004:*   Purchased plant for £10,200.

- *1 June 2005:*   Sold plant for £3,800.

- *30 November 2005:*   Sold private motor car for £2,800 and purchased replacement motor car for £13,500.

41

- *10 December 2005:* Extended the freehold premises using his own materials and labour at a cost of £6,700. The extension would have cost £10,000 if the work had been carried out externally.

Planned incorporation details:

- All the assets of the business will be transferred to Lexon Ltd.

- Consideration will consist of 1,000 £1 ordinary shares in Lexon Ltd and a loan account balance of £10,000.

- The estimated market value of the business assets at 31 December 2006 are as follows:

	£
Goodwill	40,000
Freehold premises	75,000
Lorry	4,300
Plant	8,200
Motor car	11,500
Net current assets	21,000
	160,000

VAT issues for return for quarter ended 30 November 2006:

- Completed a contract for a customer on 20 May 2006, and raised an invoice for £9,400 (inclusive of VAT) on 15 June 2006. Customer paid £2,350 on 30 June 2006, and the balance was due to be paid within 10 days of the invoice date. Now considered to be a bad debt.

- Has not been claiming the input VAT on plant which is leased for £475 (inclusive of VAT) per month. The same amount has been paid since commencement of business on 1 October 2003.

- Invoiced a customer for £3,400 (excluding VAT) on 30 September 2006. Was offered a 5% discount for payment within 30 days. This was not taken and full amount was paid on 28 November 2006.

Required

(a) (i) Calculate Alex's trading profits assessment for 2006/07. You should ignore NIC. **(7 marks)**

    (ii) Advise Alex of the capital gains tax implications of incorporating his business on 31 December 2006. **(7 marks)**

    (iii) Advise Alex of the VAT implications of incorporating his business on 31 December 2006. **(2 marks)**

You should include any tax planning points that you consider relevant.

(b) Advise Alex how he should deal with the VAT issues for the return for the quarter ended 30 November 2006. **(5 marks)**

(Total = 21 marks)

Helping hand

1 A good place to start for part (a) would be to work out the capital allowances computation as a working. Set out your proforma and feed in the figures from the question.

2 With incorporation it is a good idea to brainstorm the different taxes to trigger some ideas. Here you were given specific taxes to consider (CGT and VAT) but you were also asked for tax planning points – did you come up with any? Remember incorporation relief is pretty flexible as you can manipulate the amount of consideration not taken as shares to generate a gain to use the annual exemption, taper relief and any losses.

3 You can answer the VAT requirement in part (b) first if VAT is a comfortable topic for you.

7 Anne Parr

70 mins

Anne Parr was made redundant from Cleves plc on 1 April 2006. Anne received £88,000 on 15 September 2006 made up of a bonus of £14,000 in respect of the year ended 31 March 2006 and an unexpected *ex gratia* payment of £74,000 as compensation for loss of office.

On 1 October 2006 Anne set up her own consultancy business from home. She had submitted a business plan to her bank on the basis that she would be self-employed which showed the following projected profit figures.

Period 1 October 2006 – 30 June 2007	£27,750 (net of depreciation of £3,200)
Year to 30 June 2008	£42,800 (net of depreciation of £2,560)

The depreciation charges relate to the purchase of a motor car for £11,000 and a computer system costing £5,000 in October 2006. The private use of the motor vehicle is 70%. No other items included in the net profit figures require adjustment for trading income purposes. The business is 'small' for capital allowances purposes.

In the business plan Anne also forecast the following pattern of standard-rated supplies (exclusive of VAT).

1 October 2006 – 31 March 2007	£4,200 per month
1 April 2007 onwards	£5,800 per month

She has negotiated a six month contract with Longhorn Ltd, for a fixed fee of £36,000. Anne was not in a position to undertake any other work during the assignment. A large part of the current assignment was carried out at Longhorn Ltd's premises and the company provided Anne with the use of an assistant while she was there. Anne was expected to report on the progress of her assignment on a weekly basis to the managing director. Anne has not so far obtained any firm promises of work from other companies, but Longhorn Ltd has indicated that it might well be in a position to offer her further work.

Longhorn Ltd is a trading company, with no associates, which is expected to pay corporation tax at the small companies' rate. It is expected to make standard-rated supplies of £220,000 pa, zero-rated supplies of £30,000 pa, and exempt supplies of £70,000 pa for VAT purposes (all amounts are stated exclusive of any VAT). Longhorn Ltd's annual input VAT (disregarding any payments to Anne) is currently expected to be £34,743 of which £4,700 will be directly attributable to the exempt supplies and £8,900 will relate to general overheads.

All payments to Anne would be regarded as part of general overheads for VAT purposes. All of the company's input VAT relates to expenditure which is allowable in computing taxable profits.

Longhorn Ltd's draft profit before tax figure for the year ended 31 March 2007 has been calculated at £149,000, after crediting or deducting the following items.

	£
Depreciation of fixed assets	16,225
Amortisation of intangible asset acquired 1 July 2006	3,650
Directors' remuneration	
(including £14,000 accrued but not due to be paid until 31 March 2008)	56,000
Medical insurance paid for employees	9,250
Fine in respect of breach of trading standards	3,850
Release of specific provision for bad debts	4,500
Profit on sale of office	
(capital gain computed for tax purposes is £28,070)	42,875
Profit on sale of government security	850
Gifts of £250 each to employees passing professional examinations	2,000
Gifts of brandy to customers (costing £14 per customer)	2,268
Subscription to political party which has promised	
to reduce costs for UK businesses	10,000
Advisers' fees in relation to issue of new shares	3,750
Interest paid on loan to acquire overseas investment	3,020
Dividend received from overseas investment	
(gross amount – inclusive of 10% foreign withholding tax)	4,800
Bank interest receivable from non-trade funds	2,850

No capital allowances were due in respect of plant and machinery for the period. Any potential tax implications arising from payments to Anne are to be disregarded for these purposes.

In August 2006 Longhorn Ltd bought a site costing £175,000, including legal fees of £8,750; in the course of the year, the company built a sports pavilion on the site for its employees at a cost of £280,000, including architect's fees of £14,000. All of the costs were capitalised in the accounts of the company.

In October 2006 the company made a qualifying investment of £27,000 under the Corporate Venturing Scheme.

Required

(a) Explain the taxation treatment of the two sums received by Anne, indicating whether your analysis would be different if she had been contractually entitled to receive the payment of £74,000. **(3 marks)**

(b) Prepare a report for Anne concerning her consultancy business. The report should be in three sections, addressing the issues set out below, and should, where appropriate, include supporting calculations.

    (i) Self employed status

        Discuss whether Anne is likely to be classified as employed or self-employed in respect of her contract with Longhorn Ltd.

        Explain the factors that HMRC are likely to consider. **(7 marks)**

    (ii) Projected taxable trading income

        Advise Anne what her trading income assessments will be for the first three tax years of her business assuming that she is classified as self-employed in respect of her consultancy activities.

        You should also indicate the amount of any overlap profits arising and how they can be relieved. **(6 marks)**

    (iii) VAT

        State the date from which Anne would be obliged to register for VAT and the date on which she should start charging VAT.

        You should assume that the current VAT registration threshold will remain unchanged.

        Indicate the main consequence for Anne if she fails to register by the due date. **(4 marks)**

(c) Compare the annual after-tax cost to Longhorn Ltd of using Anne's services on the alternative assumptions that:

    (i) Anne is an employee of the company who will receive a salary of £36,000 pa and who will not be contracted out for NIC purposes, and

    (ii) Anne is a self-employed contractor who will charge the company annual fees of £36,000 plus VAT. **(7 marks)**

(d) Compute the corporation tax payable by Longhorn Ltd for the accounting period ended 31 March 2007, briefly explaining why you have allowed or disallowed each item of expenditure and income.

    You should assume that all amounts are stated inclusive of any irrecoverable VAT. **(10 marks)**

Appropriateness of the format and presentation of the report and the effectiveness with which its advice is communicated. **(2 marks)**

You may assume that the tax rates and allowances for the tax year 2006/07 and the financial year to 31 March 2007 for will continue to apply for the foreseeable future.

(Total = 39 marks)

8 Ming Khan and Nina Lee

49 mins

Your manager has had a meeting with Ming Khan and Nina Lee, who are in partnership running a music recording studio, and has sent you a copy of the following meeting notes.

To   The files
From   Tax manager
Date   1 November 2006

Subject Ming Khan and Nina Lee – partnership

This was the first meeting with Ming Khan (MK) and Nina Lee (NL). They provided the following information:

MK and NL – background

MK was previously employed by a music company with an annual salary of £42,000. She was made redundant on 28 February 2005, and received an *ex gratia* redundancy payment of £60,000.

NL was previously a student. She had inherited an investment property on the death of her parents and sold this for £125,000 on 31 March 2005 in order to finance her partnership capital. The disposal resulted in a chargeable gain of £39,600. Until March 2005 NL received rental income of £6,250 pa.

Partnership – background

The partnership commenced trading on 1 May 2005. Profits and losses are shared between MK and NL 60:40.

The partnership is registered for VAT and all of its supplies are standard rated.

Their first accounts for the 15 month period to 31 July 2006 show a tax adjusted trading loss (*before* capital allowances) of £71,250.

Capital expenditure

On 12 May 2005 the partnership purchased a freehold building and converted it into a recording studio during May and June of 2005 at a cost of £211,500, made up as follows:

	£
Land and building	69,500
Recording equipment	70,300
Installation of electrical system for the recording equipment	19,400
Sound insulation	13,200
Replacement doors and windows	2,500
Heating system	5,100
VAT	31,500
	211,500

MK and NL have decided not to claim first year allowances in respect of any or the above expenditure but will claim full writing down allowances for the fifteen month period to 31 July 2006.

Partnership's financial position

The partnership needs to purchase computer equipment costing £61,100, but does not have sufficient funds to do so outright. The computer equipment can either be leased for three years at a cost of £28,200 pa or can be bought on hire-purchase for an initial payment of £11,100 (including VAT of £9,100), followed by 35 monthly payments of £2,000.

The computer equipment will be replaced after three years use, at which time it will be worthless. MK and NL want to know the tax implications of each alternative method of financing the computer equipment.

All figures are inclusive of VAT where relevant.

Tax manager

An extract from an email from your manager is set out below.

Please prepare a memorandum for me, incorporating the following:

1   Calculations to show how the partnership's trading loss for the 15 month period to 31 July 2006 will be allocated between MK and NL for 2005/06 and 2006/07.

2   State the possible ways of relieving the trading loss.

3   Advise MK and NL on the most beneficial loss relief claims for them. Calculate the tax refunds that they will receive.

4   Advise MK and NL of the income tax and the VAT implications of acquiring the computer equipment by hire purchase or leasing.

Tax manager

Required

(a)   Prepare the memorandum requested by your manager.

Marks are available for the four components of the memorandum as follows:

1   Calculation of the partnership's trading loss for the 15 month period and its allocation to the 2005/06 and 2006/07 tax years.

Your calculations should be made on a monthly basis.   **(3 marks)**

2   Stating the options for relieving the trading loss   **(4 marks)**

3   Advising on the most beneficial claims for MK and NL and calculating the tax refunds that will be due to them.

You should ignore the possibility of any repayment supplement being due.   **(9 marks)**

4   Explaining the income tax and VAT implications for the partnership of hire purchasing or leasing the computer equipment.

You should ignore the implications of SSAP 21: *Accounting for leases and Hire-Purchase Contracts.*
(6 marks)

Appropriateness of the format and presentation of the memorandum and the effectiveness with which the information is communicated.   **(2 marks)**

You may assume that the rates and allowances for the tax year 2006/07 apply for all relevant years. Ignore taper relief.

(b)   Set out briefly the steps you would take when commencing to act for MK, NL and the partnership. **(3 marks)**

(Total = 27 marks)

9 Tim Aylsbury

41 mins

Tim Aylsbury traded as a manufacturer of reproduction furniture from 1 June 2004 until his business was affected by increased competition and he closed down on 31 December 2007. His profits (after capital allowances) had steadily declined as shown below:

	£
Period ended 31 October 2004	13,750
Year ended 31 October 2005	15,000
Year ended 31 October 2006	5,000
Year ended 31 October 2007	(10,000)
2 months to 31 December 2007	(6,000)

In 1999 Tim had inherited shares worth £150,000. These produced gross dividend income of £6,000 in 2003/04, increasing by £500 each fiscal year since then. He sold the shares in May 2007, realising a gain after taper relief of £20,800. No dividends were paid between 6 April 2007 and the date of sale.

Tim has been offered employment with an antique furniture reproductions company from April 2008. His package will be as follows:

Salary — £15,000 pa

Bonus — he has been told that this is guaranteed to be a minimum of £5,000

Share options — he will be able to buy shares in the company at a 50% discount to the current market price, as long as he does this before 31 December 2011. The current market price is £3 per share and the company expects the price to rise by 20% pa. Tim will probably purchase 2,000 shares under the scheme in three years time.

Furniture — Tim will be able to take new sample products and keep them at his home to test their durability. They would then be returned to the company after approximately one year when they would be sold as 'seconds'. He estimates the value of the samples would be worth £2,500 to buy new but would only be sold for £800 a year later. He would have the option to buy the samples himself for £500.

The company has a subsidiary based in Ruritania which produces furniture for the local market. Tim has been told that he will be able to get a two year secondment to work there after a qualifying period. The salary he would earn has a sterling equivalent of £18,000 and he would be provided with accommodation with an annual value of £4,500. Ruritania has no system of income tax, but Tim is concerned that he will be worse off under this arrangement.

Required

Write a letter to Tim, assuming the current date is mid January 2008, detailing:

(a)   The options for his trading loss, with supporting computations, concluding as to the most beneficial way of relieving the loss.   **(9 marks)**

(b)   The tax implications of his remuneration package.   **(6 marks)**

(c)   The tax and other implications of accepting the secondment in Ruritania.   **(6 marks)**

Appropriateness of the format and presentation of the notes and the effectiveness with which their content is communicated.   **(2 marks)**

You may assume that the rates and allowances for the tax year 2006/07 continue to apply for the foreseeable future.

(Total = 23 marks)

10 Amy (ATAX 12/04)

40 mins

Amy is 43 years old. She is single and does not have any children.

The following information has been extracted from client files and from meetings with Amy. Assume that today's date is 1 May 2007.

Amy:

- Resident and ordinarily resident in the UK.
- Domiciled overseas.
- Pays £5,000 into personal pension each year.
- Has not made any lifetime transfers of assets before this year.
- Concerned about future inheritance tax liabilities.

2006/07 remuneration package:

- Salary of £20,000 (PAYE deducted of £5,085).
- Diesel company car, list price of £15,000 and an emission rate of 175 grams per km.
- Fuel for both private and business use.

Investment income:

- National Savings & Investments easy access account interest of £180 (amount received).

- UK bank deposit account interest of £400 (amount received).

- Dividend of £1,800 (amount received) from 50,000 £1 ordinary shares in Red plc, a UK quoted company.

- Dividend of £1,300 (amount received) from Black Inc, a company quoted overseas. Withholding tax of 35% had been deducted at source. Only £650 of this net dividend was remitted to the UK.

Property business income:

Overseas property

- £850 rent per month.
- Withholding tax of 15% deducted at source.
- Full net amount remitted to the UK.
- Gifted to her brother, Michael, on 6 November 2006 (see below).

UK property

- £1,340 rent per month (net of letting expenses).
- Not her main residence and has never been used as a business asset.
- £140 per month interest paid on loan taken out to purchase the property.
- Gifted to her brother, Michael, on 6 January 2007 (see below).

Gifts made to her brother, Michael, during the year to 5 April 2007:

- *1 June 2006:* 50,000 £1 ordinary shares in Red plc, quoted at 221–229p, with daily bargains of 219p, 220p and 225p. Inherited in April 2004 (probate value £20,000) from her aunt, who bought them in March 2000 for £17,200. Amy has never worked for Red plc and holds less than 5% of the shares.

- *6 November 2006:* the overseas property, market value £245,000; purchased August 2002 for £220,000.

- *6 January 2007:* the UK property, market value £125,000; purchased in June 1995 for £67,000.

Future plans:

- Intends to gift her main residence to her niece, Erica, on 1 June 2007.
- Current market value is £400,000; purchased in January 2001 for £235,000.
- Has always been Amy's main residence and intends to continue to live there after the gift.

Required

(a)   (i)   State the basis on which Amy will be charged to income tax (IT), capital gains tax (CGT) and inheritance tax (IHT) given her UK residence and ordinary residence and non-UK domicile status.

(3 marks)

(ii)   Calculate Amy's IT, CGT and IHT payable for 2006/07, clearly identifying any actions she can take to defer the chargeable gains that have arisen.   **(13 marks)**

Relevant retail price index figures are:

June   1995   149.8
April   1998   162.6

(b)   (i)   Explain the inheritance tax (IHT) implications of Amy making the gift of her main residence to her niece, and calculate the IHT arising if Amy should die on 1 September 2011. Assume that the value of the property will still be £400,000, that Amy retains her non-UK domicile for the purpose of inheritance tax and that the tax rates and allowances for 2006/07 apply throughout.   **(5 marks)**

(ii)   Suggest a way by which the IHT liability calculated in (i) above could be reduced and indicate any other tax implications arising from this advice.   **(1 mark)**

(Total = 22 marks)

11 Preparation question with helping hand: Rowan Sorbus

38 mins

Rowan Sorbus, aged 47, died on 23 March 2007.

The following information has been extracted from client files and from meetings with Rowan.

Rowan Sorbus:

- Rowan made no gifts during his lifetime, other those detailed below.

Domestica Limited shares:

- Owned 30% of the £1 ordinary shares of this unquoted trading company at the date of his death.

- Remaining shares were held as follows:

National Charity	25%
Rowan's son	10%
Unconnected persons	35%

- Originally acquired a 65% holding in April 2005 for £650,000.

- Gifted the charity's shareholding to it on 10 July 2006.

- Gifted his son's shareholding to him on 20 July 2006.

- Values of the shares have been agreed by HMRC as follows:

% holding	July 2006 £	March 2007 £
65%	2,100,000	2,250,000
55%	1,450,000	1,500,000
40%	850,000	900,000
30%	650,000	700,000
25%	500,000	550,000
10%	150,000	175,000

Other assets owned at date of death:

- 100% of the shares in Aria Limited, an unquoted trading company. Acquired for £1,000 in October 2003. Value on 23 March 2007 has been agreed by HMRC at £100,000.

- Property used in Domestica Limited's trade, acquired in April 2005 for £200,000. Valued in March 2007 at £750,000.

- Property used in Aria Limited's trade, acquired in September 2004 for £100,000. Valued in March 2007 at £175,000. Outstanding mortgage of £75,000.

- Other net assets valued for IHT purposes on 23 March 2007 at £650,000, after taking account of outstanding personal tax liabilities owed at this date.

Other information:

- Residue of estate left to his son.
- Son sold all his shares in Domestica Limited in December 2007 for £1,500,000.

Required

(a)   Explain the inheritance tax implications resulting from Rowan's death on 23 March 2007. Your answer should include a calculation of any inheritance tax liabilities arising and also an explanation of the basis for valuing his shares in Domestica Limited and of any reliefs which are available.   **(13 marks)**

(b)   Explain the capital gains tax implications arising as a result of the gifts in July 2006 and the sale by Rowan's son in December 2007. Your answer should include a calculation of any chargeable gains arising, assuming that all reliefs available to minimise these gains are claimed, and include an explanation of those reliefs and why they are beneficial.

You should assume that the rates and allowances for 2006/07 apply throughout this part of the question.

(8 marks)

(Total = 21 marks)

Helping hand

To ensure you don't make mistakes and lose marks, it is best to do this question twice – first thinking IHT only the second time thinking CGT only. It is easy to confuse the two taxes. You need to approach your answer in a way that helps you to avoid confusion. The steps you should follow in a question like this are:

Step 1   Deal with the IHT implications of each lifetime gift in date order.

Step 2   Then return to each gift to consider the death tax implications for each, again chronologically.

Step 3   Deal with the death estate.

Step 4   Now return to each lifetime gift but considering CGT. There is no CGT on death.

---

12 Question with analysis: Christopher (ATAX 6/06)   36 mins

Christopher **died** suddenly on 5 February 2007.

Death = IHT

The following information has been extracted from client files and from meetings.

Christopher:

- Widower, aged 76.
- One child, Eleanor, who is 44 years old and single.

As Christopher paid will need to gross up to calculate the IHT due

Lifetime gifts:

- *9 August 1999:*   Gift of property worth £250,000 to a **discretionary trust**.
- *10 April 2002:*   Gift of £75,000 cash into the same **discretionary trust**.
- **Christopher paid any tax** due on the gifts.

CLT so IHT due

Probate values of assets in death estate:

- Residence – £550,000.
- ISA account – £12,000.
- Cash deposits – £40,000.
- Shares in Penfold Limited – £85,000.
- Shares in Boise plc (see below).

Cash deposits and Penfold Limited shares:

QSR will apply

- Received £30,000 in cash and 5,000 shares in Penfold Limited, with a probate value of £14 each, from his **deceased uncle's estate in August 2005**.

BPR due

- Penfold Limited is an **unquoted UK trading company**.

- The 5,000 shares (which had been owned by Christopher's uncle for **five years** prior to his death) represent 5% of the company's share capital.

- £75,000 inheritance tax was paid on his uncle's total chargeable estate of £450,000.

Boise plc shares:

- 15,000 ordinary £1 shares in Boise plc, a UK quoted company.

Need to value these shares

- Holding represents 2% of the company's issued share capital.

- Cum dividend price per share on 5 February 2007 was 700p – 708p, with marked bargains at 701p, 702p and 707p.

All of Christopher's assets go to Eleanor, who is his daughter so no exemptions

- A dividend of 18p per share had been declared on 15 January 2007.

- This was received on 20 February 2007.

Eleanor:

- **Sole beneficiary** of Christopher's estate.

- Wealthy in her own right paying income tax at the higher rate.

- Intends to gift assets worth £50,000 to her friend, Sam and is considering three options (see below).

- Has made no previous lifetime gifts.

Part disposal for CGT

Three options for gift to Sam:

IHT and CGT problem

- Three **paintings** valued at £50,000. Eleanor paid £25,000 for a set of four paintings in June 1995. Sold one painting for £9,000 in January 2001, when remaining paintings were valued at £31,000.

IHT problem only – no CGT on cash

- **Cash** of £50,000 from the inheritance she is shortly to receive following the death of her father.

IHT and CGT

- 5,000 **shares** representing a 5% holding in Grange Limited, an unquoted UK trading company. Acquired by Eleanor for £17,500 in May 1993.

Required

(a) Calculate the inheritance tax (IHT) liability arising as a result of Christopher's death. **(11 marks)**

(b) Evaluate the capital gains tax (CGT) and inheritance tax (IHT) implications of each of the three options being considered by Eleanor, and recommend the most tax efficient solution. Assume that Ignore the AE any gift will be made in June 2007, that Eleanor will have **already utilised her CGT annual exemption** for the tax year 2007/08 and that **gift relief will not be claimed**. **(9 marks)**

No gift relief

You should assume that the rates and allowances for the tax year 2006/07 apply throughout this question.

Relevant retail price index figures are:

May	1993	141.1
June	1995	149.8
April	1998	162.6

(Total = 20 marks)

13 Jimmy Generous (ATAX 06/03)

40 mins

Jimmy Generous is a wealthy individual aged 57, in good health and married to Jane, aged 54 and also in good health. The couple have two children, Jack, aged 34 and Jill, aged 37, who both have children of their own. You should assume that today's date is 4 June 2007.

The following information has been extracted from client files and from meetings with the shareholders.

Jimmy:

- Currently owns 60% of the issued chare capital of JG Limited, a UK resident trading company (see below).
- Works as a part-time director of JG Limited.
- Receives gross annual salary of £22,500.
- Contributed £3,750 to JG Limited's registered occupational pension scheme.
- Received £45,000 net dividend income from JG Limited.
- Received £8,000 net building society interest.
- Subscribed £20,000 for 20,000 £1 ordinary shares in Pail Ltd, a small unquoted trading company.
- Paid £1,000 of interest on a loan of £20,000 that he took out to pay for the shares in Pail Ltd.
- Has no other income or outgoings in 2006/07.

JG Ltd:

- Set up by Jimmy in 1983.
- Remaining shares are held 20% by his daughter Jill and 20% by unconnected third parties.
- The company has been very successful in recent years.

Lifetime gifts:

- Jimmy agreed that he would pay any Inheritance Tax arising on these gifts.

- *4 June 1999* £291,000 cash gift to a discretionary trust created for the benefit of his grandchildren.

- *4 March 2001* £10,000 cash as a wedding gift to his son Jack.

- *4 March 2001* 20% of the shares in JG Limited to his daughter Jill. At this time the JG Limited shares were valued as follows:

Shareholding	Value
	£
20%	100,000
60%	450,000
80%	600,000
100%	800,000

4 June 2005 A further £100,000 cash gift to the discretionary trust created on 4 June 1999.

Required

(a) Discuss the tax reliefs available for the purchase of shares in Pail Ltd and for the interest on the share purchase loan. **(4 marks)**

(b) Assuming that he obtains the most beneficial relief under part (a) calculate Jimmy's 2006/07 income tax and national insurance contribution liabilities. **(7 marks)**

(c) Explain the Inheritance Tax implications arising from the gifts made between 4 June 1999 and 4 June 2005. Your answer should include a calculation of any Inheritance Tax payable and an explanation of any exceptions or reliefs available. You are not required to consider the implications for the trustees of the discretionary trust.

You should assume that the rates and allowances for 2006/07 apply throughout this part of the question.

(11 marks)

(Total = 22 marks)

14 Paul and Sharon (ATAX 6/06)

52 mins

Your manager has had a meeting with Paul and Sharon Potter and has sent you a copy of the following memorandum.

To   The files
From   Tax manager
Date   12 July 2007
Subject Paul and Sharon Potter – Tax issues

Paul Potter (PP)

- Resigned from Memphis plc on 1 June 2007.

- Holds options over 5,000 company shares, granted to him on 25 June 2004.

- The options are part of an approved company share option plan (CSOP), and the exercise price was agreed at £3.50 per share. The current market value of the shares is £6, and this is unlikely to change in the short term.

- Has one month from the date of his resignation in which to exercise the share options and sell the shares, which are not transferable. Intends to do so as soon as possible.

Sharon Potter (SP)

- Has been running a business as a sole trader for the past three years.

- Wishes to incorporate the business and will hold 100% of the shares issued.

- Would like part of the consideration for the business to be in cash, but only if no tax is payable as a result.

- PP will work for the newly incorporated company.

- SP estimates that the business is worth £120,000, comprising the following assets:

Asset £	Market value £	Indexed gain £
Cash	10,000	–
Goodwill	40,000	40,000
Property	70,000	40,000
Stock	10,000	–
Creditors	(10,000)	–

Trust planning

- PP wishes to set up a discretionary trust in the next few months for their children by gifting a residential property into the trust.

- This property was acquired for £70,000 in August 2005 and has a current market value of £160,000.

An extract from an email from your manager is set out below.

Please prepare a report from me to Paul and Sharon Potter setting out the following:

1   The condition that would need to be satisfied for the exercise of Paul's share options to be exempt from income tax and the tax implications if this condition is not satisfied.

Calculate Paul's tax liability if he exercises the share options in Memphis plc and subsequently sells the shares immediately.

Advise Paul how he may reduce this tax liability.

2   The conditions that must be satisfied if Sharon's business is to be sold to a company without incurring an immediate charge to capital gains tax (CGT).

Advise Sharon whether or not she will be able to take advantage of such relief.

Regardless of this advice calculate the maximum amount of cash she could receive on incorporation, without triggering a CGT liability.

Are there any disadvantages to this relief that Sharon should be aware of?

Is there an alternative relief she could use?

3   All of the capital taxation issues Paul needs to be aware of for the discretionary trust for the children.

Tax manager

You have extracted the following further information from client files.

- Paul and Sharon are both aged 38.
- Have two children, Gisella, aged 5 and Gavin aged 2.
- Both Paul and Sharon are higher rate taxpayers
- Neither Paul nor Sharon has made any capital disposals in the tax year 2007/08.
- Paul made a gross chargeable transfer of £185,000 in May 2003.
- The property acquired by Paul in August 2005 generates net rental income of £4,000 per annum.

Required

Prepare the report for Paul and Sharon requested by your manager. The report should be in three sections, addressing the issues set out below, and should, where appropriate, include supporting calculations.

(1)   Paul's share options

State the condition that would need to be satisfied for the exercise of Paul's share options in Memphis plc to be exempt from income tax and the tax implications if this condition is not satisfied.

Calculate Paul's tax liability if he exercises the share options in Memphis plc and subsequently sells the shares in Memphis plc immediately, as proposed, and show how he may reduce this tax liability. **(6 marks)**

(2)   Incorporation of Sharon's business

State the conditions that must be satisfied if Sharon's business is to be sold to a company without incurring an immediate CGT charge, and advise Sharon whether or not she will be able to take advantage of such relief.

Assuming the relief **is** available, advise Sharon on the maximum amount of cash she could receive on incorporation, without triggering a CGT liability.

State any disadvantages to the relief that Sharon should be aware of, and identify and describe another relief that she might use. **(10 marks)**

(3)   Capital tax implications of the discretionary trust

Explain the capital tax issues that Paul needs to be aware of when he sets up a trust for Gisella and Gavin and the potential charges that could arise whilst the trust is in existence. Calculate the stamp duty land tax on the gift into the trust. **(11 marks)**

Appropriateness of the format and presentation of the report and the effectiveness with which its advice is communicated. **(2 marks)**

You may assume that the rates and allowances for the tax year 2006/07 continue to apply for the foreseeable future.

(Total = 29 marks)

Questions 15 to 22 cover the taxation of companies. This is the subject of Chapters 15 to 22 of the BPP study text.

15 Miller Plc

49 mins

Your manager has had a meeting with Fred Kildow, the finance director of Miller plc, and has sent you a copy of the following memorandum.

To	The files
From	Tax manager
Date	1 June 2007
Subject	Miller Plc

To simplify the group finance function Fred Kildow has moved all companies in the group to the same accounting year end. Miller plc's accounting date during 2007 has therefore changed from 31 July to 31 March.

1 August 2006 to 31 March 2007

The profit and loss account for the period from 1 August 2006 to 31 March 2007 shows a profit of £450,000 after accounting for the following items:

	£
Loss on disposal of machinery (Note 1)	30,000
Gift Aid donation accrued (paid 1 April 2007)	10,000
UK rental income	45,000
Advertising (Note 2)	60,000
Interest charged on overdue corporation tax	3,000
Dividend income (Note 3)	75,000
Debenture interest receivable (Note 3)	9,000

Note 1

The machinery had been used in the business and capital allowances had been claimed. It had originally cost £86,000 in January 1997 and was sold for £62,800 in October 2006. At the time of purchase, installation costs of £10,000 were charged in addition to the purchase price.

Note 2

The advertising included £37,750 for the hire of a corporate entertainment box at a sporting event. The cost was for the hire of the box and all food and drink. During the event, Miller plc displayed its corporate logo in the window of the box.

Note 3

In September 2006, Miller plc received a dividend of £12,500 from Bode Ltd, £28,000 from Hillman Ltd and £34,500 from Vogtli Inc. The dividend from Vogtli Inc was received gross as it was not subject to any withholding tax. Miller plc also received interest of £9,000 on a debenture loan to Bode Ltd.

Items not included in the profit and loss account

Miller plc incurred general expenses of £11,550 from the management of its various investments.

Miller plc sold its entire holding in Vogtli Inc for £120,000 on 31 January 2007.

Capital acquisitions

Miller plc purchased a Mercedes car on 1 June 2006 for £28,000. The Mercedes car was purchased for one of the directors with estimated private usage of 25%. On 1 September 2006 Miller plc also purchased a low carbon dioxide emission Jaguar car for £30,000 and new office furniture at a cost of £61,250.

Forecast group results – year ended 31 March 2008
Fred Kildow will be sending a copy of the group's forecast results for the year ended 31 March 2008.

He advised that Bloom Ltd is likely to break-even in 2009. From 2010 onwards Bloom Ltd expects to reach trading profit levels of at least £500,000 per annum.

The other group companies do not expect their income levels to change.

The capital loss shown for Weinbrecht Ltd arose on the sale of an office building in November 2007 to a non-associated company.

Tax manager

An extract from an email from your manager is set out below.

Please prepare a report to Fred Kildow setting out the following:

1   Corporation tax liability

Provide a calculation of Miller plc's corporation tax liability for the period ended 31 March 2007.

I have calculated the indexed rise on the folding in Vogtli Inc from March 1997 to January 2007 to be £9,725.

2   Group issues

State, with reasons, the nature of the relationships that exist between the various companies for corporation tax purposes in the year ending 31 March 2008.

On the basis that Fred Kildow wants to minimise the group's tax liability over the long term, explain the options available to utilise the losses within the group in the year ending 31 March 2008 and state the optimum use for each loss.

You do not need to calculate the corporation tax payable.

3   VAT

Advise on the benefits of a VAT group and explain which companies, if any, should or should not be included in a VAT group registration.

You have extracted the following further information from client files.

- The Miller plc group operates a variety of related businesses aimed at retail customers.
- The group is as follows:

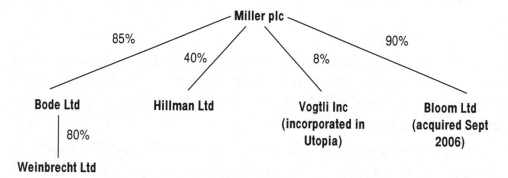

- Miller plc had brought forward trading losses of £95,000 at 1 August 2006.
- Miller plc qualifies as a medium sized enterprise for capital allowances purposes.
- The tax written down value of Miller plc's general pool on 1 August 2006 was £450,000.

- The holding in Vogtli Inc was acquired in March 1997 at a cost of £35,000.

- For VAT purposes Miller plc, Bode Ltd, and Hillman Ltd all make wholly standard rated supplies within the UK.

- 95% of Bloom Ltd's sales are to large businesses in the European Union.

- Weinbrecht Ltd specialises in the supply of insurance services and is therefore wholly exempt from VAT.

A copy of the forecast results arrives showing the following.

	Miller plc £	Bode Ltd £	Hillman Ltd £	Weinbrecht Ltd £	Bloom Ltd £
Trading profit / (Loss)	320,000	125,000	76,000	101,000	(600,000)
Chargeable gains / (Loss)	100,000			(45,000)	35,000
Property business income	70,000				
Interest income	10,000	60,000			20,000
Trading losses b/f					(50,000)

Required

Prepare the report requested by your manager to Fred Kildow. Marks are allocated as follows.

1   Corporation tax liability

     Calculate Miller plc's corporation tax liability for the period ended 31 March 2007.   **(11 marks)**

2   Group issues

     State, with reasons, the nature of the relationships that exist between the various companies for corporation tax purposes in the year ending 31 March 2008 and briefly outline the consequences.   **(4 marks)**

     Explain the options available to utilise the losses within the group in the year ending 31 March 2008 and state the optimum use for each loss.   **(5 marks)**

3   VAT

     Advise on the benefits of a VAT group.

     Explain which companies, if any, should or should not be included in a VAT group registration.   **(5 marks)**

Appropriateness of the format and presentation of the notes and the effectiveness with which their content is communicated.   **(2 marks)**

You may assume that the rates and allowances for the financial year 2006 continue to apply for the foreseeable future.

(Total = 27 marks)

16 Flop Ltd (ATAX 6/05)

40 mins

You have recently been approached by Fred Flop. Fred informs you that he is experiencing problems in dealing with aspects of his company tax returns. The company accountant has been unable to keep up to date with matters, and Fred also believes that mistakes have been made in the past. Fred needs assistance.

The following information has been extracted from client files and from meetings with the shareholders. Assume that today's date is 10 May 2007

Fred Flop:

- 100% shareholder of Flop Limited.
- Managing director.

Flop Limited:

- UK trading company.
- 'Large' for capital allowances purposes for the year ended 31 March 2005.
- Taxable profits of £595,000 in the year ended 31 March 2004.
- Has one wholly owned subsidiary.
- Both companies have a 31 March year-end.

Corporation tax return (CT600) for the year ended 31 March 2005:

- The corporation tax return for this period was not submitted until 2 November 2006, and corporation tax of £123,500 was paid at the same time. Profits chargeable to corporation tax were stated as £704,300.

- A formal notice (CT203) requiring the company to file a self-assessment corporation tax return (dated 1 February 2006) had been received by the company on 4 February 2006.

Examination of the accounts and tax computation for the year ended 31 March 2005:

- Computer equipment totalling £50,000 had been expensed in the accounts. No adjustment has been made in the tax computation.

- A £10,000 repairs provision was made; there is no supporting information.

- £46,500 legal and professional fees allowed in full without any explanation. Fred has subsequently produced the following analysis:

  Analysis of legal & professional fees

	£
Legal fees on a failed attempt to secure a trading loan	5,000
Debt collection agency fees	12,800
Obtaining planning consent for building extension	5,700
Accountant's fees for preparing accounts	14,000
Legal fees relating to a trade dispute	9,000

- No enquiry has yet been raised by HMRC.

CT600 for the year ended 31 March 2006:

- Has not been submitted yet.

- Accounts are late and nearing completion, with only one change still to be made.

- A notice requiring the company to file a self-assessment corporation tax return (CT203) dated 27 July 2006 was received on 1 August 2006. No corporation tax has yet been paid.

- Computation currently shows profits chargeable to corporation tax of £815,000 before accounting adjustments, and any adjustments for prior years.

- A company owing Flop Ltd £50,000 (excluding VAT) has gone into liquidation, and it is unlikely that any of this money will be paid. The money has been outstanding since 3 September 2005, and the impairment loss (bad debt) will need to be included in the accounts.

VAT issues:

- VAT return for the quarter ended 31 March 2007 was submitted on 5 May 2007, and VAT of £24,000 was paid at the same time.

- Previous return to 31 December 2006 was also submitted late.

- No account has been made for VAT on the bad debt.

- VAT return for 30 June 2007 may also be late. Estimated VAT liability is £8,250.

Required

(a) (i) Calculate the revised corporation tax (CT) payable for the accounting periods ending 31 March 2005 and 2006 respectively. Your answer should include an explanation of the adjustments made as a result of the information which has now come to light and the practical steps needed to correct the position. **(6 marks)**

   (ii) State, giving reasons, the due payment date of the corporation tax (CT) and the filing date of the corporation tax return for each period, and identify any interest and penalties which may have arisen to date. **(7 marks)**

   Assume that the rates and allowances for 2006/07 apply throughout this part and interest on overdue tax is 6.5%.

(b) Explain the consequences of filing the VAT returns late and advise Fred how he should deal with the underpayment and bad debt for VAT purposes. Your explanation should be supported by relevant calculations. **(9 marks)**

(Total = 22 marks)

17 Preparation question with helping hand: Bargains Ltd
40 mins

Bargains Ltd is a close company that buys and sells antiques.

The following information has been extracted from client files and from meetings with the shareholders.

Shareholders:

- Rodney, Reggie and Del Rotter each own one third of Bargains Ltd's ordinary share capital.
- Rodney and Reggie are company directors.
- Del is not a company director or an employee.

Bargains Ltd:

- Incorporated 1 August 2005.

- Incurred advertising campaign expenditure on 1 February 2006.

- Commenced purchasing antiques for resale on 1 March 2006, but the business premises (see below) were not opened until 1 April 2006.

- On the same day the company registered for VAT and made its first sale.

- Accounts have been prepared for the period 1 August 2005 to 31 December 2006.

Capital acquisitions:

- Acquired business premises, which were in a bad state of repair, on 1 January 2006. Immediately started to repair and refurbish them.

- Bought three new motor cars costing £10,575 each (including VAT), on 1 July 2006 for the business and private use of Rodney, Reggie and Del.

- CO_2 emissions for the cars are 167 g/km. No private fuel is provided.

Interest free loan to Del:

- Made an interest free loan of £42,000 to Del on 1 October 2006.
- Del used funds to purchase a holiday villa in Spain.
- The loan has not yet been repaid.

Required

(a) (i) Set out the accounting periods for Bargains Ltd up to, and including, 31 December 2006.

    (ii) How will Bargains Ltd's expenditure on its advertising campaign and the refurbishment of its business premises be treated for the purposes of corporation tax and VAT? **(9 marks)**

(b) What are the tax implications, for both Bargains Ltd and the Rotter brothers, arising from the provision of the three company motor cars? You should ignore the implications of NIC. **(8 marks)**

(c) Advise both Bargains Ltd and Del of the tax implications arising from the provision of the interest free loan. **(4 marks)**

(Total = 21 marks)

Helping hand

1   You need to be able to spot a close company from the facts in the question. Did you spot it here?

2   If a company is a close company this may affect the taxation of the provision of benefits to participators (not employees) and there will also be a 25% penalty tax charge if loans are made to participators.

3   If you are comfortable with the close company rules, why not answer parts (b) and (c) first? You can then go back to part (a) which mainly deals with pre-trading expenditure and its treatment for corporation tax and VAT purposes.

---

18 Lorna Mill Ltd

45 mins

Your manager has had a meeting with the directors of Lorna Mill Ltd and has sent you a copy of the following memorandum.

To   The files
From   Tax manager
Date   1 June 2007
Subject   Lorna Mill Ltd

Tax position for year ended 31 March 2007

The directors informed me of the following information:

Adjusted trading profit for the year is £255,000, before considering the matters referred to below.

11 May 2006: £20,000 was spent restoring a country cottage to be lived in by Sam Bradley. It was estimated that £11,000 related to improvements, although the full expenditure had been written off in the profit and loss account.

20 February 2007: a loan of £7,100 to John Harmer, son of Frank Harmer, to assist him in purchasing a racing yacht. John will pay a market rate of interest on 30 June each year.

30 September 2006: the sale of a leasehold building for £125,000. This building was acquired by the company on 1 July 1995 for £100,000, when the lease had 30 years to run (indexed rise = 0.342).

Dividends received during the year from non group companies were £27,000.

Proposed takeover

The directors of Lorna Mill Ltd have recently been approached by representatives of Evergreen plc who want to take over the company. They are offering a package of either cash or a combination of shares and loan stock (which will be qualifying corporate bonds) in exchange for either the shares held by the members of Lorna Mill Ltd or the trade itself from the company.

Tax manager

An extract from an email from your manager is set out below.

Please prepare a letter from me to the directors of Lorna Mill Ltd, setting out the following:

---

1   Calculations to show the corporation tax position for the company and its directors for the year ended 31 March 2007.

     The appropriate lease percentage figures you will need to work with are:

     30 yrs: 87.330
     19 yrs: 70.791
     18 yrs: 68.697

2   Explanations of your treatment of each item.

3   Advice on the tax considerations arising out of the takeover offers from Evergreen plc.

4   Other issues arising in respect of the proposed takeover offers.

You have extracted the following further information from Lorna Mill Ltd's client files.

- Lorna Mill Ltd was formed in 1985.

- The ordinary issued share capital of Lorna Mill Ltd is as follows:

Don Bradley FCA	(Chairman)	13,500
Sam Bradley	(Sales Director, brother of Chairman)	3,000
Mrs Anne Bradley	(Director, wife of Chairman)	2,000
Frank Harmer ACA		4,000
Chris Justice	(Production Director)	2,500
20 unrelated members of the public		2,500
Carol Laker	(Chairman's niece, not employed by the company)	2,500
Ordinary £1 shares		40,000

- All shareholders/ directors are higher rate taxpayers.

- The building sold on 30 September 2006 had been acquired using £100,000 of the proceeds from the sale of a freehold building. The freehold building had been acquired in May 1989 for £40,000 and was sold on 28 October 1993 for £130,000 (indexed rise = 0.317).

Required

Prepare the letter requested by your manager.

Marks are available for the components of the letter as follows:

1	Relevant calculations.	**(6 marks)**
2	Clear and concise explanations of your treatment of each item.	**(6 marks)**
3	The tax considerations of Evergreen plc's takeover offer.	**(7 marks)**
4	Any other considerations for the company in respect of the takeover proposals.	**(4 marks)**

Appropriateness of the format and presentation of the letter and the effectiveness with which the information is communicated. **(2 marks)**

You may assume that the rates and allowances for the tax year 2006/07 and financial year 2006 continue to apply for the foreseeable future.

(Total = 25 marks)

19 Question with answer plan: Trent Plc

61 mins

Your firm has acted for many years as taxation advisors to Trent plc, which trades as a transportation company throughout the south of England.

The partner who deals with Trent plc's affairs has just received the following letter from Sally Kosar, the managing director.

STRICTLY PRIVATE AND CONFIDENTIAL

1 July 2007

Dear Nicholas

Proposed acquisition of Ivan Ltd

We are currently involved in negotiations with Reznik plc to purchase one of its 100% subsidiaries, Ivan Ltd, a removals firm. I would like your advice on certain aspects of this proposed acquisition and some other matters.

Method of acquisition

We have agreed in principle with Reznik plc to buy Ivan Ltd for a total of £35 million. We hope to effect the acquisition on 31 August 2007.

Ivan Ltd prepares accounts to 30 June each year, and preliminary figures suggest that as at 30 June 2007 it will have the following tax losses available to carry forward:

Trading losses	£16 million
Capital losses	£2 million
Total	£18 million

Once Trent plc has acquired Ivan Ltd we would intend to refocus its operations gradually so that it would concentrate less on their traditional residential removals market and more on supplying commercial customers. The intention would be to get to the point after about two or three years when Ivan's outlets would be engaged in much the same activities as our existing 'Trent' outlets. At that point we would want to merge the activities of the two companies so that one company could operate under a single name. We would be indifferent whether the outlets would be operated by Ivan Ltd or Trent plc.

Our financial forecasts indicate that Ivan Ltd will continue to make losses for the next two to three years so that by the time of the merger of the trades of Trent plc and Ivan Ltd I would expect the total trading losses in Ivan Ltd to have risen to £20 million.

Machinist House

We hope to be able to use a surplus freehold property, 'Machinist House', owned by Ivan Ltd, to create a further capital loss which Trent plc will be able to utilise against its anticipated capital gains.

Machinist House was purchased by Ivan Ltd for £12 million on 28 February 2000 and is currently worth about £7 million. Our valuers have indicated that they do not expect this value to change in the foreseeable future.

Trent plc has just commissioned builders to commence the construction of a new freehold headquarters for the group which will cost a total of £9 million exclusive of VAT. This new office is scheduled to be ready for occupation in the early part of the summer of 2008, and we anticipate being able to vacate and to sell our existing headquarters on or around 31 August 2008. We expect to sell the existing headquarters for a total of £13 million and would anticipate realising a capital gain on this sale of about £8 million after indexation allowance.

What I hope to do is to transfer Machinist House to Trent plc immediately after we have acquired Ivan Ltd so that it can be sold, and the capital loss realised, at about the same time we realise the capital gain on the sale of our existing headquarters. In this way I would hope to be able to shelter the bulk of the capital gain arising on the sale of the headquarters with the capital loss arising on the sale of Machinist House and the capital losses carried forward in Ivan Ltd.

VAT

Finally, our new office block will contain rather more office accommodation than we are going to need for many years. We are therefore negotiating to sub-let the surplus space and we have identified an insurance company which seems to be willing to rent this surplus from us. I understand that we are permitted to opt to tax the new building for VAT purposes and would appreciate your advice on the procedure and on the advantages and disadvantages of doing so.

It occurs to me that I have not as yet sought any tax advice on the Ivan Ltd acquisition and in particular I have assumed all of our business plans can be put into practice without any tax disadvantages and that we will have considerable freedom to use Ivan Ltd's tax losses as we wish. I do not know to what extent my assumptions are correct and I should be grateful if you could write to me and explain the tax position in relation to the various matters referred to in this letter.

Yours sincerely

Sally Kosar

Required

Draft a reply to Ms Kosar's letter. Your reply should:

(a) Explain the ways in which the various tax losses in Ivan Ltd are capable of being utilised following the acquisition of Ivan Ltd by Trent plc. **(9 marks)**

(b) Explain whether and if so to what extent Trent plc will be able to shelter its forecast capital gain on the sale of its existing headquarters using the forecast loss on the sale of Machinist House as anticipated by Ms Kosar and provide advice on alternative methods of sheltering this gain. **(7 marks)**

(c) Advise how the merger of the trades of Ivan Ltd and Trent plc should be effected, and provide advice on possible ways of improving the corporation tax position in which the Trent plc group would find itself following the acquisition of Ivan Ltd. **(9 marks)**

(d) Answer Ms Kosar's queries in relation to VAT. **(7 marks)**

Appropriateness of the format and presentation of the notes and the effectiveness with which their content is communicated. **(2 marks)**

You may assume that the rates and allowances for the financial year 2006 continue to apply for the foreseeable future.

(Total = 34 marks)

20 Spark Ltd

54 mins

Your manager has had a meeting with Joan Thompson, owner of Spark Ltd, an electrical retail company, and has sent you a copy of the following memorandum.

To	The files
From	Tax manager
Date	12 May 2008
Subject	Spark Ltd group

Spark Ltd

Spark Ltd acquired a freehold property (The Hutch) from Burn Ltd for £180,000 on 19 April 2007. The property's market value at that date was £200,000. It was immediately used for the company's trade.

Char Ltd

Last year it was decided that Char Ltd should cease investing in commercial property (as had been the case until then) and should invest instead in quoted shares in unrelated companies and in government securities. In consequence Char Ltd has carried out a number of capital transactions:

1 March 2007: – sold its leasehold interest in Watt Hall for £656,000.

– purchased shares in Blowemup plc for £300,000, and £440,000 5% Funding Stock 2013 for £300,000.

1 June 2007: – sold the freehold in its only remaining property, Place House, for £185,000.
– purchased shares in Ultracool plc for £240,000.

Fizzle Ltd

Due to poor trading conditions Fizzle Ltd sold its biggest trade freehold property, Electric House, for £800,000 on 16 May 2007. Another freehold building, Rumble House, was purchased on 22 December 2007 for £200,000, and was immediately brought into use for the company's trade.

No more purchases or sales of properties held for the use of any trade are anticipated in the foreseeable future.

Results for the year ended 31 March 2007 and 2008

Before taking into account the above transactions, the results for the group were as follows:

	Year ended 31 March 2007 £'000	Year ended 31 March 2008 £'000
Spark Ltd:		
Trading profits/(losses)	172.5	(120)
Burn Ltd:		
Trading profits	25	55
Char Ltd:		
Property business income	97.5	10
Interest income	–	22
Dividend received (including tax credit)	–	30
Fizzle Ltd:		
Trading (losses)/profits	(260)	97.5

Burn Ltd has trading losses brought forward at 31 March 2006 of £75,000. In the year ended 31 March 2006 no company in the group had a corporation tax liability in excess of the small companies' rate.

An extract from an email from your manager is set out below.

Please prepare notes for my next meeting with Joan Thompson incorporating the following:

1   Discuss the available reliefs that are available to keep the corporation tax liabilities of the group to a minimum for the two years shown.

Mention any other matters you consider relevant.

Give your reasons for accepting or rejecting any possible reliefs.

2   In the light of your conclusions, calculate the corporation tax payable by each company for the years ended 31 March 2007 and 2008.

You can ignore the effect of capital allowances.

When you come to calculate the gain on the sale of the leasehold property you will need the following percentages from the lease percentage table:

16 years: 64.116%
25 years: 81.100%

Tax manager

You have extracted the following further information from client files.

•   Burn Ltd, Char Ltd and Fizzle Ltd are 100% subsidiaries of Spark Ltd.

•   All Spark Ltd group companies make up accounts to 31 March each year.

•   Burn Ltd is a property dealing and development company which holds no property by way of investment. It was incorporated in June 2000 and had acquired The Hutch for £180,000 on 1 June 2006.

•   Char Ltd is an investment company that was incorporated in September 1992. It had purchased Watt Hall on 1 March 1998 for £400,000 when the lease had exactly 25 years to run, and had purchased Place House on 25 April 1997 for £120,000.

•   Fizzle Ltd was incorporated on 1 April 2005 and trades as a retail grocer in the north of England. Electric House had been transferred to it from Spark Ltd for its open market value of £850,000 on 1 May 2006. Spark Ltd had purchased Electric House for £325,000 in November 1999.

Required

Prepare the notes requested by your manager. Marks are available as follows.

(a)   Discussing the available reliefs to reduce to a minimum the corporation tax liabilities of the group for the two years shown.   **(16 marks)**

(b)   Discussing any other relevant matters.   **(4 marks)**

(c)   Reasons for accepting or rejecting any possible reliefs.   **(5 marks)**

(d)   Computing the corporation tax payable by each company for the years ended 31 March 2007 and 2008.   **(5 marks)**

You should assume the following indexed rises.

April 1997 to June 2007   56.6%
March 1998 to March 2007   50.6%
November 1999 to May 2006   36.0%
May 2006 to May 2007   2.2%

You may assume that the rates and allowances for the tax year 2006/07 and financial year 2006 continue to apply for the foreseeable future.

(Total = 30 marks)

21 Irroy (ATAX 12/05)

40 mins

Irroy is aged 45, and owns 75% of the ordinary share capital of two companies, Aqua Limited and Aria Limited. Her brother, Irwin, owns the remaining 25% of the shares in both companies. Assume today's date is 1 May 2007.

The following information has been extracted from client files and from meetings with the shareholders.

Aqua Ltd and Aria Ltd:

- Both companies have a 31 March year end.
- Aqua Limited makes water tanks for aquariums and has been trading for five years.
- Aria Limited makes loudspeakers and started trading on 1 April 2006.

Trading results:

- The trading profits/(losses) results for the two companies are as follows:

Year ended 31 March	2007	2008 (estimated)	2009 (estimated)
	£	£	£
Aqua Limited	140,000	175,000	200,000
Aria Limited	(30,000)	(60,000)	(20,000)

- Irroy would like to obtain tax relief for Aria Limited's trading losses as soon as possible.

Overseas expansion plans:

- In April 2008 Aqua Ltd will incorporate a subsidiary, Green Limited, in the Republic of Ireland.

- It will sell water tanks supplied by Aqua Limited from the UK.

- Year ended 31 March 2009: estimated combined taxable profits of the two companies will increase from £200,000 to £275,000.

- The group currently qualifies as a small and medium sized enterprise (SME) under European Union (EU) definitions.

- Irroy believes this will continue to be the case after incorporating Green Limited.

Republic of Ireland tax rates and information:

- Standard rate of corporation tax (CT) = 12.5%.
- Standard rate of value added tax (VAT) = 21%.
- A double tax treaty exists between the UK and the Republic of Ireland, based on the OECD model.
- Both countries are part of the EU.

Required

(a) (i)   Explain why the current corporate structure prevents the early relief of Aria Limited's losses. Advise Irroy of two alternative ways in which the current structure can be amended so as to obtain such early relief.   **(5 marks)**

(ii) Illustrate the benefit of revising the corporate structure by calculating the corporation tax (CT) payable for the year ended 31 March 2008, on the assumptions that:

(1)   no action is taken; and
(2)   an amended structure as recommended in (i) above is implemented from 1 June 2007.

(3 marks)

Assume that the corporation tax rates for the financial year 2006 apply throughout.

(b) Explain the corporation tax (CT) and value added tax (VAT) issues that Irroy should be aware of, if she proceeds with her proposal for the Irish subsidiary, Green Limited. Your answer should clearly identify those factors which will determine whether or not Green Limited is considered UK resident or Irish resident and the tax implications of each alternative situation.

You need not repeat points that are common to each situation.   **(14 marks)**

(Total = 22 marks)

69

22 Dovedale Ltd (ATAX 12/06)

38 mins

Dovedale Ltd, a company with no subsidiaries, has been a client for several years, as has Belgrove Ltd.

The following information has been extracted as at 1 January 2007 from client files and from meetings with directors.

Proposed group:

- Intends to purchase 65% of the ordinary share capital of Hira Ltd from Belgrove Ltd.
- Belgrove Ltd currently owns 100% of the share capital of Hira Ltd and has no other subsidiaries.
- All three companies have head offices in the UK and are UK resident.

Hira Ltd:

- Has £18,600 trading losses brought forward at 1 April 2006.

- Had no income or gains in the year ended 31 March 2006.

- Expects to make further tax adjusted trading losses of £55,000 before deduction of capital allowances, and to have no other income or gains in the year ended 31 March 2007.

- Tax written down value brought forward of the plant and machinery pool at 1 April 2006 was £96,000. There will be no fixed asset additions or disposals in the year ending 31 March 2007.

- A small tax adjusted trading loss is anticipated in the year ending 31 March 2008.

- Will surrender the maximum possible trading losses to Belgrove Ltd and Dovedale Ltd.

Dovedale Ltd:

- Expected tax adjusted trading profit for year ended 31 March 2007 is £875,000 and will continue at this level in the future.

- Will sell a small office building, purchased for £210,000 in March 2005, to Hira Ltd on 1 February 2007 for its market value of £234,000.

- Sold a factory in October 2004 for £277,450 making a capital gain of £84,217. A claim was made to roll over the gain on the sale of the factory against the acquisition cost of the office building.

Belgrove Ltd:

- The profits chargeable to corporation tax of Belgrove Ltd are expected to be £38,000 for the year ending 31 March 2007 and to increase in the future.

Planned overseas expansion:

- Dovedale Ltd intends to acquire the whole of the ordinary share capital of Atapo Inc, an unquoted company resident in the country of Morovia on 1 April 2007.

- Atapo Inc sells components to Dovedale Ltd as well as to other companies in Morovia and around the world.

- Atapo Inc's estimated profit before tax (and taxable profits) for year ended 31 March 2008 is £160,000 and it will pay a dividend to Dovedale Ltd of £105,000.

- The rate of corporation tax in Morovia is 9%. There is a withholding tax of 3% on dividends paid to non-Morovian resident shareholders. There is no double tax agreement between the UK and Morovia.

Required

(a) Advise Belgrove Ltd of any capital gains that may arise as a result of the sale of the shares in Hira Ltd. You are not required to calculate any capital gains in this part of the question. **(3 marks)**

(b) Explain by reference to Hira Ltd's loss position why it may be beneficial for it not to claim any capital allowances for the year ending 31 March 2007. Support your explanation with relevant calculations.

(5 marks)

(c) Calculate the expected corporation tax liability of Dovedale Ltd for the year ending 31 March 2007 on the assumption that all available reliefs are claimed by Dovedale Ltd but that Hira Ltd will not claim any capital allowances in that year. **(3 marks)**

(d) Comment on your position as accountant to both Dovedale Ltd and Belgrove Ltd. **(2 marks)**

(e) Explain whether or not Dovedale Ltd, Hira Ltd and Atapo Inc can register as a group for the purposes of value added tax. **(3 marks)**

(f) Explain in detail how the profits of Atapo Inc, both distributed and non-distributed, will be taxed in the UK. You are not required to produce any calculations for this part of the question. **(5 marks)**

You should assume that the corporation tax rates and allowances for the financial year 2006 apply throughout this question.

Relevant retail price index figures are:

March	2005	190.5
February	2007	193.9 (estimated)

(Total = 21 marks)

VAT

Questions 23 to 25 cover VAT. This is the subject of Chapters 28 and 29 in the BPP study text.

23 Yaz Pica

32 mins

Yaz Pica commenced trading as a self-employed printer on 1 January 2007.

The following information has been extracted from client files and from meetings with Yaz.

Yaz Pica:

- Was employed until 30 November 2006 on an annual salary of £42,000.
- PAYE of £5,727 deducted during 2006/07.
- He is single.
- Has no other income or outgoings.

Printing business:

- Will make up accounts to 31 December 2007.

- Has produced the following quarterly profit forecast:

	Quarter ending 31.3.07 £	Quarter ending 30.6.07 £	Quarter ending 30.9.07 £	Quarter ending 31.12.07 £	Total for year £
Sales					
Standard rated	19,400	29,600	40,200	51,200	139,400
Zero rated	5,100	7,500	9,700	12,500	34,800
	24,500	37,100	49,900	63,700	174,200
Purchases	(14,900)	(16,700)	(18,400)	(20,600)	(70,600)
Opening stock	(3,600)	(3,800)	(4,400)	(5,700)	(3,600)
Closing stock	3,800	4,400	5,700	7,200	7,200
Subcontractor costs		(3,100)	(8,800)	(12,400)	(24,300)
Expenses					
Standard rated	(9,900)	(5,200)	(5,600)	(6,100)	(26,800)
Exempt	(1,100)	(1,300)	(1,600)	(1,800)	(5,800)
Profit/(Loss)	(1,200)	11,400	16,800	24,300	50,300

Expenditure:

- Opening stock of £3,600 represents purchases made during December 2006.

- On 10 December 2006 purchased printing equipment for £14,400 and spent £1,400 on an advertising campaign that ran throughout December.

- All expenses are allowable for tax purposes.

- Expenses do not include capital allowances or cost of the advertising campaign.

VAT:

- Registered for VAT on 1 January 2007.
- VAT registration turnover limit was not exceeded until June 2007.
- All sales are to members of the general public.
- Purchases are all standard rated.

The above figures do not include VAT.

Required

(a) (i) Explain to Yaz the income tax liabilities that will be due on 31 January 2008 if he makes up his accounts for the year ended 31 December 2007.

(ii) Advise Yaz of whether it will be beneficial to make up his accounts for the three month period to 31 March 2007, rather than for the year ended 31 December 2007.

You are only expected to calculate Yaz's income tax liability for 2006/07. NIC should be ignored.

(12 marks)

(b) With hindsight, it is evident that Yaz should not have registered for VAT until 1 August 2007. Explain why this is the case, and calculate the additional profit that Yaz would have made if he had registered for VAT as from 1 August 2007 rather than from 1 January 2007.

(6 marks)

(Total = 18 marks)

24 Leo Topper   63 mins

Your manager has had a meeting with Tim Topper, son of your recently deceased client, Leo Topper, and has sent you a copy of the following meeting notes via email.

To   The files
From   Tax manager
Date   1 November 2006

Subject Leo Topper

Tim Topper (TT) provided the following information following his father, Leo's, death.

Leo Topper (LT)

- Died suddenly aged 54 on 15 June 2006.

- Was managing director of VDV Ltd, a company transferring films from VHS to DVD, earning over £200,000 a year. TT has now been appointed managing director of VDV Ltd.

- Had also carried on a sole trader film making business since July 1998, which he sold shortly before his death. Details are at Appendix A.

LT's estate

- Apart from a legacy of £100,000 to charity, all his assets were left to TT, his only son, who is also his executor.
- Values of assets held at death are at Appendix B.

Tim Topper (TT)

- Sold 17 of the 47 antiques from Leo's estate (Appendix B) and added the remaining 30 items to his own collection. The 17 items were sold for £72,000, one item being sold for £6,750, the other 14 for under £6,000 each.

- Also sold 3 items from his own collection for £4,500 each.

VDV Ltd

- TT will ask the company accountant to provide this office with a copy of the profit and loss account for the year ended 31 December 2007.

- Plans to purchase 90% of the issued share capital of MD Ltd, a company with unrelieved trading and capital losses brought forward and currently trading at a loss.

- VDV Ltd joined the annual accounting scheme for VAT in 2002 when its turnover was lower than at present. It has made monthly interim payments of £9,000 for the year ended 31 December 2006 on the due dates.

Tax manager

Appendix A – Film making business

	£
Freehold property purchased on 1 July 1998 – cost	110,000
Adjusted profit for year ended 30 June 1999	24,000
(Profits increased steadily until 2004)	
Adjusted profit for year ended 30 June 2005	52,000
Adjusted profit for period ended 31 May 2006	46,000
Freehold property disposed of on 1 June 2006 – proceeds	300,000

Appendix B – LT's death estate – probate values

	£
50,000 shares in VDV Ltd (25% of issued share capital)	500,000
10,000 shares in Film plc, a listed company (0.01% of issued share capital)	25,000
Bank account containing proceeds of sale of property used in business	300,000
Shares in an ISA	17,000
Antiques (each item under £6,000)	175,000
Freehold cottage – LT's principal private residence	437,500
Private motor car	23,500
Loan owing to Westland Bank	(150,000)

An extract from the email from your manager is set out below.

Please prepare a letter from me to Tim Topper, setting out the following:

1. Calculations to show how much IHT is due on LT's estate. TT will also need to know his administrative responsibilities.

2. Explanations of LT's income and capital gains tax liabilities in the two years before his death.

3. The criteria to be considered in deciding on the tax treatment of TT's disposals of the antiques.

4. The projected VAT and corporation tax liabilities for VDV Ltd for the year ended 31 December 2006. TT is also concerned about the tax consequences and opportunities arising to VDV Ltd following the purchase of the shares of MD Ltd.

You have extracted the following further information from client files.

- LT's only lifetime gift was a cash transfer in May 2000 to a discretionary trust. The trustees paid IHT of £49,000. The gross chargeable amount of the gift was £485,000.

- VDV Ltd operates from a factory bought new in 1998 for £300,000 excluding land. Capital allowances on plant have been calculated to be £15,900. VDV Ltd is a small business for capital allowance purposes.

- VDV Ltd is VAT registered. All its sales are standard-rated.

VDV Ltd's company accountant sends a copy of the projected profit and loss account for the year ended 31 December 2006 which shows the following information.

VDV Ltd
Profit and loss account – year ended 31 December 2006

	Notes	£	£
Sales	(1)		1,420,000
Cost of sales (videos and DVDs)			(800,000)
			620,000
Wages		210,000	
Electricity		16,000	
Entertaining of clients		7,000	
Depreciation of equipment	(2)	57,000	
			(290,000)
Operating profit			330,000
Rental income	(3)		30,000
Profit for the year			360,000

Notes to the accounts

(1) All figures are shown exclusive of VAT unless non-reclaimable.

(2) Rental income is in respect of an unused office and comprises the following.

	£	£
Rent receivable – including £3,000 owing at 31 December 2006		42,000
Business rates	4,000	
Management costs	1,500	
New air-conditioning unit (February 2006)	6,500	
		(12,000)
Net rental income		30,000

Required

Prepare the letter for Tim in respect his various tax queries. The letter should be in four sections, addressing the four sets of issues set out below, and should, where appropriate, include supporting calculations.

(a) Inheritance tax on Leo Topper's estate

Advise Tim how much IHT will be due Leo's death.

You should state the due dates of payment and submission of the IHT account and the person liable. Ignore any other taxes owing at death. **(8 marks)**

(b) Leo's income tax and CGT position

Show Leo's income tax liability arising in respect of the final year of the film making business.

Explain, with supporting calculations, the tax arising from the disposal by Leo of the freehold property used in the film making business, assuming Leo has made no other disposal in 2006/07.

Advise how these liabilities would impact your answer to (a) above. **(5 marks)**

(c) Disposals of antiques

State the criteria to be considered in deciding on the tax treatment of Tim's disposals of antiques.

For both of the two possible tax treatments identify the taxes which could be payable by Tim. **(7 marks)**

(d)   VDV Ltd

State the VAT payable by VDV Ltd in respect of the year ended 31 December 2006 along with the due date of payment and submission of the return, and comment briefly on the VAT position for the following year. Ignore VAT on the rental activities.   **(4 marks)**

Compute the corporation tax payable by VDV Ltd for the year ended 31 December 2006.   **(3 marks)**

State the taxation consequences and opportunities arising to VDV Ltd following the purchase of the shares of MD Ltd.   **(6 marks)**

Appropriateness of the format and presentation of the notes and the effectiveness with which the information is communicated.   **(2 marks)**

You may assume that the rates and allowances for the tax year 2006/07 and financial year 2006 continue to apply for the foreseeable future.

(Total = 35 marks)

25 Tay Limited (ATAX 6/06)   38 mins

Assume today's date is 1 May 2007.

Tay Limited is an unquoted trading company with a 31 March year end. It acquired 100% of the shares of another company, Trent Limited, on 1 September 2006. Both companies manufacture engine components.

The following information has been extracted from client files and from meetings with shareholders.

Tay Limited:

- £250,000 trade profits in year ended 31 March 2007.

- Incurred expenditure of £250,000 on intellectual property on 1 January 2007. Does not depreciate this amount so has not claimed any writing down allowances for the expenditure.

- Lacks capacity to take on more work, so intends to transfer several orders to Trent Limited.

- Planning to sell a capital asset in September 2007 that will realise a capital gain of £75,000. Has suggested that Trent Limited sell its building (see below) at the same time to take advantage of the capital loss that would arise.

Trent Limited:

- At 1 January 2006 had tax losses of £300,000 (including £60,000 relating to the year ended 31 December 2005).

- Losses for year ended 31 December 2006 are £120,000.

- Anticipated profits, following transfer of orders, are £50,000 for the year to 31 December 2007, with greater profits expected in subsequent years. Hopes to utilise its existing corporation tax losses.

Building owned by Trent Limited:

- Purchased in September 1996 for £400,000. Tax life had expired at this date.
- Always used for trade purposes.
- Valued at £300,000 on 1 September 2006.
- Current market value is £250,000.

Proposed overseas investment by Tay Limited:

- Has recently identified an opportunity to purchase either the shares or the assets of Tagus LDA, an engineering company based in Portugal.

- Tagus LDA's business will remain Portuguese resident irrespective of the acquisition route taken.

- Portuguese companies and businesses pay tax on profits at the rate of 27.5%

Trent Limited's VAT return for quarter ended 31 March 2007:

- Recent investigation by Trent Limited's finance director has revealed an error in this return.

- Input VAT was correctly calculated at £40,000, but the output VAT was under declared by £55,000 as £87,500.

- The additional VAT due has not yet been paid.

Required

(a) (i)   State, giving reasons, whether or not Tay Limited is entitled to claim a tax allowance in respect of the purchased intellectual property.   **(2 marks)**

(ii) Calculate the corporation tax (CT) payable by Tay Limited for the year ended 31 March 2007, taking advantage of all available reliefs.   **(3 marks)**

(iii) Explain the potential corporation tax (CT) implications of Tay Limited transferring work to Trent Limited, and suggest how these can be minimised or eliminated.   **(2 marks)**

(b) Advise on the capital gains implications should Trent Limited's old building be sold as proposed. Support your advice with relevant calculations.   **(3 marks)**

(c) Briefly outline the corporation tax (CT) issues that Tay Limited should consider when deciding whether to acquire the shares or the assets of Tagus LDA. You are not required to discuss issues relating to transfer pricing.   **(6 marks)**

(d) Advise Trent Limited of the consequences arising from the submission of the incorrect value added tax (VAT) return, assuming that the company has previously had a good compliance record with regard to accounting for VAT, and comment on any action you should take.   **(5 marks)**

(Total = 21 marks)

TAX PLANNING

Questions 26 to 32 cover tax planning. This is the subject of Chapter 30 in the BPP study text.

26 Question with analysis: Andrew (ATAX 6/06)   38 mins

Andrew is aged 38 and is employed as a consultant by Bestadvice & Co.

The following information has been extracted from client files and from meetings with Andrew.

Andrew:

<table>
<tr><td>

Large salary – obviously paying income tax at 40%
</td></tr>
</table>

- Single.

- Has earnings of **£300,000**.

- Contributes 6% of his annual salary to the Bestadvice & Co registered occupational pension scheme. The firm contributes 8%.

<table>
<tr><td>CGT re disposal?</td></tr>
</table>

- Is considering investing in a new business, Scalar Limited, so has recently **disposed of a number of assets** to fund the investment.

<table>
<tr><td>Special CGT rules for leases</td></tr>
</table>

Capital disposals:

<table>
<tr><td>Gilts are exempt for CGT</td></tr>
</table>

- *12 May 2007:*   Assigned **short leasehold** interest in a residential property for £90,000. Originally paid £50,000 for a 47 year lease in May 1996.

- *14 March 2007:*   Sold £10,000 7% **Government Stock** for £11,250. Originally purchased on 1 June 2000 for £9,980. **Interest is payable half-yearly on** 20 April and 20 October.

<table>
<tr><td>Accrued income scheme</td></tr>
</table>

Scalar Limited:

- UK based manufacturing company.

- Three investors (including Andrew) have been identified to **subscribe** for ordinary shares in the company, but a fourth investor may also be invited to subscribe for shares.

<table>
<tr><td>EIS will be available</td></tr>
</table>

- Investors are all unconnected, and would subscribe equally for shares.

- Has advised investors that they can take advantage of various tax reliefs on this investment.

- Will raise £450,000 in this way and a further £50,000, in the form of loans, from the investors.

Required

(a) (i)   Calculate the chargeable gain arising on the assignment of the residential property lease in May 2007.   **(2 marks)**

(ii)   Advise Andrew of the tax implications arising from the disposal of the 7% Government Stock, clearly identifying the tax year in which any liability will arise and how it will be paid.
   (3 marks)

<table>
<tr><td>This part of question is stand alone and you could do first</td></tr>
</table>

(b) (i)   Advise Andrew of the income tax (IT) and capital gains tax (CGT) reliefs available on his investment in the ordinary share capital of Scalar Limited, together with any conditions which need to be satisfied. Your answer should clearly identify any steps that should be taken by Andrew and the other investors to obtain the maximum relief.   **(11 marks)**

(ii)   State the taxation implications of both **equity and loan finance** from the point of view of a company.   **(2 marks)**

<table>
<tr><td>

Equal to earnings but annual limit of £215,000 for tax relief

</td></tr>
</table>

(c)   Advise Andrew of the **maximum contributions** he may make to a personal pension, together with any limits he should be aware of both now and in the future, and how he may obtain tax relief for both the occupational and personal pension contributions.   **(3 marks)**

You should assume that the rates and allowances for the tax year 2006/07 apply throughout this question.

Relevant retail price index figures are:

May 1996   152.9
April 1998   162.6

Relevant extracts from the leasehold depreciation tables are as follows:

36 years   92.761
47 years   98.902

(Total = 21 marks)

27 Question with analysis: Bluetone Ltd   36 mins

<table>
<tr><td>

Business property relief for IHT available

</td></tr>
</table>

Bluetone Ltd is an **unquoted trading company** that manufactures compact discs.

The following information has been extracted from client files and from meetings with shareholders.

Bluetone Ltd:

<table>
<tr><td>

Close company

</td></tr>
</table>

*   Has four full-time working directors, **each of whom owns 25%** of its share capital of 200,000 £1 ordinary shares.

*   Shareholdings are currently valued as follows:

Shareholding	Value per share £
15%	9.00
25%	11.00
35%	12.50
50%	15.00

*   Forecast profits chargeable to corporation tax for year ended 31 March 2007 are £1,100,000.

*   Has no chargeable non-business assets.

Melody Brown:

*   Recently appointed a director of Bluetone Ltd after inheriting 50,000 shares from her father, Tony.

*   Melody wants to retain the full 25% holding so she will personally account for any IHT liability (see below).

Tony Brown's death estate:

IHT on death

- **Died** on 15 February 2007.

- Owned the following assets at date of death:

Asset	Value
50,000 Bluetone Ltd shares, purchased 12 November 2006	See above
42,000 50p ordinary shares in Expanse plc	Quoted at 312p – 320p
	Bargains of **282p, 288p, 306p and 324p.**
26,000 units in World-Growth, a unit trust.	**Bid price**: 80p; offer price 84p
Building society deposits	£29,000
Mini-cash ISA with building society	£3,000
Main residence	£125,000 (outstanding repayment mortgage of **£42,000**)
Life assurance policy on his own life	£53,000 open market value
	£61,000 proceeds received on 4 March 2007

Need this info to value the assets

Exempt from IT and CGT but **not** IHT

Include insurance policy proceeds in value of the death estate

Deduct mortgage from value of the property

- Had an **income tax liability** of **£6,600**, **gambling debts** of £1,200 and funeral expenses came to £3,460.

Deduct from estate value

Not deductible from estate value

Tony Brown's will:

- Bluetone Ltd shares left to Melody **bearing their own IHT**.
- Residue left to Melody's brother.

This means Melody pays the tax on this inheritance

Tony Brown's lifetime gifts:

- *10 February 2003:* £30,000 to Melody on her **wedding day**. — Think marriage exemption
- *4 June 2003:* £172,000 to a **discretionary trust**.

This is a chargeable lifetime transfer

Liam and Opal White

- Married, aged 37 and 32 respectively.

- Have been directors and shareholders of Bluetone Ltd since its incorporation on 1 October 1991; acquired their shares at par.

- On 20 March 2007 Liam will sell 30,000 of his shares in Bluetone Ltd **to their son** for £75,000.

Use market value as sale proceeds since it's a connected person

- Liam is a 40% taxpayer.

- Has not previously made any lifetime gifts of assets.

Noel Green

- Aged 52.

- Has been a director and shareholder of Bluetone Ltd since its incorporation on 1 October 1991; acquired the shares at par.

- For the past two years he has disagreed with the other directors of Bluetone Ltd over the company's business policies.

- Will resign as a director on 31 March 2007.

This is a purchase of own shares	• Has been agreed that Bluetone Ltd will **purchase his shareholding** for £550,000. HMRC has given advance clearance that the purchase qualifies for the special treatment applying to a company's purchase of its own shares, and can therefore be treated as a capital gain.
So tax capital gain at 40%	• **40% taxpayer**.

Required

2 taxes to consider here	(a) Calculate Melody's IHT liability and state when this will be due. **(8 marks)**

(b) Advise Liam of the **CGT and IHT** implications of selling the 30,000 shares in Bluetone Ltd to his son. You should assume that reliefs are claimed in the most favourable manner on the basis that Liam wishes to defer gains where possible. **(8 marks)**

(c) Advise both Bluetone Ltd and Noel of whether it will be beneficial to have the purchase of Noel's 25% shareholding treated as a capital gain under the special treatment, rather than as a distribution by Bluetone Ltd. **(4 marks)**

The rates and allowances for 2006/07 should be used throughout. RPIs October 1991 = 135.1; April 1998 = 162.6.

(Total = 20 marks)

28 Bill and Ben (ATAX 6/06)   40 mins

(a) For this part, assume today's date is 1 March 2007.

Bill and Ben each own 50% of the ordinary share capital in Flower Limited, an unquoted UK trading company that makes electronic toys. Bill and Ben have received an offer from a rival company, which they are considering.

The following information has been extracted from client files and from meetings with Bill and Ben.

Bill and Ben:

• Each currently receives a gross salary of £3,750 per month from Flower Limited.

• Part of the offer terms is that Bill and Ben would be retained as employees of the company on the same salary.

• Neither has used their CGT annual exemption for the 2006/07.

Flower Limited:

• Incorporated on 1 August 2006 with 1,000 £1 ordinary shares.

• Commenced trading on the same day.

• The company has accumulated a large cash balance of £180,000, which is to be used to purchase a new factory.

Two alternative offers from rival company:

• Option 1: £480,000 for the company, inclusive of the £180,000 cash balance.

• Option 2: £300,000 for the company, assuming the cash available for the factory purchase is extracted prior to sale.

Required

(i) Advise Bill and Ben which of the following means of extracting the £180,000 from Flower Limited on 31 March 2007 will result in the highest after tax cash amount:

(1) payment of a dividend, or
(2) payment of a salary bonus.

You are not required to consider the corporation tax (CT) implications for Flower Limited in your answer. **(5 marks)**

(ii) Following on from your answer to (i), evaluate the two purchase proposals, and advise Bill and Ben which course of action will result in the highest amount of after tax cash being received by the shareholders if the disposal takes place on 31 March 2007. **(3 marks)**

(iii) State how your answer in (ii) would differ if the sale were to be delayed until August 2007. **(3 marks)**

(b) For this part, assume today's date is 1 May 2010.

Repurchase of company shares:

- Bill and Ben decided not to sell the company, and instead expanded the business themselves. Ben, however, is now pursuing other interests, and is no longer involved with the day to day activities of Flower Limited.

- Bill believes that the company would be better off without Ben as a voting shareholder, and wishes to buy Ben's shares.

- However, Bill does not have sufficient funds to buy the shares himself, and so is wondering if the company could acquire the shares instead.

- The proposed price for Ben's shares would be £500,000.

- Both Bill and Ben pay income tax at the higher rate.

Required

Write a letter to Ben:

(1) stating the income tax (IT) and/or capital gains tax (CGT) implications for Ben if Flower Limited were to repurchase his 50% holding of ordinary shares, immediately in May 2011, and

(2) advising him of any available planning options that might improve this tax position. Clearly explain any conditions which must be satisfied and quantify the tax savings which may result.

(11 marks)

Assume that the corporation tax rates for the financial year 2006 and the income tax rates and allowances for the tax year 2006/07 apply throughout this question.

(Total = 22 marks)

29 Graeme (ATAX 12/05)

40 mins

Graeme, aged 57, is married to Catherine, aged 58. Graeme has come to you for some tax advice.

The following information has been extracted from client files and from meetings with Graeme.

Graeme's family:

- Both Graeme and Catherine work as medical consultants.
- Both are higher rate taxpayers.
- Have one son, Barry, aged 32.
- All are UK resident, ordinarily resident and domiciled.

Graeme's Thistle Dubh Limited shareholdings:

- *December 1986:* inherited 10,000 £1 ordinary shares on the death of his grandmother. Probate value 360p per share.

- *March 1992:* took up a 1 for 2 rights issue. The price paid for the rights shares was £10 per share.

- *October 1999:* company underwent a reorganisation whereupon Graeme received 'T' and 'D' ordinary shares (details below).

- *May 2007:* sold 12,000 'T' shares. The market values for the 'T' shares and the 'D' shares on that day were 300p and 600p per share respectively.

- *October 2007:* Graeme sold all of his 'D' shares for £85,000.

October 1999 share reorganisation:

- The ordinary shares were split into two new classes of ordinary share – 'T' shares and 'D' shares, each with differing rights.

- Graeme received two 'T' and three 'D' shares for each original Thistle Dubh Limited share held.

- The market values for the 'T' shares and the 'D' shares on the date of reorganisation were 135p and 405p per share respectively.

Thistle Dubh Limited:

- Unquoted UK trading company.
- Provides food supplies for sporting events.
- Current market value of the 'T' shares is 384p per share.

Holiday cottage:

- Graeme and Catherine own a UK holiday cottage let out as furnished holiday accommodation.

- Considering selling the cottage and purchasing a holiday villa abroad.

- Plan to let villa out on a furnished basis.

- Following their anticipated retirement, expect to occupy the property for a significant part of the year themselves, possibly moving to live in the villa permanently.

Required

(a) Calculate the total chargeable gains arising on Graeme's disposals of 'T' and 'D' ordinary shares in May and October 2007 respectively.
(6 marks)

(b) Explain the capital gains tax (CGT) and inheritance tax (IHT) implications of Graeme gifting his remaining 'T' ordinary shares at their current value either:

(i) to his wife, Catherine, or

(ii) to his son, Barry.

Your answer should be supported by relevant calculations and clearly identify the availability and effect of any reliefs (other than the CGT annual exemption) that might be used to reduce or defer any tax liabilities arising. **(8 marks)**

(c) Advise Graeme of the potential CGT and income tax implications of selling the UK country cottage and replacing it with a holiday villa abroad as proposed.

You are not required to discuss the income tax treatment of the UK country cottage. **(8 marks)**

Relevant retail price index figures are:

December	1986	99.6
March	1992	136.7
April	1998	162.6

(Total = 22 marks)

30 Reisling Ltd

52 mins

Reisling Ltd is a trading company that produces German wine in the UK. It also produces special shaped bottles that are characteristic of German wine, the majority of which are distributed to other manufacturers. This has been a very successful business which looks set to continue, although the wine production business has not proved so efficient. The rising costs of importing grapes have created substantial losses in the past four years.

The company has been a client for several years, as have the directors who each have significant shareholdings.

On 23 October 2006, the board of Reisling Ltd are approached by Chardonnay Ltd, a very successful company in the wine producing business, and negotiations have commenced for the purchase of the wine production trade.

The company has always kept information separate for the two trades and the following information relates only to the wine production side of the business:

Losses brought forward at 1 January 2006 were £290,000, and the adjusted trading loss for the year ended 31 December 2006 are expected to be £60,000.

At 1 January 2006, there were capital losses brought forward of £42,000.

Projected Balance sheet of Reisling Ltd as at 31 December 2006 (wine production only)

	£'000
Fixed assets	
Freehold factory	80
Freehold winery	40
Plant and machinery	30
Motor vehicles	30
	180
Net current assets	70
	250

Originally the freehold factory had been used for bottle production but it was replaced 3 years ago by a larger factory with all the latest technology. The factory was then transferred to the wine production side of the business and had been used for storing the finished goods before distribution.

The proposals are as follows:

Step 1   On 1 January 2007 a wholly owned subsidiary, Plonk Ltd, will be formed and the assets and undertaking of the wine production trade will be hived down.

Step 2   All assets will be transferred to Plonk Ltd except the freehold winery which Chardonnay Ltd will sell to a third party for £50,000. No liabilities will be transferred to Plonk Ltd except the hire purchase liabilities which relate entirely to plant and motor vehicles.

Step 3   The consideration for the trade transferred will be the issue of shares in Plonk Ltd, which will be immediately sold to Chardonnay Ltd for £475,000.

Following the disposal of the wine production business, the directors are considering increasing the range of bottles produced, and exporting them. Some of the exports will be to manufacturers in the EU, and some to manufacturers in the New World.

Required

Prepare notes for a forthcoming meeting with the board of Chardonnay Ltd outlining the tax and other implications of the above proposals. Your notes should be in four sections, addressing the four sets of issues set out below, and should, where appropriate, include supporting calculations.

(a)   The transfer of Reisling Ltd's wine production trade to Plonk Ltd

Comment on the tax position for Reisling Ltd if the transfer of Reisling Ltd's wine production trade to Plonk Ltd (steps 1 and 2 of the hive down, above) takes place.

Provide a calculation of the available trade losses on the basis that they will be restricted by the excess of 'relevant liabilities' over 'relevant assets'. Relevant assets are assets vested in the transferor company immediately before the transfer and not transferred, plus any consideration for the transfer.

Explain how these trading losses and the capital losses may be used by Plonk Ltd, if at all. You should not consider any anti-avoidance rules at this stage.   **(9 marks)**

(b)   The sale of Plonk Ltd to Chardonnay Ltd

Advise the company of the tax consequences of this aspect of the proposal.

Evaluate the likelihood of any anti-avoidance rules applying to the transaction.   **(6 marks)**

(c)   Other considerations

Advise the company of the effects of the proposal on existing staff, customers and suppliers.

At this point, you should also comment on any other issues that you think may be relevant to the disposal of the production business.   **(8 marks)**

(d)   Export of wine bottles

Explain the VAT implications of exporting wine bottles.   **(4 marks)**

Appropriateness of the format and presentation of the notes and the effectiveness with which the information is communicated.   **(2 marks)**

You may assume that the rates and allowances for the tax year 2006/07 and financial year 2006 continue to apply for the foreseeable future.

(Total = 29 marks)

31 Mr Royle

32 mins

Your client, Mr Royle, is considering acquiring the business of a local company.

The following information has been extracted from client files and from meetings with Mr Royle.

Mr Royle

- Made redundant by his employer last year.
- Received a large cash payment.
- Will use this cash to buy the business.
- Considering either buying the assets of the company or buying the whole of the shares in the company.

The company

- Has previously been profitable.
- Owns various items of machinery and a factory.
- Has made losses in the last two years due to the ill-health of the managing director.

Managing director

- Is also the majority shareholder.

Mr Royle is confident that he can turn the business around and make it profitable again.

Required

Write a letter to Mr Royle outlining the advantages and disadvantages of buying:

(a)   the assets of the business; or **(8 marks)**
(b)   the shares in the company. **(10 marks)**

Your answer should consider all relevant taxes. **(Total = 18 marks)**

32 Stuart and Rebecca (ATAX 12/05)

47 mins

Your manager has had a meeting with Stuart and Rebecca Lundy and has sent you a copy of the following memorandum.

To   The files
From   Tax manager
Date   21 November 2007
Subject   Stuart and Rebecca Lundy – Estate planning

Stuart has recently been diagnosed with a serious illness. He is expected to live for another two or three years only. He is concerned about the possible inheritance tax that will arise on his death. Rebecca is in good health.

In November 2007 Stuart sold a house in Plymouth for £422,100. Stuart had inherited the house on the death of his mother on 1 May 1995 when it had a probate value of £185,000. The subsequent pattern of occupation was as follows:

1 May 1995 to 28 February 1996   Occupied by Stuart and Rebecca as main residence
1 March 1996 to 31 December 1999   Unoccupied
1 January 2000 to 31 March 2002   Let out (unfurnished)
1 April 2002 to 30 November 2002   Occupied by Stuart and Rebecca
1 December 2002 to 30 November 2007   Used occasionally as second home

Both Stuart and Rebecca had lived in London from March 1996 onwards. On 1 March 2002 Stuart and Rebecca bought a house in London in their joint names. No other capital disposals were made by Stuart in the tax year 2007/08. He has £29,500 of capital losses brought forward from previous years.

Stuart intends to invest the gross sale proceeds from the sale of the Plymouth house, and is considering two investment options, both of which he believes will provide equal risk and returns. These are as follows:

(1)   acquiring shares in Omikron plc, a listed UK trading company, with 50,250,000 shares in issue. Its shares currently trade at 42p per share, or

(2)   acquiring further shares in Omega plc. The issued share capital of Omega plc is currently 10,000,000 shares. The share price is quoted at 208p – 216p with marked bargains at 207p, 211p, and 215p

Stuart and Rebecca's assets (following the sale of the Plymouth house but before any investment of the proceeds) are as follows:

Assets	Stuart £	Rebecca £
Family house in London	450,000	450,000
Cash from property sale	422,100	–
Cash deposits	165,000	165,000
Portfolio of quoted investments	–	250,000
Shares in Omega plc	see files	see files
Life insurance policy	note	note

Note. The life insurance policy will pay out a sum of £200,000 on the death of the first spouse to die.

Tax manager

An extract from an email from your manager is set out below.

Please prepare a letter from me to Stuart incorporating the following:

1   State the taxable capital gain on the sale of the Plymouth house in November 2007, setting out the amounts of any reliefs claimed.

2   Given his recent diagnosis, advice for Stuart on which of the two proposed investments (Omikron plc/Omega plc) would be the more tax efficient alternative.

     Give reasons for your choice.

3   Assuming that Stuart:

     (i)   uses proceeds from the house sale to purchase 201,000 shares in Omega plc on 3 December 2007; and

     (ii)   dies on 20 December 2009,

     calculations of the potential IHT liability which would arise if Rebecca were to die on 1 March 2010, and no further tax planning measures were taken.

     Assume that all asset values remain unchanged.

4   Advice on any lifetime IHT planning that could be undertaken to help reduce the potential liability calculated above.

Tax manager

You have extracted the following further information from client files.

●   Stuart is a self-employed business consultant aged 58. He is married to Rebecca, aged 55.

●   They have one child, Sam, who is aged 24 and single.

●   Both Stuart and Rebecca have wills whose terms transfer all assets to the surviving spouse.

- On 1 January 2003 Stuart and Rebecca elected for their London house to be their principal private residence with effect from that date, up until that point the Plymouth property had been their principal private residence.

- Omega plc was formerly Omega Ltd and Stuart and Rebecca helped start up the company. The company was formed on 1 June 1990, when they each bought 24,000 shares for £1 per share. The company became listed on 1 May 1998. On this date their holding was subdivided, with each of them receiving 100 shares in Omega plc for each share held in Omega Ltd.

- Neither Stuart nor Rebecca has made any previous chargeable lifetime transfers for IHT purposes.

Required

Prepare the letter requested by your manager.

Marks are available for the four components of the letter as follows:

1   Relevant calculations of the taxable capital gain on the sale of the Plymouth house in November 2007.

(8 marks)

2   Advice on which of the two proposed investments would be more tax efficient alternative.   **(3 marks)**

3   Calculations of the potential IHT liability which would arise if no further tax planning measures are taken and Rebecca dies in March 2010.   **(6 marks)**

4   Advice on any lifetime IHT planning that could be undertaken for both Stuart and Rebecca to help reduce their potential IHT liability (in three above).   **(7 marks)**

Relevant retail price index figures are:

May	1995	149.6
April	1998	162.6

Appropriateness of the format and presentation of the report and the effectiveness with which its advice is communicated.   **(2 marks)**

You may assume that the rates and allowances for the tax year 2006/07 continue to apply for the foreseeable future.

(Total = 26 marks)

33 Karen Wade   63 mins

Your manager has had a meeting with Karen Wade, who runs her own catering business, and has sent you a copy of the following memorandum.

To   The files
From   Tax manager
Date   1 June 2007
Subject   Karen Wade – tax issues

(1)   *Year ended 31 December 2006*

Karen Wade (KW) provided a copy of the accounts for the year ended 31 December 2006 (see attached).

She also provided the following information in connection with the accounts.

(i)   Both her nephew and son work for her. Her nephew works full-time earning £9,600 (employer's NICs are £584). Her son, aged 19, works approximately 40 Saturdays each year from 8 am until 6 pm. He will shortly be going to university to study engineering.

(ii)   Electricity and other household expenses represent the allowable percentage agreed with HMRC of the total costs at Karen's home.

(iii)   Motor expenses represent the total costs, excluding depreciation, of the car and the van.

(2)   *Motor vehicle*

Karen uses her car for both business and private use.

Her annual mileage figures are 12,500 for business and 2,500 private.

(3)   *Capital purchases*

Recent purchases of assets are as follows.

2006		£
January	Delivery van – 100% business use	10,000
February	New office equipment	4,000
August	Motor car (to replace Karen's original car which was sold for £7,600)	9,600
September	New refrigerator	1,800
October	New coffee machine	1,300
November	Computer and printer	1,700

(4)   *Other income*

Dividends from quoted shares – amounts received	22,536
Dividends on shares within an ISA	4,000
Interest on National Savings & Investments Bank – investment account	320
Premium Bond prize	500

(5)   *New contract*

From 1 January 2007 Karen will commence a new contract to supply catering to a local hotel at £3,185 per month for the next twelve months. She will not need additional staff but, to assist with deliveries, she has agreed that from 1 July 2007 her nephew will be allowed to use the van for travel to and from work and at weekends.

(6)   *Investment strategy*

Karen has surplus income of approximately £10,000 per annum. Nearly all of her wealth is invested in quoted shares and she is concerned that they may fall in value. She is considering selling a proportion of her portfolio in order to acquire an investment property.

Her brother-in-law has suggested contributing to a personal pension scheme.

Accounts for the year ended 31 December 2006

	£	£
Turnover		44,710
Expenses		
Wages		
Self	12,000	
Nephew	10,184	
Son	1,600	
Electricity	1,400	
Other household expenses	2,219	
Catering materials	1,307	
Depreciation		
Equipment	1,300	
Car	700	
Van	500	
Loss on sale of car	200	
Motor expenses		
Car	800	
Van	1,200	
		(33,410)
Profit		11,300

An extract from an email from your manager is set out below.

Please find attached a copy of the notes from the meeting with Karen Wade, along with a copy of her accounts for the year ended 31 December 2006.

Please prepare a report from me to Karen setting out the following:

1   VAT

- The rules for determining when she will need to register for VAT.
- Let her know specific dates and her administrative responsibilities.
- Explain how her VAT liability will be calculated.

2   Income tax and NIC

- Advise on the income tax consequences of the change of use of the van from 1 July 2007.
- Provide a calculation of her assessable trading income for 2006/07.
- Prepare computations of her income tax and National Insurance contributions payable for 2006/07.

3   Investment strategy

- Advise Karen which of her personal circumstances may impact the investment strategy she should adopt for investing the surplus £10,000.

- Provide details of the issues to consider depending on whether she invests in quoted shares or commercial property.

- Outline the main issues of which Karen should be aware with regard to a personal pension scheme.

Tax manager

You have extracted the following further information from client files.

- Karen is 42 and divorced.

- Started the business in 1998.

- Customers include private individuals and businesses.

- The tax written down values for capital allowances purposes at 1 January 2006 are:

Miscellaneous equipment pool	£12,000
Karen's motor car	£7,000

- Karen has made a payment of £350 pa to Oxfam, a registered charity, for the past three years. A copy of the signed gift aid declaration is on file.

- Karen has never made any pension contributions.

Required

Prepare a report for Karen as requested by your manager. The report should be in three sections, addressing the three sets of issues set out below, and should, where appropriate include supporting calculations.

(a) VAT

Advise Karen when she needs to register for VAT and of her associated administrative responsibilities.

Explain how her VAT liability for the year ended 31 December 2007 will be calculated. **(6 marks)**

(b) Income tax and NIC

Advise on the income tax consequences of the change of use of the van from 1 July 2007. **(2 marks)**

Compute her assessable trading income for 2006/07. **(6 marks)**

Prepare computations of the income tax and National Insurance contributions payable in respect of Karen's income for 2006/07. **(6 marks)**

(c) Investment strategy

    (i) Investing the surplus £10,000

        Advise Karen which of her personal circumstances may impact the investment strategy she should adopt.

        Identify any further personal information required. **(3 marks)**

    (ii) Investment in quoted shares compared with commercial property

        Provide Karen with details of the issues to consider depending on whether she invests in quoted shares or commercial property.

        You should consider all aspects of the investments including the taxation treatment of each.

        (6 marks)

    (ii) Personal pension schemes

        Outline the main issues of which Karen should be aware with regard to a personal pension scheme.

        (4 marks)

Appropriateness of the format and presentation of the notes and the effectiveness with which their content is communicated. **(2 marks)**

You may assume that the rates and allowances for the tax year 2006/07 continue to apply for the foreseeable future.

(Total = 35 marks)

34 Alasdair (ATAX 12/05)

40 mins

Alasdair is considering investing in property, as he has heard that this represents a good investment.

The following information has been extracted from client files and from meetings with Alasdair.

Alasdair:

- Aged 42 and is single.

- Wants to extract cash from his personal company, Beezer Limited, with the minimum amount of tax payable, to raise funds to buy a property.

- Partner at a marketing firm, Gallus & Co.

- Estimated profit share for 2007/08 will be £30,000.

- Has not made any capital disposals in the current tax year.

Beezer Ltd:

- Formed on 1 May 2000 with £1,000 of capital issued as 1,000 £1 ordinary shares.
- Alasdair sold the trade and related assets on 1 January 2007.
- Only asset is cash of £120,000.
- Makes up accounts to 31 December.

Extraction of profits from Beezer Ltd:

- Option 1: paying Alasdair a dividend of £120,000 on 31 March 2008.
- Company would have no assets and be wound up.
- Option 2: leaving the cash in the company and then liquidating the company.
- Costs of liquidation would be £5,000.

Property investment:

- Unsure whether to invest directly in residential or commercial property, or do so via some form of collective investment.

- Gallus & Co is looking to rent a new warehouse which could be bought for £200,000.

- May buy the warehouse himself and lease it to his firm.

- Will need to borrow additional funds to buy the property.

Required

(a) Advise Alasdair whether or not a dividend payment will result in a higher after-tax cash sum than the liquidation of Beezer Limited. Assume that either the dividend would be paid on 31 March 2008 or the liquidation would take place on 31 March 2008. **(9 marks)**

Assume that Beezer Limited has always paid corporation tax at or above the small companies' rate of 19% and that the tax rates and allowances for 2006/07 apply throughout this part.

(b) (i) Advise Alasdair of the tax implications and relative financial risks attached to the following property investments:

(1) buy to let residential property,
(2) commercial property, and
(3) shares in a property investment company/unit trust. **(9 marks)**

(ii) State, giving reasons, the inheritance tax (IHT) and capital gains tax (CGT) reliefs that would be available to Alasdair if he acquires the warehouse and leases it to Gallus & Co, rather than to an unconnected tenant. **(4 marks)**

(Total = 22 marks)

35 Neil Johnson

47 mins

Your tax partner has sent you the following internal memo:

> To   Tax assistant
> From   Tax partner
> Date   12 March 2007
> Subject Neil Johnson
>
> Neil is coming in to see me first thing tomorrow morning.
>
> He has received a business proposal from a colleague, Fred Boulder, which would involve him either investing in shares in Boulder's company, or setting himself up in business to supply certain components to Boulder's company. There is no other market for these components, but apparently the combined product is technologically very advanced and has enormous potential. The company would qualify as an Enterprise Investment Scheme company. Neil's share of the profits from this venture would start at about £20,000 per annum, increasing rapidly.
>
> Either way, he reckons he would have to invest about £150,000 - £200,000. He does not wish to borrow this money, but wants to sell some of his existing portfolio of shares.
>
> He predicts that he will want to sell out after seven to ten years, and expects to realise a substantial profit.
>
> You will remember that his brother was recently killed in a car crash, leaving his financial affairs in a terrible mess. Neil is very concerned that his affairs should be tidy, and he has asked for a review for inheritance tax purposes to be carried out at the same time.
>
> I doubt if he will get married now, but it is always possible. He is not adverse to suggestions that he may wish to hand over some of his assets to some of his nephews and nieces.
>
> Please let me have detailed notes for the meeting.
>
> Tax partner

You have extracted the following further information from Neil Johnson's client files.

- He is 45 and single.

- Has two sisters, slightly younger than himself, who have children in their teens.

- He had only one brother, who died 18 months earlier leaving his whole estate (worth about £350,000) to Neil.

- Neil's other assets (all inherited from his father in 1985) are as follows:

  - Main residence, Johnson Manor, worth £515,000. It is surrounded by 150 acres of farmland, valued at £150,000, which Neil himself farms.

  - Quoted investments worth approximately £400,000. Neil has managed the investments himself. The investments are worth, on average, three times their cost.

- Neil has not worked recently (apart from on the farm), and had treated his technological designs as a hobby. It is one of these designs that Fred wants to use. Neil does not need to increase his income, other than to replace any lost investment income from the shares he will sell (assume all investments earn 5% gross).

- Farming income is roughly £15,000 per annum.

Required

Prepare the notes requested by your tax partner.

Marks are available for the components of the notes as follows:

1   Confirmation of the potential inheritance tax that would be payable if Neil died before any of these transactions are carried out. **(4 marks)**

2   Advice concerning the inheritance tax consequences of setting up as a sole trader or of investing in Boulder's company (you may assume this is unquoted.) **(4 marks)**

3   Details of the tax costs arising from the disposal of the quoted investments.

     You should assume that Neil needs to realise £200,000 net of all taxes, and that he has already realised gains covering the annual exempt amount.

     Assume an increase in the RPI over the period of ownership of the shares of 80%. **(4 marks)**

4   Any other tax advantages or disadvantages of being a sole trader, as opposed to investing in Boulder's company. **(5 marks)**

5   Your conclusion (with reasons) as to the preferable method of investment. **(2 marks)**

6   Any possible ways of mitigating tax in the future assuming your advice is taken. **(5 marks)**

Appropriateness of the format and presentation of the notes and the effectiveness with which the information is communicated. **(2 mark)**

You may assume that the rates and allowances for the tax year 2006/07 and financial year 2006 continue to apply for the foreseeable future.

(Total = 26 marks)

Answers

1 Question with answer plan: Styrax

Text references. Chapter 30 covers basic tax planning such as utilising the personal allowance. Pensions and other tax efficient investments are dealt with in Chapter 2.

Top tips. Your financial planning suggestions must be practical. Styrax and Salvia do not have much disposable income so it would be inadvisable for them to make large pension payments.

Answer plan

(a)   (i)   Main point is *Salvia's unused PA* and starting rate band

Consider:

- Employment by Styrax
- Commercial justification
- Tax saving for Styrax

3 possibilities

- Amount up to PA – tax and NIC
- Starting rate band – tax and NIC
- Amount over starting rate band

Also consider:

- ISAs
- Maxi and Mini accounts
- Benefits
- Since risk adverse = good choice

(ii)   Pension options:

- Styrax personal pension
- Salvia personal pension
- Occupational pension

(b)   **EIS – points to cover**

- Description – general terms
- Tax reducer
- Withdrawal of relief
- CGT relief
- Reinvestment relief
- Risk

VCTs – points to cover

- Description – general terms
- Risk
- Tax reducer
- Dividends
- CGT
- Withdrawal of relief

Top tip. Making a plan like this at the outset ensures you cover all the crucial points and hence gain all the main marks available.

(a) (i) **Notes for meeting with Styrax**

Use of Salvia's personal allowance

Now that Salvia has given up employed work, she does not have any source of income. This means that her personal allowance (£5,035) is being wasted as is her starting rate band of £2,150. It is not possible to transfer the benefit of either of these to Styrax. Therefore, Styrax needs to transfer some of his income to Salvia. Styrax could do this by employing Salvia in his business (the question states that she does not want to be a partner so this is not considered).

Salvia's salary must be commercially justifiable for the work that she will do. Styrax will then be able to deduct the salary from his trading profits. This will save income tax at 22% and also reduce his Class 4 NICs at 8%.

The salary up to £5,035 will be free of income tax and Class 1 NICs. This will therefore save tax and NICs of 30%.

If Styrax were to pay an additional £2,150 to enable Salvia to use her starting rate band, this would be subject to 10% income tax and employee 11% Class 1 NICs in the hands of Salvia. Styrax will also have to pay 12.8% employer Class 1 NICs. Therefore the overall tax rate is 33.8%. However, Styrax would also save income tax and NICs at approximately the rate of 33.8% (income tax of 22%, Class 4 NICs at 8%, and income tax and Class 4 NICs on the employers Class 1 contributions which would be 12.8% × (22% + 8%) = 3.84%). Therefore, it would not be advantageous to pay this additional amount.

If the salary exceeded the starting rate band for Salvia, this would not be tax efficient as both Styrax and Salvia would be basic rate tax payers and the Class 1 NIC costs would outweigh the tax saving for Styrax.

Savings income

The couple should take advantage of Individual Savings Accounts.

Each of them can invest up to £7,000 per tax year. This can be in a Maxi-account (which can all be in shares or a mixture of cash (maximum £3,000, and the balance in shares). Alternatively, separate Mini-accounts can be opened (£3,000 cash, £4,000 shares). The income generated by the accounts is tax free as are any gains on shares.

Since the couple are risk adverse, shares are not a suitable investment for them. Each of them should open a Mini-cash ISA (Styrax would need to transfer £3,000 to Salvia). This would save income tax of £300 × 20% = £60.

(ii) **Future pension provision**

Styrax and Salvia could both start personal pensions.

The maximum tax relievable contributions that Styrax could make would be the higher of:

(1) £3,600 or

(2) 100% × his earnings

Salvia could make contributions up to £3,600 even though she has no earnings.

Alternatively, if Salvia becomes an employee of Styrax, he could set up an occupational pension scheme for her.

Since the couple only have disposable income of £3,000 per year, they would probably not wish to spend all of it on pension provision! Possibly both of them could try to invest a small amount per month (say £50).

(b) **Memorandum**

Enterprise Investment Scheme

The Enterprise Investment Scheme (EIS) is designed to promote enterprise and investment. It helps high-risk, unlisted trading companies raise finance by issuing ordinary shares to unconnected individuals.

If you subscribe for EIS shares you may be entitled to both income tax and capital gains tax reliefs. For income tax, you can claim a tax reducer of the lower of:

(i)   20% of the amount subscribed for qualifying investments (maximum qualifying investments are £400,000 in 2006/07) and

(ii)   your tax liability for the year after deducting VCT relief (described below).

For example, if you subscribed the maximum of £400,000, you could claim a tax reducer of £400,000 × 20% = £80,000. However, if your tax liability is less than £80,000, you can only bring that liability down to nil.

You must hold the shares for at least three years if the income tax relief is not to be withdrawn or reduced. The main reason for the withdrawal of relief will be the sale of the shares by you within the three year period mentioned above.

Where shares qualify for EIS income tax relief there are also special rules for capital gains purposes:

(i)   Where shares are disposed of after the three year period any gain is exempt from CGT. If the shares are disposed of within three years any gain is computed in the normal way.

(ii)   If EIS shares are disposed of at a loss at any time, the loss is allowable but the acquisition cost of the shares is reduced by the amount of EIS relief attributable to the shares. The loss is eligible for a special type of loss relief which enables you to set the loss off against income.

EIS deferral relief may be available to defer chargeable gains if you invest in EIS shares in the period commencing one year before and ending three years after the disposal of an asset. The deferred gain will become chargeable, for example when the shares are disposed of (subject to a further claim for the relief being made). It is not necessary for the shares acquired to be subject to the EIS income tax relief.

The amount of the gain (before taper relief) that can be deferred is the lower of:

(i)   The amount subscribed by the investor for his shares, which has not previously been matched under this relief, and

(ii)   The amount specified by the investor in the claim. This can take into account the availability of losses, taper relief and the annual exemption.

The gain may come back into charge, for example if you dispose of the shares or if you become non resident, broadly within three years of the issue of the shares (except if employed full time abroad for up to three years and retaining the shares until your return to the UK).

EIS investments are high risk because there is total exposure to unquoted companies engaged in risky trades.

Venture capital trusts (VCTs)

Venture capital trusts (VCTs) are listed companies which invest in unquoted trading companies and meet certain conditions. The VCT scheme differs from EIS in that you can spread your risk over a number of higher-risk, unquoted companies. However, it is still a moderately high risk investment.

If you invest in a VCT, you will obtain the following tax benefits on a maximum qualifying investment of £200,000 in 2006/07:

(i)   A tax reduction of 30% of the amount invested.
(ii)   Dividends received are tax-free income.
(iii)   Capital gains on the sale of shares in the VCT are exempt from CGT (but losses are not allowable).

If the shares in the VCT are disposed of within five years of issue, then:

(i)   If the shares are not disposed of under a bargain made at arm's length, the tax reduction is withdrawn.

(ii)   If the shares are disposed of under a bargain made at arm's length, the tax reduction is withdrawn, up to the disposal proceeds × 20%.

There is no deferral relief available for VCT investments.

If a VCT's approval is withdrawn within three years of the issue any tax reduction given is withdrawn.

2 Charles Choice

> **Text references.** Chapters 4 and 5 deal with employment income and Chapter 2 looks at pensions.
>
> **Top tips.** It was important to allocate your time so that you made a good attempt at each part of the question.
>
> **Easy marks.** The employment benefits calculations should have provided very easy marks at this stage of your studies.

Marking scheme

			Marks	
(a)	*Accepting the company motor car*			
	Car benefit	1		
	Fuel benefit	1		
	Contributions	1½		
	Total annual cost	1		
	Accepting the cash alternative			
	Income tax liability	1½		
	Class 1 NIC	1		
	Mileage allowance	1		
	Running and leasing costs	1		
	Authorised mileage rates	1		
	Conclusion	1		
			11	
(b)	(i) Any amount	1		
	Tax relief up to earnings	1		
	Likelihood of maximum contributions	1		
	AVCs/personal pension	1		
			4	
	(ii) Personal pension:			
	Basic rate relief	1½		
	Occupational pension:			
	Deduct from earnings/ net	1½		
			3	
	(iii) Maximum contribution	1		
	Annual allowance	1		
	Tax charge on excess	1		
	Higher rate relief	1		
			4	
			22	

(a) Accepting the company motor car

The annual cost of accepting the company car is:

	£
Car benefit £15,400 × 18 % (diesel)	2,772
Less: contributions 12 × £35 (50 − 15)	(420)
	2,352
Fuel benefit (no deduction for partial reimbursement) £14,400 × 18%	2,592
	4,944

	£
Additional income tax liability at 22%	1,088
Contributions 12 × £50	600
Total annual cost to employee	1,688

Accepting the additional salary

The annual cost of accepting the additional salary is:

	£	£
Salary		2,800
Less: Income tax at 22%	616	
Class 1 NIC (below UEL still)		
£2,800 at 11%	308	
		(924)
		1,876
Mileage allowance (8,000 at 23p)		1,840
Tax relief on expense claim £1,360 × 22% (see below)		299
Additional income		4,015
Running costs	1,650	
Leasing cost (12 × £285)	3,420	
		(5,070)
Total annual cost to employee		1,055

Based on purely financial criteria, the cash alternative appears to be the most beneficial as it results in a saving of £633 (£1,688 – £1,055).

Charles can take advantage of the authorised mileage allowance. The mileage allowance of £1,840 is less than the tax free amount laid down under the scheme:

	£
8,000 × 40p	3,200

This means the £1,840 Charles receives is tax free and an expense claim can be made by Charles to deduct the excess of £1,360 (£3,200 – £1,840).

(b) (i) **Maximum contributions**

Charles can contribute any amount to a pension regardless of the level of his earnings.

However tax relief will only be given for contributions up to his earnings for the tax year.

As Charles' salary is £23,500 he can contribute up to this amount to either a personal or occupational pension and obtain tax relief. However it is unlikely that he will wish to pay his entire earnings into his pension and he might therefore decide instead to continue paying the same amount as he was previously paying into his personal pension.

If he joins the occupational scheme he will already have made contributions of £1,410 (£23,500 @ 6%) and his employer will also have made contributions of the same amount. He might therefore choose to pay an additional £1,590 ([12 × £250] – £1,410) into a pension. He could make these payments to his occupational scheme, by way of Additional Voluntary Contributions, or instead decide to continue funding his personal pension.

(ii) **Tax relief**

If Charles makes payments to his personal scheme he will automatically be given basic rate tax relief as he will pay contributions net of 22%. This means that he will pay only 78% of the gross payment into the pension. The government pays the extra 22% on his behalf to the pension provider.

Charles will only need to pay £1,240 (£1,590 × 78%). The payment does not affect his income tax computation.

If he makes the contribution to the occupational pension he will normally make the payment gross and it will be deducted from his employment income on the face of his income tax computation.

(iii) **Salary of £223,500**

If Charles had a salary of £223,500 this would have the following impact:

(1) he could make tax-relievable contributions up to £223,500;
(2) if so, his contributions would exceed the annual allowance of £215,000 for 2006/07;
(3) there would be a 40% tax charge on the excess.

In terms of the tax relief available, Charles would be entitled to higher rate relief. This is given by extending the basic rate band for the year by the amount of his gross contribution.

3 Question with analysis: Benny Fitt

Text references. All aspects of employment income are dealt with in Chapters 4 and 5.

Top tip. An excellent question to really get to grips with employment income. It is not exam standard but provides you with the opportunity to test your knowledge, and your ability to direct your answer appropriately at your target audience, in this case the director of a company.

Always keep your figures in an Appendix whether you are producing a report, letter, notes or a memorandum. It gives a far more professional impression.

Easy marks. Work though the question calculating the benefits one by one. Leave any calculations you cannot do – return to these if you have time. Cross off the relevant sections on the exam paper as you deal with them. This approach ensures you gain marks quickly and systematically.

Marking scheme

				Marks
(a)	*Employment benefits*			
	Car benefit		2	
	Other benefits		2	
	Expense claim		1	
	Income tax liability		1	
	Usine Ltd			
	Capital allowances		2	
	Deductible expenses		1	
	Class 1A NIC		1	
	Private petrol			
	Tax saving		1	
		Max		8
(b)	*Lump sum payments*			
	Wages in lieu of notice		1	
	Taxable amount		2	
	Lump sum on taking up employment			
	Beneficial loan		1	
	Relocation costs		2	
	Accommodation			
	Additional benefit		2	
	Furniture/running costs		1	
				9
(c)	CSOP conditions (1 mark for each relevant point)	Max		4
	Format/ presentation			2
		Max		23

PRIVATE AND CONFIDENTIAL

[Our address]

[Your address]
[Date]

Dear Benny

USINE LTD – BENEFITS FOR EMPLOYEES

This letter deals with the income tax implications of providing various benefits to you, as managing director. It also covers the tax treatment of payments made to the departing sales director and those payments and benefits provided to the new sales director. Finally the conditions for a share option scheme to be approved are detailed.

(a)   **Employment benefits**

Benny Fitt

You will have a total taxable benefit charge in respect of the provision of the company car, credit card and computer of £8,260 (see Appendix 1).

You will be able to claim a deduction from your general earnings for the expense payments of £1,100.

The total tax due on these benefits for 2006/07 will be £2,864 (£8,260 – £1,100 = £7,160 @ 40%).

There is no NIC for you as an employee on the value of the benefits.

Usine Ltd

Capital allowances are available to Usine Ltd on the cost of the motor car. The writing-down allowance on the car is initially restricted to £3,000 per annum as it costs more than £12,000.

A 50% first year allowance of £1,500 will be available for the expenditure on the computer as Usine Ltd is a small company for capital allowances purposes.

The credit card expenses of £1,265 (£460 + £380 + £425) are allowable deductions from trading profits. However, the cost of client entertaining is not deductible.

Class 1A NIC of £916 will be due on 19 July 2007.

Private petrol

If you reimburse Usine Ltd the £180 paid for your private petrol there would be no assessable fuel benefit.

This would reduce your income tax liability by £922 (£2,304 at 40%). The net saving for you would therefore be £742 (£922 – £180).

Usine Ltd's Class 1A NIC liability will also be reduced by £295 (£2,304 at 12.8%).

(b)   **Sales director changes**

Redundancy payment to departing sales director

Each component of the redundancy payment is treated differently for tax purposes.

The statutory redundancy element is completely exempt from income tax and NIC.

Any payment that the sales director was contractually entitled to is taxable income. This means that the holiday pay is subject to income tax and NIC.

The agreement not to work for a rival company is a 'restrictive covenant'. This is taxable. Income tax and NIC are due on this amount.

Unless there is a contractual entitlement to receive a payment in lieu of notice such payments are treated as 'ex gratia'. The first £30,000 of ex gratia payments are exempt. However any statutory redundancy payment received reduces this amount.

Consequently £15,000 of the £45,000 redundancy payment is taxable (see Appendix 2).

Payments and benefits on new sales director taking up employment

    (i)   Lump sum payment

        The lump sum payment of £10,000 to the new sales director will be taxable as a 'golden hello' unless the payment represents compensation for a right or asset given up on taking up the employment.

    (ii)   Beneficial loan

        In 2006/07 there will be a taxable benefit of £625 (£50,000 × 5% × 3/12).

    (iii)   Relocation costs

        There will be no taxable benefit in respect of eligible removal expenses up to £8,000. The exemption covers such items as legal and estate agents' fees, stamp duty land tax, removal costs, and the cost of new domestic goods where existing goods are not suitable for the new residence.

    (iv)   Accommodation

        There will be a taxable benefit in respect of the accommodation in 2006/07 of £2,795 (Appendix 2).

(c)   **Company Share Option Plan**

    To obtain HMRC approval, a Company Share Option plan must satisfy the following conditions:

    (i)   The shares over which the options are granted must be fully paid ordinary shares.

    (ii)   The price of the shares must not be less than their market value at the time of the grant of the option.

    (iii)   Participation must be limited to employees and full-time directors but not all such individuals need be eligible to participate.

    (iv)   An employee can only hold options up to a market value of £30,000.

    (v)   If the company has more than one class of shares, the majority of shares of the class over which the scheme operates must not be held by directors/employees (except for an employee controlled company) nor a holding company (unless scheme shares are quoted).

    (vi)   Anyone who has, within the preceding 12 months held over 25% of the shares of a close company whose shares may be acquired under the scheme, must be excluded from the scheme.

If you can provide any further information please let me know.

Yours sincerely

Tax manager.

Appendix 1 – Benny Fitt

Employment benefits

	£
Car benefit (£28,400 + £700 − £2,500) × 32% (W) × 6/12	4,256
Fuel benefit (£14,400 × 32% × 6/12)	2,304
Expense payments (£380 + £720)	1,100
Computer £3,000 × 20%	600
	8,260

Working

Taxable car benefit percentage

225 (rounded down) − 140 = 85 ÷ 5 = 17% + 15% = 32%

Class 1A NIC for Usine Ltd

Taxable benefits (£8,260 − 1,100 =) £7,160 at 12.8%   £916

Appendix 2 – Sales director payments and benefits

Redundancy payment to departing sales director

	£	£
General earnings		
Holiday pay	2,800	
Restrictive covenant	3,000	5,800
Specific employment income		
Payment in lieu of notice (if not contractual)	3,100	
Compensation	34,000	
	37,100	
Less: exempt £(30,000 – 2,100)	(27,900)	9,200
Taxable as employment income		15,000

Accommodation benefit for new sales director

	£
Annual value (£4,400 × 3/12)	1,100
Additional benefit (£105,000 – £75,000) = £30,000 at 5% × 3/12	375
Furniture (£10,400 × 20% × 3/12)	520
Running costs (£3,200 × 3/12)	800
	2,795

4 Benny Korere

Text references. Employment income aspects in Chapters 4 and 5. CGT liability covered in Chapters 11 to 13. The income tax computation is covered in Chapter 1.

Top tips. You would be best to look at each section of the requirements carefully and separately. Work through each part one by one. Keep your answers well presented, clear and well spaced out.

Easy marks. Three marks for standard employment income computation. It is well worth getting to grips with this topic as there can be lots of easy marks available.

Marking scheme

				Marks
(a)	Salary		½	
	Payment in lieu of notice taxable in full		½	
	Payment for agreeing not to work for competitors		½	
	Car benefit		1½	
				3
(b)	(i)	Grant of option – no income tax	½	
		Exercise of option:		
		Amount chargeable to tax	1	
		Tax year/rate of tax	½	
		Risk exposure:		
		Identification of potential problem	1	
		Shares could be worth less than price paid	½	
		Income tax paid	½	
				4
	(ii)	Additional information – 5 × ½	2½	
		Flat in different location:		
		Recognition that benefit is likely to increase	1	
		Statement of how increase calculated	1	
		Max		4
(c)	(i)	January 2005 acquisition	1	
		FA 1985 pool: Proceeds	½	
		Cost	1	
		Indexation	1½	
		Taper relief	1	
		Annual exemption	½	
		CGT at 40%	½	
				6
	(ii)	Tax saved by delaying sale		
		Additional year of taper relief	½	
		Rate of tax in 2007/08	2½	
				3
				20

(a)   Employment income for 2006/07

	£
Salary (£32,000 × 11/12)	29,333
Payment in lieu of notice (Note)	8,000
Payment for agreeing not to work for competitors	17,500
Car benefit (W)	3,621
Employment income	58,454

Note . As the payment in lieu of notice is made in accordance with Benny's contractual arrangements with Golden Tan plc, it will be treated as a payment in respect of services provided and will be taxable in 2006/07, the year in which it is received.

Working

Car benefit

	£
List price (£22,360 – £5,000)	17,360
Percentage (185 – 140)/5 = 9	
15 + 9	× 24%
	× 11/12
	3,819
Contributions for private use (£18 × 11)	(198)
	3,621

BPP Tutorial Note. Although Benny paid £6,100 as a capital contribution towards the car only £5,000 can be deducted from the cost of £22,360.

(b)   (i)   **The share options**

There are no income tax implications when the share options are granted.

In the tax year in which Benny exercises the options and acquires the shares, the excess of the market value of the shares over the price paid, ie £11,500 ((£3.35 – £2.20) × 10,000) will be subject to income tax.

Benny's financial exposure arises due to the rule of the share option scheme obliging him to hold the shares for a year before he can sell them. If the company's expansion into Eastern Europe fails, and its share price consequently falls to below £2.20 before Benny has the chance to sell the shares, Benny's financial position may be summarised as follows:

- Benny will have paid £22,000 (£2.20 × 10,000) for shares which are now worth less than that.
- He will also have paid income tax of £4,600 (£11,500 × 40%).

(ii)   **The flat**

The following additional information is required in order to calculate the employment income benefit in respect of the flat.

- The flat's annual value.
- The cost of any improvements made to the flat prior to 6 April 2007.
- The cost of power, water, repairs and maintenance etc borne by Summer Glow plc.
- The cost of the furniture provided by Summer Glow plc.
- Any use of the flat by Benny wholly, exclusively and necessarily for the purposes of his employment.

Note. The market value of the flat is not required as Summer Glow plc has owned it for less than six years.

One element of the employment income benefit in respect of the flat is calculated by reference to its original cost plus the cost of any capital improvements prior to 6 April 2007. If Benny requests a flat in a different location, this element of the benefit will be computed instead by reference to the cost of the new flat, which in turn equals the proceeds of sale of the old flat.

Accordingly, if, as is likely, the value of the flat has increased since it was purchased, Benny's employment income benefit will also increase. The increase in the employment income benefit will be the flat's sales proceeds less its original cost less the cost of any capital improvements prior to 6 April 2007 multiplied by 5%.

(c)   (i)   **Capital gains tax liability – Sale of shares in Mahana plc**

The shares sold are matched with the acquisition in January 2005 and then with shares in the FA 1985 pool.

Acquisition in January 2005

	£
Disposal proceeds (£24,608 × 1,300/5,800)	5,516
Less: Cost	(2,281)
	3,235

FA 1985 pool

	£
Disposal proceeds (£24,608 × 4,500/5,800)	19,092
Less: Cost (W1)	(3,286)
Less: Indexation (£5,159 – £3,286)	(1,873)
	13,933

Capital gains tax liability

	£
Acquisition in January 2005	3,235
(No taper relief as held for less than three years)	
FA 1985 pool (65% × £13,933)	9,056
(Non-business asset – 8 years plus bonus year)	
Less: Annual exemption	(8,800)
Taxable gains	3,491
Capital gains tax at 40% (Note)	1,396

Note. Benny has employment income of £58,454 in 2006/07 (see part (a)) and is therefore a higher rate taxpayer.

(ii)   **Tax saved by delaying the sale until mid-April 2007**

- There would be an additional 5% taper relief.
- Capital gains tax would be charged at 20% (W2) rather than 40%.

	£
Acquisition in January 2005	3,235
FA 1985 pool (60% × £13,933)	8,360
(Non-business asset – 9 years plus bonus year)	
Less: Annual exemption	(8,800)
Taxable capital gains	2,795
Capital gains tax at 20% (W2)	559
Capital gains tax saved (£1,396 – £559)	837

Workings

(1)   *FA 1985 pool*

	Shares No	Cost £	Indexed cost £
June 1988 Acquisition	8,400	6,744	6,744
Indexation to February 1996			
150.9 – 106.6/106.6			2,803
February 1996 Sale of rights		(610)	(610)
	8,400	6,134	8,937
Indexation to April 1998			
162.6 – 150.9/150.9			693
	8,400	6,134	9,630
March 2007 Sale	(4,500)	(3,286)	(5,159)
	3,900	2,848	4,471

Note. The proceeds from the sale of the rights are regarded as small because they are less than £3,000. Accordingly, there is no disposal and the proceeds are deducted from the cost in the pool.

(2) *2007/08 taxable income and marginal tax rate*

	£
Salary (£39,000 × 7/12)	22,750
Benefit in respect of flat (£11,800 × 7/12)	6,883
Rental income	4,000
Statutory total income	33,633
Personal allowance	(5,035)
	28,598
Upper limit of basic rate band	33,300
Remainder of basic rate band	4,702

5 Nui Neu

Text references. Chapter 1 covers the income tax computation, which should be second nature to you. Chapter 4 deals with national insurance contributions for employees and chapter 22 covers the calculation of corporation tax liabilities.

Top tips. Comparison questions require discipline – you must spend the time doing the calculations first in order to be able to produce a sensible conclusion. However, calculations alone will not allow you to pick up all the available marks – you must explain your answer, as expected in the requirement.

Easy marks. The calculations of tax were very straightforward provided that you dealt with each separately and then brought them together for the conclusion in part (b). This question is not exam standard but is useful to practice your ability to make quick and accurate calculations in the exam.

Marking scheme

		Marks
(a)	**Sole trader**	
	Income tax liability	1
	Class 2 NIC	1
	Class 4 NIC	1
	Net spendable income	1
	Director's remuneration	
	Income tax liability	1
	Employee's Class 1 NIC	1
	Employer's Class 1 NIC	1
	No corporation tax liability	1
	Net spendable income	1
	Dividends	
	No income tax payable	1
	No employee's Class 1 NIC liability	1
	Corporation tax liability	2
	Net spendable income	1
		14
(b)	Conclusion	2
	Mix of dividends and salary	2
		4
		18

(a) **Income tax, national insurance and corporation tax liabilities**

   (i) **Sole trader**

   If Nui operates the shop as a sole trader any drawings taken are irrelevant as a sole trader is taxed on the entire profits of the business. The whole of the £30,000 profits is therefore taxable on Nui as non savings income. As a sole trader Nui will need to pay both Class 2 and Class 4 national insurance contributions.

   Her net spendable income would be £22,660 (see Appendix 1).

   (ii) **Company – salary £25,000**

   If Nui sets up a company to run the shop any salary paid to Nui will be taxable on her as non savings income and there will also be Class 1 primary (Nui) and secondary (the company) NIC contributions due. The salary and secondary Class 1 NIC (but not he primary Class 1 NIC) are deductible expenses for the company for corporation tax purposes.

   Her net spendable income in this case would be £20,650 (see Appendix 1).

   (iii) **Company – dividends £25,000**

   If Nui sets up a company to run the shop and receives dividends she will be taxable on the gross dividend (ie net dividend × 100/90). As Nui is a basic rate taxpayer (she has no other taxable income) the dividends are taxed at 10% and come with a 10% tax credit, so there is no further income tax liability.

   There are no NICs either for Nui or the company on the dividends. Her liability is therefore £nil. However, dividends are not deductible for the company and therefore the full profit is taxable in the hands of the company.

   Her net spendable income in this case would be £24,300 (see Appendix 1).

(b) **Conclusion**

Based on the above calculations, it appears that running the business through a company, with Nui taking dividends, appears to be most beneficial as it results in more profits after tax and NIC and gives Nui more net cash in her hands.

However, Nui may wish to consider taking a combination of salary and dividends to further increase her net spendable income. A salary of £5,035 would use the personal allowance but would not be subject to NIC. The balance of the profit could then be paid out as a dividend. The salary would also reduce the company's taxable profits.

Nui's net spendable income would therefore be £25,257 (see Appendix 2), which would give Nui and additional £957 (£25,257 – £24,300) of spendable income.

Appendix 1

Sole trader:	*Non- savings*
Income tax	£
Trading profit (N)/STI	30,000
Less: Personal allowance	(5,035)
Taxable income	24,965
Tax	£
£2,150 @ 10%	215
£22,815 @ 22%	5,019
Income tax payable	5,234
National insurance contributions	£
Class 2 £2.10 × 52	109
Class 4 (£30,000 − £5,035) @ 8%	1,997
	2,106
Net spendable income	£
Profit	30,000
Less: Income tax and NIC (£5,234 + £2,106)	(7,340)
Net income	22,660

Company – salary £25,000	*Non-savings*
Income tax for Nui	£
Employment income/STI	25,000
Less: Personal allowance	(5,035)
Taxable income	19,965
Tax	£
£2,150 @ 10%	215
£17,815 @ 22%	3,919
£20,105	
Income tax payable	4,134
NIC	
Class 1 primary (£25,000 − £5,035) @ 11%	£2,196
Corporation tax	£
Trading income	30,000
Less: salary	(25,000)
Less: employer's Class 1 NICs on salary (£25,000 − £5,035) @ 12.8%	(2,556)
PCTCT	2,444
Tax @ 19%	464
Net spendable income:	£
Profit	30,000
Less: Income tax and NIC (£4,134 + £2,196)	(6,330)
Employer's NIC	(2,556)
Corporation tax	(464)
Net income	20,650

Company – dividends £25,000

	Dividend/Total income £
Income tax for Nui	
Dividend income × 100/90/STI	27,778
Less: Personal allowance	(5,035)
Taxable income	22,743
Tax	
£22,743 @ 10%	2,274
Less: tax credit £22,743 @ 10%	(2,274)
Income tax	0
NIC – none	
Trading income/PCTCT	£30,000
Tax @ 19%	£5,700
No employer's NIC	

Net spendable income:	£
Profit	30,000
Less: Income tax and NIC	0
Employer's NIC	0
Corporation tax	(5,700)
Net income	24,300

Appendix 2

Company – salary £5,035, dividends £19,965

	Non-savings £	Dividends £
Income tax for Nui		
Employment income	5,035	
Dividend income × 100/90		22,183
Less: Personal allowance	(5,035)	
Taxable income	Nil	22,183
Tax		£
£22,183 @ 10%		2,218
Less: tax credit £22,183 @ 10%		(2,218)
Income tax		0
NIC – none		
Corporation tax		£
Trading income		30,000
Less: salary		(5,035)
Less: employer's Class 1 NICs on salary		Nil
PCTCT		24,965
Tax @ 19%		4,743

Net spendable income:		£
Profit		30,000
Less: Income tax and NIC		Nil
Employer's NIC		Nil
Corporation tax		(4,743)
Net income		25,257

6 Preparation question with helping hand: Alex Zong

Text references. Trading profits are covered in Chapter 6. Incorporation of a business is covered in Chapter 30. The VAT aspects of the question are in Chapters 28 and 29.

Top tips. Take care with taper relief. It is deducted **after** current and brought forward capital losses. Consider how much of this question requires nothing more than your basic Paper 2.3 tax knowledge.

Easy marks. The trading profits calculation in part (a) should have been very easy marks, so long as you knew your basis period rules for opening, continuing and closing years. If you pick up these easy marks you do not have to score so highly on the more complex incorporation and VAT issues.

(a)   (i)   **Trading profits assessments**

The trading profits for each accounting period are:

		£
P/E 30.6.04	£28,000 – £8,050 (W)=	19,950
Y/E 30.6.05	£44,000 – £2,388 (W)=	41,612
Y/E 30.6.06	£53,000 – £3,007 (W)=	49,993
P/E 31.12.07	£29,000	29,000

Overlap profits on commencement were.

	£
1.10.03 to 5.4.04 (£19,950 × 6/9)	13,300
1.7.04 to 30.9.04 (£41,612 × 3/12)	10,403
	23,703

Alex's taxable trading profits assessment for 2006/07 will be as follows.

	£
Y/E 30.6.06	49,993
P/E 31.12.06	29,000
	78,993
Relief for overlap profits	(23,703)
	55,290

Working

Capital allowances

	FYA £	Pool £	Private use £		Allowances £
Period ended 30.6.04					
Additions	19,000		4,000		
FYA @ 40% /WDA (25% × 9/12)	(7,600)		(750)	× 60%	8,050
TWDV c/f		11,400	3,250		
Year ended 30.6.05					
Disposal		(3,800)			
		7,600	3,250		
WDA – 25%		(1,900)	(813)	× 60%	2,388
WDV c/f		5,700	2,437		
Year ended 30.6.06					
Disposal			(2,800)		
Balancing charge			363	× 60%	(218)
Addition			13,500		
WDA 25%/(restricted)		(1,425)	(3,000)	× 60%	3,225
TWDV c/f		4,275	10,500		3,007

Note 1

FYAs are obtained at 40%. The 50% rate applies for the period 6/4/06 to 5/4/07.

Note 2

Alex should elect to transfer plant to Lexon Ltd at its written-down value. This avoids the balancing charges that would otherwise arise in the final period. The market values of the lorry and plant (£4,300 + £8,200 = £12,500) and the motor car (£11,500) both exceed their respective written-down values.

(ii) **Capital gains tax**

The assets will be deemed to be disposed of at their market values:

	£	£
Goodwill		
Proceeds		40,000
Cost		nil
Capital gain		40,000
Freehold premises		
Proceeds		75,000
Cost	32,000	
Enhancement expenditure	6,700	
		(38,700)
Gain		36,300

Total gains (before taper relief) total £76,300 (40,000 + 36,300).

Incorporation relief applies automatically as the business is being transferred as a going concern, and all of the business assets are being transferred. However since Alex is receiving some shares and some cash (loan account) not all of the gain can be rolled over. Alex will have a chargeable gain before taper relief of £4,769 (£76,300 × 10,000/160,000) which will be completely extinguished by the capital losses made in the year.

However, to avoid wasting taper relief and the annual exemption. Alex should consider increasing the amount of the loan account to £100,026:

	£
$£76,300 \times \dfrac{100,026}{160,000} =$	47,700
Less: Capital loss	(12,500)
Net gain for year	35,200
	£
Gain remaining after taper relief (£35,200 × 25%)	8,800
Less: Annual exemption	(8,800)
	Nil

Alex is currently entitled to maximum business asset taper relief. If he does not think he will hold the shares for at least two years (the holding period to obtain that same level of taper relief again) he could consider making an election for incorporation relief not to apply.

(iii) **Value added tax**

The incorporation of a business is outside the scope of VAT. This means there will be no VAT charged on any assets transferred to Lexon Ltd.

Lexon Ltd will be able to take over Alex's VAT registration number if it wishes. However, if this is done then the company assumes Alex's VAT liabilities.

(b)   (i)   **Bad debt**

Bad debts relief is given six months after the time that payment was due, provided that the debt has been written off. Since an invoice was not raised until 15 June 2006, bad debt relief cannot be claimed in the VAT return for the quarter ended 30 November 2006. The amount of the relief to be claimed in the following VAT return will be £1,050.

(ii)   **Refund of VAT**

A claim must be made for the repayment of the VAT underclaimed. The amount due cannot just be put through on the next VAT return, since the error exceeds £2,000. Claims for the refund of VAT are subject to a three year time limit, and so the claim will cover the period 1 December 2003 to 30 November 2006. The repayment will be for £2,547 (£475 × 36 × 17.5/117.5).

(iii)   **Discount**

Where a discount is offered for prompt payment, VAT is due on the net amount even if the discount is not taken. The output VAT due is £565 (£3,400 × 95% × 17.5%).

7 Anne Parr

Text references. Chapter 5 covers the taxation of termination payments. The employment vs self employment factors are discussed in Chapter 4. Trading income is in Chapter 6. The basic VAT rules are in Chapter 28 and the partial exemption rules are in Chapter 29. Chapters 21 and 22 cover the calculation of corporation tax liabilities, with capital allowances in Chapter 7.

Top tips. The requirement for part (b) provides you with three useful headings so use in your report so use them to help structure your answer.

Make sure you do the calculations for part (c) before you jump in and write your answer so that you can compare the results of each option and write a sensible conclusion.

Easy marks. Part (d) required a calculation for 10 marks. Do your workings first, such as the capital allowances, and reference them in clearly to pick up all the available marks.

Marking scheme

			Marks

(a) **Compensation payment**

Bonus = reward for services	½	
Taxable 2006/07	½	
Ex gratia partially exempt	1	
£30,000 exempt	1	
If contractual = taxable	½	
Max		3

(b) **Employment vs self employment**

Contract of/ for services	½	
No single factor conclusive	½	
Factors – 1 mark per sensible comment	6	
Conclusion	1	
Max		7

Taxable trading income

Adjusted profits	1	
Capital allowances	1½	
2006/07	1	
2007/08	1	
2008/09	½	
Overlap profits	1	
When can be relieved	1	
Max		6

VAT dates

Threshold exceeded	1	
Register by 30 November	1	
Charge from 1 December	1	
Liable for VAT if fails to register	1	
		4

Format/ presentation   2

(c) **After-tax cost of using Anne's services**

Employer's NIC	½	
Partial exemption percentage	1	
Irrecoverable VAT – excluding Anne's services	2½	
Irrecoverable VAT – including Anne's services	3½	
Corporation tax saving	1	
Max		7

(d) **Longhorn Ltd CT liability**

Adjusted trading profits (½ mark for each correct adjustment)	5½	
IBAs	2	
Interest income	1½	
Overseas income	½	
Gains	½	
CT rates	½	
DTR	1	
CVS relief	½	
Max		10
		39

(a) **Compensation payment**

The bonus due to Anne forms part of her normal earnings as it is a reward for past services performed and will be fully liable to tax. It will be taxable in the tax year of receipt, ie 2006/07.

The *ex gratia* payment does not arise from her employment contract but is instead made in respect of the loss of her employment. Only the excess of the payment over £30,000 (ie £44,000) is taxable.

If Anne were to receive a contractual termination payment, this would again be fully taxable since it would arise from her employment.

(b) **Report**

To: Anne Parr
From: A Adviser
Date: [date]
Subject: Self employment status

This report covers tax issues relating to:

(i)   Factors in deciding employment or self-employment
(ii) Projected taxable trading income
(iii) VAT registration

(i) **Factors in deciding employment or self-employment**

The key test of employment as against self-employment is the existence of a contract *of* service, compared with a contract *for* services. There are a number of other factors which should be considered. No single factor is likely to be conclusive.

HMRC are likely to consider the following factors:

- Degree of control
- Mutuality of obligations
- Correction of work
- Degree of financial risk
- Provision of equipment
- Conditions of pay
- Client portfolio
- Integration into business organisation

Factors indicating self-employment

With regard to your own circumstances, you appear to be acting as an external consultant, as opposed to performing an integral function in Longhorn Ltd's business.

You are receiving a fixed fee for work done, rather than payment for time spent on the company's behalf.

While Longhorn Ltd is currently your only paymaster you are not formally tied to it beyond the span of your six month assignment and it appears that you are seeking other clients; this probably outweighs the fact that in practice you cannot currently work for others.

You have no obligation to accept further work from Longhorn Ltd nor does Longhorn Ltd have to provide such work. This shows there is no mutual obligation.

Longhorn Ltd does not seem to have control over the conduct of your work, assuming that your presence on the premises is merely a practical requirement; the obligation to report to the managing director does not appear to imply supervision of your work as such.

Factors indicating employment

Office space and assistance is provided by Longhorn Ltd. However, you will presumably also make use of your home office. It is therefore arguable that these are temporary arrangements which are a necessary feature of this particular line of work.

Conclusion

Taking all these factors into account, it therefore seems likely that you would be regarded as having self-employed status.

(ii) **Projected taxable trading income**

Your first tax year of trade will be 2006/07 when the taxable trading profits will be £18,554. The taxable trade profits in 2007/08 and 2008/09 will be £38,847 and £44,065 respectively.

The overlap profits that will arise as a result of double taxation of trade profits in 2006/07 and 2007/08 will be £29,570, which you will be able to offset either on a change of accounting date or when the business ceases.

Please see Appendix 1 for my calculations of the above figures.

(iii) **VAT registration**

You will exceed the registration threshold of £61,000 by the end of October 2007 as follows:

		£
November 2006 – March 2007	5 × £4,200	21,000
April 2007 – October 2007	7 × £5,800	40,600
Exceeds threshold		61,600

You will be required to register with HMRC by 30 November 2007.

You should start charging VAT on your supplies from 1 December 2007.

Failure to register for VAT

If you to fail to register on time you would still be liable to account for VAT due on supplies made from the date on which you were obliged to register (from 1 December 2007).

(c) **After-tax cost to Longhorn Ltd of using Anne's services**

As an employee, the cost to the company comprises Anne's salary and Class 1 secondary contributions, both of which are allowable deductions in the company's corporation tax computation.

As a self-employed contractor the company will pay her fees, but will consequently incur irrecoverable input VAT relating to general business overheads. Both costs are allowable deductions in the company's corporation tax computation.

The after tax cost to the company will be £3,182 (£35,553 – £32,371) greater if it hires Anne on a self employed basis (see Appendix 2).

(d)   **Longhorn Ltd – Corporation tax computation – period ended 31 March 2007**

	£
Taxable trading profits (W1)	139,538
Interest (W3)	680
Overseas income (dividends)	4,800
Chargeable gains	28,070
PCTCT	173,088
Corporation tax (£173,088 × 19% (W4))	32,887
Less Double tax relief (W5)	(480)
	32,407
Less Corporate Venturing Scheme relief (£27,000 × 20%)	(5,400)
Corporation tax payable	27,007

Workings

(1)   *Taxable trading profits*

	£	£
Profit per accounts		149,000
Add back		
Depreciation of fixed assets	16,225	
Directors' remuneration (Note (i))	14,000	
Fine for breach of law	3,850	
Gifts of drink to customers	2,268	
Subscription to political party	10,000	
Fees in relation to issue of shares	3,750	
Interest on loan to acquire investment	3,020	
		53,113
Deduct		
Non-trade interest	2,850	
Profit on sale of office	42,875	
Profit on gain of government security	850	
Dividend from overseas investment	4,800	
		(51,375)
Adjusted profit before capital allowances		150,738
Less IBAs (W2)		(11,200)
Taxable trading profits		139,538

Notes

(i)   The directors' remuneration is allowable if paid within nine months of the year end. As £14,000 is not paid within nine months, it must be disallowed in this period's computation, but will be allowed in the following year when paid.

(ii)   The amortisation of intangible assets is an allowable deduction for companies.

(2)   *IBAs allowances on sports pavilion*

Sports pavilions provided for the welfare of employees qualify for industrial buildings allowances.

Building costs (including fees but excluding cost of land) (£280,000 × 4%)	£11,200

(3)   *Interest*

	£
Bank interest	2,850
Profit on sale of government security	850
Interest paid on loan to acquire overseas investment	(3,020)
Interest	680

The income/expenditure and profits/losses on all loan relationships entered into for non-trade purposes are aggregated. A net credit is taxed as interest income.

(4) *Corporation tax rate – 12 months ended 31 March 2007*

PCTCT = 'profits'   £173,088

The company has not received any franked investment income and the 'profits' are therefore the same as the PCTCT

FY2006

Upper limit	£1,500,000
Lower limit	£300,000
	Small companies' rate applies

(5) **Double tax relief**

	£	£
Double tax relief available on the overseas dividend is the lower of:		
(i) Foreign tax suffered (£4,800 × 10%)	480	
(ii) UK tax on overseas income (£4,800 × 19%)	912	
Double tax relief		480

Appendix 1

Taxable trading profits

	£
2006/07	
1 October 2006 – 5 April 2007 (actual basis)	
£27,831 (W1) × $^6/_9$	18,554
2007/08	
1 October 2006 – 30 September 2007 (first 12 months)	
£27,831 + (£44,065 × $^3/_{12}$)	38,847
2008/09	
Year ended 30 June 2008 (current year basis)	44,065

Overlap profits

	£
1 October 2006 to 5 April 2007 (£27,831 × $^6/_9$)	18,554
1 July 2007 to 30 September 2007 (£44,065 × $^3/_{12}$)	11,016
	29,570

Workings

(1) *Adjusted profits*

	Nine months to 30 June 2007 £	Year ended 30 June 2008 £
Profits	27,750	42,800
Add Depreciation	3,200	2,560
Less Capital allowances (W2)	(3,119)	(1,295)
Tax adjusted profits	27,831	44,065

(2)   *Capital allowances*

	FYAs £	General pool £	Private use car £		Allowances £
9 m/e 30 June 2007					
Additions without FYA			11,000		
WDA @ 25% $\times ^3/_{12}$			(2,063)	× 30%	619
Additions with FYA: computer (note)	5,000				
FYA @ 50%	(2,500)				2,500
WDV c/f		2,500	8,937		
Total allowances					3,119
Y/e 30 June 2008					
WDA @ 25%		(625)	(2,234)	× 30%	1,295
WDV c/f		1,875	6,703		
Total allowances					1,295

Note. Anne's business is a small business for capital allowance purposes and therefore eligible for 50% FYA on plant and equipment purchased between 6 April 2006 and 5 April 2007.

It may be advantageous for the new computer to be treated as a short-life asset if it is envisaged that it will be disposed of within five years, and a balancing allowance will crystallise on its disposal. If the election is made, a separate column is set up for the computer. However, the allowances will remain the same in this nine month accounting period.

Appendix 2

After-tax cost to Longhorn Ltd of using Anne's services

	Employee £	Self-employed £
Payment – salary/fees	36,000	36,000
Employer's NIC (W1)	3,964	
Irrecoverable VAT cost (W2)		7,892
	39,964	43,892
Less Corporation tax saving @ 19%	(7,593)	(8,339)
After-tax cost to the company	32,371	35,553

Workings

(1)   *Employer's NIC*

Class 1 secondary contributions = (£36,000 – £5,035) × 12.8% = £3,964

Note.   For annual calculations the primary threshold of £5,035 should be used in the examination.

(2)   *Irrecoverable VAT cost*

Recoverability of input VAT

Excluding supplies from Anne as a VAT registered trader

	Total £	Recoverable £	Irrecoverable £
Re exempt supplies	4,700		4,700
Re general overheads (W3)	8,900	7,031	1,869
Re taxable supplies (bal fig)	21,143	21,143	
	34,743	28,174	6,569

Average exempt input tax falls below £625 per month and is less than 50% of the total input tax. Therefore all exempt input VAT is recoverable, ignoring Anne's supplies.

Taking Anne's supplies into account

	£	Total £	Recoverable £	Irrecoverable £
Re exempt supplies		4,700		4,700
Re taxable supplies		21,143	21,143	
Re general overheads				
As before	8,900			
Supplies from Anne				
(£36,000 × 17.5%)	6,300			
Allocation (79%:21%) (W3)		15,200	12,008	3,192
		41,043	33,151	7,892

Exempt input tax is now in excess of de minimis limits so no exempt input VAT is recoverable. Recoverable VAT would be £33,151.

Irrecoverable VAT of £7,892 represents an additional cost to the company but, as it relates to general business overheads, it is an allowable deduction for corporation tax purposes.

(3) *Indirectly attributable input VAT*

Recoverable input VAT on general overheads =
$$\frac{220,000 + 30,000}{220,000 + 30,000 + 70,000} \times 100\%$$

Recoverable input VAT on general overheads = 79% (round up to nearest whole %)

Irrecoverable input VAT on general overheads = 21%

8 Ming Khan and Nina Lee

Text references. Partnerships are covered in Chapter 9. Capital allowances are in Chapter 7. Loss relief is in Chapter 8. Ethics are in Chapter 30.

Top tips. Chargeable gains are taxed at 10% if they fall within the starting rate band and at 20% if they fall within the basic rate band. They are, however, taxed at 40% to the extent that, when added to taxable income, they are at or above the higher rate threshold.

Easy marks. There are a lot of different things to do in this question. You do not have to answer the question in order. For example, part (c) is a stand alone part. For easy marks tackle the parts of a question you feel most comfortable with first. However, allocate your time carefully between the sections.

				Marks
(a)	(1)	Capital allowances	2	
		Allocation of loss	2	
		Max		3
	(2)	Section 385 ICTA 1988	1	
		Section 380 ICTA 1988/Section 72	2	
		Section 381 ICTA 1988	1	
				4
	(3)	*Ming Khan*		
		Loss relief claims	1	
		Refund 2004/05	3	
		Refund 2003/04	2	
		Nina Lee		
		Refund 2004/05	3	
		Loss relief claims	1	
		Max		9
	(4)	*Computer equipment – Hire-purchase*		
		Capital allowances	1	
		FYA @ 50%/40%	1	
		Finance charge	1	
		VAT	1	
		Computer equipment – Leasing		
		Lease rental payments	1	
		VAT	1	
				6
	Format/ presentation			2
(b)	Client identification		1	
	Communication with previous accountant		1	
	Engagement letter		1	
				3
				27

(a)

To	The files
From	Tax assistant
Date	[date]
Subject	Ming Khan and Nina Lee – partnership

This memorandum covers tax issues relating to the partnership run by Ming Khan (MK) and Nina Lee (NL).

Allocation of partnership trading loss

The trading loss is £105,000 (71,250 + 33,750 (W)).

This is shared £63,000 to MK and £42,000 to NL, and allocated to tax years as follows.

	Ming (60%) £	Nina (40%) £
2005/06 (1.5.05 to 5.4.06)		
£63,000/£42,000 × 11/15	46,200	30,800
2006/07 (Balance of loss)	16,800	11,200
	63,000	42,000

The trading profit assessments for 2005/06 and 2006/07 will be nil.

Working

Capital allowances	General Pool £
Recording equipment	70,300
Electrical system	19,400
Sound insulation	13,200
Heating system	5,100
	108,000
WDA (25% × 15/12)	(33,750)
TWDV carried forward	74,250

The building is not an industrial building hence no IBAs are due on its cost.

Use of trading losses

The trading losses can be relieved in the following ways:

(i) Carrying it forward under s 385 ICTA 1988 to set against future trading profits.

(ii) Claiming relief against total income under s 380 ICTA 1988. The loss for 2005/06 can be set against total income for 2005/06 and/or 2004/05. The loss for 2006/07 can be set against total income for 2006/07 and/or 2005/06. Provided, in any particular year, that a s 380 claim is made first, a claim could also be made under s 72 FA 1991 to extend the set off to chargeable gains of the same year.

(iii) Claiming relief under s 381 ICTA 1988 against total income of the three years preceding the year of the loss, earliest year first. Thus the 2005/06 loss can be carried back to: 2002/03, 2003/04 and 2004/05 and the 2006/07 loss can be carried back to 2003/04, 2004/05 and 2005/06

Specific loss relief claims and repayments generated

Ming Khan

MK should claim under s 380 ICTA 1988 to set the loss of £46,200 for 2005/06 against her total income for 2004/05.

	£	£
Employment income – Salary (£42,000 × 11/12)		38,500
Compensation	60,000	
Exemption	(30,000)	
		30,000
		68,500
Less: Loss relief (S 380)		(46,200)
		22,300
Personal allowance		(5,035)
Taxable income		17,265

This will result in a tax repayment of:

	£
16,035 (£33,300 − £17,265) @ 22%	3,528
30,165 @ 40%	12,066
46,200	15,594

MK does not have any income for 2005/06 or 2006/07, and so a claim under s 380 ICTA 1988 in respect of her loss for 2006/07 is not available. She should therefore make a claim under s 381 ICTA 1988 against her total income for 2003/04.

	£
Employment income – Salary	42,000
Loss claim (s 381)	(16,800)
	25,200
Personal allowance	(5,035)
Taxable income	20,165

This will result in a tax repayment of:

	£
£13,135 (£33,300 − £20,165) @ 22%	2,890
£3,665 @ 40%	1,466
16,800	4,356

Nina Lee

NL's taxable income for 2002/03 and 2003/04 is £1,215 (£6,250 − £5,035). A claim under s 381 ICTA 1988 is not beneficial as it would waste personal allowances in these years and only save a small amount of tax.

NL should utilise her loss of £30,800 for 2005/06 by claiming under s 380 ICTA 1988 against her total income for 2004/05. Although this does waste personal allowances it also allows her to set the loss against her chargeable gain and obtain an immediate repayment of CGT.

	£
Rental income	6,250
Less: Loss relief (S 380)	(6,250)
	nil
Tax refund: £1,215 at 10%	122

	£
Chargeable gain	39,600
Less: Loss relief (£30,800 − £6,250)	(24,550)
	15,050
Annual exemption	(8,800)
	6,250

Capital gains tax due:	£
£2,150 × 10%	215
£4,100 × 20%	820
	1,035

Previously paid on £30,800 (£39,600 − £8,800)

£935 (£2,150 − £1,215) × 10%	(94)
£29,865 @ 20%	(5,973)
Repayment due	(5,032)

NL's loss of £11,200 for 2006/07 should be carried forward under s 385 ICTA 1998 against her trading profits for 2007/08 (year ended 31 July 2007

Acquisition of computer equipment

Hire-purchase

The partnership will be able to claim capital allowances on the cost of the computer equipment of £52,000 (£61,100 × 100/117.5). A first year allowance of 50% will be available if the purchase occurs between 6 April 2006 and 5 April 2007 and at 40% thereafter.

The finance charge of £20,000 (36 × £2,000 = £72,000 − £52,000) will be a deductible expense for the partnership, and will be allocated to periods of account using normal accounting principles.

The input VAT of £9,100 will be reclaimed on the VAT return for the period in which the computer equipment is purchased.

Leasing

The lease rental payments of £24,000 pa (£28,200 × 100/117.5) will be a deductible expense for the partnership, and will be allocated to periods of account in accordance with the accruals concept.

The input VAT of £4,200 (£28,200 × 17.5/117.5) included in each lease rental payment will be reclaimed on the tax return for the period during which the appropriate tax point occurs.

No capital allowances can be claimed by the partnership.

Tax assistant

(b)   When commencing to act for MK, NL and the partnership you must:

- Obtain proof of identity. For MK and NL this would be one item of photographic ID, such as a passport, and proof of address, eg a recent utility bill. A partnership need have no formal documentation, but you should obtain some proof of existence such as a bank statement, or certificate of registration for VAT. You have already confirmed the identities of the partners.

- Communicate with the former accountant, if any. If either MK or NL has previously had a tax adviser you should request permission to write to them, and you should ask MK or NL to authorise the previous adviser to communicate with you. If this permission is not forthcoming you need to decline to act.

- Prepare a letter of engagement for each of MK, NL and the partnership setting out your own and their responsibilities.

- In instances where you are acting for all the parties you need to ensure that no conflict of interest arises. You will need to monitor the situation regularly to ensure that you identify any threat as soon as it arises.

9 Tim Aylsbury

Text references. Trading income is dealt with in Chapter 6. Loss relief is in Chapter 8. Employment income is covered in Chapter 4 with share related income in Chapter 5. Overseas aspects of income tax are in Chapter 10 and the overseas aspects of chargeable gains are in Chapter 15.

Top tips. You should have been able to calculate the loss of the final year of trade and the amount available for terminal loss relief without problem. If you are finding the calculations tricky you must practise using appropriate proformas as not many marks will be available for them in the exam and you must be able to do them quickly.

Easy marks. This is not an exam standard question so there were lots of easy marks, but it is still useful to help you practice writing your answer in an appropriate format with figures contained in an Appendix.

Marking scheme

			Marks
(a)	Income calculation	1	
	Opening year rules	1	
	Overlap	½	
	Cessation rules	1	
	Loss of 2007/08	1	
	Use of loss in current year/ carry back/ gains	1½	
	Terminal loss calculation	1	
	Use of terminal loss	1	
	Tax savings	1	
	Recommendation	1	
		Max	9
(b)	Tax collected under PAYE for earnings	½	
	Self assessment	½	
	Salary and bonus	1	
	Share options unapproved	1	
	Tax on exercise	½	
	Base cost for CGT	½	
	Taper relief from exercise	½	
	Business asset	½	
	Furniture use	½	
	Keep furniture	½	
			6
(c)	Absence covers complete tax year	½	
	NR and NOR for period	½	
	UK income taxable	½	
	Foreign income not taxable	½	
	No CGT	½	
	Could sell shares	½	
	Temporary non residence	½	
	Gain/ loss in year of return	½	
	Taper relief	½	
	Practical issues		
	Cost and standard of living	½	
	Can rent out home in UK	½	
	Different environment	½	
			6
	Format/presentation		2
			23

[Our address]

[Your address]

[Date]

Dear Mr Aylsbury

LOSS RELIEF AND YOUR NEW EMPLOYMENT

I was sorry to hear of the closure of your business, but I am pleased to see that you have found employment in the same line of trade.

I have set out below the options for your recent losses, together my comments on your new remuneration package and the implications of working abroad. All calculations are in the Appendix to this letter.

Loss options

As you are ceasing to trade, the loss of your final year of trade (2007/08) of £22,250 (W2) cannot be carried forward as there are no future profits of the same trade to use them against. The alternatives available to you are:

(1)   (a)   Set against your capital gain for the year of £20,300. This will save you tax at 10% and 20%, but you will lose some of the benefit of your annual exemption.

      (b)   Alternatively, the loss could instead be set against the income of £12,500 of 2006/07. This would not save tax as the dividends would be taxed at 10% (personal allowance set against trading income and thus left with dividend income in charge to tax), which is covered by the 10% tax credit. This would result in a loss of personal allowance and would provide no tax benefit.

(2)   The £20,583 loss of the last 12 months of trade can be set against your trading profits only of 2006/07, 2005/06 and 2004/05 (in that order). This will generate re-payments of tax previously paid in respect of your trading income (at 10% and 22%).

I would recommend that you take this second form of loss relief as, although it does waste your personal allowances for both years, it provides greater tax savings than the first option.

The balance of loss available of £1,667 (£22,250 – £2,053) can be used against your gains in 2007/08, saving tax at 20%.

New remuneration package

Your salary and any taxable benefits (see below) will be taxed each month through the pay-as-you-earn scheme. This is different, of course, from your old business where you paid tax only twice a year.

Your salary and bonus will be taxable as earnings.

The share option scheme will not be HMRC approved as there is a large discount to the current market price. There are no tax implications of being granted the right to buy the shares, but a taxable benefit will arise on exercising that right in three years' time.

Assuming that the share price increases by 20% each year over the next 3 years to £5.18 (£3 x 1.23), you will be assessed on a benefit of £7,360 (2,000 shares @ [5.18 - 1.50]). The shares will have a base cost of £5.18 when you eventually sell them. Taper relief will run from the date of exercise at the business asset rate, as you work for the company.

You will be taxed on the furniture that you take home. The taxable benefit will be 20% of the value, which in this case amounts to £500 pa. There are no further tax implications if you give back the furniture.

If you decide to keep the furniture, there will be an additional benefit. HMRC will tax you on the value of the furniture when first used by you less the amount assessed for using it (£2,500 - £500), or the value at the time of the outright gift (£800) if higher.

In this case you would be assessed on £2,000, less the amount you are required to pay (£500), a total of £1,500.

Secondment abroad

As you would be going abroad to work for two years, this would cover at least one entire tax year. Consequently HMRC would treat you as not resident and not ordinarily resident in the UK for the entire duration of the secondment.

As a result, you would only be liable to income tax on any income generated in the UK. Your income from Ruritania would not be taxed in the UK.

You would also not be liable to capital gains tax while seconded abroad, which would give you an opportunity to sell your shares from the share option scheme without incurring an immediate tax liability.

However, as you will not be outside the UK for at least five years any gain (or loss) will be taxable (or allowable) in the tax year of your return under the temporary non residence rules. Taper relief, where applicable, will run to the actual date of disposal, as normal, and not to the date the gain is taxed.

It is difficult to establish whether you will be better off by accepting the secondment. You need to bear in mind the cost and standard of living in Ruritania, whether you could rent out your home here and the experience of a different environment. It would be worth speaking to employees who have been there in order to determine the suitability of the opportunity to you.

I trust that the above has clarified matters for you, but if you have any queries please do not hesitate to contact me.

Yours sincerely

A Adviser

Appendix: Statement of total income and gains before loss relief

	2004/05	2005/06	2006/07	2007/08
	£	£	£	£
Trading profit (W1)	20,000	15,000	5,000	Nil
Dividend income	6,500	7,000	7,500	–
Total income	26,500	22,000	12,500	Nil
Capital gains (20,300 – 8,800)	–	–	–	11,500

Workings

(1) *Trading profit*

2004/05 – actual basis

1.6.04 – 5.4.05			
1.6.04 – 31.10.04		13,750	
1.11.04 – 5.4.05	5/12 × £15,000	6,250	20,000

2005/06 – y/e 31.10.05   15,000

2006/07 – y/e 31.10.06   5,000

2007/08 – y/e 31.10.07	(10,000)	
Add: 2 m/e 31.12.07	(6,000)	
Less: overlap (1.11.04 – 5.4.05)	(6,250)	(22,250)
		ie nil trading profit

(2) *Calculation of terminal loss*

Last 12 months of trade

	£
2007/08: 6.4.07 – 31.12.07 (9m)	
Trade loss	
6,000 + ($^7/_{12}$ × 10,000)	11,833
Add: overlap relief	6,250
2006/07: 1.1.07 – 5.4.07 (3m)	
Trade loss	
$^3/_{12}$ × 10,000	2,500
	20,583

(3) *Application of terminal loss*

	£
2007/08	Nil
2006/07	5,000
2005/06	15,000
2004/05	583
	20,583

10 Amy

Text references. Income tax elements of question dealt with in Chapters 1 to 4 with the overseas aspects covered in Chapter 10. CGT, including the overseas aspects, is covered in Chapters 11 to 15. IHT knowledge contained in Chapters 17-19.

Top tips. Part (a) (ii) required you to deal with three different taxes. In questions like this ensure that you do deal with all of the taxes mentioned otherwise you will throw away many easy marks.

Easy marks. If you knew the answer to part (b)(ii) it was worth doing this early on to ensure you picked up the mark available. However, remember you only have about 1½ minutes to spend on one mark.

Marking scheme

				Marks
(a)	(i)	Income tax	1	
		Capital gains tax	1	
		Inheritance tax	1	
				3
	(ii)	*Income tax:*		
		Car benefit	1	
		Fuel benefit	½	
		UK rental income	½	
		Overseas rental income	1	
		NS&I interest	½	
		Bank interest	½	
		UK dividends	½	
		Overseas dividends	1	
		Income tax (before DTR) including W3	2	
		DTR (½ + ½)	1	
		Tax deducted at source	½	
		CGT:		
		June gain (½ + ½)	1	
		November – no gain	½	
		January gain (½ + ½)	1	
		Tapered gains (½ + ½)	1	
		Annual exemption/tax liability	½	
		IHT	½	
		Deferral of gains:		
		Not eligible for gift relief	½	
		Qualifies for EIS relief	½	
		EIS deferral relief details	½	
			Max	13
(b)	(i)	Gift with reservation – identification	½	
		– treatment	1	
		Potential double charge	½	
		Calculate ignoring PET:		
		June – annual exemptions	½	
		November – not chargeable	½	
		Estate at death – liability	½	
		Calculation with gift as PET:		
		Annual exemption	½	
		Tax liability	½	
		Taper relief	½	
		Higher charge used	½	
	(ii)	Pay market rent	½	
		IHT saving as not GWR	½	
		Rent charge	½	
			Max	6
			Total	22

131

(a) (i) **Basis of charge to tax:**

Income tax – Amy will be chargeable to income tax on all of her UK source income but as she is not UK domiciled she will only be liable to income tax on such amount of her foreign income as is remitted to the UK.

Capital gains tax – Amy will be chargeable to capital gains tax on any gains made on the disposal of UK situated assets but as she is not UK domiciled she will only be liable to capital gains tax on any gains on the disposal of non-UK situated assets that are remitted to the UK. No relief is available for losses on non-UK situated assets.

Inheritance tax – As Amy is not UK domiciled she is only liable to inheritance tax on transfers of assets that are situated in the UK. It should be noted that if Amy has been UK resident for 17 out of the last 20 tax years she will be treated as UK domiciled and so liable to inheritance tax on transfers of all of her assets, wherever situated.

(ii) **Amy income tax computation 2006/07**

	Non savings income £	Savings (excl dividend) income £	Dividends income £	Total £
Salary	20,000			
Benefits (W1)	7,350			
NS&I easy access		180		
Deposit interest (£400 × 100/80)		500		
UK Dividends (£1,800 × 100/90)			2,000	
Foreign dividends (£650 × 100/65)			1,000	
Foreign rents £850 × 7 × 100/85	7,000			
UK rents ((£1,340 – 140) × 9)	10,800			
	45,150	680	3,000	48,830
Less Personal allowance	(5,035)			
	40,115	680	3,000	43,795

Income tax liability	£
£2,150 × 10%	215
£37,560 (W2) × 22%	8,263
£405 × 40%	162
£680 × 40%	272
£3,000 × 32.5%	975
	9,887
Less DTR	
On rent £7,000 × 15% (no restriction)	(1,050)
On dividends £1,000 × 32.5% (restricted to UK tax)	(325)
	8,512
Less tax deducted:	
PAYE	(5,085)
Bank interest	(100)
Dividends	(200)
Income tax payable	3,127

Capital gains tax computation 2006/07

	£
Red plc shares	
Proceeds (market value) 50,000 × £2.22 (W3)	111,000
Cost (probate value)	(20,000)
	91,000
Gain after taper relief (NBA held for 2 years) £91,000 × 100%	£91,000

Overseas property

The property is gifted to Michael so no proceeds are remitted to the UK and no chargeable gain arises.

UK property

	£
Proceeds (market value)	125,000
Cost	(67,000)
	58,000
Less indexation allowance	
$\dfrac{(162.6-149.8)}{149.8} = 0.085 \times £67,000$	(5,695)
	52,305
Gain after taper relief (8 years + bonus year)	
£52,305 × 65%	33,998

	£
Total gains £(91,000 + 33,998)	124,998
Less annual exemption	(8,800)
Taxable gains	116,198
CGT payable £116,198 × 40%	£46,479

As neither the shares nor the UK property qualify as business assets, gift relief is not available. The only way in which Amy can defer the gains arising is by subscribing for shares under the enterprise investment scheme (EIS). The investment must be made within three years of the disposal, and the amount of the gain that can be deferred is the lower of the amount invested, the amount of the gain, or the amount claimed.

IHT: the gifts to Michael are PETs and will only be chargeable to IHT should Amy die within seven years of the gifts.

Workings

(1) **Benefits** £

Car benefit (175 − 140)/5 = 7 + 15 = 22 + 3 (diesel) = 25%

Benefit £15,000 × 25%	3,750
Fuel benefit £14,400 × 25%	3,600
	7,350

(2) **Basic rate band**

Contributions: £5,000 ×100/78 = £6,410 gross

Basic rate band = £31,150 + £6,410 = £37,560

(3) **Market value**

¼ up 221 + ¼ × (229 − 221) =223

Average bargain ½ × (225 + 219) = 222

(b) (i) If Amy gives her main residence to her niece Erica on 1 June 2007 but continues to live in the property, then this will be treated as a gift with reservation of benefit. However as a lifetime gift to an individual it is treated as a PET. Also, as Amy dies without having moved out of the property the house is treated as part of her estate on death.

There will be an IHT charge, being the higher of:

- the charge on the PET ignoring the house in the death estate, and
- the charge on the house in the death estate ignoring the PET.

IHT computation

Lifetime transfers	£
1 June 2006 Red plc shares	
Value	111,000
Less annual exemptions 2006/07	(3,000)
2005/06	(3,000)
	105,000

Covered by nil rate band. No IHT payable.

6 November 2006 Overseas property

The gift is not chargeable as Amy is not UK domiciled.

6 January 2007 UK property

Value	£125,000

Covered by nil rate band. No IHT payable.

GWR

Charge PET and ignore house in estate

1 June 2007 House

	£
Value	400,000
Less annual exemption 2007/08	(3,000)
	397,000

£105,000 + £125,000 = £230,000 of nil band used, £55,000 remaining	£
£55,000 @ Nil	–
£342,000 @ 40%	136,800
Less taper relief (4 – 5 years) 40% × £136,800	(54,720)
	82,080

Ignore PET and charge house in estate

1 September 2011 House

Value	£400,000

£105,000 + 125,000 = £230,000 of nil band used, £55,000 remaining	£
£55,000 @ Nil	
£345,000 @ 40%	138,000
The highest charge will apply so the IHT payable is	138,000

(ii) If Amy paid Erica a full market rental for occupying the house it would not be a gift with reservation of benefit, it would be a PET and would not be in Amy's estate on death. The IHT payable as a result of Amy's death would be £82,080.

Erica would be liable to income tax on the rent receivable, less any expenses that she incurred.

11 Preparation question with helping hand: Rowan Sorbus

Text references. Chapters 11-13 for the CGT aspects in the question. Chapters 17-19 for IHT knowledge required.

Top tips. When dealing with unquoted company shares, the related property rules for IHT are often tested. In this case, it was important to spot that the shares given to the charity were related property.

Marking scheme

		Marks
(a)	*Lifetime transfers*	
	Charity exemption	½
	PET to son – no lifetime tax	1
	Charge on death	½
	Related property rules/loss to donor	1
	Calculation of loss to donor	2
	Annual exemptions	½
	IHT calculation	1
	No BPR – explanation	1
	Death estate	
	Charge	½
	Domestica Limited shares	1
	Aria shares	1
	Property used by Domestica Limited	1
	Property used by Aria Limited	1
	Other assets	½
	IHT calculation	½
		13
(b)	*July 2006 gifts*	
	Charity – exempt	1
	Gift to son – MV	½
	Gain on gift	½
	Gift relief	1
	December 2007 sales	
	Matching rules	1
	March 2007 acquisition: cost	1
	no taper	½
	July 2006 acquisition: cost	1
	IHT deduction	1
	taper relief	1
	Annual exemption	½
	Max	8
	Total	21

(a) **Lifetime transfers**

10 July 2006

This was an exempt transfer to charity and there is no IHT implication.

20 July 2006

This transfer to his son was exempt to the extent of the annual exemptions for 2006/07 and 2005/06. The remainder of the transfer was a potentially exempt transfer (PET) because it was a transfer between individuals. There is no lifetime tax payable on a PET because it is treated as exempt during Rowan's lifetime.

The PET becomes chargeable on Rowan's death within 7 years.

The value of the transfer needs to take account of the related property rules and the loss to donor principle. Only the shares owned by the charity will be counted under the related property rules, not those owned by his son.

The value of the transfer is:

	£
Before transfer:	
$\dfrac{40}{40+25} \times £2,100,000$ (value of 65% holding)	1,292,308
After transfer:	
$\dfrac{30}{30+25} \times £1,450,000$ (value of 55% holding)	(790,909)
Loss to donor	501,399
Less: AE 2006/07	(3,000)
AE 2005/06	(3,000)
PET now chargeable	495,399
Tax	
£285,000 × 0%	0
£210,399 × 40%	84,160
	84,160

No taper relief (death within 3 years).

Although Domestica Ltd is an unquoted trading company, there is no business property relief (BPR) available on the transfer because the shares were not owned by Rowan for 2 years before the transfer.

Death estate

There is a charge to IHT on the death estate of Rowan as follows:

	£	£
Domestica Ltd shares		
$\dfrac{30}{30+25} \times £1,500,000$ (value of 55% holding)		818,182
Aria Ltd shares	100,000	
Less: BPR @ 100% (owned 2+ years)	(100,000)	0
Property used by Domestica Ltd (no BPR – not owned 2 years)		750,000
Property used by Aria Ltd	175,000	
Less: charge secured on property	(75,000)	
	100,000	
Less: BPR @ 50% (N)	(50,000)	50,000
Other assets		650,000
Chargeable estate		2,268,182
IHT @ 40% (nil band used by lifetime transfer)		907,273

Note. The property used by Aria Ltd attracts 50% because it has been owned for at least 2 years and Aria Ltd is controlled by Rowan.

(b) **Gifts by Rowan in July 2006**

10 July 2006

This is a disposal by Rowan to a charity and therefore take place at no gain, no loss.

20 July 2006

This is disposal between connected persons and so is deemed to be at market value. The gain is:

	£
MV of 10% holding in July 2006	150,000
Less: cost to Rowan	
10/65 × £650,000	(100,000)
Gain	50,000

Note. The market value used does not take account of any related property.

This gain can be deferred into the base cost of Rowan's son by gift relief. This is because the shares are in an unquoted trading company. Although Rowan's son does not achieve an increase in the rate of taper relief on his disposal, the claim is beneficial since it allows the IHT on the gift to be deducted from the chargeable gain on the disposal.

Disposals by Rowan's son in December 2007

The disposal of shares is matched with each acquisition on a last in, first out basis as follows:

March 2007 acquisition

	£
Proceeds 30/40 × £1,500,000	1,125,000
Less: cost (as ascertained for IHT)	(818,182)
Gain	306,818

No taper relief because not owned for 1 whole year.

July 2006

	£	£
Proceeds 10/40 × £1,500,000		375,000
Less: cost	150,000	
less: gift relief	(50,000)	(100,000)
		275,000
Less: IHT paid on original gift		(84,160)
Gain		190,840
Gain after taper relief (1 year – business asset @ 50%)		95,420
Total gains £(306,818 + 95,420)		402,238
Less: annual exemption		(8,800)
Taxable gains		393,438

12 Question with analysis: Christopher

Text references. Basic IHT is in Chapters 17 and 18 with deeds of variation covered in Chapter 19. Basic CGT including part disposals are in Chapters 11 and 12 with share disposals in Chapter 13.

Top tips. Do not confuse items that are exempt for one tax but not for another. The ISA would be tax free for income tax purposes but forms an asset in the death estate – so is subject to IHT.

Regarding Eleanor's part disposal, you were not asked to calculate the gain on the first disposal. However you did need to calculate how much of the original cost was used up by that first disposal.

Easy marks. Make sure you read the question and the question requirements carefully. Here you were told to ignore both gift relief and the annual exemption for Eleanor's CGT calculations. Do not waste time and effort on these.

Examiner's comments. This question was answered well. It covered the clearly well-practiced area of inheritance tax (IHT), with some trickier capital gains tax (CGT).

Most candidates coped well with the calculation of IHT on both lifetime gifts and the estate on death. The most common error was a failure to calculate correctly the nil rate band available for each gift/estate on death. Candidates appeared to forget to consider all chargeable gifts made in the previous seven years. Arguably the trickiest calculation – the quick succession relief – was spotted, and well attempted by the majority of candidates.

Part (b) produced the widest variation in answers. Some were extremely good, showing a sound appreciation of both the CGT and IHT implications of a particular course of action. This is an important skill for this paper. Several failed to read the question properly, and included gift relief, despite being specifically told this would not be claimed. The gift of the paintings gave the most problems. While many understood the issue and produced correct calculations a significant minority calculated the wrong gain – on the earlier, first part disposal, which was not required and therefore wasted time.

The question specifically asked you to recommend the most tax efficient solution, and it was pleasing to see most candidates did this. You should remember that as long as your conclusion is consistent with the points you have made, and figures you have calculated previously, the marks will be given.

		Marks
(a)	Gifts into trust are chargeable lifetime transfers	½
	First gift: two annual exemptions (correct years)	½
	calculation of nil rate band remaining	½
	Second gift: two annual exemptions (correct years)	½
	correct gross-up calculation	1
	40% death rate	½
	Taper relief/rate (2 × 0.5)	1
	Less: lifetime tax paid	½
	Christopher's estate on death:	
	quoted shares – correct valuation	1
	– no BPR	½
	unquoted shares	½
	100% BPR	1
	ISA	½
	cash/residence	½
	correct restriction of nil rate band	½
	tax at 40%	½
	Quick succession relief:	
	awareness	½
	correct percentage	½
	correct calculation basis	1
	Max	11

(b)   Gift of paintings:

part of set/part disposal rules	½
cost disposed of previously/cost remaining	½
indexation	½
taper relief/non business/rate (2 × 0.5)	1
CGT at 40%	½
PET for IHT	½
availability of two annual exemptions	½
no IHT/within nil band	½
falls out of account after seven years	½
Gift of cash	
exempt for CGT purposes	½
PET if made direct by Eleanor	½
alter will so that gift passes directly from estate	½
result is that IHT paid re estate is not affected	½
Gift of shares	
part of FA1985 pool	½
indexation – disposal cost	½
taper relief/business asset	½
CGT at 40%	½
PET but 100% BPR available	½
Recommend gift of cash by varying will	½

Max
$\dfrac{9}{20}$

(a)   IHT

Lifetime gifts

(i)   9/8/99 – CLT

	£
Gift	250,000
Less: AE 99/00	(3,000)
AE 98/99	(3,000)
	244,000

Below nil band (£285,000)

Therefore no tax due

(ii)   10/4/02 – CLT

	£	£
Gift		75,000
Less: AE 02/03		(3,000)
AE 01/02		(3,000)
		69,000
Less: nil band	285,000	
Less: chargeable transfers in previous 7 years	(244,000)	
		(41,000)
		28,000
Tax @ $^{20}/_{80}$		7,000
Gross chargeable transfer : £69,000 + £7,000		£76,000

Death tax

(i)   9/8/99 – more than 7 years before death therefore no death tax

(ii)   10/4/02 – CLT

	£	£
GCT		76,000
Less: nil band	285,000	
Less: chargeable transfers in previous 7 years	(244,000)	
		(41,000)
		35,000
Tax @ 40%		14,000
Less: taper relief @ 40%		(5,600)
[4.02-2.07 = 4-5 yrs]		8,400
Less: lifetime tax		(7,000)
Tax due		1,400

Death estate

	£	£
Residence		550,000
ISA		12,000
Cash		40,000
P Ltd shares	85,000	
Less: BPR @ 100%	(85,000)	
B Plc shares (W1)		105,300
Chargeable estate		707,300
Tax £(707,300 – 209,000) @ 40% (W2)		199,320
Less: QSR (W3)		(4,000)
Tax due		195,320

> **Top tips.** Always deal with the lifetime gifts first – lifetime tax (if relevant), then death tax on these gifts – and only then move onto the death estate. If you follow this method you will increase your chances of picking up all the available marks.

Workings

(1)   *B Plc shares*

Lower of:

(i)   ¼ up rule: $\dfrac{708 - 700}{4} + 700$ = 702p

(ii)   average: $\dfrac{707 + 701}{2}$ = 704p

702p × 15,000   = £105,300

(2)   *Remaining nil rate band on death estate*

	£
Nil rate band	285,000
Less 10 April 2002 CLT	(76,000)
	209,000

The transfer on 9 August 1999 is more than 7 years before death.

(3) *QSR*

QSR is available on the cash received from Christopher's uncle's estate. (Not on the shares as they are subject to BPR).

$$QSR = \text{Tax paid on uncle's transfer} \times \frac{\text{net tfr to Christopher}}{\text{total tfr by uncle}} \times \%$$

$$= £75,000 \times \frac{30,000}{450,000} \times 80\% \text{ (1-2 years)}$$

$$= \underline{£4,000}$$

(b) Gifts to Sam in June 2007

(i) Painting

IHT

	£
Transfer of value	50,000
Less: AE × 2 (07/08 and 06/07)	(6,000)
PET	44,000

No tax during lifetime

CGT

	£
Deemed proceeds (MV)	50,000
Less: cost (W1)	(19,375)
Less: IA	
$\frac{162.6 - 149.8}{149.8} = 0.085 \times £19,375$	(1,647)
Gain before taper	28,978
Chargeable gain: 9 yrs + bonus year = 10 yrs: 60%	17,387
Tax @ 40%	6,955

(ii) Cash

IHT

	£
As above – PET	44,000

CGT

Cash is not a chargeable asset therefore no CGT

Eleanor can make a deed of variation to effectively change her father's will so that the cash goes directly to Sam. The cash will therefore not form part of her estate and will not be treated as a PET. The deed of variation must be made within 2 years of her father's death.

(iii) G Ltd shares

IHT

	£
Transfer of value	50,000

Potential BPR at 100% provided Sam still owns the shares at Eleanor's death
PET so no tax during lifetime

CGT

	£
Deemed proceeds (MV)	50,000
Less: cost	(17,500)
Less: IA	
$\dfrac{162.6 - 141.1}{141.1} \times £17,500$	(2,667)
Gain before taper	29,833
Chargeable gain: 9 yrs (business asset) = 25%	7,458
Tax @ 40%	2,983

Advice

Option 2 with a deed of variation is best from a tax perspective as there are no IHT implications, as the cash is not treated as being Eleanor's. In addition there is no CGT to pay on the gift.

Working – painting base cost

	£
Original part disposal January 2001:	
Original cost (June 1995)	25,000
Less: Cost used:	
$25,000 \times \dfrac{9,000}{9,000 + 31,000}$	(5,625)
Cost for future disposal	19,375

Top tips. If the question asks for your advice…give it, even if you are not sure that you are right!

---

13 Jimmy Generous

Text references. EIS is covered in Chapter 1 as is the IT computation. NIC is in Chapter 4. IHT on lifetime gifts is dealt with in Chapter 17.

Top tips. Make a good effort at all parts of a multi-tax question like this one. Parts (a) and (b) are on income tax and national insurance and do not affect part (c) on capital taxes.

Easy marks. The income tax computation was very straightforward and the examiner made the IHT computations easier by using up the nil rate band in the first chargeable lifetime transfer.

Examiner's comments. (Part (a) has been amended).

Part (b) was reasonably well attempted by most candidates although a sizeable minority continue to make basic errors such as grossing up interest at 22% and dividends at 20%. Also many muddled the relief for the contributions to the occupational pension scheme with the way relief is given for contributions paid into personal pension schemes. This sort of confusion really needs to be eliminated by the time of the examination.

Part (c) was again reasonably attempted by most candidates. Some, however, muddled chargeable lifetime transfers (CLTs) with potentially exempt transfers (PETs). Some thought that transfers to discretionary trusts were PETs whilst those to individuals were CLTs. Perhaps unsurprisingly, candidates making this kind of fundamental error scored very poorly with this question part. Other common errors included the omission of annual exemptions, the incorrect application of the loss to the donor principle and the failure to identify (and properly explain) the availability of business property relief where appropriate.

Marking scheme

		Marks	
(a)	EIS relief	1	
	Conditions	2	
	Interest relief	1	
			4
(b)	Salary	½	
	Payroll giving	1	
	Pension contribution deducted from employment income	1	
	Interest	½	
	Dividends	½	
	PA	½	
	Income tax computation	2	
	NICs	1	
			7
(c)	*4 June 1999*		
	CLT	1	
	AEs	½	
	IHT	½	
	4 March 2001 – Jack		
	PET	2	
	AE/ME	1	
	Death	1	
	4 March 2001 – Jill		
	Valuation	1½	
	BPR	1	
	4 June 2005		
	Grossing	½	
	IHT	1	
	Death	1	
			11
			22

(a) Jimmy may be able to obtain EIS income tax relief on the shares subscribed for. The relief is given as a tax reducer and is the lower of 20% x £20,000 = £4,000 and Jimmy's income tax liability.

For EIS relief to be available the following conditions must be satisfied:

(i) The shares must be subscribed for in cash

(ii) Jimmy must not be connected with Pail Ltd, ie broadly he must not own more than 30% (including holdings of associates ie spouse or child, but not a brother or sister) of the issued share capital

(iii) Pail Ltd must be unquoted and the funds raised must be used in carrying out a qualifying trade. At least 80% of the money raised by the EIS share issue must be so used within twelve months of the issue, and the remainder within a further twelve months (ie within twenty-four months).

(iv) The gross assets of the company must not exceed £7m prior to nor £8m after the investment.

If the shares are disposed of within three years the relief will be withdrawn.

If EIS relief is available, no relief is given for the interest paid on the share purchase loan. If EIS relief is not given, interest relief will be due if Pail Ltd is a close trading company and Jimmy holds a more than 5% interest in the share capital or works full time as a manager or director of the company.

(b)   **Jimmy Generous – Income Tax 2006/07**

	Non-savings income £	Savings (excl. dividend) income £	Dividend income £	Total income £
Salary	22,500			
Less: Pension	(3,750)			
Employment income	18,750			
BSI £8,000 × $^{100}/_{80}$		10,000		
Dividends £45,000 ×$^{100}/_{90}$			50,000	
STI	18,750	10,000	50,000	78,750
Less: Personal allowance	(5,035)			
Taxable income	13,715	10,000	50,000	73,715

Tax

	£
£2,150 × 10%	215
£11,565 × 22%	2,544
£10,000 × 20%	2,000
£9,585 ×10%	959
£40,415 × 32½%	13,135
	18,853
Less: EIS relief	(4,000)
Income tax liability	14,853

Jimmy Generous – Class 1 NICs 2006/07

£(22,500 – 5,035) × 11%	£1,921

Note. No deduction for pension contribution.

(c)   **Inheritance tax**

4 June 1999

Chargeable lifetime transfer

	£
Gift	291,000
Less: AE 1999/00	(3,000)
AE 1998/99 b/f	(3,000)
CLT	285,000

This is within the nil rate band of £285,000 (2006/07 rates used as standard in examination questions) so no lifetime IHT payable.

4 March 2001

Potentially exempt transfer

	£
Gift	10,000
Less: AE 2000/01 (N)	(3,000)
Marriage exemption	(5,000)
Potentially exempt transfer	2,000

Gifts between individuals are potentially exempt transfers. There will be no IHT liability if Jimmy survives until 4 March 2008. If he survives between 3 and 7 years, taper relief of between 20% and 80% will be available to reduce the death tax. There is no grossing up required.

Note. The annual exemption has been allocated in full to this transfer since the same day transfer to Jill attracts 100% BPR.

4 March 2001

Potentially exempt transfer

Note. On 4 June 2007 we are told Jimmy owned 60% of shares. Thus when he gives his daughter a 20% holding in March 2001 this means that prior to the gift he held 80% of the shares.

	£
Before 80% holding	600,000
After 60% holding	(450,000)
Loss to donor	150,000
Less: 100% BPR	(150,000)
PET	0

The value of the transfer is the loss to the donor, using the value of Jimmy's shareholding before and after the gift. BPR at 100% is available as this is a gift of unquoted trading company shares owed for at least 2 years. No IHT will be payable if Jimmy survives until 4 March 2008 or dies before that time and Jill still owns the shares (or certain replacement business property).

4 June 2005

Chargeable Lifeline transfer

	£
Gift	100,000
Less: AE 2005/06	(3,000)
AE 2004/05 b/f	(3,000)
CLT	94,000

Nil rate band of £(285,000 − 285,000) = 0 available as reduced by transfer in previous 7 years.

£94,000 × $^{20}/_{80}$ = £23,500

The transfer must be grossed up to find the loss to donor as Jimmy agrees to pay the IHT due (stated in question).

If Jimmy dies before 4 June 2012, additional tax may become payable by the trustees, subject to taper relief.

14 Paul and Sharon

Text references. Incorporation is dealt with in Chapters 14 and 30. Gift relief for CGT is also in Chapter 14. Share options are dealt with in Chapter 5 with NIC for employees in Chapter 4. Trusts are covered in Chapter 20.

Top tips. Incorporation is a topic which the examiner can use to test many aspects of the syllabus. Ensure you are happy with this topic.

There is a big difference between an approved and an unapproved share scheme. You were told this scheme was approved. So act accordingly and do not waste time and effort mentioning unapproved schemes.

Easy marks. The three parts were stand alone. You should attempt the part you feel most comfortable with first to gain the easy marks available.

For good marks don't just outline all you know about a subject eg incorporation relief but rather make it specific to the question facts.

Examiner's comments. This question produced the poorest answers on the paper.
[The part on the share scheme] was generally answered badly. On the whole, candidates were unclear as to the precise tax implications (IT and CGT) of approved and unapproved share options schemes, and answers were very confused, leading to a failure to pick up many marks.

Most candidates were able to state the main conditions for incorporation relief to apply, although several failed to advise Sharon as to whether or not it would be available to her, as specifically required. Most had a brave attempt at calculating the maximum cash she could take, picking up at least half marks, while a significant minority, who had clearly practised this, obtained the full 3 marks. Many candidates were able to identify the major disadvantages of incorporation relief, and suggest gift relief as a suitable alternative. However, several suggested rollover relief, which would not have been suitable in this scenario, as she was not planning to buy further assets. Candidates must consider what is appropriate in the given scenario, not just what is available generally.

Marking scheme

			Marks
(1)	Approved options CGT treatment	½	
	Requirement to exercise after three years	½	
	If condition not met, exercise treated as unapproved	½	
	Taxed as employment income on exercise if before 25 June 2007	½	
	Amount taxed is market value price paid on exercise	½	
	Calculation: amount taxable	½	
	income tax at 40%	½	
	national insurance at 1%	½	
	If exercise after 25 June no tax on exercise, capital gains treatment on sale	½	
	No taper relief/runs from date of exercise/not available	½	
	Calculation: gain	½	
	annual exemption	½	
	capital gains tax at 40%	½	
		Max	6
(2)	Transfer must be by a person	½	
	Business must be transferred as a going concern	½	
	Transfer must comprise all assets apart from cash	½	
	Transfer wholly or partly in exchange for shares	½	
	Application to Sharon	½	
	Availability of annual exemption	½	
	Availability of taper relief at business rates	½	
	Taper relief rate (75%)	½	
	Calculation of gain required/held over	½	
	Formula for calculating gain to be rolled over	½	
	Calculation of potential tax-free consideration	1	
	Must put all assets into the company	½	
	Double tax on property: sale/extraction of proceeds	½	
	Loss of taper relief history on incorporation	½	
	Sale within two years gives higher tax	½	
	Deferral, not reduction in tax	½	
	Gift relief: awareness	½	
	Gain deferred set against base cost of new asset	½	
	Potential for double tax charge	½	
	Not all assets need to be transferred	½	
		Max	10

(3) IHT: creation: chargeable lifetime transfer   ½
                 annual exemptions   ½
                 nil rate band remaining   ½
                 tax at 25%   ½
                 payment date   ½
                 gross chargeable amount   ½
                 additional tax if dies within 7 years   ½
                 taper relief   ½
         during: exit charge when assets leave trust   1
                 principal charge every 10 years   1
    CGT: creation: chargeable disposal   ½
                 deemed market value/connected persons   ½
                 gain before taper relief deferred   ½
                 gift relief available   ½
                 chargeable lifetime transfer for IHT purposes   ½
                 deferral of liability only   ½
                 settlor interested trust implications   ½
    SDLT: Gift: nil   2

                                Max   11

Format/Presentation   2

                                          29

Report

To: Paul and Sharon Potter
From: A Adviser
Date: [date]
Subject: Share options, incorporation and trust planning

This report covers tax issues relating to:

(i)   Paul's share options
(ii)   Incorporation of Sharon's business
(iii) Capital tax implications of setting up a trust

(1) Paul's share options

There is no income tax charge on the exercise of approved share options so long as the exercise does not occur within three years of the date of grant. As your share options were granted on 25 June 2004 you will need to wait until 25 June 2007 to exercise the options without an income tax charge.

If you do not wait, the exercise will be treated as an exercise of unapproved options.

If you exercise the options immediately, there will therefore be an income tax charge on the difference between the market value at the date of exercise and the exercise price of £5,000, along with a National Insurance Contribution charge of £125.

There would be no chargeable gain.

If you do wait until 25 June 2007 there will be no income tax charge. There will be a CGT charge of £1,480.

You will therefore save a total of £3,645 (5,000 + 125 − 1,480) by delaying the exercise until 25 June 2007.

Please see Appendix 1 for the calculation of the above figures.

(2) **Incorporation of Sharon's business**

If you sell your business to a company you will make a disposal of all the business's assets. You can avoid an immediate charge to capital gains tax through incorporation relief.

This applies automatically when:

- There is a transfer of a going concern
- All assets (except cash) are transferred
- The transfer is by an individual to a company
- In return wholly or partly for share consideration from the company

If the above conditions are satisfied you would need to elect for the relief **not** to apply.

The full gain may be deferred where all of the consideration is received as shares. If any of the consideration is received in cash (or loan notes or left on a loan account) a proportion of the gain will remain chargeable.

The maximum amount of cash that you could receive without triggering a gain is £52,800 (Appendix 2).

The disadvantages to incorporation relief are as follows.

- The base cost of the shares that you will be able to use when you eventually dispose of the shares will be reduced by the relief given to £22,400 (£67,200 – £44,800). Your gain would therefore be higher.

- Any business asset taper relief earned so far (which is the maximum available as you have held the sole trader business assets for more than 2 years) will be lost. You will therefore need to hold the shares for at least two years before you attain the same rate of taper relief.

- You will have had to transfer every asset (except cash) even if you did not want to.

- The transfer of assets (such as property) may lead to a double tax charge in the future as corporation tax would be due from the company on the disposal of the asset and then when the proceeds are paid out to the shareholders there will be a further tax charge (eg income tax on dividends).

As an alternative, you could consider gift relief. In this case you would need to gift the business's assets to the company and you would therefore be able to choose which assets to transfer and which to retain, eg the property.

Gift relief defers your gain by reducing the base cost of the asset for the recipient ie the company. The company would then have a lower base cost when it comes to sell the assets and therefore a higher gain.

(3) **Capital tax implications of the discretionary trust**

> *BPP Note.* The original question included an Accumulation & Maintenance trust, the rules for which were significantly changed by Finance Act 2006 and are not examinable in Paper P6. The question has therefore been modified to reflect this change and instead refers only to a discretionary trust.

There will be both inheritance tax (IHT) and capital gains tax (CGT) implications when you set up the discretionary trust.

IHT

The creation of the trust will be a chargeable lifetime transfer for IHT purposes.

The transfer of value will be the market value of the property ie £160,000, which will be reduced by the annual exemptions of £3,000 each for 2006/07 and 2007/08.

As you made a gross chargeable transfer within the last seven years part of your nil rate band will be used, leaving you £100,000 which partially covers the gift to the trust. The balance will be taxed at 25% (20/80) assuming you pay the tax. You will therefore have an IHT liability of £13,500 (Appendix 3).

This is due for payment by the end of the month six months following the gift. So, if you make the gift in, say, July 2007 the tax will be due by 31 January 2008.

You should be aware that if assets are passed from the trust by the trustees to the children there will be an exit charge for IHT purposes. In addition, if the assets remain in the trust there will be a principal charge on every ten year anniversary of the trust. The maximum charge is 6%.

CGT

The creation of the trust will also be a deemed disposal at market value of the trust property for CGT purposes. The CGT payable is £36,000.

Gift relief is not available as the trust is a settlor interested trust, Paul's minor children being beneficiaries.

SDLT

No SDLT arises on the transfer since there is no consideration.

Once the trust is in place, if the trustees decide to sell the property while the children are still unmarried minors (under age 18), the gains will be taxed on Paul.

Appendix 1 – Share option exercise

Exercise immediately

Income tax

	£
MV at exercise: £6 × 5,000	30,000
Less: exercise price: £3.50 × 5,000	(17,500)
Chargeable as employment income	12,500
Tax @ 40%	5,000
Class 1 employees' NICs: 1% of £12,500	125

CGT

	£	£
Sale		
Proceeds		30,000
Less: cost	17,500	
Add: amount subject to IT	12,500	(30,000)
Chargeable gain		Nil

Delay until 25 June 2007

No income tax charge

CGT

	£
Proceeds: £6 × 5,000	30,000
Less: cost: £3.50 × 5,000	(17,500)
Gain before taper	12,500
Chargeable gain (No taper relief as <1 year since exercise)	12,500
Less: AE	(8,800)
	3,700
Tax @ 40%	1,480

> **Top tips.** Make sure that you know the conditions for a scheme to be approved for tax purposes. If it is approved there are usually only CGT implications. Any other scheme will lead to income tax charges, which are usually higher than CGT due to the availability of CGT taper relief.

Appendix 2 – Maximum cash consideration to take on incorporation

	£
Total consideration	120,000
Less: share consideration (W1)	(67,200)
Cash consideration	52,800

Workings

(1)   *Share consideration*

	£
We want relief of (W1) :	44,800
Gain before taper is:	80,000
Total consideration is:	120,000

Therefore share consideration must be:

$$\frac{44,800}{80,000} \times 120,000 \qquad\qquad £67,200$$

(2)   *Relief to bring gain to nil* (hint: work backwards!)

	£
Total gain before taper:	
Goodwill	40,000
Property	40,000
	80,000
Less: incorporation relief	(44,800)
Gain before taper	35,200
Chargeable gain – business asset > 2yrs: 25%	8,800
Less: AE	(8,800)
Taxable gain	Nil

Appendix 3 – Discretionary trust – capital tax issues

IHT

	£	£
Transfer of value		160,000
Less: 2 × annual exemptions		(6,000)
Chargeable		154,000
Less: nil rate band	285,000	
Less: May 2003 gift (in previous 7 years)	(185,000)	(100,000)
Taxable		54,000
Tax @ 20/80		13,500

CGT

	£
Deemed proceeds (MV)	160,000
Less: cost (8/05)	(70,000)
Chargeable gain (no taper relief, held < 3 years) (AE already used)	90,000
CGT @ 40%	36,000

Note. If Paul exercises his share options before 25 June 2007 his CGT annual exemption will be available to set against this gain.

15 Miller Plc

Text references. The calculation of corporation tax is covered in Chapters 21 and 22. Trading losses are in Chapter 24. Groups are in Chapter 26. VAT is in Chapters 28 and 29.

Top tips. You could have attempted the VAT part of the question first if you were confident in that area. Just remember to put your answer in the correct order before you hand it in – you don't want to make the examiner hunt around to give you marks.

Easy marks. The calculations were straightforward. The examiner has said that he may test the computation of PCTCT so ensure you can do so quickly and efficiently, and then tie the figures into your answer.

Marking scheme

				Marks
(a)	*Corporation tax calculation*			
	Trading profit (1/2 mark for each adjustment)	Max	2½	
	Capital allowances		2	
	Trading loss b/f		½	
	Chargeable gain		1	
	Interest income		1	
	Property income		½	
	Foreign income		½	
	Deduct management expenses		1	
	Add back accrued donation/ no tax deduction for Gift Aid		1	
	CT limits		½	
	Tax at 30%		½	
				11
(b)	*Group relationships*			
	Associates		1	
	Loss group 1		1	
	Loss group 2		1	
	Gains group		1	4
	Use of group losses			
	Cannot surrender Bloom's loss b/f		½	
	Carry forward only in Bloom		½	
	Cannot carry forward if major change rules apply		½	
	Surrender Bloom's current year loss		½	
	Current year claim in Bloom		½	
	Carry forward in Bloom		½	
	Cannot surrender Weibrecht's capital loss		½	
	Carry forward against future gains		½	
	Election for deemed transfer of asset		½	
	Conclusion for use of losses		½	
	Calculation of loss relief		½	
		Max		5
(c)	*Advantages of VAT group*			
	Intra-group supplies exempt		½	
	One VAT return		½	
	Include companies making exempt supplies		½	
	Group registration			
	Hillman Ltd excluded – holding		½	
	Bloom Ltd repayment trader – implications		1	
	Weibrecht exempt – implications		1	
	Conclusion		1	
				5
	Format/Presentation			2
		Max		27

Report

To: Fred Kildow, Miller plc group finance director
From: Tax manager
Date: [date]
Subject: Tax issues for the Miller plc group

This report covers tax issues relating to:

(a)   Miller plc's corporation tax liability for the period ended 31 March 2007
(b)   Group issues
(c)   VAT

(a)   **Miller plc's corporation tax liability for the period ended 31 March 2007**

Miller plc's corporation tax liability for the eight month period from 1 August 2006 to 31 March 2007 is £100,618 (Appendix 1).

(b)   (i)   **Group relationships**

Miller Plc is associated with all the companies under its control ie Bode Ltd, Weinbrecht Ltd, and Bloom Ltd. The consequence of this is that the small companies limits' are divided by 4.

Miller Plc is in a loss group with Bode Ltd, and Bloom Ltd because Miller Plc has a direct and indirect/effective interest of at least 75% in each company. This enables group relief to be claimed for trading and other losses.

There is a second loss group of Bode Ltd and Weinbrecht Ltd.

Miller Plc is in a gains group with Bode Ltd, Weinbrecht Ltd and Bloom Ltd because it has a direct holding of at least 75% and an indirect/effective interest of > 50%. This enables assets to be transferred around the group without crystallising chargeable gains.

(ii)   **Group Losses**

Bloom Ltd's brought forward loss

Bloom Ltd cannot surrender its brought forward trading loss.

The trading loss will instead be carried forward and must be set against the first available trading profits from the same trade.

If there has been a major change in the nature or conduct of Bloom Ltd's trade or if there is deemed to be a revival of trade after it has been negligible then the trading losses incurred before September 2006 (date of change of ownership of Bloom Ltd) cannot be carried forward against post acquisition profits.

Bloom Ltd's current year loss

Bloom Ltd can surrender its current year trading loss to Miller plc or Bode Ltd.

Alternatively Bloom Ltd could itself make a current year claim to set the loss against its own income and gains.

The loss should be used in the most effective way possible by offsetting it in the company with highest marginal rate of tax.

As Bloom Ltd will be taxed at 30% in 2010, any loss which will save tax at less than 30% this year, should be carried forward by Bloom Ltd.

Weinbrecht Ltd's capital loss

The capital loss itself cannot be surrendered.

The capital loss could be carried forward in Weinbrecht Ltd and set against any future gains.

Alternatively an election could be made to treat the asset as having been transferred to another group company prior to disposal so that the loss is deemed to have arisen in another group company.

The capital loss should be utilised against the capital gain in the company with the highest marginal rate of tax, ie Miller Plc.

Conclusion

The optimum use of Bloom Ltd's losses would entail surrender of £110,000 to Bode Ltd and £380,000 to Miller plc. This would bring both companies' PCTCT to the small companies' rate level, so that each company would be paying tax at 19% (see Appendix 2).

The capital loss will reduce Miller Plc's PCTCT to £455,000.

Trading losses of £160,000 (remainder of the current year loss of £110,000 plus the £50,000) will be carried forward within Bloom Ltd to the year ended 31 March 2009.

(c) **VAT group**

The following are benefits of a VAT group:

- No VAT is charged on intra-group supplies

- Only one VAT return is required, providing an administration saving as you could easily centralise this function

- Can exclude companies that only make exempt supplies

Hillman Ltd is not eligible to be included in the group registration as Miller Plc does not hold at least 50% of the shares.

As an exporter to large businesses, Bloom Ltd's customers are likely to be VAT registered. Therefore 95% of the sales will be zero rated. Bloom Ltd is thus a repayment trader. Bloom Ltd should be excluded from the VAT group otherwise the cash flow advantage of a monthly VAT repayment will be lost.

Weinbrecht Ltd provides wholly exempt supplies. Including Weinbrecht Ltd in the group will make the whole group partially exempt. This may limit its recovery of input VAT if the total exempt input VAT of the group exceeds the de minimis limits.

The VAT group should include Miller Plc and Bode Ltd. Weinbrecht Ltd should only be included if it does not reduce the total input VAT recoverable by the group.

Appendix 1 – Corporation tax computation for the period ended 31 March 2007

	£
Trading profit (W1)	280,717
Less: Trading losses brought forward	(95,000)
	185,717
Property business income	45,000
Foreign income	34,500
Chargeable gain (W3)	75,725
Interest income (W4)	6,000
	346,942
Less: general management expenses	(11,550)
Less: Gift Aid paid	–
PCTCT	335,392
Corporation tax (W5)	
£335,392 @ 30%	100,618

Workings

(1) *Trading profit*

	£
Tax adjusted profits	450,000
Loss on disposal of fixed asset	30,000
Gift aid accrued	10,000
Interest on overdue corporation tax	3,000
Client entertaining	37,750
UK rental income	(45,000)
Dividend from Bode Ltd	(12,500)
Dividend from Hillman Ltd	(28,000)
Dividend from Vogtli Inc	(34,500)
Interest received	(9,000)
Capital allowances (W2)	(121,033)
Taxable trading profit	280,717

(2) *Capital allowances*

	£	Main Pool £	Mercedes Car £	Allowances £
WDV b/f		450,000		
Additions (No FYA)				
– Mercedes car			28,000	
Disposal – Machine		(62,800)		
		387,200		
WDA @ 25% × 8/12		(64,533)		64,533
WDA £3,000 × 8/12			(2,000)	2,000
Additions qualifying for FYA				
Low emission car	30,000			
FYA @ 100%	(30,000)			30,000
Office furniture	61,250			
FYA @ 40%	(24,500)			24,500
		36,750		
				121,033
WDV c/f		359,417	26,000	

(3) *Capital gain on disposal of Vogtli Inc*

Substantial shareholding exemption does not apply as Miller Plc's holding is < 10%.

	£
Proceeds	120,000
Less cost	(35,000)
Unindexed gain	85,000
Less Indexation allowance	(9,725)
Chargeable gain	75,275

(4) *Interest income*

	£
Gross debenture interest from Bode Ltd	9,000
Interest charged on overdue corporation tax	(3,000)
	6,000

(5) *Corporation tax rate*

Limits ÷ 4 associates

		£
PCTCT		335,392
FII (£27,000 × 100/90)		30,000
'Profits'		365,392
Upper limit (£1,500,000/4) = 375,000 × 8/12		250,000
Lower limit (£300,000/4) = 75,000 × 8/12		50,000

Full rate company

Appendix 2 – use of losses within the Miller plc group

	M Plc £	Bode Ltd £	Bloom Ltd £
Trading profit	320,000	125,000	–
Property business income	70,000		–
Interest income	10,000	60,000	20,000
Chargeable gain (100,000 – 45,000)	55,000		35,000
PCTCT pre loss-relief	455,000	185,000	55,000
CT rate (4 associates)	30%	32¾%	19%
Surrender order	2	1	–
Surrender until CT rate @ 19%	(380,000)	(110,000)	
Revised PCTCT	75,000	75,000	55,000
Revised CT rate	19%	19%	19%

16 Flop Ltd

Text references. CT computations in Chapters 21 and 22 with payment of CT dealt with in Chapter 23. VAT penalties are covered in Chapter 28 and bad debts in Chapter 29. Ethics are in Chapter 30.

Top tips. Do not give FYAs to a large company. Read the question carefully to determine what size company you are dealing with.

Easy marks. Learn your administration rules for the different taxes – they are often tested in the exam. Make sure you do not confuse the rules for companies and those for individuals.

Examiner's comments. While candidates were broadly successful in identifying the main items to be disallowed in part (a), three main errors cropped up. Firstly, capital allowances were incorrectly claimed, with too many candidates not realising that as a large company, first year allowances were not available. In addition, the second year's figures were not adjusted for additional capital allowances. Finally, candidates had little awareness of what legal and professional fees were allowable. The tendency was to disallow both the planning consent fees and the fees on attempting to secure a loan. The latter cost is specifically allowed by legislation.

The second element of part (a) asked candidates to state the dates for payment of tax and filling of the relevant tax returns. Far too many candidates confused corporation tax administration with personal tax administration, with the resulting loss of a significant number of marks. In addition, few candidates identified the fact that a company broadly has to be large for two years in succession before it is required to make quarterly instalment payments.

In many ways part (b), relating to value added tax (VAT) issues, was less straightforward yet many candidates scored solid marks here. The surcharge liability notice, and the implications for Fred Flop of being in the surcharge period was picked up by most candidates, as was the VAT treatment of bad debts.

Marking scheme

				Marks

(a)   (i)

Computers are capital	½	
No first year allowances	½	
Calculation of allowances	½	
Provision is general	½	
General provisions – disallowed	½	
Trading loan relationship costs – allowable	½	
Trade costs – allowable	½	
Costs of £5,700 capital – disallowed	½	
Profit chargeable to corporation tax	½	
Two associates	½	
Calculation of CT	½	
Further capital allowances on computers	½	
Inclusion of bad debt	½	
Revised PCTCT	½	
Amendment of CT return	½	
Money laundering	½	
Max		6

(ii)

Awareness of no quarterly payments	½	
Reason: company was not 'large' in 2004	½	
Due date nine months one day	½	
Filing: 12 months from period of account	½	
three months from date of CT203	½	
Take later	½	
First penalty (not submit on time)	½	
Second penalty (not submit within three months)	½	
Third penalty (tax geared)	½	
Calculation of tax geared penalty	½	
Interest periods: to late payment	½	
Interest periods: to balancing payment	½	
Payment date: large for second year	½	
Quarterly payments apply	½	
Dates of quarterly payments	1	
Filing date	½	
Penalty: late submission	½	
Further penalty (submission beyond 30.6.07)	½	
Interest from date of underpaid instalments	½	
Max		7

(b) Default surcharge: awareness ½
two or more within year ½
Issue of surcharge liability notice ½
Period runs from date of notice ½
Runs to anniversary of quarter in which default ½
Return and/or payment late ½
Further defaults extend surcharge period ½
Levy 2% surcharge if late payment ½
Progressive rates thereafter ½
Compliance for one year required ½
Extension as second return late ½
Extend again if June return is late ½
Calculation of £480 ½
Exceeds de minimis level of £400 ½
Submission date to avoid surcharge ½
Saving that would result ½
Period extended though no surcharge ½
Refund of VAT on bad debt 1
Conditions for refund (0.5 each) 1
Three year time limit for claim ½
Calculation of VAT repayable ½
Net VAT repayment ½

Max 9
Max 22

(a) (i) **CT payable**

Year ended 31 March 2005

	£	£
Original PCTCT		704,300
Add: computer equipment (N1)	50,000	
repairs provision (N2)	10,000	
professional fees (N3)	5,700	65,700
		770,000
Less: CAs (W1)		(12,500)
Revised PCTCT		757,500
CT @ 30% (W2)		227,250

Year ended 31 March 2006

	£	£
Current PCTCT		815,000
Less: bad debt (N4)	50,000	
CAs (W1)	9,375	(59,375)
Revised PCTCT		755,625
CT @ 30% (W2)		226,688

Notes

1 Capital expenditure is not an allowable expense for CT purposes.

2 If there is no supporting documentation for the provision it is likely that HMRC will treat it as a general provision, which is not allowable for tax purposes. If proof can be provided to confirm that this is a specific provision against a specific debt, it would be allowable.

157

3   So long as professional fees are incurred wholly and exclusively for the purpose of the trade, and do not relate to capital items they will be allowable. Consequently all the fees should be allowable except those incurred in respect of the planning consent (capital item).

4   VAT-exclusive bad debt amount is an allowable deduction for corporation tax purposes as the VAT is dealt with separately.

5   An amendment to the corporation tax return for the year to 31 March 2005 should have been filed by 31 March 2007. Although this date has passed HMRC should be advised of the amendments.

6   A deliberate error should be reported under the money laundering regulations. If the error was innocent, the position is less clear and you should discuss it with your firm's money laundering officer.

Top tips. Always try to comment on **every** matter/issue/figure mentioned in the question. Do not ignore anything, even if it is something that you do not consider to be relevant/ taxable/ deductible, as you will miss out on the allocated marks.

Workings

1   *Capital allowances*

	Pool	Allows
Y/e 31.3.05	£	£
Additions:		
Computer equipment	50,000	
Less: WDA @ 25%	(12,500)	£12,500
TWDV c/f	37,500	
Y/e 31.3.06		
Less: WDA @ 25%	(9,375)	£9,375
TWDV c/f	28,125	

Note. FYAs are not available as Flop Ltd is not a small or medium sized company.

2   *CT limits*

Two associated companies therefore divide CT limits by 2:

	£	£
UL	1,500,000 ÷ 2	750,000
LL	300,000 ÷ 2	150,000

Therefore Flop Ltd is a large company for the first time in FY04 (y/e 31 March 2005) and also in FY05.

(ii) **Payment and filing dates**

Tax

FY04

Flop Ltd is a large company for corporation tax purposes for the first time in FY04 (it was not large in the previous year due to its level of profits).

Therefore its tax for the y/e 31 March 2005 would have been due 1 January 2006 (9 months 1 day following the chargeable accounting period). However, it did not pay its tax until 2 November 2006.

Therefore interest would have run from the due date to the date of payment (1.1.06 – 2.11.06) = 306 days late.

Interest due:

$$\frac{306}{365} \times 6.5\% \times £227,250 = £12,383.56$$

Interest will continue to run at this rate on the underpayment of £103,750 (£227,250-£123,500) until it is paid.

This interest is deductible for corporation tax purposes.

FY05

Flop Ltd is a large company for corporation tax purposes again in FY05.

Therefore its tax for the y/e 31 March 2006 will be due via quarterly instalments of 25% of the current year's estimated CT liability.

The amounts due on each of these dates is:

£226,688 ÷ 4 = £56,672

The due dates are:

- 14 October 2005
- 14 January 2006
- 14 April 2006
- 14 July 2006

As it is now 10 May 2007, the company is late paying its first 4 payments.

Interest will run from the due date to payment date at base + 1% up to the traditional nine month due date at which point more punitive rate of base + 2.5%.

Return

The company's returns are due on the later of:

(1)   12 months after the end of the period of account, and
(2)   3 months after the notice to complete a return has been issued.

For the y/e 31 March 2005, the due date will therefore be the later of:

(1)   31 March 2006, and
(2)   1 May 2006 ie 1 May 2006.

For the y/e 31 March 2006, the due date will therefore be the later of:

(1)   31 March 2007, and
(2)   27 October 2006 ie 31 March 2007.

If a return is filed up to 3 months late, a fixed penalty of £100 is imposed (or £500 for a third consecutive late return). If the return is over 3 months late, the fixed penalty is £200 (or £1,000 for a third consecutive late return).

If the return is filed between 18 and 24 months after the end of the accounting period, an additional tax geared penalty is imposed of 10% of the unpaid tax. If the return is filed more than 24 months after the end of the accounting period, the penalty is 20% of the unpaid tax.

The company is therefore over 6 months late in submitting the return for the y/e 31 March 2005 and will incur a £200 penalty.

If the company submits the return for the y/e 31/3/06 before 30 June 2007, the penalty will remain at £100.

Note that late filing penalties can be forgiven if there is a reasonable excuse for the failure.

Top tips. Do not ignore the tax **administration** rules as these are often examined as part of a question.

(b)   **VAT**

Filing a VAT return late leads to the issue of a Surcharge Liability Notice (SLN), as will the late payment of VAT. There is no separate system of interest for underpaid VAT.

When the 31 December 2006 return was submitted late an SLN would have been issued, running to 31 December 2007. No penalty would have arisen at that point as this was the first default.

When Flop Ltd defaults for the q/e 31 March 2007, which falls within the SLN period, there will be a surcharge of 2% of the outstanding tax, ie £480 (£24,000 × 2%). The SLN period will be extended until 31 March 2008.

If Flop Ltd is late in submitting its June 2007 return the surcharge will be 5% of the unpaid VAT (as it is the second default within the SLN period) ie £8,250 × 5% = £412.50, and the SLN period will be extended until 30 June 2008.

Only if Flop Ltd submits all its returns within the SLN period to 30 June 2008 on time, and pays all of its VAT on time, will the SLN be discharged.

Bad debt

Flop Ltd must write off the bad debt by making the appropriate entry in its 'refunds for bad debts' account.

If at least six months (but not more than three years and six months) have elapsed since the later of the date of supply or the due date for payment, the VAT may be reclaimed.

As the debt has been outstanding for just over 20 months, Flop Ltd may claim the following bad debt relief:

£50,000 × 17.5% = £8,750

17 Preparation question with helping hand: Bargains Ltd

Text references. CT basics in Chapters 21 and 22. Revenue and capital item treatment in Chapters 6 and 7. VAT is dealt with in Chapters 28 and 29. Employment benefits are covered in Chapter 4. Close companies are dealt with in Chapter 25.

Top tips. The rules treating benefits to participators in close companies as distributions only apply when the normal employment income rules taxing benefits do not apply.

(a)   (i)   The company's first accounting period will run from the start of trade on 1 April 2006 to its accounting date, 31 December 2006. Any deductible pre-trading expenditure will be treated as incurred on the first day of trading, and will therefore be deductible in this accounting period.

        (ii)   The pre-trading expenditure on advertising will be deductible for corporation tax purposes. The expenditure on refurbishment will also be deductible except to the extent that it is capital expenditure. Expenditure needed to make the premises fit for use will be capital expenditure *(Law Shipping Co Ltd v CIR 1923)*. Expenditure leading to significant improvements, such as the installation of a heating system where there was none before, will also be capital expenditure. Expenditure on routine repairs and redecoration, on the other hand, will be revenue expenditure.

                 The VAT incurred on both the advertising expenditure and the refurbishment expenditure will be recoverable, because it is VAT on services supplied not more than six months before registration.

(b)   Rodney and Reggie will be taxed on earnings as follows.

165 (rounded down) − 140 = 25 ÷ 5 = 5

The benefit is $(15\% + 5\%) \times £10{,}575 \times \dfrac{9}{12} = £1{,}586$

There will be no employment income charge on Del, but the provision of a car to him will be treated as a distribution of £1,586 net. Del will be taxed as if he had received a dividend of this amount, giving him gross income of £1,586 × 100/90 = £1,762, a tax credit of £176 and no further tax liability unless he is a higher rate taxpayer. The actual cost of providing the car will be a disallowable expense for the company. The company will be treated as though it had paid a dividend of £1,586. Any motor expenses incurred by the company in respect of Del's car will be disallowable.

The VAT on the cars will not be recoverable because of the private use. Capital allowances will be available on the full cost (including VAT) of the cars provided for Rodney and Reggie, but not on the cost of the car provided for Del because its provision is treated as a distribution. The annual writing down allowances will be 25% on a reducing balance basis. Because the first accounting period is only 9 months long, the allowance in that period will be 2 × £10,575 × 25% × 9/12 = £3,966. Any motor expenses incurred by the company in respect of servicing, insurance and general running of both Rodney and Reggie's cars will be tax deductible for the company.

(c)   On making the loan to Del, the company will become liable to account for an amount of tax of £42,000 × 25% = £10,500. This is, in general, due nine months after the end of the accounting period, so it is due by 1 October 2007. However, if the company becomes a large company the tax will be subject to the quarterly payments on account regime. This tax is recovered when the loan is repaid.

Del will only be taxed on the loan as income to the extent that it is written off. He will then be treated as receiving a net dividend equal to the amount written off.

Del will, however, be treated as receiving (and the company will be treated as paying) a dividend equal to the taxable benefit for interest-free loans. This will be the interest which Del would have had to pay at the official rate. The tax consequences will be the same as for the deemed distribution in respect of Del's car.

18 Lorna Mill Ltd

Text references. Chapters 21 and 22 cover the calculation of corporation tax liabilities. Close companies are covered in Chapter 25. Chargeable gains on takeovers are in Chapter 13 and leases are in Chapter 15. The tax implications of a sale of shares compared with a sale of assets can be found in Chapter 30.

Top tips. Do your calculations in an Appendix then feed the results into your written answer. Use headings and subheadings and keep paragraphs short and snappy to maximise your marks.

Easy marks. Once again the calculations and the presentation marks are the easy marks. Remember your proformas and presentation formats to get them.

Marking scheme

			Marks

(i) Calculations

CT computation

Add back capital expenditure	½	
Chargeable gains	½	
FII	½	
CT limits/rate	½	
Tax calculation	1	

Gain on leasehold property

Indexed gain	½	
Cost × lease percentage	1	

Frozen gain crystallised

Original gain	½	
Rollover relief	1	
		6

(ii) Explanations

Corporation tax liability	½	
Payment date	½	
Cottage	2	
Loan	2	
Sale of leasehold building	2	
Max		6

(iii) Tax considerations for takeover

Sale of shares

Taking cash	1	
Taking shares and loan notes	1	
Effect on taper relief	1	

Sale of assets (ie trade)

Gain	1	
Double tax charge on shareholders	1	
Transfer of stock	1	
Transfer of capital assets	1	
Close investment holding company	2	
VAT TOGC	1	
Max		7

(iv) Other considerations

Future income/capital streams	1	
Continues employment with new company	1	
Repayment of John Harmer's loan (if buys shares)	1	
Retain liabilities (if buys trade)	1	
Conflict of interest	1	
Max		4
Format/presentation		2
Max		25

PRIVATE AND CONFIDENTIAL

[Our address]

[Your address]
[Date]

Dear Sirs

TAX POSITION YEAR ENDED 31 MARCH 2007 AND TAKEOVER IMPLICATIONS

This letter deals with the matters that will affect the Corporation Tax computation for the year ended 31 March 2007 and the tax and other implications of the proposed takeover by Evergreen plc.

(a)   **Year ended 31 March 2007**

The company must pay £70,371 corporation tax which is due on 1 January 2008 (see Appendix 1).

The following matters were taken into account in arriving at this figure.

(i)   *Country cottage to be lived in by Sam Bradley*

The £11,000 relating to improvements will need to be added back to the adjusted trading profit. It is assumed that the remaining £9,000 is accepted as revenue expenditure.

Sam Bradley is the sales director of the company. As such he will be assessed on the benefit of the provision of the cottage. This will be based on the annual value, and there will be an additional charge if the cottage cost (including improvements) more than £75,000.

(ii)   *Loan to John Harmer*

As Lorna Mill Ltd is a close company, the loan to John Harmer attracts a 25% tax charge (a 'penalty tax'). The tax due to HMRC is £1,775 (25% × £7,100) and is due on the same day as the regular corporation tax liability ie 1 January 2008.

When the loan is repaid the tax will also be repaid to the company. The repayment will be received nine months after the accounting period in which the loan is repaid. This penalty tax cannot be offset against the company's tax liability.

If the loan is written off, the tax will be repaid, as above, and John will be treated as receiving a net distribution equal to the amount written off.

(iii)   *Sale of leasehold building*

This gives rise to a chargeable gain of £17,019. Note that as the leasehold building is a wasting asset, its original purchase price is reduced when calculating the gain.

A further consequence will be that the gain arising on the sale of the freehold building in 1993 now crystallises as the gain was deferred into the acquisition of a replacement depreciating asset. This means that an additional gain of £47,320 is chargeable this year. Detailed calculations are contained in Appendix 2.

(b)   **Considerations on proposed take-over**

(i)   *Tax considerations*

Capital gains tax issues for disposal of shares

If the takeover is structured so that the shareholders of Lorna Mill Ltd sell their shares for cash, they will each crystallise a capital gain based on the excess of the cash received over the cost of their shares (with an allowance for inflation).

If shareholders choose to take the shares and loan stock package, no gain will arise. Instead, the original cost of the shares in Lorna Mill Ltd will be apportioned between the new securities acquired in the ratio of their respective market values at the date of the take-over.

The gain arising in respect of the shares received does not need to be calculated at the date of the takeover but instead will be deferred until the shares are sold. Taper relief will continue to apply from the original date of acquisition. The shareholders will obtain taper relief for the new shares at the business asset rate so long as they either continue to work for the Evergreen plc or hold at least 5 % of the shares.

If the shares become non business assets, this will be reflected in the rate of taper given on disposal as the gain will need to be apportioned between business and non business periods.

The gain arising in respect of the QCB loan notes received will need to be calculated at the date of the takeover and frozen until the loan notes are redeemed. Any gain arising from the eventual redemption (ie disposal) of the QCB loan notes is exempt from CGT but at that date the frozen gain will become chargeable with its original taper relief. Any future non business taper relief periods will therefore not impact the taper relief available.

Tax aspects of a sale of Lorna Mill Ltd's trade

Gains will crystallise on the disposal of chargeable assets in the company which will then be subject to corporation tax.

From the shareholders' perspective, they will effectively suffer a double charge to CGT as the company will suffer corporation tax on the disposal of the assets and the shareholders will pay CGT on the disposal of their shares (as the proceeds will reflect the increase due to the sale of the assets at a profit).

Stock will be transferred at market value, giving rise to additional trading profit at the take-over date, although an election can be made to treat the stock as transferred at book value.

Any assets qualifying for capital allowances will also be transferred at market value, potentially giving rise to balancing charges.

Lorna Mill Ltd will be left with no trading assets so will become a close investment holding company. This means that it will pay corporation tax at 30% on its taxable income, irrespective of the size of that income.

If the company becomes an investment holding company, this will impact the taper relief position on a future disposal by the shareholders as the shares will become non business assets.

The transfer of the trade is likely to be a transfer of a going concern and will therefore be outside the scope of VAT, assuming Evergreen plc is VAT registered.

If Lorna Mill Ltd ceases to make taxable supplies the company will have to notify HMRC within 30 days. It will then be deregistered.

(iii) *Other considerations*

The shareholders must compare the consideration being offered with the potential income and capital streams from retaining the shares. They will of course want to maximise wealth now and in the future, so the total value of the package must be considered.

Will the employees and directors of Lorna Mill Ltd be able to retain their jobs if the company or trade is taken over? If so, what will their new terms of employment be, compared to their present position? As we have seen above, this could seriously affect their taper relief position.

If Evergreen plc takes over the company (as opposed to the trade) it is likely to demand repayment of the loan made to John Harner. Will this cause difficulties to him?

By selling the trade, Lorna Mill Ltd (and hence the shareholders) will retain responsibility for any liabilities, especially any bank loans which may have personal guarantees to cover them. This may not be a desirable outcome.

As can be seen the takeover proposals have different advantages and disadvantages for different directors, shareholders and employees, and for the company. They may wish to consider taking independent advice about their own tax positions.

We trust that the above clarifies the points raised by you, but please contact us if we may be of further assistance.

Yours faithfully

Tax Manager

Appendix 1: Corporation tax computation – year ended 31 March 2007

	£
Trade profits (£255,000 + £11,000)	266,000
Chargeable gains (Appendix 2)	64,339
Profits chargeable to corporation tax	330,339
FII: $£27,000 \times \dfrac{100}{90}$	30,000
'profits'	360,339
PCTCT × 30%	99,102
Less: marginal relief $11/400 \times [1,500,000 - 360,339] \times \dfrac{330,339}{360,339}$	(28,731)
CT due 1 January 2008	70,371

Appendix 2: Chargeable gains

	£
Sale of leasehold	
Proceeds	125,000
Cost: $£100,000 \times \dfrac{(\%18y3m)\ 70.268\ *}{(\%30y)\ 87.330}$	(80,463)
Indexation: 0.342 × £80,463	(27,518)
Gain	17,019
*30yrs - 11 yrs 3m = 18 yrs 9m	
%19 yrs: 70.791	
%18 yrs: (68.697)	68,697
$2.094 \times \dfrac{9}{12} =$	1,571
	70,268

	£
Gain on freehold now crystallising	
Proceeds	130,000
Cost	(40,000)
0.317 × £40,000	(12,680)
	77,320
Less: rollover relief (frozen gain now crystallising)	(47,320)
Gain chargeable at date of disposal ie proceeds not reinvested	
£130,000 - £100,000 =	30,000
Total gains £(17,019 + 47,320)	64,339

19 Question with answer plan: Trent plc

> **Text references.** The basics of chargeable gains are in Chapters 11 and 12. Rollover relief is in Chapter 14. Groups and the implications of transfers of a trade are dealt with in Chapter 26. You should also study Chapter 30 on tax planning. VAT is covered in Chapters 28 and 29.
>
> **Top tip.** You must use the correct terminology in your answers. For example it would have been incorrect to discuss a mere change in the nature or conduct of trade – you must use the word 'major' to obtain the available mark.
>
> Do not be afraid to submit your answer plan with your answer. It will show that you have taken the time to really think about the question and the examiner can give you credit for your ideas.
>
> **Easy marks.** This was a complex question testing a number of issues that often crop up in the context of corporate restructuring, whether on a new acquisition or on the reorganisation of an existing group. The more you practise questions like this the easier the marks will be to obtain as you will be considering the same areas time and time again.

Answer plan

(a)   Group diagram

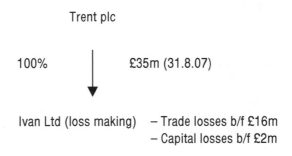

Trent plc

100%   £35m (31.8.07)

Ivan Ltd (loss making)   – Trade losses b/f £16m
                          – Capital losses b/f £2m

(b)   Losses

- Trent will change nature or conduct of trade

    –   if < 3 yrs trade losses b/f cannot be used

- £4m post acquisition losses (£20m - £16m)

    –   can be group relieved to Trent

    –   cannot carry back to period prior to change of ownership if 'major change in nature or conduct of trade'

(c)   Building & gains/losses

Trent

- new building cost £9m (1 yr's time)
- selling old building for £13m → gain of £8m
- new building will be partly rented out ∴ restriction on rollover relief

Ivan

- Machinist House: cost £12m, value £7m (ie loss of £5m)
- Pre-acquisition ∴ can't use against assets passed from Trent to sell
- Capital loss of £2m cannot be given to Trent

(d)   VAT

- New building to be rented to insurance company (exempt supplier)
- Wants to waive exemption
  - how to do it?
  - advantages and disadvantages?

PRIVATE AND CONFIDENTIAL

[Our address]

[Your address]

[Date]

STRICTLY PRIVATE AND CONFIDENTIAL

Dear Sally

Purchase of Ivan Ltd

I am writing in reply to your letter of 17 July, asking for tax advice on the purchase of Ivan Ltd.

Use of Ivan Ltd's tax losses

Ivan Ltd's trading losses unrelieved at 31 August 2007 can only be carried forward against future profits from the same trade. However, if Trent plc makes a major change to the nature or conduct of Ivan Ltd's trade before 31 August 2010, then the carry forward of the losses will be denied. Any minor changes would be ignored.

In my opinion your proposals regarding Ivan Ltd's future will constitute a major change of trade and my advice would be to delay this until after 31 August 2010 if commercially possible.

Any trading losses incurred by Ivan Ltd after 31 August 2007 can be group relieved to Trent plc to reduce its own profits for the corresponding accounting period. Alternatively these losses could be set against any income or gains of Ivan Ltd for the period of the loss, and then the previous twelve months.

If you change the nature or conduct of the trade, then the post-acquisition losses could not be carried back to any accounting period before 31 August 2007, although it appears unlikely that there are any profits against which to obtain loss relief before 31 August 2007.

The capital losses at the date of acquisition (£2m) cannot be used to shelter any capital gains of assets owned by Trent plc, as these losses arose prior to the acquisition. They can only be set off against gains on assets owned by Ivan Ltd at the date of acquisition or purchased subsequently from a third party.

There is no question of the capital losses realised by Ivan Ltd being transferred to Trent plc.

Proposals to shelter gain on sale of old headquarters

As described above, Trent plc will not be able to utilise Ivan Ltd's capital loss of £2m as these losses cannot be transferred to Trent plc, and in any case they arose prior to acquisition of Ivan Ltd. A similar restriction applies where capital losses are realised after a company joins a group on assets held by the company on joining the group.

It may be possible to utilise some of the capital loss anticipated on the sale of Machinist House if the property is transferred to Trent plc prior to the sale. Although there is unlikely to be a large change in the value of the property in the next year so that it could be argued that the full loss in value arises prior to Ivan Ltd being acquired, the law allows the pre-acquisition loss to be computed on a time basis if it benefits the taxpayer.

Thus, with a proposed sale date of 31 August 2008, we can treat approximately £588,000 (Appendix 1) as a post-acquisition loss and, if realised by Trent plc, this can be set off against the gain on the sale of its headquarters.

As an alternative, the gain of £8m could be partly deferred by claiming rollover relief on the purchase of your new headquarters. Not all of the gain can be deferred however. Normally, the proceeds not used for the purchase of the new building of £4m (£13m – £9m) would remain chargeable, but in this case, not all of the new headquarters will be used in Trent's trade (as it will be subletting space). Thus only a proportion of the £9m will be allowed as qualifying cost, thus increasing the chargeable gain.

A further alternative is to delay the sale of Machinist House in order to increase the amount of post-acquisition loss which could be used by Trent plc. It is important to note, however, that the sale will need to be made in the same accounting period as the gain is realised on the headquarters. Any delay beyond this period would prevent the capital loss being used in this way.

Merger of trades of Ivan Ltd and Trent plc

The transfer of Ivan Ltd's trade to Trent plc would allow the trading losses of Ivan Ltd to be used in future (but only against profits of its trade).

No capital gains would arise on the transfer, as Ivan Ltd is at least 75% owned by Trent plc, and no balancing adjustments would arise on the transfer of assets qualifying for capital allowances - whichever way around the transfer was effected.

If Trent plc's trade was transferred to Ivan Ltd, then there would be no restriction against the losses being set against the profits of Trent's trade now transferred.

However if Ivan Ltd's trade is transferred to Trent plc, and it becomes dormant, its capital losses will be wasted.

For this reason (and the impact of setting off Ivan Ltd's losses brought forward as described above) I would recommend that Trent plc's trade is transferred to Ivan Ltd, so that the capital losses can be utilised by Ivan Ltd against gains on assets it already owns or buys after the transfer.

As stated above, in order to preserve Ivan Ltd's trade losses at the date of acquisition, you should ensure that you do not change the nature or conduct of its trade prior to September 2010.

VAT position on letting out part of the headquarters

In order to waive exemption on (or opt to tax) the new building, Trent plc needs to send a notice of election to HMRC which will be effective immediately. This notice must be sent within 30 days of making the election.

The advantage to Trent plc waiving the exemption is that it will be able to recover all of its input tax on any purchases or supplies received in relation to the building including the VAT charged on the purchase price.

If it did not opt to tax, then the rent charged would be an exempt supply, making Trent Ltd partially exempt. This would cause problems in recovering the full input VAT on the purchase price and on any repairs or expenses relating to the part let out. A further consequence of not opting to tax is that the 'capital goods scheme' would apply, leading to annual adjustments of the input tax recovery over the next ten years to reflect changes in the use of the building for making exempt supplies.

The main disadvantage of opting to tax is that Trent plc would have to charge VAT on the rent, which the insurance company would be unable to recover as it makes exempt supplies. This could make the rent uncompetitive with similar landlords who have not waived the exemption on their buildings and could jeopardise the arrangements.

Another disadvantage (albeit not of immediate concern), is that Trent plc would have to charge VAT on the eventual sale of the building, and if this is to an exempt supplier it would increase the 'cost' of the building to them, making it uncompetitive as discussed above.

I trust that the above clarifies the points raised in your letter, but should you have any further queries, please do not hesitate to contact me.

Yours sincerely

Tax Adviser

Appendix 1 – post acquisition loss on sale of Machinist House

	£
Anticipated proceeds	7,000,000
Less: cost	(12,000,000)
Loss	5,000,000
Time owned since purchased (28.2.00-31.8.08) =	8½ years
Post-acquisition period (1.9.07-31.8.08) =	1 year

$$\therefore \text{ Post acquisition loss} = £5m \times \frac{1}{8\frac{1}{2}} = \underline{£588,235}$$

20 Spark Ltd

Text references. The calculation of PCTCT and the corporation tax computation are in Chapters 21 and 22. Losses are in Chapter 24. Gains are covered in Chapters 11 and 12. Reliefs for chargeable gains are in Chapter 14. Corporate groups are in Chapter 26. VAT is in Chapters 28 and 29.

Top tips. The key here is to deal with the property transactions and establish the PCTCT for each company for each year. Burn Ltd's loss brought forward should be dealt with first, before considering Fizzle's loss and making an initial conclusion on the best available relief. Finally, consider Spark's loss bearing in mind the use of Fizzle's loss.

Easy marks. This is a tough question and there are no easy marks as such. You really need to think about the loss relief rules and how they apply within a group and be methodical when writing your answer.

Marking scheme

				Marks
(a)	Burn Ltd's brought forward losses		1	
	Options for Fizzle Ltd's loss	Max	4	
	Conclusion		1	
	Options for Spark Ltd's loss	Max	4	
	Conclusion		1	
	Spark Ltd purchase of The Hutch		1	
	Spark Ltd transfer of Electric House		1	
	Burn Ltd's transfer of The Hutch		1	
	Char Ltd sale of Watt Hall lease		1	
	Char Ltd sale of Place House		1	
	Fizzle Ltd sale of Electric House		2	
	No rollover available due to proceeds not reinvested		1	
		Max		16
(b)	*Other matters*			
	Claim requirements		1	
	Order of relief		1	
	Availability of rollover relief		1	
	VAT aspects		1	
				4
(c)	Rejecting/accepting loss relief claims			5
(d)	*Corporation tax computations*			
	Spark Ltd		1½	
	Burn Ltd		1	
	Char Ltd		1½	
	Fizzle Ltd		1½	
		Max		5
				30

Notes for meeting

(a) **Available reliefs to reduce Spark Ltd group's corporation tax liability**

Burn Ltd's trading losses brought forward

- Must use these before any other available losses.

- Leaves no profit for y/e 31.3.07 and remaining loss of £30,000 (£75,000 – £(25,000 + 20,000) to carry forward.

- Burn Ltd's profit y/e 31.3.08 of £55,000 (no profit arises on the transfer of The Hutch as the transfer takes place at no gain/ no loss) is reduced by the loss carried forward of £30,000 to £25,000. There is no other option for dealing with loss.

Fizzle Ltd's loss £260,000 for y/e 31.3.07

- Can be used in the following ways:

  (i) Group relief to Spark Ltd: save tax @ 32.75% until profits reach £75,000, then 19% thereafter. Maximum loss used £172,500.

  (ii) Group relief to Burn Ltd: not an option as Burn will have used its loss b/fwd already.

  (iii) Group relief to Char Ltd: has profits of £97,500 and a gain of approximately £179,800 (W2), a total of £277,300. Loss will save tax @ 32.75% until profits reach £75,000 (ie on £202,300) then @ 19% on remainder. Max loss to use: £260,000.

  (iv) Combination of (i) & (iii)

  ie use loss to bring Spark Ltd profits down to £75,000, by using £97,500 of loss, then group relief to Char Ltd remaining loss of £162,500. This has advantage of saving tax @ 32.75% on entire loss in current year.

  (v) Bring Char Ltd profits to £75,000 first, then group relief remaining loss to Spark Ltd – same effect as in (iv) above, leaving Spark Ltd with profit of £114,800 (W3).

  (vi) Carry back loss (no current year profits) in Fizzle Ltd to year ended 31.3.06. Relief obtained earlier than (i)-(v) above but maximum relief 19%. Interest will be paid on any corporation tax repaid. Rejected due to low rate of relief and insufficient profits to absorb loss.

  (vii) Carry loss forward against Fizzle Ltd's trading profit for year 31.3.08 – save tax at 32.75% on £97,500 (no relief available against gain of £348,300 in that year). Rejected as it delays relief.

On balance options (iv) and (v) offer best combination of earliest relief and highest tax savings. Of these, option (v) will be best in view of treatment of Spark Ltd's loss (see below).

Spark Ltd's loss of £120,000 for y/e 31.3.08

- Can be used in the following ways:

  (i) Carry back to y/e 31.3.07 (no profits in y/e 31.3.08). Saves tax @ 32.75% until profits reach £75,000, saving 19% thereafter. This will interact with option (v) above. Spark would have remaining profits of £114,800 (W3), so that 32.75% tax is saved on losses up to £39,800 (£114,800 – £75,000), leaving £75,000 losses attracting relief at 19%, and £5,200 losses to be relieved elsewhere.

  (ii) Group relief to Burn Ltd:

  Burn Ltd has profits of £25,000 remaining in y/e 31.3.08 (see above). Relief would only be 19% and is therefore rejected as better relief could be obtained elsewhere.

(iii)   Group relief to Char Ltd

Char Ltd is now a close investment holding company (probably since 1.3.07 when it ceased to invest wholly or mainly in land and building) and will pay tax on its profits at the full rate of 30%. For y/e 31.3.08, it could utilise loss of £32,000 to save tax @ 30%. This is rejected to minimise tax liabilities.

(iv)   Group relief to Fizzle Ltd

Fizzle Ltd has profits of £445,600 (£97,500 + £348,300 (W3)) and so relief would be initially at 30%. This would apply for losses of up to £70,800 (£445,800 - £375,000). Thereafter, relief would be at 32.75%.

(v)   Carry forward the loss against Spark Ltd's future trading profits This is rejected as there is no indication of the level of those profits, whilst also delaying possible relief.

Conclusion

- Take option (v) for Fizzle Ltd's loss for y/e 31.3.07 discussed above.

- Group relief £80,200 of Spark Ltd's loss to Fizzle Ltd to save tax at 30/32.75%, then carry back the remaining loss of £39,800 against Spark Ltd's profit for y/e 31.3.07 to bring that profit down to £75,000, saving tax @ 32.75% with the bonus of interest on repaid corporation tax. This gives the best combination of early relief and maximum tax saving.

Other matters

- Group relief requires a written claim within two years of the end of the claimant company's accounting period. Carry back of losses requires a written claim within two years of the end of loss making period.

- Some of the capital gains may be rolled over if reinvestment into qualifying assets is made within three years of the relevant disposals. There is still time left to do this and it would obviously change the planning discussed above. Note that reinvestment could be undertaken by any of the group companies as long as the asset is used for business purposes, which seems to exclude Char Ltd.

- Technically the group relief claim should be made before the carry back claim to restrict the loss to be carries back. But in practice HMRC will accept a simultaneous claim.

- Sale of commercial buildings under 3 years old is a standard rated supply. Any other sale is exempt unless any of the companies has waived exemption in which case 17½% VAT would have to be added to the sale price. If a group registration exists, the transfer of property between group companies within the registration will be outside the scope of VAT.

(b)   **Corporation tax computation**

Spark Ltd

y/e 31.3.07	£
Trading profit	172,500
s.393A loss c/back	(39,800)
Group relief (W3)	(57,700)
PCTCT	75,000
Tax @ 19% =	14,250

y/e 31.3.08
CT = Nil

Burn Ltd

y/e 31.3.07

CT = <u>Nil</u>

y/e 31.3.08

Trading profit = <u>£25,000</u> (see part (a))

Tax @ 19% = <u>£4,750</u>

Char Ltd

	£
y/e 31.3.07	
Property business income	97,500
Gains	179,800
	277,300
Group relief (W3)	(202,300)
PCTCT	75,000
Tax @ 19% =	£14,250
y/e 31.3.08	
Property business income	10,000
Interest income	22,000
PCTCT	32,000
	£
Tax @ 30% (CIC)	9,600

Fizzle Ltd

y/e 31.3.07

CT = <u>Nil</u>

	£
y/e 31.3.08	
Trading profit	97,500
Gains (W2)	348,300
	445,800
Group relief	(80,200)
PCTCT	365,600
Tax @ 30%	109,680
Less: taper relief	
11/400 × £[375,000 − 365,600]	(259)
CT payable	109,421

Workings

(1) *Group structure*

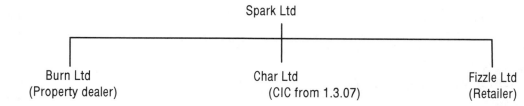

FY 07 and FY 08

$$UL = \frac{1,500}{4} = 375,000$$

$$LL = \frac{300}{4} = 75,000$$

(2) *Property transactions*

Spark Ltd

y/e 31.3.08

- Purchased building 'The Hutch' from Burn Ltd 19.4.07 – deemed cost £200,000 (see below).

y/e 31.3.07

- Transfer of building 'Electric House' to Fizzle Ltd (1.5.06) (no gain/no loss rules automatically apply)

Burn Ltd:

Sale of 'The Hutch' to Spark Ltd

- The Hutch was held as trading stock and is treated as appropriated to fixed assets immediately before the transfer at its market value of £200,000. This leads to additional trading profit to £20,000. The transfer to Spark Ltd is a no gain/no loss transfer.

Char Ltd

- Investment company – no rollover relief

y/e 31.3.07

Sale of lease

	£
Proceeds	656,000
Cost	
$400,000 \times \dfrac{64.116\,(\%16)}{81.100\,(\%25)}$	(316,232)
	339,768
Indexation	
$50.6\% \times £316,232$	(160,013)
Gain	179,755

(say £179,800)

y/e 31.3.08

Sale of Place House

	£
Proceeds	185,000
Cost	(120,000)
	65,000
Indexation	
(56.6% × £120,000) = £67,920 max	(65,000)
Indexed gain	Nil

Note. Indexation cannot create a loss.

Fizzle Ltd

y/e 31.3.08

Sale of 'Electric House'

	£
Base cost: cost to Spark Ltd	325,000
Indexation to May 06:	
36% × £325,000	117,000
	442,000

	£
Proceeds	800,000
Cost	(442,000)
Indexation	
2.2% × £442,000	(9,724)
Gain	348,276
(say £348,300)	

Purchased 'Rumble House' on 22.12.07, cost £200,000 (no rollover relief possible on sale of 'Electric House' - proceeds not reinvested of £600,000 (£800,000 − £200,000) exceed the gain.

(3) *Option (v) for Fizzle Ltd's loss:*

- Loss used against Char Ltd's profit = £(277,300 − 75,000) = £202,300
- Remaining loss relieved against Spark Ltd = £(260,000 − 202,300) = £57,700
- Spark Ltd's remaining profits = £(172,500 − 57,700) = £114,800

21 Irroy

Text references. Group relief of losses is covered in Chapter 26 and transfer pricing is dealt with in Chapter 21. Overseas aspects of CT is in Chapter 27 and overseas aspects of VAT is in Chapter 29.

Top tip. This question required a lot of writing for the answer, with minimal calculations. Answer plans are essential.

The two companies are associated with each other so don't forget to divide the small companies' limit by 2. Even through they are owned by a person rather than a company they are still associated for upper and lower limits purposes.

Easy marks. To pick up lots of marks (and to not confuse yourself or the examiner along the way) when considering two alternatives take it one at a time. Discuss the pros and cons of one alternative and then move onto the second. Where an answer keeps flicking from one alternative to another and then back it can be confusing and you may lose marks if the examiner cannot easily follow your answer.

Examiner's comments. A Corporation Tax (CT) question concerning groups. This question required candidates to suggest alternative group structures which would allow the companies to claim group relief, and also to explain the different CT and Value Added Tax (VAT) implications of an overseas subsidiary being treated as UK resident, or alternatively, overseas resident. It had a very high written component, as opposed to computational content, and was generally poorly done by the relatively few candidates who chose it.

In part (a) most candidates were able to recognise the problem with the current structure, and suggest at least one alternative, but still didn't include enough detail to gain more than half marks.

A surprising number of candidates slipped up in (a)(ii) by not recognising that the two companies were associated, therefore reducing the small companies' limits. This lost easy marks.

Part (b) was not well done. There were a lot of relevant points a candidate could have made in this question, some straightforward, some less so. The key was to adopt a structured, logical approach, but too often the answers adopted a haphazard, scattergun approach. When comparing two alternative situations (here, whether Green Ltd is UK resident or Irish resident), candidates must make it clear which scenario they are talking about when making their points. It is not enough to state a fact, then leave it to the marker to decide which of the alternatives it applies to. This will not gain marks.

Marking scheme

				Marks
(a)	(i)	Companies not part of a group	½	
		Inability to surrender losses	½	
		Ability to use losses in future	½	
		Shareholding requirements to make a group	½	
		Share for share: possibility	½	
		no immediate CGT consequences	½	
		commercial requirements	½	
		clearance procedure available	½	
		dormant company not an associate	½	
		Straight sale: consideration of CGT issues	½	
		availability of business taper relief	½	
		availability of annual exemptions	½	
		Existing tax losses v future trading profit only	½	
			Max	**5**
	(ii)	Awareness of associated companies	½	
		No planning: Corporation tax at 30%	½	
		Marginal relief calculation	½	
		Planning: Restriction of group relief	½	
		Corporation tax at 19%	½	
		Calculation of tax saved	½	
				3

(b) Residence:

	incorporation not necessarily sufficient	½
	central management/control	½
	conduct meetings outside UK	½
if resident UK:	taxed on worldwide income	½
	PE in ROI	½
	consequences	½
if resident ROI:	dividends/overseas income	½
	still associated	½
	no group relief	½
Double tax relief:	relief for withholidng tax	½
	relief for underlying tax	½
	10% plus holding	½
	double tax: lower of	½
Transfer Pricing:	identify issue	½
	arms length	½
	applies in UK/exemption if SME	½
	applies if Irish resident/exemption if SME	½
CFC issues:	identify issue	½
	dependent subsidiary	½
	material difference in tax rates	½
	conclusion: ROI low tax country	½
	deemed distribution	½
	requirement to self-report	½
	£50,000 exemption	½
	acceptable distribution policy	
	– identify exemption	½
	– 90%/details	½
VAT issues:	making taxable supplies in ROI	½
	UK zero rated	½
	VAT paid in ROI	½
	proof of supply required	½
	invoice to bear both VAT numbers	½
	alternative domestic treatment	½
	need for an ESL	½
	penalties	½

Max

$$\frac{14}{25}$$

(a) (i) Aqua Ltd and Aria Ltd are both owned 75% by Irroy and 25% by Irwin.

Although both companies are under the control of Irroy they do not form a group for group relief purposes, and so it is not possible to claim group relief. To be part of a group, companies must be controlled by another company, not an individual. Had a group existed, Aria Ltd could have surrendered its trading loss to Aqua Ltd. This would have been set against Aqua's profits of the same accounting period.

Instead the losses of Aria Ltd can only be carried forward against future profits arising from the same trade which are not anticipated to arise before the year ended 31 March 2010 at the earliest.

The current structure could be amended by:

(1) Irroy and Irwin transferring their shareholdings in both companies to a third company in return for that company issuing shares to Irroy and Irwin in the same proportions. Aqua Ltd and Aria Ltd would each be wholly owned subsidiaries of the third company, so satisfying the conditions for group relief. The share exchange would be treated for capital gains purposes as a 'paper for paper' transaction, but it would be advisable to obtain advance clearance from HMRC.

(2) Irroy and Irwin transferring their shareholdings in one company, say Aria Ltd, to the other, say Aqua Ltd. Aria Ltd would then be a wholly owned subsidiary of Aqua Ltd, so again the conditions for group relief would be satisfied. As Irroy and Irwin are 75% and 25% shareholders in Aqua Ltd, their interests in Aria Ltd would be in the same proportions. Although the transfer would be a disposal for capital gains purposes it would appear unlikely that any gain would arise as Aria Ltd has made losses from the outset. If a gain did arise, business assets taper relief would be available, and also Irroy's and Irwin's annual exemptions.

If a group structure is set up, only losses arising after that date can be relieved, using time apportionment if it occurs during an accounting period (unless some other method of apportionment would give a just and reasonable result).

(ii) (1) If no action is taken, there are two associated companies, as they are controlled by Irroy.

The corporation tax payable for the year to 31 March 2008 is:

	Aqua Ltd £	Aria Ltd £
PCTCT (loss c/f 60,000 + 30,000 b/f = £90,000)	175,000	NIL
CT payable £175,000 × 30%	52,500	
Less MR 11/400 × (750,000 – 175,000)	(15,812)	
	36,688	NIL

(2) If an amended structure is implemented from 1 June 2007 there will still be two associated companies, assuming that if a holding company is interposed it does not trade and so can be disregarded for this purpose. Group relief can only be surrendered for the 10 month period 1 June 2007 – 31 March 2008.

The corporation tax payable for the year to 31 March 2008 is:

	Aqua Ltd £	Aria Ltd £
Profits	175,000	
Less group relief 10/12 × 60,000	(50,000)	
PCTCT (loss c/f 60,000 – 50,000 + 30,000 b/f = £40,000)	125,000	NIL
CT payable £125,000 × 19%	23,750	NIL

The corporation tax saved by implementing the group structure is £36,688 – £23,750 = £12,938, although the losses carried forward in Aria Ltd are reduced by £50,000.

(b) **Charge to corporation tax**

If Green Ltd had been incorporated in the UK it would have been resident in the UK. However Green Ltd is to be incorporated in the Republic of Ireland. It may still be treated as resident in the UK if its central management and control is exercised in the UK, such as through the holding of directors' meetings in the UK.

If Green Ltd is treated as UK resident, then it will be taxed in the UK on all of its worldwide profits, wherever arising. If any corporation tax were paid in the Republic of Ireland, then double tax relief would be available by allowing the Irish corporation tax as a credit against the UK corporation tax. Any dividends paid by Green Ltd to Aqua Ltd would be disregarded for UK corporation tax purposes.

If Green Ltd is not UK resident, then it will only be taxable in the UK on any income arising in the UK. If it pays any dividends to Aqua Ltd, then those dividends would be taxable on Aqua Ltd as foreign income. As Green Ltd will be a subsidiary of Aqua Ltd, Aqua will be entitled to double tax relief for any underlying foreign tax as well as for any withholding tax charged on the dividends paid.

As Green Ltd will be trading in the Republic of Ireland it is likely that the Irish authorities will consider it to be resident in the Republic of Ireland on the grounds that it has a permanent establishment there. It will then be liable to Irish corporation tax on its trading profits, and on any other income arising anywhere.

Since the rate of Irish corporation tax is lower than the rate of UK corporation tax it would seem to be preferable for Green Ltd to be treated as resident in the Republic of Ireland, and not in the UK. The net effect would be that all trading profits would be taxed at the Irish corporation tax rate of 12.5%, with this being topped up to Aqua Ltd's marginal rate of corporation tax only on those profits distributed to the UK.

It should be noted that Green Ltd will be treated as an associated company, so reducing the small companies' limits, regardless of residence.

Anti-avoidance legislation

Transfer pricing

Green Ltd will be selling water tanks supplied by Aqua Ltd. As the companies are under common control, it would be possible to manipulate the prices charged, so redirecting profits to the lower tax paying company. The transfer pricing rules are designed to prevent such manipulation. They can apply where there are transactions between companies under common control at non-arm's length prices, even if both companies are UK resident. However, the group is expected to continue to qualify as a small and medium sized enterprise, and the transfer pricing legislation does not generally apply to small and medium sized enterprises.

It may still apply if one party is not resident in the UK but is resident in a country which has a double tax treaty with the UK which does not contain a non discrimination clause. This is not the case here. It may also apply to a medium sized enterprise if HMRC issues a transfer pricing notice in respect of a particular transaction or series of transactions.

Controlled foreign companies

The controlled foreign companies' legislation applies where a company which is controlled by a UK company is resident in a 'low tax country', ie one where the rate of tax is less than 75% of the UK rate. As the rate of Irish corporation tax is 12.5% compared to the UK small companies rate of 19%, this would appear to apply if Green Ltd is resident in the Republic of Ireland (12.5% ÷ 19% = 66%).

The consequence of the controlled foreign company legislation applying would be that Green Ltd's profits would be apportioned to Aqua Ltd, and subject to UK corporation tax at the full rate of corporation tax. Double tax relief would be given for any Irish tax paid on those profits.

The controlled foreign company legislation will not apply if Green Ltd's profits are less than £50,000, or if at least 90% of the profits are distributed to Aqua Ltd no later than 18 months after the end of the accounting period.

VAT

Green Ltd will be making taxable supplies in the Republic of Ireland and will be required to register for VAT, unless its supplies fall below the taxable limits. Green Ltd will be required to charge Irish VAT at the rate of 21% on its supplies.

Aqua Ltd will be making supplies to another EU member state, to a customer registered for VAT in that member state. Provided it obtains Green Ltd's VAT number and quotes it on invoices issued, Green Ltd's supplies will be zero rated in the UK. Depending on the volume of sales, Aqua Ltd may be required to complete a UK sales list.

As the supplies have been zero rated, Green Ltd will be required to account for Irish VAT on those supplies at the Irish rate of 21%. It can, however, claim credit for the Irish VAT paid against the Irish VAT that it must charge on its supplies.

22 Dovedale Ltd

> **Text references.** Capital allowances are covered in Chapter 7. CT is in Chapters 21 to 24 with group aspects dealt with in Chapter 26. Overseas aspects of CT is dealt with in Chapter 27. VAT groups are covered in Chapter 28, and Ethics in Chapter 30.
>
> **Top tips.** Make sure you look at the marks available in each part of the question and allocate your time and effort accordingly.
>
> **Easy marks.** You must show your workings clearly and explain why you have done what you did – marks for all of this. Keep calm, don't panic or rush – work through the question carefully to maximise marks.

Marking scheme

			Marks
(a)	Gain on shares	½	
	Substantial shareholding exemption	½	
	Three conditions	1½	
	Possible degrouping charge	½	
	No gain, no loss transfers within six years	½	
	Max		3
(b)	Losses to be surrendered:		
	Calculation of group relief	1	
	Calculations of consortium relief	1½	
	Losses remaining:		
	Must be carried forward	½	
	No offset before year ending 31 March 2009	½	
	Change of ownership and trade	1	
	Capital allowances:		
	Claiming would increase unrelieved losses	½	
	Not claiming would increase next year's loss	½	
	Consortium relief available	½	
	Max		5
(c)	Trading profit and consortium relief	½	
	Chargeable gain:		
	Cost	1	
	Unindexed gain	½	
	Indexation	½	
	Rate of corporation tax	½	
	Corporation tax liability	½	
			3
(d)	Conflict of interest	1	
	Resolution	1	
			2
(e)	Dovedale Ltd and Hira Ltd:		
	Control	½	
	Established in the UK with reason	1	
	Atapo Inc:		
	Control	½	
	Established in the UK	½	
	Fixed establishment in the UK with meaning	1	
	Max		3

(f)

May be CFC	½	
Definition	½	
Effect of being CFC	1	
Exceptions not satisfied	1	
Exempt activities	½	
Motive test	½	
Not CFC – not taxed in UK	½	
Taxed on dividends received	½	
Adjust for withholding tax and underlying tax	1	
Double tax relief	1	
	Max	5
		21

(a) **Capital gains that may arise on the sale by Belgrove Ltd of shares in Hira Ltd**

Belgrove Ltd will realise a capital gain on the sale of the shares unless the substantial shareholding exemption applies. The exemption will be given automatically provided all of the following conditions are satisfied.

- Belgrove Ltd has owned at least 10% of Hira Ltd for a minimum of 12 months during the two years prior to the sale.

- Belgrove Ltd is a trading company or a member of a trading group during that 12-month period and immediately after the sale.

- Hira Ltd is a trading company or the holding company of a trading group during that 12-month period and immediately after the sale.

Hira Ltd will no longer be in a capital gains group with Belgrove Ltd after the sale. Accordingly, a capital gain, known as a degrouping charge, may arise in Hira Ltd. A degrouping charge will arise if, at the time it leaves the Belgrove Ltd group, Hira Ltd owns any capital assets which were transferred to it at no gain, no loss within the previous six years by a member of the Belgrove Ltd capital gains group.

(b) **The advantage of Hira Ltd not claiming any capital allowances**

In the year ending 31 March 2007 Hira Ltd expects to make a tax adjusted trading loss, before deduction of capital allowances, of £55,000 and to surrender the maximum amount possible of trading losses to Belgrove Ltd and Dovedale Ltd.

For the first nine months of the year from 1 April 2006 to 31 December 2006 Hira Ltd is in a loss relief group with Belgrove Ltd. The maximum surrender to Belgrove Ltd for this period is the lower of:

- the available loss of £41,250 (£55,000 × 9/12); and
- the profits chargeable to corporation tax of Belgrove of £28,500 (£38,000 × 9/12).

ie £28,500. This leaves losses of £12,750 (£41,250 – £28,500) unrelieved.

For the remaining three months from 1 January 2007 to 31 March 2007 Hira Ltd is a consortium company because at least 75% of its share capital is owned by companies, each of which own at least 5%. It can surrender £8,938 (£55,000 × 3/12 × 65%) to Dovedale Ltd and £4,812 (£55,000 × 3/12 × 35%) to Belgrove Ltd as both companies have sufficient taxable profits to offset the losses. Accordingly, there are no losses remaining from the three-month period.

The unrelieved losses from the first nine months must be carried forward as Hira Ltd has no income or gains in that year or the previous year. However, the losses cannot be carried forward beyond 1 January 2007 (the date of the change of ownership of Hira Ltd) if there is a major change in the nature or conduct of the trade of Hira Ltd. Even if the losses can be carried forward, the earliest year in which they can be relieved is the year ending 31 March 2009 as Hira Ltd is expected to make a trading loss in the year ending 31 March 2008.

BPP
LEARNING MEDIA

Any capital allowances claimed by Hira Ltd in the year ending 31 March 2007 would increase the tax adjusted trading loss for that year and consequently the unrelieved losses arising in the first nine months.

If the capital allowances are not claimed, the whole of the tax written down value brought forward of £96,000 would be carried forward to the year ending 31 March 2008 thus increasing the capital allowances and the tax adjusted trading loss, for that year. By not claiming any capital allowances, Hira Ltd can effectively transfer a current period trading loss, which would be created by capital allowances, of £24,000 (25% × £96,000) from the year ending 31 March 2007 to the following year where it can be surrendered to the two consortium members.

(c) **Dovedale Ltd – Forecast corporation tax computation for the year ended 31 March 2007**

	£
Trading profit	875,000
Chargeable gain (W1)	37,289
	912,289
Less: Consortium relief (from (b))	(8,938)
Profits chargeable to corporation tax	903,351
Corporation tax liability	
£903,351 × 30% (W3)	271,005

Note. The two companies are not in a capital gains group as Dovedale Ltd owns less than 75% of Hira Ltd. Accordingly, Dovedale Ltd will realise a gain on the sale of the building.

Workings

W1 Chargeable gain on sale of office building

	£
Disposal proceeds	234,000
Less: Cost (W2)	(193,233)
	40,767
Less: Indexation	
(193.9 – 190.5)/190.5 = 0.018 × £193,233	(3,478)
Chargeable gain	37,289

W2 Base cost of office building

	£
Initial cost	210,000
Less: Rollover relief claimed	
Gain on factory £84,217	
Proceeds not invested £277,450 – £210,000 = £67,450	
Rollover relief claimed (£84,217 – £67,450)	(16,767)
	193,233

W3 Rate of corporation tax

Dovedale Ltd has one associate, Hira Ltd, for the year ending 31 March 2007. Accordingly, the upper limit will be £750,000 (£1,500,000 ÷ 2) such that Dovedale Ltd is a large company.

(d) If you are asked to act in respect of a matter which affects two clients there may be a conflict of interests.

You need to consider carefully the advice that each client requires, and whether the advice given to one client would be detrimental to the other client. In that case it is likely that you should only act for one of the clients, and you would have to explain to the other that you could no longer act.

There may be instances where it is still possible to act for both clients if their interests do not conflict. This may be the case here, if both Dovedale Ltd and Belgrove Ltd are agreed on the terms of the sale. You should, however, advise each of them that you act for the other, and seek their consent to your acting for both. It may be advisable to suggest to one or both of them that they may like to take independent advice regarding the sale.

(e)   Dovedale Ltd and Hira Ltd can register as a group for the purposes of value added tax (VAT) because Dovedale Ltd controls Hira Ltd and both companies are established in the UK in that their head offices are in the UK.

Dovedale Ltd will also control Atapo Inc. However, Atapo Inc cannot be part of a group registration unless it is established in the UK or has a fixed establishment in the UK. It will be regarded as established in the UK if it is centrally managed and controlled in the UK or if its head office is in the UK. A fixed establishment is a place where the company has staff and equipment and where its business is carried on.

(f)   Atapo Inc appears to be a controlled foreign company (CFC) in that:

- it is resident outside of the UK in Morovia; and
- it is controlled by Dovedale Ltd, a UK resident company; and
- the rate of corporation tax in Morovia is less than three quarters of that in the UK.

If Atapo Inc is a CFC its profits will be attributed to Dovedale Ltd and must be included in Dovedale Ltd's corporation tax return. The whole of the profits of Atapo Inc would be taxed at 30% with relief given for the Morovian tax suffered.

Atapo Inc will not be regarded as a CFC if it satisfies one of the exceptions. Three of the exceptions do not apply as Atapo Inc is not a quoted company, its profits exceed £50,000 and it does not intend to pay at least 90% of those profits to Dovedale Ltd. However, there are two further exceptions that it may be able to satisfy.

Atapo Inc will be regarded as carrying out exempt activities if:

(i)   it has a genuine physical presence in Morovia, as appears to be the case; and

(ii)   less than half of its gross trading receipts arise from transactions with Dovedale Ltd or other associated entities.

Alternatively, Atapo Inc may be able to satisfy the motive test. This test is satisfied if it can be argued that Atapo Inc was not formed in order to divert profits from the UK or reduce a UK tax liability.

If Atapo Inc is not a CFC it will not be taxed in the UK on its profits as it does not have a permanent establishment in the UK. However, Dovedale Ltd will be taxed on the dividends received from Atapo Inc.

The dividends received will be included in the corporation tax computation gross of underlying tax (the Morovian tax paid in respect of the profits distributed) and the tax withheld on the dividends paid. The underlying tax is included because Dovedale Ltd owns at least 10% of Atapo Inc.

The corporation tax at 30% on the gross dividend will then be reduced by double tax relief. The double tax relief will equal the underlying tax and the withholding tax on the dividend, as the total Morovian tax suffered is less than 30% of the gross dividend.

Note. If Atapo Inc is a CFC the tax payable by Dovedale Ltd on the profits apportioned to it will be reduced because it has received dividends from Atapo Inc.

23 Yaz Pica

Text references. Trading profit aspects are dealt with in Chapter 6. Capital allowances are in Chapter 7. Income tax is covered in Chapter 1. VAT registration is dealt with in Chapter 28.

Top tips. Do the computations of income tax and NIC liability first and then write your answer around your findings. This is the best approach for all questions where supporting calculations are required.

Marking scheme

		Marks	
(a)	Earnings	1	
	Trading profits adjustment	2	
	Taxable income	1	
	Tax liability	1	
	Final payment/payment on account	1½	
	Trading loss	1	
	S 381 ICTA 1988 claim	1	
	Income tax refund	1	
	Tax liability/payment on a/c	1½	
	Conclusion	1	
			12
(b)	*Additional profit*		
	Income	1	
	Output/Input VAT on goods sold	3	
	Pre-trading expenditure	2	
			6
			18

(a)　(i)　*Payments of income tax*

Total income tax due of £2,066 (W) will be due on 31 January 2008.

This payment will be the full payment of income tax for 2006/07 of £1,377 (W). No payments on account will have been paid because the 2005/06 liability was paid via PAYE.

In addition, the first payment on account for 2007/08 of £689 (W) will be due on this date.

Working

Income tax 2006/07

		Non savings Income
	£	£
Earnings (8/12 × £42,000)		28,000
Trading profits		
Profits per accounts (y/e 31.12.07)	50,300	
Less:　Pre-trading expenditure	(1,400)	
First year allowance 50% × £14,400	(7,200)	
	41,700	
2006/07 taxable profits (£41,700 × 3/12)		10,425
STI		38,425
Less:　Personal allowance		(5,035)
Taxable income		33,390
Tax on non-savings income		£
£2,150 ×　10%		215
£31,150 ×　22%		6,853
£90 ×　　40%		36
		7,104
Less:　PAYE		(5,727)
Tax for 2006/07		1,377
Add:　payment on account 2007/08 – 50%		689
Total tax due 31.1.08		2,066

(ii)   Yaz is likely to be in a refund position if he makes up accounts to 31 March 2007.

This is due to the taxable trading profit for 2006/07 being £nil as a loss will arise (W). Under s 381 ICTA 1988 the loss can be set against the total income of the preceding three years on a first in, first out basis ie against income of 2003/04 first. If Yaz's income was sufficiently high in that tax year, this could result in an income tax refund of up to £(9,800 × 40%) = £3,920.

In addition, no payment on account will be needed for 2007/08, since the tax in 2006/07 will be covered by the PAYE deducted.

No income tax will be due until 31 January 2009 which provides a cashflow advantage for Yaz.

Yaz should be aware, however, that these advantages will be offset by a higher liability for 2007/08 if the profit forecast is correct.

Working

	£
Loss per accounts	1,200
Pre trading expenditure	1,400
First year allowance	7,200
Loss for 2006/07	9,800

(b)   (i)   As Yaz exceeded the VAT registration limit in June 2007, he should have applied to be registered by 30 July 2007 and then would have been registered from 1 August 2007.

In this case, as his sales to the general public would have been at the same selling price, output tax would have been additional income.

The input tax on the stock purchased in December 2006 (to the extent retained at 1 July 2007); the printing equipment; and the standard rated expenses incurred in the six months before registration (unless consumed or related to supplies made before 1 July 2007), can be recovered. However, the input tax on the advertising campaign could not be recovered as it was incurred more than six months before registration.

Assuming no restriction on the standard rated expenses incurred in the six months before registration, the additional profit is therefore:

		£	£
Output VAT			
q/e 31.3.07 £19,400× 17.5%			3,395
q/e 30.6.07 £29,600 × 17.5%			5,180
			8,575
Less: (1) *input tax on goods sold*			
q/e 31.3.07 £(14,900 + 3,600 – 3,800) = £14,700 × 17.5%		2,573	
q/e 30.6.07 £(16,700 + 3,800 – 4,400) = £16,100 × 17.5%		2,817	
(2) *input tax on advertising not recoverable*			
£1,400 × 17.5%		245	(5,635)
Increased profit			2,940

24 Leo Topper

Text references. Chapters 17 to 19 deal with IHT. Trading income is in Chapter 6 with IBAs in Chapter 7. The basic rules for gains are in Chapters 11 and 12. VAT is in Chapter 28. Corporation tax is in Chapters 21 and 22 with groups in Chapter 26.

Top tips. It is unlikely that you will get so many computations in one question in the exam. Use this question to make sure that you can perform straightforward calculations quickly and efficiently using standard proformas, feeding your results into your written answer.

Easy marks. Set up your letter to obtain the easy presentation mark. For part (b) be sure to discuss how your answer impacts part (a).

			Marks
(a)	Lifetime gift		
	Valuation of death estate	½	
	Availability of BPR	3	
	Debt	½	
	Exempt legacy	½	
	Nil band	½	
	Tax rate	½	
	Tax due date	1	
	Person liable	½	
	Return due date	1	
			8
(b)	*Income tax*		
	Cessation rules	1	
	Overlap (opening year rules)	1	
	Higher rate taxpayer	½	
	CGT		
	Gain before taper relief	½	
	Taper relief	½	
	Annual exemption	½	
	CGT @ 40%	½	
	Impact on IHT liability	1	
	Max		5
(c)	½ mark for each criterion and explanation (max)	3	
	Taxation if capital disposal		
	CGT (no indexation or taper)	1	
	Chattels rules	1	
	Taper relief	1	
	Taxation if trading income		
	Income tax	½	
	NIC	1	
	VAT	1	
	Max		7

(d)   *VAT*

Supplies	½	
Video tapes	½	
Electricity	½	
Wages	½	
Entertaining	½	
VAT due – annual accounting	1	
y/e 31 December 2008	1	
Max		4

Corporation tax

Adjustment of profits	1	
IBAs	1	
Property business income	1	
CAs on property business equipment	1	
Corporation tax	1	
Max		3

Implications for purchase of shares

Associates	1	
CT groups and implications	2	
Current year losses	1	
Brought forward losses	2	
Capital losses	1	
Group VAT registration	1	
Max		6
Format/ presentation		2
		35

PRIVATE AND CONFIDENTIAL

[Our address]

[Your address]

[Date]

Dear Tim

TAX ISSUES

This letter deals with the tax position for your father and his estate, as well as tax issues arising for VDV Ltd.

(a)   **Inheritance tax on your father's estate**

The IHT arising on your father's estate on death will be £291,200 (see Appendix 1).

You will note that Business Property Relief (BPR) is not available for the quoted company shares, as your father did not have a controlling interest in the company. Nor is BPR available for the cash proceeds received from the sale of his business. The relief is only available if the business had been owned at the date of death and there was no binding contract for sale.

The tax must be paid by you, as the Executor of the estate, by 31 December 2006 to avoid interest running from this date until the actual date of payment. You have until 30 June 2007 to submit the IHT account.

You will need to declare the lifetime gift to the discretionary trust on the IHT return, but any additional IHT that may be due is the responsibility of the trustees.

(b) **Your father's income tax and CGT position**

Your father's earnings from his directorship with VDV Ltd make him a higher rate tax payer.

His income tax liability for the year of his death is £9,600 and his CGT liability is £15,480.

See Appendix 2 for our calculation of these figures.

These may both be deducted from your father's estate, so reducing the IHT liability by £10,032 ((£9,600 + £15,480) @ 40%)

(c) **Your disposals of antique furniture**

HMRC look at several criteria to decide whether proceeds from the disposals should be treated as capital proceeds (and therefore assessed to capital gains tax) or trading receipts (assessed to income tax).

The criteria relevant to you are as follows.

Factors to consider	Indicative of a capital gain or trading income?
Profit motive	The profit motive is not clear. You inherited the items, some of which you did not wish to add to your own personal collection. As you did not purchase them with the intention of selling them at a profit this could be treated as not trading. However, you also sold three of your own items for a profit. A profit motive would indicate trade.
Subject matter	Antiques are normally acquired for personal pleasure or for their investment potential, which is not indicative of trading.
Length of ownership	You did not own the antiques for long as the disposal was shortly after you acquired/inherited them. If assets are only held for a short period, this suggests a trading profit. However, they were bought by your father and inherited (not bought) by you.
Frequency of transactions	Isolated transactions would be treated as a capital gain. However, more than one similar transaction (as in this case) could be indicative of trading.
Supplementary work	No supplementary work is carried out. This suggests a capital disposal, not a trading activity.
Reason for sale	As an unwanted legacy, the disposal appears to be a result of a personal choice between items. This does not suggest a trading activity.

Overall, it is likely that these transactions will be treated as capital disposals. This is mainly because:

- You are not personally involved in the antiques trade, and
- The acquisition of the personal assets was a result of a legacy (not a purchase by you with a view to profit).

If the sales are treated as capital disposals:

- CGT will be due if the proceeds exceed the probate value (MV at date of death)
- Chattels costing and sold for under £6,000 are exempt. Chattels sold for ≥ £6,000 would be chargeable but a restriction (5/3rds rule) would apply.
- There would be no indexation allowance (as acquired after 5 April 1998) and no taper relief (as not held for at least three years).

If instead they are treated as trading income:

- The excess of proceeds over probate value will be liable to income tax. No chargeable gains arise on the disposal of the assets as they are treated as trading stock.

- If the profit exceeds the lower limits, Class 2 and Class 4 National Insurance contributions would be payable.

- As the turnover exceeds £61,000, the business might need to register for, and charge, VAT.

(d) (i) **VDV Ltd VAT payable – y/e 31 December 2006 (ignoring VAT on rental activity)**

The projected VAT due for the year ended 31 December 2006 is £105,700 (Appendix 3).

As VDV Ltd is registered under the annual accounting system, the due dates for payment are as follows:

	£
Interim monthly payments	
30 April 2006 to 31 December 2006 (inclusive) (9 × £9,000)	81,000
Final payment – 28 February 2007	24,700
	105,700

The VAT return must be submitted by 28 February 2007.

VAT position for year ended 31 December 2007

VDV Ltd's taxable turnover (£1,420,000) currently exceeds the limit for joining the annual accounting scheme (£1,350,000) but falls below the limit where withdrawal from the scheme is required (£1,600,000).

As a result VDV Ltd can remain within the scheme and will pay nine monthly interim payments of £10,570 (£105,700 ÷ 10) starting on 30 April 2007.

(ii) **Corporation tax – y/e 31 December 2006**

The projected corporation tax payable by VDV Ltd for the year ended 31 December 2006 is £89,750 (see Appendix 3).

(ii) **Purchase of an 85% interest in the shares of MD Ltd**

Taxation consequences

Associated companies

VDV Ltd will have an associated company. The limits for determining the rate of corporation tax payable by each company must be halved.

This could increase the rate of tax payable by VDV Ltd. (MD Ltd is currently loss-making and therefore unlikely to be paying corporation tax.)

Group definition – Capital gains group and group relief group

As MD Ltd will be a 75% subsidiary, both companies form a group for capital gains and group relief purposes.

Opportunities for use of trading and capital losses

Current year trading losses in MD Ltd

Group relief claims are possible between the companies in any direction, but for current year trading losses only. Brought forward trading losses cannot be group relieved.

Brought forward trading losses in MD Ltd

MD Ltd's brought forward trading losses can only be carried forward and utilised in that company. However, it is important to remember that where there is a major change in the nature or conduct of trade in the following three years, the use of these losses is denied.

Therefore care should be taken to avoid a major change in the nature or conduct of trade of MD Ltd.

Capital losses in MD Ltd

Capital losses brought forward in MD Ltd cannot be group relieved/transferred to VDV Ltd. They can only be utilised by MD Ltd against future capital gains.

Furthermore, the use of these 'pre-entry capital losses' is restricted in the future. These losses cannot be matched against gains realised on assets transferred to MD Ltd intra-group at nil gain/nil loss.

Other opportunities

Capital gains privileges available

- Inter-group transfers at nil gain/nil loss possible.

- Group roll-over relief claims possible.

- Minimisation of group corporation tax by electing for gains to crystallise in the company paying the lowest marginal rate of tax, and use of post-acquisition capital losses as soon as possible.

Group VAT registration possible

Both companies can form a VAT group and submit one group VAT return, which saves on administration and allows companies to ignore accounting for VAT on any inter-group transactions.

If you have any further queries or would like to discuss the above further, please do not hesitate to contact me.

Yours sincerely

Tax manager

Appendix 1 – Inheritance tax liabilities

Gift to discretionary trust – May 2000

	£
Gross chargeable amount (given)	485,000

Uses nil rant band

Note. You were asked to calculate the IHT due on LT's estate, not the additional IHT (if any) due from the trustees of the discretionary trust.

Death estate

	£	£
VDV Ltd shares	500,000	
Less BPR (100%)	(500,000)	
		Nil
Film plc shares		25,000
Bank account		300,000
Shares in an ISA		17,000
Antiques		175,000
Cottage		437,500
Motor car		23,500
		978,000
Less debts – loan to bank		(150,000)
		828,000
Less exempt legacies – charity		(100,000)
Gross chargeable estate		728,000
IHT on estate at death (£728,000 × 40%)		291,200

(No nil rate band available).

Appendix 2 – income tax and CGT liabilities 2006/07

Trading income

	£
2006/07 year of cessation	
1 July 2005 – 31 May 2006	46,000
Less overlap profits (W)	(18,000)
	24,000
Tax @ 40% (higher rate taxpayer)	£9,600

Disposal of freehold property

	£
Sale proceeds (June 2006)	300,000
Cost (July 1998)	(110,000)
Gain before taper relief	190,000
Gain after taper relief (BA held > 2 yrs: 25%)	47,500
Less Annual exemption	(8,800)
Taxable gain	38,700
CGT £38,700 × 40%	£15,480

Working

Overlap profits

		£
1998/99	Opening year – actual profits	
	1 July 1998 – 5 April 1999	
	($^{9}/_{12}$ × £24,000)	18,000
1999/00	Second year – 12 months ending in the tax year	
	y/e 30 June 1999	24,000
Overlap profits	(1 July 1998 – 5 April 1999)	18,000

Appendix 3 – VDV Ltd tax liabilities year ended 31 December 2007

VAT payable

	£
VAT on outputs	
Standard rated supplies (£1,420,000 × 17½%)	248,500
VAT on inputs	
Purchases of videos and DVDs (£800,000 × 17½%)	(140,000)
Wages (Note 1)	Nil
Electricity (£16,000 × 17½%)	(2,800)
Entertaining customers (Note 2)	Nil
Depreciation (Note 3)	Nil
VAT payable for the year	105,700

Notes

1 Wages are outside the scope of VAT.

2 VAT incurred in respect of entertaining customers is not recoverable.

3 Depreciation is not a supply of goods or services for VAT purposes. VAT incurred on the purchase of equipment would have been recovered at the date the equipment was acquired.

Corporation tax payable

	£
Trading profit (W1)	366,100
Property business income (W3)	33,900
PCTCT	400,000
Corporation tax (W5) (£400,000 × 30%)	120,000
Less Marginal relief $^{11}/_{400}$ × (£1,500,000 – £400,000)	(30,250)
Corporation tax payable	89,750

Workings

(1) *Trading profit*

	£
Operating profit per accounts	330,000
Add Entertaining clients	7,000
Depreciation	57,000
	394,000
Less Capital allowances	
Plant and machinery (given)	(15,900)
Industrial building (W2)	(12,000)
Adjusted trading profit	366,100

(2) *Industrial buildings allowances*

A writing down allowance (WDA) of 4% is available on the cost of the factory (excluding land) within its tax life.

WDA = £300,000 × 4%	£12,000

(3) *Property business income*

	£
Rental income per accounts (amounts receivable)	42,000
Less Allowable deductions	
Business rates	(4,000)
Management costs	(1,500)
Capital allowances (W4)	(2,600)
Property business income	33,900

(4)   *Capital allowances – rental property*

		£
Air-conditioning unit		6,500
FYA (40%) (Note)		(2,600)
WDV c/f		3,900

Note. A first year allowance of 40% is available on the air-conditioning unit as VDV Ltd is a small business and the purchase is before 1 April 2006.

(5)   *Corporation tax rates*

			£
PCTCT = Profits (as no dividends received)			400,000
Small companies	– upper limit		1,500,000
	– lower limit		300,000
			Marginal relief

25 Tay Limited

Text references. Group aspects covered in Chapter 26. VAT penalties are dealt with in Chapter 28. Overseas aspects of groups is covered in Chapter 27. Capital allowances are in Chapter 7. Use of corporation tax losses are in Chapter 24.

Top tips. This required a highly written answer. Watch your time – don't overrun. A plan may help especially to ensure you don't forget some of your first thoughts as you get bogged down in writing your answer.

There are often more marks available than those stated in the requirements. You do not need to cover every single point in your solution, as we have in the model answer, to pass the question: you just need to get the main points.

In part (d) submission of an incorrect VAT return leads to a misdeclaration penalty. Penalties and VAT are very popular exam topics.

Easy marks. Write brief, to the point, concise comments to secure the marks. Don't waffle and only make your point once – no extra marks for saying the same thing twice.

Part (b) specifically asked for calculations as well as advice. Marks are awarded specifically for the numbers – make sure you do them.

In part (c) the examiner specifically asked you to ignore transfer pricing. So ignore it!

Examiner's comments. This question, which primarily concerned a UK company acquiring a UK subsidiary, and considering investment in a company overseas, produced a wide range of answers.

In part (a)(i) very few candidates were aware of the rules on capital allowances for intangible assets. A significant number confused intellectual property with industrial buildings (presumably due to the word 'property'!), and referred to the allowances available to these.

In calculating the corporation tax (CT) in (a)(ii), most candidates correctly reduced the small companies' rate limits as a result of having gained an associate. Most realised group relief would be available, but failed to calculate it correctly, as being from the date of acquisition to the end of the loss-making period only.

Virtually no candidates recognised the issue in (iii) which was regarding the possible restriction in carrying forward a trading loss following the change in ownership of the company, but, admittedly, this is a tricky area.

It was surprising in part (b) how few candidates recognised the problem of the pre-entry capital loss, most just discussing, often in considerable detail, the rules for offsetting losses against gains in a gains group, and thereby missing out on several marks.

In part (c) most candidates seemed to be aware of the issues, but didn't always make it clear in their answer which alternative (purchase of shares or assets) they were dealing with. Subheadings are useful here. You cannot leave it to the marker to guess whether a particular point you are making relates to a share purchase or an asset purchase. Several marks were undoubtedly lost unnecessarily in this way.

Knowledge of the VAT issues in part (d) was, in the main, very sketchy. Several candidates used words such as 'surcharge' and 'misdeclaration', but without appearing to understand the context in which they used them. This is textbook stuff, and should be learned accurately.

Marking scheme

				Marks
(a)	(i)	Allowances usually equal to amortisation	½	
		Alternative 4% allowance where no depreciation	½	
		Time limit for election	½	
		Election irrevocable	½	
				2
	(ii)	Deduction for IP allowance	½	
		Group relieve only post-acquisition loss	½	
		'Lower of' calculation (2 × ½)	1	
		Corporation tax at 30%	½	
		Marginal relief calculation	½	
				3
	(iii)	Change of ownership and nature of trade	½	
		Three year time limit	½	
		Losses blocked at date of acquisition	½	
		Quantify losses/tax at risk (2 × ½)	1	
		Advice and recommendation	½	
			Max	2
(b)		Awareness of pre-entry losses	½	
		Formula basis: Statement/explanation	1	
		Calculation of allowable loss	½	
		Pre-entry proportion	½	
		Alternative election: treatment and effect	½	
		calculation of pre-entry loss	½	
		Recommend making the election	½	
		Use of pre-entry loss – possibilities	½	
			Max	3
(c)		Acquisition of shares:		
		associated company	½	
		limits reduced, possibly increased tax	½	
		profits taxed in Portugal	½	
		remitted profits taxed as overseas income	½	
		double tax relief for withholding tax	½	
		double tax relief for underlying tax	½	
		requirement for 10% plus holding	½	
		relief is lower of UK/Portuguese tax	½	
		losses cannot be relieved against UK profits	½	
		Acquisition of assets		
		permanent establishment, so no extra associate	½	
		taxed in UK as extension of trade	½	
		permanent establishment: taxed in Portugal	½	
		DTR available	½	
		capital allowances can be claimed	½	
		loss offset automatically as part of UK company	½	
			Max	6

(d) Default surcharge: issue surcharge notice   ½
                          runs to anniversary   ½
                          further defaults extend period   ½
                          further late payments will incur a penalty   ½
                          2% initially rising to 15%   ½
     Misdeclaration penalty:
        awareness of potential penalty   ½
        significant understatement: definition   ½
                                     calculation   ½
        penalty rate of 15% of VAT lost   ½
        voluntary disclosure   ½
        next return/period of grace   ½
        in writing/ASAP   ½
     Default interest: chargeable even with voluntary disclosure   ½
                         basis period   ½
     Ethical issues   1
                                                              Max   5
                                                                                    ──
                                                                                    21
                                                                                    ══

(a)   (i)   **Tax allowances**

Intellectual property is an intangible asset. The writing down allowances on intangible assets are usually equal to the depreciation charge in the accounts. If there is no depreciation charge in the accounts an alternative is available.

Tay Limited will be entitled to claim capital allowances for the intellectual property it purchased.

The allowance will be 4% of the cost ie 4% × £250,000 = £10,000 p.a. for 25 years.

The irrevocable election for the capital allowances must be within 2 years of the end of the accounting period.

      (ii) Corporation Tax y/e 31 March 2007

	£
Trade profit	250,000
Less: Allowance	(10,000)
PCTCT	240,000
Less: group relief (W1)	(40,000)
Revised PCTCT	200,000
Tax @ 30%	60,000
Less: Marginal relief (W2)	
11/400 × (750,000 − 200,000)	(15,125)
CT due	44,875

Workings

(1) *Group relief*

Trade losses may be shared between the two companies but only for the corresponding accounting periods since Trent joined the group ie for the period 1.9.06 to 31.12.06.

Loss available for group relief is therefore the lower of:

Profit of Tay Ltd £240,000 × $^4/_{12}$ = £80,000
Loss of Trent Ltd £120,000 × $^4/_{12}$ = £40,000 ie £40,000

(2) *CT limits*

£1,500,000/2	£750,000
£300,000/2	£150,000

Therefore Tay Limited is a marginal relief company

(iii) Transferring work to Trent Limited

The problem with transferring orders to Trent Limited is that HMRC may argue that there has been a 'major change in the nature or conduct' of Trent Limited's trade which would result in the corporation tax losses not being able to be carried forward in Trent Limited to use against profits from the orders.

This treatment is applied if, within **three** years of a change in ownership, there is a major change in the trade.

A change in customers could be a fundamental change for these purposes and it is therefore essential that Trent Limited maintains its original suppliers, pricing policies etc to avoid a successful attack by HMRC.

If there is a major change in the trade within 3 years then losses of £380,000 (£300,000 + $^8/_{12}$ × £120,000) will be wasted, with potential tax reductions of £114,000 (£380,000 × 30%). The charges should be delayed until 1 September 2009 if possible.

(b) **Capital gains implications for sale of buildings**

The two companies are in a gains group for corporation tax purposes. This means that assets may be transferred around the group at no gain/ no loss in order to take advantage of lower tax rates or capital losses available elsewhere in the group.

The issue for Trent Limited and Tay Limited is that Trent Limited had the unrealised loss when it was acquired by Tay Limited and therefore the pre-entry element of the loss will not be available for use against Tay Limited's gain.

The available loss would be limited to the amount of loss that has arisen since the group was formed. This can be done on a time basis or based on the market value when Tay Limited joined the group.

On the time basis, the available loss would be calculated as follows:

	£
Proceeds	250,000
Less: cost	(400,000)
Loss	(150,000)

Time since joined group: 1.9.06 – 1.9.07 = 1 yr

Total ownership: 9.96 – 9.07 = 11yrs	£
$^1/_{11}$ × (150,000)	(13,636)

On the market value basis, the available loss would be calculated as follows:

	£
Proceeds	250,000
Less: MV when joined group	(300,000)
Loss	(50,000)

The company would clearly choose the market value basis to obtain a larger loss. Assuming Tay Limited's asset is transferred to Trent Limited prior to sale, or an election is made to treat the gain as having been made in Trent Limited, the remaining gain would be taxed at Trent Limited's marginal rate (19%), as follows:

	£
Gain	75,000
Less: capital loss	(50,000)
Chargeable gain	25,000
Tax @ 19%	4,750

The balance of the loss (£100,000) can only be used in Trent Limited against gains arising on sales of its own assets.

(c)   **Acquiring shares or assets of Tagus LDA**

If Tay Limited acquires the shares of Tagus LDA it would be acquiring a overseas subsidiary company; if it acquires the assets and continues the business in Portugal it would be acquiring a overseas permanent establishment.

The corporation tax (CT) issues that Tay Limited should consider are therefore:

CT issue	Overseas subsidiary	Overseas permanent establishment (ie branch)
Associates	There will be another associate for CT purposes. CT limits will need to be divided by three.	Not an associate.
Losses	Losses made by EU subsidiaries may be relieved against the profits of UK group companies, but only where all possibilities for the losses to be relieved at any time against profits in the subsidiary's own country have been exhausted.	Not in a group relief group but in any case, overseas losses will be set against UK profits.
Capital gains group	Will not be part of the UK gains group.	Overseas gains will be included in UK company's trade profits
Profit	Will not be taxed in the UK unless dividends paid to UK owner.	Will be included as part of the UK company's profits.
DTR	Lower of UK tax (average rate) and overseas tax, which includes both withholding and underlying tax (as owns > 10%).	Lower of UK tax (average rate) and overseas tax (27.5%).
P&M	Will continue with Portuguese method.	FYAs available (where applicable), then WDAs at 25%.
Interest deduction	No trade deduction for loan interest incurred in connection with purchase.	Interest paid will be deductible so long as money borrowed wholly and exclusively for the trade.
Sale of shares/ assets	Substantial shareholding exemption may apply if sell shares after at least 12 months.	Gain on assets sold; base cost will be market value when acquired by UK company

Top tips. It is perfectly acceptable to use a table, like the one above, where you are comparing or contrasting two areas. It may even help you to brainstorm the issues

(d)   **Incorrect VAT return**

As the error is greater than £2,000, Trent Limited should notify HMRC (or complete Form 652) to avoid a possible Misdeclaration Penalty (MP) being imposed.

Interest will still be charged.

If Trent Limited does not notify HMRC before HMRC discover the error there will be an MP if the misdeclaration is higher than the greater of:

(i)   £1 million; or

(ii)   30% of the Gross Amount of Tax (GAT).

GAT is the total of the correct output VAT plus the correct input VAT:

	£
Total output VAT	
– reported	87,500
– under-reported	55,000
Correct output VAT	142,500
Correct input VAT	40,000
GAT	182,500
@ 30%	54,750

As the misdeclaration was £55,000, which exceeds £54,750, an MP will apply.

The penalty is 15% × error:

£55,000 @ 15% = £8,250.

As part of the tax liability for the quarter to 31 March 2007 is paid late, HMRC may issue a surcharge liability notice. Therefore if an VAT is paid late, or return made late in the next four quarters a surcharge will apply, starting at 2% × unpaid tax.

You should advise Trent Ltd that it should notify its error to HMRC at the earliest opportunity. If Trent Ltd agrees you need take no further action, assuming the under declaration was a genuine error. If Trent Ltd refused to notify the error, then you would be obliged to refuse to act for the company as this would be the concealment of a tax irregularity. You should also report the matter to your firm's money laundering officer.

26 Question with analysis: Andrew

Text references. CGT on leases is in Chapter 15. Accrued income scheme is in Chapter 3. EIS is in Chapters 1 and 2 with EIS CGT deferral relief in Chapter 14. Pensions are looked at in Chapter 2. Types of finance are dealt with in Chapter 31.

Top tips. The question in part (a)(i) asked for a **chargeable gain** – this is after taper relief but before deducting the annual exemption.

The examiner prefers to see questions with several parts presented with the parts in the correct order; you don't need to have done the earlier parts to do the later parts but make sure you answer all parts and put them in the correct order when you're done.

Easy marks. Show all your working to achieve maximum marks. Plus if you've made a mistake you can gain some marks for your workings.

When answering a question asking for general rules such as part (b)(i) keep points short and snappy. Make a new point on a new line. This lets the marker see your points clearly set out and allocate marks accordingly.

Along a similar line if you can answer using a table (such as in (b)(ii) here) then do so – again great presentation and it all helps gain easy marks.

Examiner's comments. This was a mixed question, largely discursive, on a variety of investment and finance issues for both an individual and companies.

In part (a)(i), many candidates produced a correct calculation of the chargeable gain on assignment of a short lease. Note that a 'chargeable gain' is after deducting taper relief, but before deducting the annual exemption. Failure to appreciate this led to a failure to gain all marks, or time being wasted.

Surprisingly few candidates knew that government stock was exempt from CGT, with most calculating an unnecessary gain. Virtually no-one mentioned the accrued income scheme, although those who appreciated that there were income tax implications in respect of the interest did gain marks.

Part (b) was generally well done, with many candidates showing a good, detailed knowledge of the conditions for and impact of EIS relief. However many then spoiled this somewhat by going on to discuss VCTs in equal detail.

				Marks
(a)	(i)	Restriction of cost	½	
		Indexation	½	
		Taper relief: non business asset rate (2 × ½)	1	
				2
	(ii)	Exempt from CGT	½	
		IT under accrued income scheme	½	
		Nominal value >£5,000	½	
		Taxed when next interest payment due	½	
		Year 2006/07	½	
		Income accrued on a daily basis to 14 March	½	
		Paid gross/taxed at 40% via self assessment	½	
		Ongoing source within half-yearly payments	½	
		Max		3
(b)	(i)	Identification of EIS relief	½	
		Qualifying individual:		
		not employee	½	
		not director at time of issue	½	
		No material (≥30%) interest	½	
		Timing requirements	½	
		Relevant date definition	½	
		Currently connected	½	
		Investment by fourth individual advisable	½	
		Eligible shares		
		New and fully paid up	½	
		Not redeemable for three years	½	
		No preferential rights to dividends	½	
		Qualifying company		
		Unquoted	½	
		Not controlled by another company	½	
		Qualifying trade, wholly/mainly in UK (2 × ½)	1	
		Time limits/% reinvestment (2 × ½)	1	
		Income tax:		
		Tax reducer	½	
		20%	½	
		£400,000 limit	½	
		≤50% of investment pre-6 Oct carried back	½	
		Capital gains tax:		
		EIS shares exempt	½	
		Capital losses allowable, reduced by relief	½	
		Deferral relief for any gains	½	
		Set loss against income	½	
		Timing requirements	½	
		income tax relief not essential	½	
		Application to Andrew	½	
		Relief withdrawn if:		
		Shares sold within three year period	½	
		Value received from company	½	
		Individual or company ceases to qualify	½	
		Repayment of loans possible issue	½	
		Max		11

(ii) *Equity:*

Costs of issuing share capital are not tax deductible	½	
Costs of making distributions are not tax deductible	½	
Distributions themselves not tax deductible	½	
Loan finance/debt:		
Interest on loan to finance business is allowable	½	
Capital costs not deductible as trading expense	½	
Incidental costs of raising loan finance are allowable	½	
Max		2

(c)			
	Current contributions	½	
	Relief for contributions	1	
	Maximum	½	
	Annual allowance	½	
	Lifetime allowance	½	
			3
	Total		25

(a) (i) **Assignment of lease**

	£
Proceeds	90,000
Less cost (W)	(46,895)
Less: IA	

$$\frac{162.6 - 152.9}{152.9} = 0.063 \times £46,895 \qquad (2,954)$$

	40,151
Chargeable gain 6.4.98 – 5.07 = 9yrs + bonus = 10yrs: 60%	24,091

Working

$$\text{Cost} \times \frac{\%36\text{yrs}}{\%47\text{yrs}}$$

	£
$£50,000 \times \dfrac{92.761}{98.902}$	46,895

(ii) **Disposal of government stock**

Government stock is exempt from CGT.

It is, however, a security for the purposes of the accrued income scheme, if it has a nominal value in excess of £5,000.

As a result, when Andrew received the first interest payment in the year that he bought the stock, he would have obtained some relief from tax for the period before he actually held the stock

Similarly, in the year that he sold the stock he would have been taxed on the income that had accrued up to the date that he sold it, even though he did not actually receive it.

2000/01

First interest payment received – 20/10/00

	£
7% × £10,000 × ½	350
Less: rebate relief [21.4.00 – 1.6.00]	
42/183 × 350	(80)
Taxable interest	270

2005/06 – year of sale

	£
Interest received 20/4/05	350
Interest received 20/10/05	350
Taxable interest	700

2006/07
No interest payment received 20.4.06
But interest accrued from 21.10.05 – 14.3.06

	£
145/182 × 350	279
Taxable as interest income	279
Reported in self assessment tax return for 2006/07 and taxed at 40% =	£112

Top tips. This was a difficult part of the question – it was only worth 3 marks so hopefully you had a stab and then moved on. Don't waste time stressing over one requirement when there are so many more that you **can** get marks for.

(b)   (i)   **Investment in Scalar Ltd**

If Andrew invests in Scalar Ltd (S Ltd), which is an Enterprise Investment Scheme (EIS) company, he will be entitled to the following reliefs:

EIS income tax relief

A tax reducer of 20% × his investment (maximum £400,000).

May carry back up to 50% × investment (maximum £50,000) to obtain relief in the prior year, where made before 6 October.

This can reduce his tax liability to nil but not create a repayment.

EIS CGT exemption

Any shares attracting the above income tax relief will be exempt from CGT if they are sold after a minimum holding period of 3 years.

EIS CGT deferral relief

If an individual disposes of any asset at a gain he can defer the gain (along with its original taper relief) where he purchases EIS shares in the period 12 months before to 3 years after the disposal.

Unlike the above two reliefs, there is no maximum amount that can be deferred. The investor may choose the optimum amount of relief in order to preserve the annual exemption, losses and taper relief.

Loss relief

If an investor sells EIS shares at a loss, that loss may be used as a normal capital loss or it may be used against income.

Conditions

There are a number of conditions that must be satisfied both by the company and Andrew in order for the income tax relief and CGT exemption to be available:

S Ltd

Must be an unquoted (AIM is included for these purposes) trading company performing qualifying activities.

Prohibited activities include land, financial, legal, accountancy and property-back trades.

The company must have gross assets of ≤ £7 million before and ≤ £8 million after the share issue.

80% of the funds raised must be used by the company (or a 90% subsidiary) in the first 12 months and the balance in the following 12 months.

The trade must take place wholly or mainly in the UK.

The shares issued must be new, ordinary shares. They must be fully paid up and not redeemable.

The above conditions must continue to be satisfied for at least three years from the share issue.

Andrew (& other investors)

Must subscribe for the shares (ie cannot simply purchase them from the stock market) wholly in cash.

Must not be 'connected' with the company ie cannot be an employee or own more than 30% of the shares/ voting rights/ rights to assets on a winding up, along with their 'associates' (e.g. spouse or child but not brother or sister).

Note that if there were only three investors they would all have >30% of the shares and so the relief would not be available.

This rule applies for the period of one year before and three years after the share issue.

If the investor receives 'value' from the company in this period the relief can be adjusted/ withdrawn.

The interest received from the company in respect of the proposed loans could be considered to be 'value' if it is not at a commercial rate.

It would be advisable for the company to issue the shares and then obtain the loans from the investors to avoid the loan interest being treated as a return of value.

Conclusion

If there are four investors who subscribe for the shares prior to making loans to the company and all the above conditions are satisfied, the immediate relief available to each will be: £112,500 @ 20% = £22,500 tax reducer.

(ii) **Equity and loan finance tax implications**

	Equity finance	Loan finance
Legal costs	Not tax deductible	Tax deductible
Return to investors	Dividends – not deductible for tax purposes	Interest paid will be part of a trading or non-trading loan relationship (depending on reason for raising money). Deductible in both cases

(c) Even though Andrew and his employer contribute to his occupational pension he may still contribute to a personal pension.

His current contributions are:

	£
Andrew: 6% × £300,000	18,000
Employer: 8% × £300,000	24,000
Occupational pension	42,000

He is not taxed on the employer contributions ie they are not treated as salary or a taxable benefit.

He will obtain tax relief at his marginal rate (40%) for his own contributions as they will reduce the amount of employment income he will need to report on his tax return:

	£
Earnings	300,000
Less: contributions	(18,000)
Employment income	282,000

The maximum that he may contribute to a pension in the year is the greater of:

(i)   £3,600; and

(ii)   100% × earnings

        ie £300,000.

However, there is a 40% charge if he contributes more than the annual allowance, which is £215,000 (2006/07).

To avoid any charge Andrew may therefore contribute:

	£
Annual allowance	215,000
Less: total occupational pension contributions	(42,000)
Available contributions	173,000

If he makes this contribution it will be paid net of basic rate tax ie 78% × £173,000 = £134,940. In this way he receives basic rate tax relief automatically.

As he is a higher rate taxpayer he will also obtain higher rate relief by extending his basic rate band by the gross contribution. This amount will be taxed at the basic rate of tax rather than the higher rates. He will therefore obtain 18% (40% – 22%) relief in this way.

In terms of limits for the future, Andrew should be aware that there is a lifetime allowance that applies to the amount of contributions he can make over his lifetime. This is currently £1,500,000.

> **Top tips.** The 2007 exams are the first time that the new pension rules can be examined – make sure that you are aware of the new rules and can write sensibly about them.

27 Question with analysis: Bluetone Ltd

> **Text references.** IHT aspects of question covered in Chapters 17 to 19. CGT gift relief is in Chapter 14 and the CGT computation is in Chapters 11 and 12. Purchase of own shares is dealt with in Chapter 23.
>
> **Top tips.** You may need to use two different values for the same asset in a question: one for CGT (usually the market value), the other for IHT (the loss to donor or diminution in value). They are frequently tested in the same question; do not confuse the two!
>
> **Easy marks.** Ensure you show all of your workings, eg for the share valuations and how you calculated the average IHT rate. Never do a working in your head/on your calculator without writing it down on your answer script. There are marks available for workings.

Marking scheme

			Marks
(a)	Wedding gift	½	
	Chargeable lifetime transfer	½	
	Shares in Expanse plc	1	
	Shares in Bluetone Ltd/units in Word-Growth	1	
	BPR not available	1	
	Building society deposits/life policy	1	
	Income tax/funeral expenses	1	
	House	1	
	IHT liability/IHT due by Melody	1	
	Due date/instalments	1½	
	Max		8
(b)	*CGT:*		
	Gift relief	2	
	Deemed consideration	1	
	Cost/Indexation	1	
	Taper relief	1	
	Annual exemption/CGT	1	
	IHT:		
	Value transferred	2	
	BPR	1	
	Max		8
(c)	Capital gain	1	
	Taper relief	1	
	Additional income tax liability on distribution	2	
	Conclusion	1	
	Max		4
			20

(a) *Melody's IHT liability*

The lifetime gifts made by her father will affect Melody's IHT liability as they will use up part of the available nil rate band. The amount of the lifetime gifts are:

		£
PET		30,000
Less:	Marriage exemption	(5,000)
	Annual exemption (02/03)	(3,000)
	Annual exemption (01/02)	(3,000)
		19,000

		£
Chargeable lifetime transfer		
Gift		172,000
Less:	Annual exemption (03/04)	(3,000)
		169,000

The available nil band on death is therefore £(285,000 − 19,000 − 169,000) = £97,000:

Death estate

Personalty

	£	£
Bluetone Ltd Shares (Note 1) £11 × 50,000		550,000

Expanse plc shares

Lower of

$$\frac{1}{4} \text{ up } \frac{320 - 312}{4} + 312 = 314$$

and

$$\text{mid-bargain } \frac{324 + 282}{2} = 303$$

	£	£
ie 303p × 42,000		127,260
World-Growth units (80p × 26,000)		20,800
Building society deposits (39,000 + 3,000) (Note 2)		32,000
Life policy (proceeds)		61,000
		791,060
Less: income tax	6,600	
Gambling debts (Note 3)	Nil	
Funeral expenses	3,460	(10,060)
		781,000
Realty		
House	125,000	
Less: secured debt	(42,000)	83,000
Chargeable estate		864,000

Notes

1   No BPR is available as Melody's father did not own the Bluetone Ltd shares for at least two years prior to his death.

2   No IHT exemption is available for an ISA, only for IT and CGT.

3   Gambling debts are not deductible.

IHT on estate

£(864,000 − 97,000) = £767,000 × 40% = £306,800

Melody's IHT

$$\frac{550,000}{864,000} \times £306,800 = \underline{£195,301}$$

£195,301 is all due for payment on 31 August 2007 (or the delivery of the IHT account, if earlier).

Melody can elect to pay the tax in 10 equal annual interest-free instalments of £19,530. The first instalment is due on 31 August 2007.

(b)   *CGT on Liam's gift*

	£
Deemed proceeds (£9 × 30,000)	270,000
Less: cost	(30,000)
Unindexed gain	240,000
Less: IA to April 1998	
$$\frac{162.6 - 135.1}{135.1} \times £30,000$$	(6,107)
Indexed gain	233,893

Gain immediately chargeable to CGT (excess proceeds):

£(75,000 − 30,000) = £45,000

	£
Gain after taper relief (25% × £45,000)	11,250
Less: Annual exemption	(8,800)
Taxable gain	2,450
Tax @ 40%	980

Gift relief £(233,893 − 45,000) = £188,893

No taper relief is available to reduce the gain deferred. Liam's son's qualifying period for taper relief will run from 20 March 2007. Thus the remainder of Liam's taper relief will be lost.

IHT on Liam's gift

The value of the lifetime transfer will be:

		£
Before:	50,000 × £15 (part of 50% holding with Opal)	750,000
After:	20,000 × £12.50 (part of 35% holding with Opal)	(250,000)
		500,000
Less:	Proceeds paid	(75,000)
Gift		425,000

BPR will be available at 100% as these are unquoted trading company shares. However, the relief will be withdrawn if Liam dies within seven years and his son does not own the shares as business property at the date of Liam's death (unless the shares have been sold and replaced with other business property).

(c)   *Noel*

If repurchase treated as distribution:

£(550,000 − 50,000) = £500,000 net

	£
Grossed up 100/90 × £500,000 =	555,556
Tax @ 32.5%	180,556
Less: credit	(55,556)
Tax to pay	125,000

If treated as CGT disposal:

	£
Proceeds	550,000
Less: cost	(50,000)
Unindexed gain	500,000
Less: IA to April 1998	
$\dfrac{162.6 - 135.1}{135.1} \times £50,000$	(10,178)
Indexed gain	489,822
Gain after taper relief (25% × £489,822)	122,455
Less Annual exemption	(8,800)
Taxable gain	113,655
Tax @ 40%	£45,462

Therefore it is better to use the CGT route (which is mandatory if the relevant conditions are satisfied in any case). Neither option has any effect for Bluetone Ltd.

28 Bill and Ben

Text references. Extraction of value from a company is looked at in Chapter 30. CGT and shares is dealt with in Chapter 13. Purchase of own shares is covered in Chapter 23.

Top tips. Bill and Ben are sharing equally. Divide the sums between them and then do the necessary calculations for just one of them. State the answer will equally apply to the other. This is the easiest way to approach this question in part (a).

Comparison questions are common in the exam – make sure that you work through all the calculations quickly but carefully. Above all, don't panic!

Easy marks. In part (a) don't just calculate the tax liabilities. Make sure you go a step further and calculate the 'after tax cash' as required by the examiner for extra easy marks.

A letter was asked for thus each marks for producing an answer using that format.

Examiner's comments. Answers to part (a) could either have been done for Bill and Ben separately, by dividing the £180,000 equally between them, (probably the easier way), or it could have been done in total, as a single computation. However, in this case, you had to remember to deduct 2 x personal allowances, 2 x starting rate band etc. Candidates who adopted this approach usually overlooked this fact. The question asked for a calculation of the after-tax cash for each option. Easy marks were therefore available for doing this extra step, rather than stopping at the tax liability.

Most candidates coped reasonably well with the CGT calculations in parts (a)(ii) and (iii).

In part (b) the most surprising thing was that a large number of candidates failed to produce anything resembling a letter! Candidates should be aware that there are presentation marks available in a question like this, which they can achieve just by producing the letter in a professional letter format, regardless of the content!

Many were clearly unaware of the purchase of own share rules, producing only a calculation of a capital gain, and, what they had obviously learned as a generally available means of relieving/deferring any gain, by reinvesting in companies which qualified for EIS or VCT relief. From the facts in the question it would appear that these were not appropriate in this scenario. There is no suggestion at all that Ben is looking to further invest.

Marking scheme

			Marks	
(a)	(i)	Calculation of income	½	
		Personal allowance	½	
		Calculation of basic rate band remaining	½	
		Gross up dividend	½	
		Tax at 10%/32.5%	½	
		Use of tax credit	½	
		Income tax at 22/40%	½	
		National insurance at 11%/1%	1	
		Conclude that dividend is better	½	
				5
	(ii)	Proceeds less cost	½	
		No taper relief available	½	
		Annual exemption	½	
		CGT (2 × 0.5)	1	
		Total cash after tax P1 and P2 correct rates	½	
		Conclude P2 better	½	
		Max		3

(iii)	Taper relief: business asset	½	
	correct number of years/rate	½	
	Revised taxable gain	½	
	Conclude P1 now better (2 × 0.5)	1	
	Deferral of CGT now payable 31 January 2009	½	
			3

(b)	Shares not held for five years	½
	Income tax, not capital gains treatment	½
	Income distribution dividend	½
	Net distribution	½
	Gross distribution	½
	Income tax at 32.5%	½
	Calculation of after-tax income	½
	Included in self assessment tax return	½
	Income tax payable by 31 January 2012	½
	Defer repurchase	½
	Further conditions:	
	– unquoted trading company	½
	– individual is UK resident/ord resident	½
	– trade benefit test	½
	– includes buying out of dissenting shareholder	½
	– not part of scheme to avoid tax	½
	– 75% share reduction test	½
	– 30% connection test	½
	Calculation of gross capital gain	½
	Taper relief – business asset rate (2 × 0.5)	1
	Annual exemption	½
	Calculation of after tax cash	½
	Capital gains treatment better	½
	Payment date	½
	Clearance application available	½
	Time limit to respond	½
	Independent advice	1
	Presentation/format	2

Max   11
                                                         22

(a)   (i)   **Extraction of £180,000**

2006/07

	£
Income tax	
Salary (8 × £3,750)	30,000
Less personal allowance	(5,035)
Taxable income	24,965

Remaining basic rate band (£33,300 – 24,965) = £ 8,335

Class 1 national insurance

Assuming Bill and Ben are directors

Remaining 11% band (£33,540 – 30,000) = £3,540

The dividend would be the most tax efficient method of extracting the £180,000 from the company as it leaves Bill and Ben with £15,129 each more post-tax cash, as follows

Bonus

	£
Earnings (each)	90,000
Less: Tax @ 22% (on £8,335)	(1,834)
Less: Tax @ 40% (on £81,665)	(32,666)
Less: NIC @ 11% (on £3,540)	(389)
Less: NIC @ 1% (on £86,460)	(865)
Net cash	54,246

Dividend

	£
Net div (each)	90,000
Add: Tax credit @ 10%	10,000
Less: Tax @ 10% (on £8,335)	(834)
Less: Tax @ 32.5% (on £91,665)	(29,791)
Net cash	69,375

Note that the question asks candidates to ignore CT implications.

(ii) **Purchase proposals**

Package 1 – £480,000 in full

	£
Proceeds (each)	240,000
Less: cost £1 × 500	(500)
Gain before taper	239,500
Chargeable gain: 1.8.06 - 31.3.07 (no taper relief as <1yr)	239,500
Less: AE	(8,800)
Taxable gain	230,700
Tax £8,335 @ 20%	1,667
£222,365 @ 40%	88,946
	90,613
Post-tax cash	240,000
Proceeds	(90,613)
Less: tax	149,387

Package 2 – £300,000 and £180,000 pre-sale dividend

	£
Proceeds (each)	150,000
Less: cost £1 × 500	(500)
Gain before taper	149,500
Chargeable gain: 1.8.06 - 31.3.07 (no taper relief as <1yr)	149,500
Less: AE	(8,800)
Taxable gain	140,700
Tax @ 40%	56,280

Note. There is no basic rate band left due to the dividend.

Post-tax cash	
Proceeds of share sale	150,000
Less: CGT	(56,280)
Add: net cash from dividend (see(a))	69,375
	163,095

Therefore it is better to take the pre-sale dividend as this leaves them each with £13,708 (£163,095 – 149,387) more post-tax cash.

(iii) **Delay until August 2007**

If the sale is delayed until August 2007 the gains will attract a year's worth of business asset taper relief, which will reduce the chargeable gain to 50%.

As Bill and Ben will continue to work for the company their salaries of £45,000 (12 × £3,750) will use up the whole of the basic rate band. Therefore, all of the gains and dividend will be taxed at the higher rates.

The tax due, if the whole amount were taken in exchange for the shares, would be reduced to £44,380 (see below) thus increasing the post-tax cash to £195,620, whilst the post tax amount in the pre-sale dividend scenario would increase to only £191,120.

Therefore if they waited until August 2007 it would be better to take the whole amount in exchange for cash rather than taking the pre-sale dividend.

The delay until August 2007 will also mean that the tax on the gain will be payable by 31 January 2009 rather than 31 January 2008.

	£
Proceeds (each)	240,000
Less: cost £1 × 500	(500)
	239,500
Chargeable gain: 1.8.06 - 1.8.07 (business asset 1yr: 50%)	119,750
Less: AE	(8,800)
Taxable gain	110,950
Tax @ 40%	44,380
Post-tax cash	240,000
Proceeds	(44,380)
Less: tax	195,620

	£
Proceeds (each)	150,000
Less: cost £1 × 500	(500)
	149,500
Chargeable gain: 1.8.06 – 1.8.07 (business asset 1yr: 50%)	74,750
Less: AE	(8,800)
Taxable gain	65,950
Tax @ 40%	26,380
Post-tax cash	
Proceeds of sharesale	150,000
Less: CGT	(26,380)
Add: net cash from dividend (W1)	67,500
	191,120

Working 1	£
Net dividend	90,000
Tax credit	10,000
	100,000
Less tax @ 32.5%	(32,500)
	67,500

Top tips. Usually when a question suggests delaying a sale of an asset, this will be to ensure a further year of taper relief is obtained. This is particularly important for business assets where the rates of taper relief are very generous and waiting a year can be the difference between having an effective CGT tax rate of 20% (40% × 50% after one year) and 10% (40% × 25% after two years).

(b)

Your address   Our address

                                                                                                Date

Dear Ben

COMPANY REPURCHASE OF OWN SHARES

If Flower Ltd (F Ltd) purchases your shares there will be various income tax and CGT implications, which are set out below.

Income tax

The usual treatment of shareholders who sell their shares back to the issuing company is to treat the gain as a net dividend and tax it at the shareholder's marginal rate, with no taper relief or annual exemption, where applicable, to reduce the taxable amount.

Assuming the company pays the proposed price of £500,000 this will lead to a tax charge of £124,875, payable by 31 January 2012. This leaves you with a post-tax income of £375,125 (see Appendix 1).

Capital treatment

It is possible in certain circumstances for the gain to be taxed under the CGT rules. The conditions for this capital treatment are:

- The company must be unquoted

- The repurchase or 'buy back' must be taking place to benefit the trade

- The vendor must be resident and ordinarily resident in the UK

- The shares must have been held for at least 5 years prior to the buy back

- The vendor's holding must be reduced by at least 25% (yours will be reduced by 100%)

- After the buy back the vendor must hold no more than 30% of the shares (you will own no shares after the buy back).

- The repurchase is not part of a scheme to avoid tax

At present you have not satisfied the ownership requirement, having only owned the shares for 4 years 9 months (from August 2006 to May 2011).

The tax due under this capital treatment if the sale were postponed until the five years has elapsed would be £46,430, leaving you with post-tax cash of £453,570 (see Appendix 1), which is considerably higher than the income treatment.

Advice

It would therefore be worth waiting a further three months before selling your shares back to the company, if this is agreeable to Bill. (Bill may wish to take advice as to whether this delay would cause any disadvantages to him or the company.) At that point you should satisfy the conditions for capital treatment and you will receive an additional £78,445 cash as a result.

It is possible to apply for advance clearance, to ensure that the required tax treatment is applied. HMRC will respond to the clearance application within 30 days.

I trust you find this information useful in your decision. If you have any further queries please do not hesitate to contact me.

Kind regards

A Adviser

Appendix 1

Income treatment

	£
Proceeds	500,000
Less: subscription cost	(500)
	499,500
× 100/90	555,000
Tax @ (32.5% − 10%)	124,875
Post tax cash	
Proceeds	500,000
Less: tax	(124,875)
	375,125

Capital treatment

	£
Proceeds	500,000
Less: cost	(500)
	499,500
Chargeable gain: 25% (BA >2yrs)	124,875
Less: AE	(8,800)
	116,075
Tax @ 40%	46,430
Post tax cash	
Proceeds	500,000
Less: tax	(46,430)
	453,570
Additional cash using capital treatment (£453,570 − 375,125)	78,445

Top tips. If the question asks for a letter there will be at least one mark available for the format so don't miss that easy mark. In addition, any computations should be included in a separate appendix. A great way to approach the question is to do the appendix first then write the body of the letter around your findings.

---

29 Graeme

Text references. Basic CGT is covered in Chapters 11-12. Shares and securities are dealt with in Chapter 13. CGT reliefs are in Chapter 14 and the overseas aspects dealt with in Chapter 15. IHT on lifetime gifts is covered in Chapter 17. Furnished holiday lettings are covered in Chapter 3.

Top tips. You need to calculate the value of the shares when first disposed of because we use this to apportion the cost and indexed cost on reorganisation.

Read the question requirements carefully. The question says ignore the CGT annual exemption – so ignore it. Similarly the question told you not to discuss the IT treatment of the cottage – don't discuss it.

Rollover relief does not apply to overseas assets and foreign property does not qualify as FHL so is not a business asset for taper relief purposes.

Easy marks. You can lose marks by confusing CGT and IHT. It is best to write your answer to each tax separately. So cover all your IHT points and then all CGT (or the other way around if you find this easier). It helps to reduce your confusion.

Examiner's comments. This question had a heavy emphasis on CGT. Candidates had to calculate gains on disposals of shares following a reorganisation of share capital, and advise on both CGT and IHT implications of gifting further shares, and on the CGT and income tax (IT) implications of replacing a UK holiday cottage with a villa abroad.

Share for share exchanges was examined in part (a) which produced some very confused answers. Many candidates were clearly not familiar with this topic.

Part (b) was answered better, but again highlighted the confusion which exists in a significant number of candidates between CGT and IHT. The fact that the question specifically instructed candidates to ignore the CGT annual exemption did not prevent a good number from mentioning it.

Part (c) was generally poorly answered. This was largely due to a failure to read the question. It specifically said that you were not required to discuss the IT treatment of the country cottage, yet many candidates' answers did little else. In many cases they included a detailed description of the furnished holiday letting rules, which were not required, and therefore could not be awarded marks.

A reasonable number were aware of the availability of rollover relief for furnished holiday lettings, but few realised that this is only available where the replacement asset is in the UK, so the holiday villa abroad would not qualify.

Marking scheme

			Marks
(a)	Indexation to March 1992		½
	Rights issue: shares, cost		½
	Indexation to April 1998		½
	Reorganisation: correct basis of apportionment		1
	number/value of 'T' shares		½
	'T' share costs		½
	number/value of 'D' shares		½
	'D' share costs		½
	'T' shares: disposal cost		½
	indexation		½
	Taper relief: business asset, rate		½
	'D' shares: disposal cost		½
	indexation restricted		½
		Max	6

(b) Transfers to Catherine: no gain/no loss disposal   ½
                              spouse inherits tax history   ½
                              exempt from IHT   ½
     Transfers to Barry: connected persons   ½
                              proceeds (MV)   ½
                              cost   ½
                              indexation allowance   ½
                              taper relief   ½
                              availability of gift relief   ½
                              unquoted trading company   ½
     Effect of deferring gain: Barry's base cost reduced   ½
                              Graeme's loss of taper relief   ½
                              time to regain full taper   ½
                              jointly written claim   ½
                              time limit for claim   ½
     Inheritance tax: 100% business property relief   ½
                              if held by Barry from gift until Graeme's death   ½
                              PET for IHT purposes   ½
                              annual exemption up to × 2   ½
                              taper relief 3-7 years   ½
                                                                                    Max   8

(c) *Sale of existing property*
     Capital gains: indexation available to April 1998   ½
                     taper relief: non-business asset   ½
                     taper relief: business asset while FHL   ½
                     apportionment of gain on time basis   ½
                     qualifying asset for rollover relief   ½
                     proportion of gain while FHL   ½
                     need to acquire further qualifying asset within qualifying period   ½
                     overseas villa not a qualifying asset   ½
     Acquisition of overseas property
     Residence: UK residents therefore taxed on worldwide income   ½
                     significant periods of absence will not per se change   ½
                        residence status
                     criteria for becoming non-resident (2 × ½)   1
     Income tax: Overseas income   ½
                     DTR: availability   ½
                            lower of UK/foreign tax   ½
                     villa: does not qualify as FHL   ½
                            reason/situated outside UK   ½
                     not relevant income for pension purposes   ½
                     trading loss offset facility not available   ½
     Capital gains: does not qualify as a business asset   ½
                                                                                    Max   8
                                                                                                    ──
                                                                                                    22

(a)   **Thistle Dubh Ltd shares FA 1985 pool**

		Number	Cost £	Indexed cost £
December 1986	Acquisition	10,000	36,000	36,000
March 1992	Indexed rise			
	(136.7 − 99.6)/99.6 × 36,000			13,410
				49,410
Rights		5,000	50,000	50,000
		15,000	86,000	99,410
April 1998	Indexed rise			
	(162.6 − 136.7)/136.7 × 99,410			18,835
		15,000	86,000	118,245
October 1999	Reorganisation:	30,000 T shares		
		45,000 D shares		

		Value	Cost £	Indexed Cost £
May 2007	Sale of T shares			
	30,000 T shares @ 300p	90,000	21,500	29,561
	45,000 D shares @ 600p	270,000	64,500	88,684
		360,000	86,000	118,245

The shares are unquoted so the cost and indexed cost are apportioned in the ratio of the values at the time of the first disposal

Chargeable gains computation

		£
May 2007	12,000 T shares proceeds 12,000 × 300p	36,000
	Cost 12,000/30,000 × 21,500	(8,600)
	Indexation allowance 12,000/30,000 × (29,561 −21,500)	(3,224)
	Indexed gain	24,176
	Tapered gain 24,176 × 25%	6,044
October 2007	45,000 D shares proceeds	85,000
	Cost	(64,500)
	Indexation allowance (88,684 − 64,500) restricted	(20,500)
	Indexed gain	NIL

> **Top tips.** Set out your FA 1985 Pool performance carefully. Remember that you need to index up to the date of a rights issue and that indexation is not rounded in the pool.

(b)   Graeme now holds 18,000 T shares with a cost of £12,900 and an indexed cost of £17,737.

   (i)   If Graeme gifts the shares to Catherine she will acquire them with the same cost and indexed cost as Graeme, as transfers between spouses are made on a no gain no loss basis. There will be no capital gain. She will also inherit his period of ownership for taper relief purposes

   The gift is an exempt transfer for inheritance tax purposes.

   (ii)   If Graeme gifts the shares to Barry there will be a disposal for capital gains tax purposes. The chargeable gain before taper relief would be 18,000 × 384p = 69,120 − 17,737 = £51,383. After taper relief the gain would be £12,846.

   Graeme and Barry could make a joint election to hold over the gain on the gift since the shares are unquoted shares in a trading company. There would be no chargeable gain but Barry's base cost would be £17,737. Thus any gain would be deferred until Barry sells the shares, but Barry must hold them for two years to obtain the maximum 75% taper relief.

The gift is a potentially exempt transfer for IHT purposes and will be exempt if Graeme survives seven years. If Graeme has made no other gifts, however, his annual exemption for the current year and the previous year would first be set against the gift.

If Graeme should die within seven years of the gift 100% BPR will be available provided Barry still holds the shares (or previously died still holding them) and they are still unquoted. Should business property relief not be available and inheritance tax be due on the gift, then the tax will be tapered if death occurs between three and seven years after the gift.

> **Top tips.** Try and consider the CGT and IHT issues separately to avoid confusion. You can then put the 'pieces' back together in your answer. An answer plan would help with a question like this.

(c)   If Graeme and Catherine sell their UK country cottage a capital gain will arise. Taper relief will be available to reduce the gain. The cottage will qualify as a business asset for taper relief purposes for any period during which it qualifies as furnished holiday lettings, and will qualify as a non-business asset for the remaining period. The gain will be time apportioned between business and non-business use and taper relief applied, calculated based on the whole period of ownership.

Had Graeme and Catherine decided to acquire a new business property in the UK any gain attributable to the use as furnished holiday lettings could be rolled over against the acquisition, but roll over relief is not available against the purchase of the villa abroad.

The foreign villa will be a chargeable asset for capital gains tax purposes and if it should be sold whilst Graeme and Catherine are still UK resident any gain would be chargeable. If they should become non-resident and subsequently sell the property the gain would not be chargeable to UK capital gains tax unless they resumed UK residence.

If the property is let whilst Graeme and Catherine are UK resident they will be liable to UK income tax on any profit. The profit will be based on the rental income less any expenses of letting, but relief cannot be claimed for any proportion of expenses incurred which relate to periods during which Graeme and Catherine are using the property. If foreign tax is payable, then relief for this will be given against any UK tax due.

If Graeme and Catherine become non-resident then they will not be liable in the UK on the rental profits. They will have to take care as they will be categorised as UK resident if they are in the UK for 6 months in any year or for more than 3 months pa averaged over a four year period.

Properties abroad do not qualify as furnished holiday lettings so Graeme and Catherine will not qualify for any of the tax reliefs which apply to such properties in the UK, such as offset of losses against income, business assets taper relief or rollover relief.

30 Reisling Ltd

> **Text references.** Hive downs are covered in Chapter 26. Tax planning in Chapter 30.
>
> **Top tips.** The question helpfully set out the scenario for you and even told you how to calculate the available losses. An answer plan is essential. You should be able to come up with the tax issues by brainstorming the different taxes. The non-tax issues are common sense.
>
> **Easy marks.** Stick to the basics, stating fundamental points such as 'Reisling Ltd and Plonk Ltd will be in a gains group (direct ownership ≥75%)' to pick up easy marks. Don't struggle to get the difficult marks.

Marking scheme

			Marks
(a)	**Transfer of assets to Plonk Ltd**		
	Gains group	1	
	No gain/no loss transfer	1	
	Disposal of winery	1	
	Cannot transfer capital losses	1	
	CAs continue	1	
	Trading losses can be carried forward	1	
	VAT – TOGC	1	
	Corporation tax – associate affects tax rate	1	
	SDLT	1	
			9
(b)	**Sale of Plonk Ltd to Chardonnay Ltd**		
	No chargeable gain	1	
	VAT	1	
	Stamp duty	1	
	Anti avoidance		
	Degrouping charge	2	
	Major change in nature and conduct of trade	1	
			6
(c)	**Other considerations**		
	Redundancy payments deductible for employer	1	
	Statutory redundancy tax free for staff	1	
	Contractual termination payments taxable	1	
	Ex gratia payments £30,000 exemption	1	
	Tell customers/suppliers	1	
	Roll over relief may be available	1	
	Ethical issues	2	
			8
(d)	**Exports**		
	Non EU – zero rated	2	
	EU – zero rated to registered customers	1	
	– standard rated to non-registered customers	1	
			4
	Format/presentation		2
	Max		29

Notes for meeting

Date: [date]
Subject: Chardonnay Ltd's proposed acquisition of Reisling Ltd's wine making business

These notes cover tax issues relating to:

(a)   The transfer of Reisling Ltd's wine production trade to Plonk Ltd
(b)   The sale of Plonk Ltd to Chardonnay Ltd
(c)   Other considerations

(a) **The transfer of Reisling Ltd's wine production trade to Plonk Ltd**

Chargeable gains

Reisling Ltd and Plonk Ltd will be in a gains group (direct ownership ≥75%). Consequently the transfer of the assets will take place at no gain/no loss.

The only asset not transferred, ie the winery, will be sold to a third party for £50,000. Subject to the amount of indexation allowance, this will crystallise a chargeable gain in Reisling Ltd, which will be available to offset against the £42,000 capital losses brought forward in that company.

Capital losses

The unrelieved capital losses will remain with Reisling Ltd.

Capital allowances

The assets will be automatically transferred at their tax written down value for capital allowance purposes.

Trading losses

The trade is treated as continuing so Plonk Ltd will inherit the tax affairs of Reisling Ltd in relation to carried forward trading losses and will be available to set against future profits of the same trade.

The amount of loss available to transfer is £(29,000 + 60,000) unless any part of the current year's loss is relieved against Reisling Ltd's other income.

VAT

The transfer of the business as a going concern will be outside the scope of VAT.

Corporation tax

For year ended 31 December 2007 Reisling Ltd will have had an associated company for part of the year. This will impact on the small companies' limits for corporation tax and potentially the tax rate payable by the company.

Stamp duty land tax

Stamp duty land tax relief may be available for the intra-group transfer of land and buildings.

(b) **Sale of Plonk Ltd to Riesling Ltd**

Chargeable gains

No chargeable gain will arise on the sale of the shares to Riesling Ltd as the shares are being sold at their cost of £475,000 (ie the market value at the date of issue). The substantial shareholding exemption is not available as the shares have not been held for at least 12 months.

VAT

A sale of shares is exempt from VAT.

Stamp Duty

A sale of shares attracts stamp duty at 0.5%.

Anti avoidance

Riesling Ltd must ensure that the improvements it makes to the trade in order to make it profitable again does not constitute a major change in the nature or conduct of trade, or the trading loss being carried forward will be extinguished.

The gains deferred by the no gain/no loss treatment on the transfer of the assets from Reisling Ltd to Plonk Ltd will crystallise in Plonk Ltd in the accounting period that it leaves the group, as this occurs within six years of the transfer of assets.

It is unlikely that the parties would agree that the charge should accrue to the other group member ie Reisling Ltd.

(c)   **Other considerations**

As a result of the reorganisation it is likely that Reisling Ltd will have to make some staff redundant. The redundancy costs are an allowable expense for corporation tax purposes for the company.

The staff will receive statutory redundancy pay free of tax.

Management may have service contracts. Termination may trigger termination payments which, due to being contractual, will be fully taxable. Any *ex gratia* payments will be exempt up to £30,000 (although any statutory redundancy pay will use part of this exemption).

Existing trade customers and suppliers need to be told of the proposals.

If the chargeable gains arising on the disposal of the winery cannot be relieved against capital losses, the gain may be rolled over if reinvested into a qualifying assets within three years of the disposal.

The directors are all shareholders of Riesling Ltd and will need to consider the effects of the proposed sale on their investment as well as on their roles as directors. Some of the directors may hope to become directors of Plonk Ltd or Chardonnay Ltd, whilst some may prefer to remain with Riesling Ltd.

As the interests of the different directors may conflict they may like to take independent advice.

(d)   **Exports**

The VAT treatment of exports depends on whether the export is to an EU member state or to a non-EU country.

If the export is to a non-EU country, the export is zero-rated.

If the export is to an EU member state, the treatment depends on whether the customer is VAT registered:

- If he is VAT registered and provides Riesling Ltd with his VAT registration number, then the export is zero-rated.

- If he is not VAT registered, or if he does not provide his VAT registration number, the export should be standard rated.

31 Mr Royle

Text references. Chapter 7 covers capital allowances and IBAs. Chapter 24 deals with corporation tax losses. Chapter 28 for VAT and an outline of the transfer of a going concern provisions. Chapter 30 is a useful chapter to revise tax planning issues.

Top tips. The mention of losses in the question should lead you to consider whether it is possible to utilise them in future. It is always important to be concise in your answers. This allows you to maximise your marks on the question concerned whilst not impinging on the time available for other questions.

Marking scheme

			Marks
(a)	Choose which assets	1	
	Capital allowances and IBAs	1	
	Consideration	1	
	No liabilities	1	
	No use of losses	1	
	VAT charge	1	
	TOGC relief	1	
	CGT base cost	1	
	SDLT	1	
	Max		8
(b)	Business carries on	1	
	Liabilities transferred	1	
	Capital allowances and IBAs	1	
	No FYAs	1	
	Losses used	1	
	Restriction on losses	1	
	Close company issues	2	
	CGT base cost	1	
	Stamp duty	1	
			10
			18

[Our address]

Mr J Royle

[Address]

[Date]

Dear Mr Royle

Purchase of business

Thank you for your enquiry about your proposed purchase. I will outline the advantages of either buying the assets of the business or shares in the company.

Purchase of assets

(a)   You will be able to choose which assets you wish to acquire, rather than the whole of the assets of the company.

(b)   You will be entitled to claim capital allowances on plant and machinery, including possible first year allowances of 50% depending on the type of asset acquired. Industrial buildings allowance may also be available on the factory.

(c)   It may be possible to maximise the use of capital allowances by allocating consideration to assets which attract more capital allowances, eg plant and machinery.

(d)   The liabilities of the company will not be passed to you.

(e)   One disadvantage is that you will not be able to utilise the existing losses of the company.

(f)   VAT may be chargeable on the assets acquired by you. If you cannot fully recover all the VAT paid on acquiring the assets, this may be unattractive.

There is a relief which provides that VAT is not chargeable on the transfer of a business as a going concern, but this may not be available if you only purchase some of the assets.

(g) The base cost of each asset for CGT purposes will be the price paid for it. The business assets rate of taper relief will be available.

(h) Stamp duty land tax will be payable on any land and buildings, including the factory. The rate of tax depends on the price paid, but would be nil if it were less than £150,000, or 1% if between £150,000 and £250,000.

Purchase of shares

(a) The business of the company will continue uninterrupted.

(b) You will be taking over the liabilities of the company as well as the assets, albeit within the company not personally.

(c) Capital allowances and industrial buildings allowance will be unaffected by the purchase. However, this means that there will be no first year allowances available.

(d) It may be possible for the losses incurred by the company to be carried forward and used against profits in future years.

However, where there is a change in ownership of a company and a major change in the nature of the conduct of the company's trade occurs within three years, trading losses cannot be carried forward. This also applies where there is a change in ownership after the scale of activities has become small or negligible before it revives.

(e) The company will be 'close' for corporation tax purposes as it is currently, and will continue to be, controlled by five or fewer participators or any number of directors.

If loans are made by the company to participators this will usually result in a penalty tax charge of 25% being due to HMRC. Any amounts written off will be taxable on the participator as a distribution. Distributions are not deductible for corporation tax purposes.

Benefits provided to non-employee participators will also be taxed as distributions from the company.

(f) The capital gains base cost of the assets in the company will be unaffected by the sale. Any gains on subsequent disposals will be taxable in the company. The base cost of the shares will be the price paid, and these will be eligible for the business assets rate of taper relief.

(h) Stamp duty will be payable on the price of the shares purchased at the rate of 0.5%.

I hope this is helpful. I suggest we meet to discuss your proposed purchase further.

Yours sincerely,

Certified Accountant

32 Stuart and Rebecca

Text references. Capital gains tax is dealt with in Chapters 11 to 13 and PPR relief is in Chapter 14. IHT is in Chapters 17 and 18.

Top tips. Read the question requirements carefully. Part 2, for example, asks you to consider two alternatives. There are no marks available for doing anything else.

Stuart's estate passes wholly to Rebecca on his death. This is an exempt transfer. State this fact. Do **not** waste time and effort in calculating Stuart's estate and exempting the total figure.

In part 4 do not discuss making changes to gifts made in the past – it is too late to change this. Consider only what can be done now.

Easy marks. The examiner expects a candidate to be able to perform easy calculations to support your answers. Part 1 for 8 marks contained such a calculation of which the majority of marks was for an easy gain computation. Ensure you can do basic gain calculations like this.

Examiner's comments. This question covered CGT, primarily Principal Private Residence (PPR) relief, and IHT computations and planning for a married couple. Overall it was done fairly well.

In part 1 a careful candidate, with a reasonable knowledge of the PPR rules, could score well. Unfortunately many candidates failed to pick up marks due to an inability to put together a basic CGT computation, and deal correctly with indexation, taper relief, capital losses, and the annual exemption. This is a fundamental requirement at this level.

In part 2 the key phrase was 'Given his recent diagnosis ...' As this indicated Stuart's death within 2-3 years, the answer was looking for the IHT implications of the two alternatives. Although a minority of candidates acquitted themselves very well, many failed to appreciate this and gave irrelevant answers.

In part 3, it was only the liability on Rebecca's death that was required.

The use of Business Property Relief (BPR) was often confused.

A good number of candidates interpreted part) as 'Write all you know about IHT planning in general', and clearly gave little, if any thought to the scenario presented.

Marking scheme

				Marks
1	Acquisition cost		½	
	Indexation		½	
	Principal private residence:			
	correct treatment of each period (× 7)		3½	
	PPR exempt gain: exempt fraction		½	
	Letting exemption:			
	awareness		½	
	calculation of let period gain		½	
	identification of other limits (½ × 2)		1	
	lowest of three		½	
	Offset of capital losses		½	
	restricted to preserve annual exemption		½	
	Annual exemption		½	
	Correct order of offset of exemptions and reliefs		½	
		Max		8
2	Holding required to get BPR for listed company		½	
	Rate of BPR that applies		½	
	Omikron small shareholding, no BPR		1	
	Omega: related property shareholdings		½	
	calculation of shares required		½	
	hold for more than two years		½	
	Reasoned conclusion		½	
		Max		3
3	Stuart: exempt estate to spouse		½	
	Rebecca: Omega shares valuation/lower of two methods		1	
	estate: value of shares		½	
	deduction of BPR		1	
	other assets: investments		½	
	cash deposits		½	
	cash (insurance policy)		½	
	residence		½	
	nil rate band		½	
	IHT at 40%		½	
				6

4	Need to use nil rate bands	½
	Stuart's will to transfer nil rate band assets to son	½
	No point gifting Omega shares as BPR is available	1
	Calculation of tax saved on first death	½
	No PETs, re Stuart	½
	Reason/reference to taper relief 3–7 years	½
	Lifetime gift/PET nil rate band re Rebecca	½
	Still should not be Omega shares/BPR	½
	Make use of annual exemptions	½
	Availability of two annual exemptions each	½
	Calculation of immediate tax saving	½
	Small exempt gifts	½
	Expenditure out of normal income – identify relief	½
	Usual standard of living/pattern of giving (2 × 0.5)	1
	Use of insurance	½

Max 7

Format/ presentation 2

26

PRIVATE AND CONFIDENTIAL

[Our address]

[Your address]

[Date]

Dear Stuart

TAX POSITION AND ESTATE PLANNING

This letter deals with the capital gains tax implications of your recent property sale and your current and potential inheritance tax liabilities.

1 **Capital gains tax on property disposal 2007/08**

The capital gain arising on the disposal of the Plymouth house is £3,358.

This is after taking account of principal private residence relief of £131,725, based on an exempt period of 90 months out of a total ownership period of 151 months, and lettings relief of £39,517.

The gain shown is after maximum non business asset taper relief, as the property has been held for nine years with an additional year given as it was held at 17 March 1998.

The calculation of the above figures can be found in Appendix 1.

2 **Proposed investment**

As you are considering making an investment in a quoted company you will only be able to obtain business property relief for inheritance tax purposes if you, together with Rebecca, control the company, ie over 50% of the shares.

You could buy approximately 1 million shares in Omikron plc. This would be in the region of a 2% holding, so no business property relief would be available.

Alternatively you could buy approximately 195,000 shares in Omega plc with the proceeds, at a cost of 216p. Currently you and Rebecca jointly hold 4.8 million shares. Provided you achieve a slightly lower price or invest slightly more so that you purchase 200,001 shares, you and Rebecca will have a controlling holding. Provided you then survive for at least two years you will achieve 50% business property relief on your Omega plc shares.

3 **Inheritance tax on Rebecca's estate 1 March 2010**

If, following your death, Rebecca were to die on 1 March 2010, and no IHT planning is implemented, the IHT liability would be £2,658,420 (Appendix 2).

4 Lifetime IHT planning

As your will leaves all of your estate to Rebecca you have not taken advantage of your nil rate band. This could be utilised by leaving assets to the value of £285,000 to beneficiaries other than to Rebecca, for example to Sam, or to a discretionary trust. The trust could include Rebecca as a beneficiary if she needs to be able to benefit from the assets.

The Omega plc shares should be left to Rebecca so that the 50% BPR would be available on her death or earlier gift of the whole shareholding.

Rebecca should consider making lifetime gifts in the hope that she will survive for seven years, so that they become PETs. If she survived more than 3 but less than seven years, and IHT was payable on the lifetime gifts, then the IHT payable would be tapered.

Both of you should make lifetime gifts utilising your annual exemptions. You may also be able to establish a regular pattern of giving to use the exemption for normal expenditure out of income. Your wealth would appear to be such that it would be simple to demonstrate that capital was not being eroded by this strategy.

It could be possible to give away the life policy before death at a lower value than the death benefit. It would then be excluded from the death estate and escape any IHT liability.

Top tips. Do not ignore easy planning points such as use of exemptions. These are easy marks – don't lose them.

Appendix 1 – disposal of Plymouth property

	£
Sale proceeds	422,100
Less cost May 1995	(185,000)
Less indexation May 1995 – April 1998	
$\dfrac{162.6 - 149.6}{149.6} = 0.087 \times £185,000$	(16,095)
	221,005
Less PPR exemption $\dfrac{90}{90+61} \times £221,005$ (W)	(131,725)
	89,280

Less letting exemption, lowest of:

(i) PPR relief given: £131,725

(ii) Gain in let period: $\dfrac{27}{90+61} \times £221,005 = £39,517$

(iii) Maximum: £40,000	(39,517)
Gain before taper relief	49,763
Less capital losses brought forward	(29,500)
	20,263
Gain after taper relief (9 + bonus year) @ 60%	12,158
Less annual exemption	(8,800)
Taxable gain	3,358

Working

Periods of occupation		*Exempt Months*	*Non-exempt Months*
1 May 1995 – 28 Feb 1996	Occupied	10	
1 March 1996 – 31 Dec 1999	Unoccupied – absence for any reason	36	
	Unoccupied		10
1 Jan 2000 – 31 Mar 2002	Let		27
1 Apr 2002 – 30 Nov 2002	Occupied	8	
1 Dec 2002 – 30 Nov 2004	Unoccupied		24
1 Dec 2004 – 30 Nov 2007	Last 36 months	36	
		90	61

> **Top tips.** Get into the habit of listing out the periods of occupation and non-occupation of a private residence to help determine the correct proportion of the gain that is exempt. This will show the examiner your understanding of the PPR rules.

Appendix 2 – Rebecca's IHT liability with no IHT planning

	£	£
London property		900,000
Cash deposits (including £200,000 from life policy)		530,000
Quoted investments		250,000
Shares in Omega plc 5,001,000 × 210p (1/4 up is lower)	10,502,100	
Less BPR @ 50%	(5,251,050)	
		5,251,050
		6,931,050
Less nil rate band		(285,000)
Taxable at 40%		6,646,050
IHT liability		2,658,420

33 Karen Wade

> **Text references.** VAT is in Chapter 28 and 29. Employment income is in Chapter 4. Trading income and NIC for the self employed is covered in Chapter 6 with capital allowances in Chapter 7. Investment issues are in Chapter 31. Pensions are in Chapter 2.
>
> **Top tips.** You must quickly and efficiently calculate the turnover for VAT for part (1) so that you can comment on the registration position. All figures should be contained in a separate Appendix – you can work on the figures first and then place the Appendix at the end of your answer. This makes your work look more professional.
>
> **Easy marks.** You should be able to write about and apply the VAT registration test rules as they are an essential planning issue for new business start ups.

Marking scheme

			Marks
(a)	Taxable supplies	½	
	Historic test	½	
	Future test	½	
	Turnover thresholds	1	
	Date by which to notify HMRC	½	
	Registration date	½	
	VAT liability	1	
	Output VAT	½	
	Motor car	½	
	Fuel scale charge	½	
	Input VAT	½	
	Blocked input VAT	½	
	Quarterly returns	½	
	Max		6

(b)   *Change of use of vans*

No consequences for Karen	½	
Costs deductible for trade purposes	½	
Taxable benefit for nephew for private use	½	
Scale charges increasing 07/08	½	
No benefit if only used for commuting	½	
	Max	2

Trading income assessment

Profit adjustments (½ mark for each item correctly adjusted)	Max 2	
Capital allowances	Max 3	
Wages allowed	½	
Private use of car	½	
Small for CA purposes	½	
	Max	6

Income tax and NIC

Calculation of income tax	4	
Class 2 NIC	1	
Class 4 NIC	1½	
	Max	6

(c)   *Investment strategy*
Surplus £10,000

Consideration (½ mark for each relevant item)	Max 2	
Required information (½ mark for each relevant item)	1	
	Max	3

Quoted shares v property

Liquidity	1½	
Risk	1½	
Capital vs income growth	1½	
Taxation	1½	
		6

Pension

£3,600 or 100% × income	½	
Annual allowance	½	
Paid net	½	
Tax recovered from HMRC	½	
Extend basic rate band	½	
Tax relief	½	
Contribute from capital (no tax relief)	½	
Income and gains grow tax free in the pension	½	
Lifetime allowance	½	
	Max	4
Format/Presentation		2
		35

Report

To:	Karen Wade
From:	Tax Manager
Date:	[date]
Subject:	Tax issues for 2006/07 tax year

This report covers tax issues relating to:

(i) VAT registration and liability

(ii) Income tax and NIC issues

(iii) Investment strategy

(a) **VAT registration and liability**

Registration

You will be liable to register for VAT if the value of your taxable supplies (standard and zero-rated) exceed the statutory limits. All of your supplies are standard-rated and therefore taxable.

You liable to register:

(i) at the end of any (relevant) month if the value of taxable supplies, in the twelve months then ended, has exceeded £61,000, or

(ii) at any time if there are reasonable grounds for believing that taxable supplies in the next 30 days will exceed £61,000.

Sales of capital assets are ignored when considering the registration limits.

You will not become liable under (ii) as your maximum turnover for a month is £6,735 (see Appendix 1).

However, your taxable supplies exceed the limits under (i) by the end of June 2007 (Appendix 1).

You must notify HMRC within 30 days of the end of the relevant month, ie by 30 July 2007.

You will be registered from the end of the month following the relevant month, ie from 1 August 2007.

There is no requirement to register under (i) above if HMRC are satisfied that the taxable supplies in the twelve months beginning 1 July 2007 will not exceed £59,000.

However, it is anticipated that these will be £61,710 (Appendix 1) (more if the catering contract continues); therefore there will be a liability for you to register.

VAT liability

You will have no VAT liability in the seven months to 31 July 2007 as you will not be registered.

From 1 August 2007 you will prepare quarterly returns of output tax (ie VAT on your taxable supplies) and input tax (ie VAT reclaimable from HMRC on goods and services purchased by you).

(1) Output VAT

The output tax (amounts owed to HMRC) on sales for the each month from August to December 2007 (assuming VAT will be added to current prices) will be £1,179 (£6,735 × 17.5%).

Output tax on sales for each month from 31 January 2008 assuming the catering contract ceases will be £621 (£3,550 × 17.5%).

Note. Business customers will be able to reclaim the VAT you charge. Private customers cannot, and you will need to check carefully whether adding output tax to your current charges will lose business. You may need to adjust prices to absorb part of the increase.

VAT on private use of motor car

No output tax is due on the private use of your car as no input tax was recoverable on the purchase of the car.

Output tax is payable, however, on the fuel provided for your private motoring. The VAT element of this is estimated by using the VAT scale charges and is dependent upon

- type of fuel (petrol/diesel)
- cylinder capacity of the car.

(2) Input VAT

You can reclaim any input tax suffered on most of the supplies you receive.

Certain input tax is never reclaimable. This includes input tax on:

- motor cars and accessories supplied with them (unless wholly used for business purposes), and

- entertaining (except of employees).

Accounting for VAT

The quarterly returns must be completed and sent to HMRC, together with any tax, within one month of the end of the quarter.

(b) **Income tax and NIC issues**

Consequences of the change of use of the van from 1 July 2007

Consequences for Karen

There are no income tax consequences for you as you do not use the van for private use.

All costs of running the van remain allowable against your trading income as they are incurred wholly and exclusively for the purposes of the business.

Consequences for your nephew

Your nephew has earnings in excess of £8,500 pa. He will therefore be assessed on the use of the van at weekends as a taxable benefit, using the scale rates, which are increasing considerably from 6 April 2007.

Note that ordinary commuting in the van is an exempt benefit, however any other private use of the van (ie at weekends) gives rise to the benefit charge. You could, therefore, allow him to use the van for travel to and from work, but prohibit any other private use.

Trading income assessment – 2006/07

Adjusted trading profit of year ended 31 December 2006

Your trading income assessment for 2006/07 will be the taxable profits of the year ended 31 December 2006 on the 'current year basis', ie £13,633 (Appendix 2).

In coming to this figure I have allowed the wages paid to your nephew and son on the assumption that these are reasonable for the work performed.

I have also estimated the private use of your car based on the private and business mileage driven ie

$$\frac{2,500}{2,500 + 12,500} = \frac{1}{6}.$$

You should note that as you satisfy the definition of a small business for capital allowances purposes (turnover < £5.6m, fewer than 50 employees), you qualify for 40% FYA on plant and machinery purchased between 6 April 2005 and 5 April 2006 and 50% FYA on plant and machinery purchased between 6 April 2006 and 5 April 2007.

Income tax and NIC – 2006/07

Your income tax for 2006/07 is £1,745, which is due under self assessment.

As a higher rate taxpayer, your basic rate band has been extended by your gross gift aid donation to £33,749 (£33,300 + £449). Both dividends received from shares in an ISA and Premium Bond prizes are exempt from income tax.

As your accounting profit exceeds the small earning limit of £4,465, you will need to pay Class 2 NICs of £109. These are payable monthly by direct debit or by quarterly demand.

Your earnings for Class 4 NIC purposes are the taxable trading profits ie £13,633. You will therefore be required to pay Class 4 contributions of £688, also by self assessment.

All figures above are shown in Appendix 3.

(c) **Investment strategy**

(i) **Investing the surplus £10,000**

The following personal circumstances will all impact on your investment strategy:

- You are 42 years old and single

- Your son is going to university shortly and you may need to contribute towards his fees and maintenance

- You have £10,000 of surplus income per annum

- You currently have a significant investment in quoted shares – assuming a yield of, say, 4%, the shares are worth approximately £563,400 (£22,536 ÷ 4%)

- You would like to reduce your exposure to risk by investing in property

In order to properly advise on an appropriate investment strategy, the following information is required regarding your plans for the future:

- Will you need to realise significant sums at short notice?
- When so you plan to retire?
- How do you intend to replace your earned income?

(ii) **Investment in quoted shares compared with commercial property**

When comparing investments, there are four factors to consider: liquidity, risk, capital growth versus income and, of course, taxation.

Liquidity

The main difference between investing in quoted shares and commercial property is their relative liquidity. Quoted shares can be realised for cash at very short notice. Commercial property, on the other hand, cannot be realised until a buyer has been found and title has been investigated. This disadvantage could be reduced by investing through a Real Estate Investment Trust (REIT) where the investor holds shares in the investment company.

Risk

Quoted shares are medium/high risk depending on the companies concerned. Commercial property may be regarded as medium risk. Again, the risk would be reduced by investing in a REiT.

Capital growth vs income

Both investments should be regarded as likely to generate capital growth in the long term. In the shorter term, depending on the companies concerned and the nature of the properties, there is also the possibility of investment income.

Taxation

Dividend income from share investments has an effective rate of taxation for a higher rate taxpayer like yourself of 25% of the dividend received. For example, a net dividend of £10,000 will give you a tax liability of £2,500. Income from property, whether directly held or via a REIT, is taxed as non savings income at the higher rate of 40%. So, income of £10,000 will give you a higher rate tax liability of £4,000. From a purely tax perspective, an investment in shares is more tax efficient.

This also applies if you are a basic rate tax payer on any part of the income (as may be the case if the new contract is not renewed). To the extent that they fall in the basic rate band no additional tax is payable on dividends, whereas basic rate income tax would be due on property income at 22%.

(iii) **Investing in a personal pension scheme**

Each tax year you can obtain tax relief on the greater of £3,600 and 100% of your relevant earnings (trading income).

- The amount you contribute will be deemed to be net of 22% income tax. The tax deducted at source will be recovered by the pension fund from HMRC.

- As a higher rate taxpayer, you will be able to extend the basic rate band by the gross contribution so that more income is taxed at the basic rather than higher rates. This will provide a minimum tax saving of an additional 18%. This will be particularly useful in 2007/08 because of the additional income from the new contract, although only a small amount of income falls in the higher rate tax band in 2006/07.

- You can also contribute additional amounts from capital, although these will not attract initial tax relief. These will not count towards the annual allowance, which is currently £215,000.

- Income and gains within the fund are tax free

- Funds can usually only be withdrawn when you reach retirement age (50 up to 5 April 2010 and 55 thereafter).

- The pension fund will be tested against the lifetime allowance when funds are vested to provide a pension and/or lump sum. Tax is payable if the fund exceeds the lifetime allowance (currently £1.5 million).

Appendix 1 – VAT taxable turnover

(1) **Taxable turnover**

Assuming turnover accrues evenly over a year and at the same rate.

	£
Normal monthly turnover = £42,600 ÷ 12	3,550
Additional turnover from 1 January 2007	3,185
	6,735

Year ended	Less earliest month £	Add next month £	Cumulative turnover for 12 months £
31 December 2006			42,600
31 January 2007	(3,550)	6,735	45,785
28 February 2007	(3,550)	6,735	48,970
31 March 2007	(3,550)	6,735	52,155
30 April 2007	(3,550)	6,735	55,340
31 May 2007	(3,550)	6,735	58,525
30 June 2007	(3,550)	6,735	61,710

(2)   Taxable turnover in the twelve months after 30 June 2007

		£
July 2007 – December 2007	(6 × £6,735)	40,410
January 2008 – June 2008	(6 × £3,550)	21,300
		61,710

Appendix 2

Taxable trading profits

	£
Net profit per accounts	11,300
Wages – self (drawings)	12,000
Depreciation	
Equipment	1,300
Car	700
Van	500
Loss on sale of car	200
Motor expenses – Karen's car – Private use disallowable ($^1/_6$ × £800)	133
	26,133
Less Capital allowances (W)	(12,500)
Trading income assessment	13,633

Working: Capital allowances – 12 months ended 31 December 2006

	£	General pool £	Car with private use (1) £	Car with private use (2) £	Capital allowances £
WDV b/f		12,000	7,000		
Addition not eligible for FYA					
August 2006				9,600	
Disposal			(7,600)		
		12,000	(600)		
Balancing charge			600 × $^5/_6$		(500)
WDA (25%)		(3,000)		(2,400) × $^5/_6$	5,000
		9,000			
Additions eligible for FYA					
Jan – Feb 2006	14,000				
FYA (40%)	(5,600)				5,600
		8,400			
Sep – Nov 2006	4,800				
FYA (50%)	(2,400)				2,400
		2,400			
WDV c/f		19,800		7,200	
Total allowances					12,500

Appendix 3

Income tax and NIC liabilities 2006/07

Income tax

	Total £	Non-savings £	Savings £	Dividends £
Earned income				
Trading income (above)	13,633	13,633		
Savings income				
NS&I interest	320		320	
Dividend income (£22,536 × $^{100}/_{90}$)	25,040			25,040
STI	38,993	13,633	320	25,040
Less PA	(5,035)	(5,035)	–	–
Taxable income	33,958	8,598	320	25,040

		£		£
Income tax				
Starting rate band:	Non-savings	2,150	@ 10%	215
Basic rate band:	Non-savings	6,448	@ 22%	1,419
	Savings	320	@ 20%	64
	Dividends	24,831	@ 10%	2,483
Extended basic rate band (Note)		33,749		
Higher rate band:	Dividends	209	@ 32½%	68
		33,958		
Income tax liability				4,249
Less Tax credit on dividends				
(£25,040 × 10%)				(2,504)
Income tax payable under self assessment				1,745

Note. Basic rate band is extended by gross gift aid donation of £449 (£350 × $^{100}/_{78}$).

NIC

Class 2: 52 × £2.10 = £109

Class 4

8% × (£13,633 – £5,035) £688

34 Alasdair

Text references. Extracting value from a company is covered in Chapter 30. Liquidation is mentioned in Chapter 30 and also in Chapter 23. Property income and other investment income is covered in Chapter 3. Basic IHT is dealt with in Chapters 17 and 18 with basic CGT in Chapters 11 and 12 and rollover relief in Chapter 14. VAT aspects are dealt with in Chapters 28 and 29. Stamp duty is in Chapter 20. IBAs are in Chapter 7. Investment products are covered in Chapter 31.

Top tips. In part (b) look at each of the three investments suggested one by one outlining both the tax consequences and financial risks as asked by the question.

Easy marks. Try and set out your answer in a logical way. Where a question asks for two of more taxes to be considered (as was asked in part (b)(ii) by the examiner) look at each tax separately. This helps to reduce the possibility of you getting confused and losing marks.

BPR only applies to IHT. It is a popular topic with lots of (easy) marks awarded to the student who knows something about it.

Examiner's comments. This question, involving primarily the IT, CGT, and IHT implications of different investments, was not well done by the relatively few candidates who attempted it.

Part (a) concerned the practical issue of stripping out the value of a company prior to liquidation by means of a dividend, or leaving the cash in the company, and facing a higher CGT charge on the deemed disposal of the shares on liquidation. It was clearly a scenario with which candidates were unfamiliar. Although the dividend option was dealt with reasonably in some cases, a very small number made references to the CGT implications of liquidation.

In part (b) many candidates' answers again suffered from a haphazard, unstructured approach. Those who thought logically, and described the fundamental rules regarding the taxation of property (eg taxable rental income, tax relief for expenses, relief for losses etc), and shares (eg taxation of dividends) scored reasonably.

Most candidates were aware of the existence of reliefs available under CGT and IHT in (b)(ii), although again the details of these, in particular BPR, were sketchy.

Marking scheme

Marks

(a) *Dividend:*
   – Personal allowance ······································· ½
   – Recognition of remaining basic rate band ········· ½
   – Gross up of dividend ··································· ½
   – Tax at 10% ··· ½
   – Tax at 32·5% ·· ½
   – Less tax credit ·· ½
   – Net cash after tax ····································· ½
   Liquidation:
   – Tax treatment of liquidation (CGT) ················· ½
   – Non-business asset taper for dormant period ······ ½
   – Split of ownership period ···························· ½
   – Deduction of liquidator's costs ····················· ½
   – Disposal cost ·· ½
   – Taper relief (2 × 0·5) ································· 1
   – Annual exemption ····································· ½
   – Extra tax payable (20%/40%) ······················· 1
   – Net cash after tax and expenses ··················· ½
   Summary/recommendation ····························· ½

Max   9

(b) (i) *Income tax: direct investment*
   – investment income as property income ············· ½
   – normal trading rules re deduction of expenses ···· ½
   – interest allowed on borrowing to purchase ········· ½
   – use of losses ·· ½
   – commercial property: possibly claim plant allowances ½
   – residential property: wear & tear allowance (furnished) ½
   – normal tax rates (10/22/40%) ······················ ½
   Income Tax: collective investment
   – distributions taxed at 10/32.5% with tax credit ···· ½
   – no relief for interest or other expenses ············ ½
   – REIT – taxed as property income ··················· ½
   CGT:
   – normal rules apply ···································· ½
   – not normally a business asset ······················ ½
   – collective investment may be ISA'd ················· ½
   VAT position on purchase
   – new, commercial/residential ························· ½
   – second hand, commercial ··························· ½
   Stamp Duty Land Tax/Stamp Duty ················· ½
   Investment risks/benefits: direct investment
   – high risk other than long term ······················ ½
   – substantial initial costs ····························· ½
   – significant ongoing running costs ··················· ½
   – illiquid investment (particularly commercial property) ½
   – cyclical market ·· ½
   – residential property historically good inflation hedge ½
   Investment risks/benefits: collective investment
   – reduced risks via diversification through large portfolio ½
   – more liquid investment ······························ ½

Max   9

Note. Additional half marks up to the maximum will be given for other relevant points.

(ii)		
Availability of BPR		1
Rate of BPR		½
Two year ownership condition		½
Availability of rollover relief		1
Operation of rollover relief		½
Requirement for replacement asset		½
Availability of business asset taper relief		½
	Max	4
		22

(a) **Extracting cash from Beezer Ltd**

Taking a dividend will result in net proceeds of £91,875 (W1), compared with net proceeds of £105,187(W2) if the company is liquidated. Alasdair should therefore liquidate the company so that he receives an additional £13,312 of net cash.

Workings

(1) *Dividend payment – income tax computation*

	£
Gross dividend £120,000 × 100/90	133,333
Income tax	
£(33,300 – (30,000 – 5,035)) = £8,335 @ 10%	834
133,333 – 8,335 = £124,998 @ 32.5%	40,624
	41,458
Less tax credit	(13,333)
Additional income tax payable	28,125

Net proceeds £120,000 – £28,125 = £91,875

(2) **Liquidation – capital gains tax computation**

	£
Proceeds (£120,000 – £5,000)	115,000
Cost	(1,000)
	114,000
Gain after taper relief (note)	
15/95 × 75% × £114,000	(13,500)
80/95 × 25% × £114,000	(24,000)
Chargeable gain	37,500
Less annual exemption	(8,800)
Taxable gain	28,700

	£
Capital gains tax	
£8,335 @ 20%	1,667
£20,365 @ 40%	8,146
CGT payable	9,813

Net proceeds £115,000 – £9,813 = £105,187

Note. Seven complete years of ownership from 1 May 2000 – 31 March 2008

Business use 80 months 1 May 2000 – 31 December 2006

Non business use 15 months 1 January 2007 – 31 March 2008

(b) (i) (1) **Buy to let residential property**

For income tax purposes Alasdair will be liable to income tax on the letting profit. This will be the excess of rents receivable over letting costs, such as agents' fees, repairs and maintenance and mortgage interest. Capital allowances are not generally available in respect of residential property (except for furnished holiday lettings), apart from on plant and machinery used to maintain the lettings. Wear and tear allowance at the rate of 10% of rents is available for property which is let furnished. If a loss should arise it will be carried forward and set against future rental profits from any UK properties (residential or commercial) as soon as they arise. Losses may arise if Alasdair finds it difficult to let the property.

When Alasdair sells the property he will be liable to capital gains tax on any increase in value of the property during his period of ownership. He will be entitled to taper relief at the non-business asset rate, although the business asset rate would be available for any period during which the property qualified as furnished holiday lettings.

VAT is not charged on the letting of residential property.

Financially Alasdair will be exposed to fluctuations in the property market. Property is illiquid, and it may not be possible to sell the property at short notice. Property should be viewed as a long term investment. There are also substantial costs associated with buying and selling, such as stamp duty land tax (at 0%, 1%, 3% or 4%), estate agents' and solicitors' fees.

(2) **Commercial property**

As for residential property, Alasdair will be liable to income tax on the letting profit. Capital allowances are generally available on plant and machinery and fixtures in the building. Industrial buildings allowance is available on certain commercial buildings such as factories, but not on buildings such as office and shops. Again losses may be carried forward against future rental profits.

When Alasdair sells the property he will be liable to capital gains tax on any increase in value of the property during his period of ownership. If the property is used for the purposes of a trade carried on by an individual, a partnership or a qualifying company he will be entitled to taper relief at the business asset rate. A qualifying company is broadly an unquoted trading company, but would also include a quoted trading company if Alasdair was an employee or held at least 5% of the shares.

If the property is less than 3 years old on acquisition or the option to tax has previously been exercised, VAT will be charged on the purchase of the building. If Alasdair also opts to tax, he may reclaim the VAT on the purchase price but must charge VAT on the rental income and on the subsequent sale of the building.

As for residential property, investment in commercial property must be regarded as long term. The commercial property market is even more exposed to external factors, and during a downtown a sale may take a significant time. Again there are significant costs associated with buying and selling commercial property.

(3) **Shares in a property investment company/unit trust**

For income tax purposes Alasdair will be liable to income tax only if dividends are paid to him. Additional tax will only be payable if he is a higher rate taxpayer. If Alasdair should have to borrow to purchase the shares or units, no tax relief is available for the interest paid.

The disposal of shares or units will be a chargeable disposal for capital gains tax purposes. Alasdair will be liable to CGT on any gain, but will be entitled to taper relief at the non-business asset rate.

Income and capital gains can be sheltered from tax if the investment is made through an individual savings account.

There are no VAT consequences on buying or selling shares or units, but stamp duty at the rate of 0.5% is payable on the purchase of shares. Purchasing units in a unit trust may incur an initial management charge, which is reflected in the difference between the buying and selling prices of units.

Shares and units are risky investments as they are dependent on the company's performance. However the risk is spread over the portfolio of properties owned by the company or trust, which is less risky than having a single investment. The investment is subject to fluctuations both in the stock market and in the property market due to the underlying investment. Provided the shares or units are quoted they are comparatively liquid as it should be possible to dispose of the shares or units at short notice.

Alasdair might also consider investing in a Real Estate Investment Trust (REIT). Any distributions received will be taxed as property income, not as company dividends and basic rate tax (22%) will be deducted at source from the distribution paid.

(ii)   If Alasdair acquires the warehouse and leases it to Gallus & Co he will be entitled to business property relief for inheritance tax purposes at the rate of 50%. The relief is given by reducing the value of the property by 50% on a transfer of value.

Normally business property relief is only available once the property has been held for two years. Relief may be available earlier if the warehouse can be regarded as replacement property for Beezer Ltd.

For capital gains tax purposes the warehouse will be occupied by a partnership which is carrying on a trade or profession. It will therefore qualify as a business asset for taper relief purposes. It is possible that the warehouse could still qualify as a business asset if occupied by a third party, but Alasdair would not have control over the activities of the tenant and would not be able to be certain that the warehouse would qualify throughout the letting.

Furthermore if the warehouse is used by Gallus & Co it would qualify for capital gains tax rollover relief, provided Alasdair reinvested the proceeds in a replacement business asset. It would not be necessary for the replacement asset to be used by Gallus & Co, Alasdair could, for example, set up a business as a sole trader and use the replacement asset in that business.

35 Neil Johnson

Text references. Chapters 17 to 19 deal with IHT. The basic rules for gains are in Chapters 11 and 12 with the deferral reliefs in Chapter 14. The comparison of operating as a sole trader versus through a company is covered in Chapter 30.

Top tips. Structure your answer using the marks available to guide you as to how much time to spend on each section. The use of a table for your answer in part (d) can be a helpful way to brainstorm a topic.

Easy marks. There were not a lot of marks available for calculations here so you had to set your answer out carefully, using lots of headings and subheadings. Did you pick up that easy mark for your presentation?

Marking scheme

			Marks
(a)	*Current IHT position*		
	Value of estate	1	
	APR	1	
	Nil band	½	
	Tax @ 40%	½	
	QSR	1	
			4
(b)	*Sole trader*		
	Value of business	½	
	Lifetime gift	½	
	BPR @ 100%	½	
	Ownership period	½	
	Death tax implications	½	
	Company investment		
	Lifetime gift	½	
	BPR @ 100%	½	
	Death tax implications	½	
	Company becomes quoted	½	
	Max		4
(c)	*Disposal of quoted investments*		
	Higher rate taxpayer	1	
	Formula to find amount to sell	1	
	Taper relief	1	
	EIS deferral relief	1	
			4
(d)	*Advantages or disadvantages of sole trader or company investment*		
	Income tax	1	
	R&D costs	1	
	NIC	1	
	CGT	1	
	Appreciation of investment	1	
			5
(e)	*Conclusion*		
	Availability of EIS deferral relief	½	
	Greater increase in value	½	
	Greater flexibility on disposal	½	
	Sheltering of income within the company	½	
			2
(f)	*Tax planning*		
	Lifetime gifts	1	
	Use of trust	1	
	Disposal of shares	1	
	No CGT on death	1	
	Remuneration	1	
	House/ farm – GWR implications	1	
	Max		5
	Format/ presentation		2
			26

NOTES FOR MEETING WITH NEIL JOHNSON ON 13 MARCH 2007

(a) **Current inheritance tax position**

If Neil dies before implementing any of the proposals his IHT liability will be £392,000 (W). This will be subject to quick succession relief because his brother's estate was liable to inheritance tax on his death 18 months ago. The rate of QSR is 80%, dropping to 60% 2 years after the death, and by a further 20% each subsequent year.

(b) **Inheritance tax consequences of investment**

(i) Sole trader

- The value of the business for IHT purposes will be the value of the underlying assets including goodwill.

- If Neil owns the business for at least two years, business property relief (BPR) will be available on death.

- If Neil was to make a chargeable lifetime transfer (CLT) of the business (ie by gifting it to a discretionary trust), BPR would also be available at 100%.

- If he dies within 7 years, any potentially exempt transfer (PET) becomes chargeable or there may be additional tax due on a CLT. The property must still be business property in the recipient's hands for the relief to be available in computing any IHT due because of Neil's death.

(ii) Company investment

- After Neil has held the shares for two years, they will qualify for BPR on his death, or on a CLT.

- If Neil dies within 7 years of a CLT or PET the shares must still be held by the recipient for the relief to be available in computing any IHT or additional IHT due because of his death.

- The rate of BPR is 100% regardless of Neil's level of shareholding.

- If the shares become quoted on the Stock Exchange, Neil would need to have control of the company to be entitled to 50% BPR. Otherwise no BPR is available.

Conclusion: Both running the business and holding the shares for two years can remove the value from the charge to IHT whether transferred during Neil's lifetime or as a result of his death.

(c) **Disposal of quoted investments**

(i) Capital gains tax payable

The disposal of quoted investments gives rise to a capital gain in Neil's hands.

The gain, expressed as a fraction of the proceeds is:

	£
Proceeds	X
Less: cost	$(1/3 \times X)$
indexation	$(80\% \times 1/3 \times X)$
Chargeable gain	$40\% \times X$

The taper relief period would run from 6 April 1998 to the date of disposal, so if Neil were to sell the investments before the end of the tax year 65% taper relief would be available (non business assets held for 8 years plus the bonus year). This gives a taxable gain of $26\% \times X$ (ie $65\% \times 40\% \times X$).

As Neil is a higher rate taxpayer (W) the CGT payable would be:

$40\% \times (26\% \times X) = 10.4\% \times X$.

Hence to realise a net sum of about £200,000, Neil would need to sell investments worth £223,214 ($£200,000 \times {}^{100}/_{89.6}$), on which he would pay tax of £23,214.

(ii)   EIS deferral relief

If Neil uses the proceeds of disposal to invest in shares in Boulder's company, then Neil would be able to claim EIS deferral relief.

Neil would only need to sell shares with a value of £200,000, and all of the resulting capital gain (26% × £200,000 = £52,000) could be deferred.

No CGT would be due as the gain would be deferred (effectively with its original taper relief) until the sale of the EIS shares or if the company ceased to be a qualifying company.

(d)   **Any other tax advantages or disadvantages of sole trader v company investment**

		Sole trader	Company investment
(i)	Income tax	Liable to income tax on all the profits arising from the business, on an actual basis (subject to opening year rules). Clearly even after taking disposals of investments into account, Neil is a higher rate tax payer, so all profits will be taxed at 40%.	Liable to income tax on salary or dividends withdrawn. Neil's rate of tax will be 40%, but profits retained in the company will be liable at 19% (small companies' rate), 30% (full rate) or 32.75% (marginal rate). Will not be able to claim EIS income tax relief on the investment if he is connected with the company either by the level of his holding (if it exceeds 30%) or if he is employed by the company. If he is not 'connected' he will be able to obtain a tax reducer of 20% × the investment, but this would be clawed back if he receives any value from the company
(ii)	Technological design	Neil may be able to claim the design costs (if revenue in nature) as pre-trading expenditure. If capital in nature, capital allowances may be available.	Neil could charge the company for his design to offset his costs against the proceeds. The company will be able to claim a tax deduction of up to 150% (depending on the size of the company) for any revenue cost, or capital allowances for any capital expenditure.
(iii)	NIC	Class 2 and Class 4 contributions payable by Neil.	Class 1 contributions payable on salary paid to Neil. Dividends are not liable to NIC. Class 1 is usually more expensive.

		Sole trader	Company investment
(iv)	CGT	Any disposals of capital assets are liable to capital gains tax. If proceeds are reinvested in replacement business assets, roll over relief may be available. Gift relief would be available if Neil gave away the business. Business asset taper relief is available on disposal if Neil runs the business for at least one complete year. The gain remaining chargeable after taper relief is 50% after one complete year and 25% for two or more years.	Any disposals of capital assets are liable to corporation tax within the company. If proceeds are reinvested in replacement business assets in the company, roll over relief may be available. A disposal of shares by Neil would be liable to capital gains tax, and would crystallise the gain deferred using EIS deferral relief. Gift relief would be available if Neil gave away the shares. Business asset taper relief is available on disposal if Neil holds the shares for at least one complete year. The rates are as for a sole trader. Note that if EIS income tax relief is available for the investment then the sale of the shares after three years would be completely exempt from tax, although the deferred gain would still crystallise.
(v)	Appreciation of investment	Neil's business as a sole trader is dependant on Boulder's company continuing to purchase the components from him. Any prospective purchaser would take this into account in valuing the business. Any dispute between Neil and Fred Boulder would have serious consequences for the business.	Since the company will be making the combined product the value of the company is likely to be greater than the value of two separate businesses would be. Neil should be able to achieve a greater appreciation in value. However it is likely that Neil will be a minority shareholder, and is still dependent on good relations with Fred Boulder. If there is a disagreement Neil may be able to sell his shares to Boulder, to a third party or back to the company.

(e)   **Choice of investment**

I would recommend that Neil should invest in shares in Boulder's company. The main reasons are:

(i)   the availability of EIS deferral (and possible income tax and CGT) relief
(ii)   the likely greater appreciation in value
(iii)   the greater flexibility on disposal
(iv)   the sheltering of income within the company.

(f) **Tax planning**

(i) Inheritance tax

After two years the shares will be relevant business property for BPR purposes and can be transferred free of inheritance tax. Although this would also apply on Neil's death, Neil intends to dispose of the business after 7 - 10 years.

Neil could therefore consider giving the shares away before they are due to be sold.

It would be possible to give the shares outright to his sisters and their children (a PET) or give the shares to a discretionary trust (a CLT) for them.

If Neil dies within 7 years of the gift, but after the shares have been sold, there will be a liability to inheritance tax as BPR would no longer be available. However it will be the value of the shares at the date of the gift to take into account, not the value at the date of death.

(ii) Capital gains tax

The gain on the disposal of the shares to the trust can be deferred using gift relief as there is also an IHT charge. It is the gain before taper relief that is deferred. The gain on an outright gift to his sisters and their children could also be deferred using gift relief as the shares are business assets. The recipients would need to hold the shares for two years to obtain maximum business asset taper relief.

If Neil died owning the shares, they would be uplifted to market value free of CGT, as there is no CGT on death.

(iii) Other matters

Neil can structure his remuneration and dividend package in a way to suit himself. He can provide for a pension for himself from the company, which can be used to provide an income stream even after the shares have been sold.

If Neil builds up a pension, he may then be able to afford to give away some of his quoted investments. This would however give rise to a capital gains tax liability, but would avoid IHT if Neil survived 7 years.

He would be unwise to divest himself of his house and farm, whilst living and farming there. Any such gift may well be a gift with reservation (unless a market rental is paid), and so would not save IHT.

Working

IHT on estate

Asset	Value (for part (a)) £	Income (for part (c)) £
Newsome Manor	515,000	–
Farm	150,000	15,000
Quoted investments	400,000	20,000
Assets inherited from brother's estate	350,000	17,500
Total	1,415,000	52,500
Less: Agricultural property relief (100%)	(150,000)	
Estate for inheritance tax purposes	1,265,000	

IHT payable:
£285,000 @ nil%
£980,000 @ 40%   392,000

Mock Exams

ACCA Professional Paper P6 – Options Module

Advanced Taxation (UK)

Mock Examination 1

Question Paper	
Time allowed	**Reading and planning: 15 minutes** **Writing: 3 hours**
This paper is divided into two sections	
Section A	**BOTH questions are compulsory questions and MUST be attempted**
Section B	**TWO questions ONLY to be attempted**

During reading and planning time only the question paper may be annotated

DO NOT OPEN THIS PAPER UNTIL YOU ARE READY TO START UNDER EXAMINATION CONDITIONS

Section A: BOTH questions are compulsory and MUST be attempted

Question 1

Camel Ltd is a trading company that acquired two 100% subsidiaries, Hump Ltd and Dromedary Ltd, both of which are trading companies, on 1 January 2007.

Camel Ltd's forecast profits chargeable to corporation tax for the year ended 31 December 2007 of £1,350,000. Its results for the last four accounting periods were as follows.

	Year to 30 June 2004 £	Six months to 31 Dec 2004 £	Year to 31 Dec 2005 £	Year to 31 Dec 2006 £
Trading profit/(loss)	100,000	80,000	(360,000)	130,000
UK property business income	30,000	62,000	64,000	66,000
Chargeable gains/(losses)	(21,800)	41,700	15,600	(3,000)

Camel Ltd had trading losses brought forward at 1 July 2003 of £13,900.

To finance the purchase of its subsidiaries, Camel Ltd sold a warehouse that had been purchased in March 1997 at a cost of £225,000. In August 2001 Camel Ltd added an extension to the building at a cost of £56,000 and made some repairs to the original building at a cost of £11,500. The whole building was sold in April 2007 for £425,000. The company incurred professional fees of £9,200, which included legal fees of £5,100 and tax adviser's fees of £1,500. The indexation allowance applicable for the period March 1997 to April 2007 can be assumed to be £62,000 and for the period August 2001 to April 2007 it can be assumed to be £9,750.

Hump Ltd intends to acquire a new factory for use in the trade during the year ended 31 December 2007 for £400,000.

Dromedary Ltd has an expected annual turnover of £280,000, inclusive of VAT at the standard rate. The company's turnover consists of 40% cash sales and 60% credit sales; credit customers are expected to pay within 30 days. Bad debts are expected to become an increasing problem in the future. The expected annual cost of raw materials is £41,000, inclusive of VAT at the standard rate. All of the company's suppliers allow two months' credit. Dromedary Ltd's does not suffer input VAT on its expenses.

Camel Ltd pays for tax advice to be provided to their directors. They have approved a report to be prepared for one of the directors, Harry Lamar, who is a higher rate taxpayer. Harry owns 10,000 shares in the company that he acquired in May 2002 at a cost of £9 per share and which are currently valued at £54 per share.

Harry also owns 50,000 ordinary £1 shares in Westplan plc, which was taken over by Eastlane plc on 7 September 2005. He had acquired the Westplan plc shares in June 2000 at a cost of £1.85 per share. He received four £1 ordinary shares in Eastlane plc together with £3 in cash for every two £1 ordinary shares held in Westplan plc. The market value of each £1 ordinary share in Eastlane plc was £1.75 on 7 September 2005. Harry has never been an employee or director of either Westplan plc or Eastlane plc, both of which are non-trading quoted companies. Harry's holding in both companies is less than 1% of the total issued shares.

Harry intends to make a gift of his shares in both companies to his daughter, Trudy, before 31 March 2007. This will be his first substantial lifetime gift. Trudy, who is aged 24 and single, currently receives a salary of £31,500 pa (subject to PAYE of £5,564) and UK bank interest (net) of £800 pa. It is expected that Trudy will receive cash dividends of £12,000 pa from the shares. Trudy pays £1,440 into her employer's registered occupational pension scheme each year.

Required

(a) Describe the options available in respect of Camel Ltd's trading losses for the year ended 31 December 2006 and compute the profits chargeable to corporation tax for the four accounting periods to 31 December 2006 on the assumption that the company wishes to claim all loss reliefs as early as possible. State the time limits for any claims that would need to be submitted.

Show the unrelieved amounts to carry forward at 31 December 2006. **(6 marks)**

(b) Explain how the capital gain arising on the sale of the office building by Camel Ltd might be deferred, indicating any potential restriction on the amount which may be deferred.

Provide a calculation of the gain in support of your answer.

Advise Camel Ltd when it must pay its corporation tax liability in respect of the accounting periods ending on 31 December 2007 and 31 December 2008. **(7 marks)**

(c) Advise Dromedary Ltd whether or not it should use the VAT cash accounting scheme.

Explain the basis of your advice. Detailed calculations are not required. **(3 marks)**

(d) Prepare a report for Harry Lamar concerning his shareholdings. The report should be in three sections, addressing the three sets of issues set out below, and should, where appropriate include supporting calculations.

    (i) Takeover of Westplan plc

        Explain the taxation consequences of the takeover of Westplan plc and state the base cost of Harry's Eastlane plc shares. **(4 marks)**

    (ii) Gift of shares to daughter

        Explain the capital taxes implications which would arise in respect of the gifts of shares in Camel Ltd and Eastlane plc, indicating how these might change if Harry were to die within the next three years. Calculations are not required for this section of the report. **(7 marks)**

    (ii) Daughter's income tax position

        Comment on the impact of the gift of shares on Harry's daughter's income tax payable for the tax year 2007/08. **(3 marks)**

(e) Comment on any issues that may arise regarding the giving of tax advice to directors. **(2 marks)**

Appropriateness of the format and presentation of the report and the effectiveness with which the information is communicated. **(2 marks)**

You may assume that the rates and allowances for the tax year 2006/07 and financial year 2006 continue to apply for the foreseeable future.

(Total = 34 marks)

Question 2

Your manager has received a letter from Geraldine Rivers as she wishes to reorganise her portfolio of assets in a tax efficient way.

STRICTLY PRIVATE AND CONFIDENTIAL

31 January 2007

Dear Tax Manager

Proposed tax efficient reorganisation of assets

My brother, Marc, has decided to start up his own interior design company, InSight Ltd, which I would like to invest in. He says I'll obtain some kind of tax relief for my investment but he didn't specify what it would be.

I'm planning to sell all of my assets at the end of March. I think Marc needs about £75,000 for the new company (which will give me a 40% stake in the business). I know I'll probably realise much more cash than this, so I will probably put it all into a high interest rate building society account.

Marc has offered to support me following the investment. He says I can move in with him and he will look after me into my old age! He is my only remaining close relative and I really want to help him out.

This is probably a good time to bring you up to date on my income and various assets:

Leasehold flat

On 29 September 2006 I sublet the flat to a new tenant who pays me an annual rental of £2,500 on the normal quarter days in advance. My aunt had been staying in the flat until she died on 31 July 2006 and she paid me rent of £50 per month at the end of each month in arrears. The flat was empty before being sub-let to the new tenant.

I spent £350 on redecorating the place on 7 April 2006, £400 on 8 August 2006 on advertising for a new tenant and £500 on electrical repairs on 9 October 2006.

Freehold warehouse

The freehold warehouse I own is now worth around £280,000. I'm still receiving quarterly rental of £10,250.

Semi detached house

This year this property was only rented out for 11 weeks, from 16 April to 30 June 2006, at £400 per week. Each letting only lasted for two weeks. It is worth about £355,300.

I paid council tax of £280 for the year and repairs and maintenance costs of £100.

Other income

During 2006/07 I received the following:

	£
UK dividends	16,500
Dividend income from ISA	500
Building society interest received	3,600
Premium bond prize	100

I think that's everything you need. If you need any further information just let me know.

I look forward to hearing from you.

Yours sincerely

Geraldine Rivers

You have extracted the following further information from client files.

- Geraldine Rivers is 48 and has never married.
- She has made a will leaving all her wealth to Cancer Research, a registered charity.
- Has never contributed to a pension.
- Her asset portfolio is as follows:

Investment properties

Leasehold flat:	Rented out unfurnished. Acquired 31 July 1998 for £10,000 when the lease had 90 years to run. The leasehold has a current value of £67,414.
Freehold warehouse:	This was acquired on 1 September 1997 for £150,000 (its then market value) from her cousin James Richardson. The indexed cost of the warehouse at 5 April 1998 was £152,000. James had constructed the building himself at a cost of £55,000 on 1 July 1991 and had rented it out continuously to Practical Products Ltd, an unquoted trading company, since then. It is still used by Practical Products Ltd, to store products.
Semi-detached house:	This is located in the Peak District and cost Geraldine £200,000 in December 2005. It has increased in value to £250,000 in the short time Geraldine has held the property.

Other investments

Performance plc:	10,000 shares (representing 1% of the share capital). Purchased 1 April 1999 for £7,000 and presently quoted at £2.00.
£25,000 9¾% Treasury Stock 2010:	This was acquired in 2001 for £20,000 but due to the recent period of low interest rates is now worth £40,500. Interest is paid half yearly on 31 March and 30 September.
1972 Rolls Royce:	This cost £15,000 in early December 1987, but today is worth £45,000.
Detached house in Hertfordshire:	Purchased on 20 February 1988 for £160,000 (indexed cost at 5 April 1998 was £172,000) and it is now worth £510,000. Geraldine has always lived there, although she did spend six months on a world cruise which she had always dreamed of doing.
Maxi-ISA:	Had invested £7,000 in 2003. Now worth £11,000.

Required

Write a letter to Geraldine detailing the tax liabilities that will arise if she proceeds with her plans and explaining how she can mitigate these tax liabilities. Show clearly any tax due for 2006/07 and give full explanations for your treatment of the income and expenses from the various properties. **(24 marks)**

You may assume that the asset values will not change in the near future.

Appropriateness of the format and presentation of the letter and the effectiveness with which its content is communicated. **(2 marks)**

You may assume that the rates and allowances for the 2006/07 tax year continue to apply for the foreseeable future.

(Total = 26 marks)

Section B: TWO questions ONLY to be attempted

Question 3

You are the tax adviser to Eyetaki Inc, a company resident in the country of Eyeland.

The following information has been extracted from client files and from meetings with shareholders.

Eyetaki Inc:

- Manufactures cameras in Eyeland.

- Has been selling these in the UK since 1 January 2007.

- Initially, Eyetaki Inc employed a UK based agent to sell their cameras and rented a warehouse in London in order to maintain a stock of goods.

- On 1 March 2007 Eyetaki Inc sent an office manager and two sales managers to the UK from their head office in Eyeland and rented an office building and showroom in London.

UK subsidiary:

- On 1 July 2007 Eyetaki Inc will form a 100% subsidiary, Uktaki Ltd.

- Will be incorporated in the UK.

- Will commence trading on 1 August 2007 and will make up its first accounts for the 18 month period to 31 December 2008.

- Will initially sell cameras on a wholesale basis, but will commence retail sales during 2008.

Purchase of freehold building:

- Uktaki Ltd will purchase a new freehold building.

- The building will be used to:

    (a)   assemble cameras from components imported from Eyeland, and
    (b)   store components prior to their assembly, and assembled cameras prior to sale.

- The building will also contain a showroom and general offices.

Camera components:

- Eyetaki Inc will export camera components to the UK at their normal trade selling price plus a markup of 25%.

- Wishes to maximise its own profits which are only subject to corporation tax at the rate of 15% in Eyeland.

Appointment of director:

- A director, currently resident and domiciled in Eyeland, will be assigned to the UK for a period of between two and three years to manage Uktaki Ltd.

- Will continue to be employed by Eyetaki Inc and will perform duties both in the UK and Eyeland.

- Has income from investments situated in Eyeland.

Tax position of Eyeland:

- No double taxation treaty between the UK and Eyeland.

- Eyeland is not currently a member of the European Union, but is expected to become a member in the near future.

Required

(a) (i) Advise Eyetaki Inc of whether or not it will be liable to UK corporation tax during the period from 1 January 2007 to 31 December 2008, and, if so, how the corporation tax liability will be calculated.

(ii) Set out Uktaki Ltd's accounting periods for the period up to, and including, 31 December 2008.

(7 marks)

(b) Explain as to what extent the new freehold building to be purchased by Uktaki Ltd will qualify for Industrial Buildings Allowance, and state the Industrial Buildings Allowance that will be available. **(4 marks)**

(c) Briefly advise Uktaki Ltd of the basis on which it will have to account for VAT on the components imported from Eyeland. Explain how this basis will alter if Eyeland becomes a member of the European Union.

(3 marks)

(d) Advise Eyetaki Inc and Uktaki Ltd of the tax implications arising from the invoicing of camera components at their normal trade selling price plus a markup of 25%. **(2 marks)**

(e) Briefly state the circumstances in which the director of Eyetaki Inc will be liable to UK income tax in respect of:

(i) Emoluments for duties performed in the UK.
(ii) Emoluments for duties performed in Eyeland.
(iii) Investment income arising in Eyeland. **(4 marks)**

(Total = 20 marks)

Question 4

You act as Sue Macker's tax accountant. Sue Macker was made redundant from her employment on 15 March 2006. She is a vintage motor car enthusiast, and so decided to take this opportunity to indulge her hobby

The following information has been extracted from client files and from meetings with Sue.

Sue Macker:

• Had no other income during the tax year 2006/07.

Premises and equipment:

• Took out a bank loan of £75,000, at an annual interest rate of 10%, on 6 April 2006.
• Rented a workshop for twelve months at £400 per month.
• Purchased equipment for £13,500.

Purchase of motor vehicles:

• Purchased four dilapidated vintage motor cars for £8,000 each on 10 April 2006.
• Completed restoration of the four cars on 1 March 2007 at a cost of £12,000 per motor car.
• Sold all of the motor cars on that day for a total of £200,000.

Change of circumstances:

• Sue was then offered employment elsewhere in the country commencing on 6 April 2007.
• Sold the equipment for £5,800 on 20 March 2007.
• Repaid the bank loan on 5 April 2007.

Tax treatment of profits:

• Believes she has just been indulging a hobby. She is adamant that the disposal of the vintage motor cars is exempt from tax and insists she will not complete self employment pages for her tax return.

• Has done some research on the Internet and has discovered that whether or not she is treated as carrying on a trade will be determined according to six 'badges of trade'.

Required

(a) State and briefly explain each of the 'badges of trade'. You are not expected to quote from decided cases.

(6 marks)

(b) Prepare notes for a meeting with Sue at which you will discuss whether or not she is likely to be treated as carrying on a trade in respect of her vintage motor cars. **(5 marks)**

(c) Calculate Sue's income tax liability and her Class 2 and Class 4 national insurance contributions for the tax year 2006/07, if she is treated as carrying on a trade in respect of her vintage motor car activities. Advise Sue what notifications should be made to HMRC, including any notification required for VAT. **(7 marks)**

(d) Explain why it would be beneficial if Sue were instead treated as not carrying on a trade in respect of her vintage motor car activities. **(2 marks)**

(Total = 20 marks)

Question 5

Mabel Porter is 76 years old and in poor health.

The following information has been extracted from client files and from meetings with Mabel.

Mabel Porter:

- Husband, Luke, died on 1 June 2006.

- Has no children.

- Mabel has capital losses of £13,000 brought forward at 5 April 2006.

- Mabel has left the whole of her estate to Bruce and Padma, her brother's children, in her will.

- Bruce and Padma have always visited Mabel regularly although, since emigrating to South Africa in January 2003, Bruce now keeps in touch by telephone.

Assets owned:

- Below is a list of Mabel's assets, showing the current market value and probate value where inherited from Luke:

	Probate value on 1 June 2006	Market value Today	Estimated at 30 June 2011
	£	£	£
House and furniture		325,000	450,000
Rolls Royce motor car		71,000	55,000
Diamond necklace		70,000	84,000
Cash and investments in quoted shares		120,000	150,000
Assets inherited from her husband, Luke:			
40,000 ordinary shares in BOZ plc	44,500	77,000	95,000
Land in the country of Utopia	99,000	75,000	75,000

Mabel's lifetime gifts:

- Only lifetime gift to date was £170,000 to a discretionary trust on 1 May 2000.

- Has decided to give a substantial presents to both Bruce and Padma on each of their birthdays on 1 February 2007 and 5 March 2007 respectively (see below).

- Does not want to gift any asset that will give rise to a tax liability prior to her death and hopes the gifts will reduce her eventual inheritance tax liability.

- Bruce and Padma have agreed to sign any elections necessary to avoid tax arising on the gifts.

- Assume the market values of the assets will not change between now and when the gifts are made.

Gift to Bruce:

- Will gift either the shares in BOZ plc or the land in the country of Utopia.

- Luke purchased the BOZ plc shares on 1 March 2003.

- BOZ plc is a quoted manufacturing company with an issued share capital of 75,000 ordinary shares. It owns investment properties that represent 8% of the value of its total assets.

- The land in Utopia consists of a small farm that has always been rented out to tenant farmers. It was purchased by Luke on 1 May 2002 and has a current agricultural value of £58,000.

Gift to Padma:

- Will gift either the Rolls Royce or the necklace.
- Purchased the Rolls Royce, new, in June 2001, for £185,000.
- Inherited the necklace from her grandmother in April 1984; its probate value at that time was £11,500.

Required

(a) Explain the immediate capital gains tax and inheritance tax implications of each of the four possible gifts. Quantify the capital gain or loss and the potentially exempt transfer in each case and comment on the availability or otherwise of any reliefs. **(10 marks)**

(b) Mabel has two objectives when making the gifts to Bruce and Padma:

　　(1)　To pay no tax on any gift in her lifetime; and
　　(2)　To reduce the eventual liability to inheritance tax on her death.

Advise Mabel which item to gift to Bruce and to Padma in order to satisfy her objectives. Give reasons for your advice.

Your advice should include a computation of the inheritance tax saved as a result of the two gifts, on the assumption that Mabel dies on 30 June 2011. **(8 marks)**

(c) Without changing the advice you have given in (b), or varying the terms of Luke's will, explain how Mabel could further reduce her eventual inheritance tax liability and quantify the tax saving that could be made.
(2 marks)

The increase in the retail prices index from April 1984 to April 1998 is 84%.

You should assume that the rates and allowances for the tax year 2006/07 will continue to apply for the foreseeable future.

(Total = 20 marks)

Answers

DO NOT TURN THIS PAGE UNTIL YOU HAVE
COMPLETED THE MOCK EXAM

A plan of attack

What's the worst thing you could be doing right now if this was the actual exam paper? Sharpening your pencil? Wondering how to celebrate the end of the exam in about 3 hours time? Panicking, flapping and generally getting in a right old state?

Well, they're all pretty bad, so turn back to the paper and let's sort out a **plan of attack**!

First things first

You have 15 minutes reading time. Make sure you spend it wisely, looking through the paper in detail working out which optional questions to do and the order in which to attack the questions. You've then got **two options**. Option 1 is the option recommended by BPP.

Option 1 (if you're thinking 'Help!')

If you're a bit worried about the paper, do the questions in the order of how well you think you can answer them. If you find the questions in Section B less daunting than the compulsory questions in Section A, start with Section B. Remember you only need to do two of the three questions in Section B. Start by deciding which question you will not do and put a line through it.

- The requirements of **question 3** are broken down, which is helpful in allocating your time. Also, you can clearly see where the marks are. If you could make a good attempt at each part of this question this may well have been worth doing first.

- **Question 4** is a sole trader question requiring a discussion of the badges of trade. If you feel confident with this area you could have selected this question first.

- If you are totally happy with chargeable gains calculations and inheritance tax calculations then start with **question 5**. If you feel you are doing these computations correctly, it will boost your confidence.

Ensure that you do not spend longer than your allocated time on Section B. When you've spent the allocated time on **two** of the three questions in Section B turn to the longer questions in Section A. Read these questions through thoroughly before you launch into them. Once you start make sure you allocate your time to the parts within the questions according to the marks available and that, where possible, you attempt the easy marks first.

Lastly, what you mustn't forget is that you have to **answer both questions in Section A and TWO in Section B**. Do not miss out more than one question in Section B and do not waste time answering three questions in Section B or you will seriously affect your chance of passing the exam.

Option 2 (if you're thinking 'It's a doddle')

It never pays to be over confident but if you're not quaking in your shoes about the exam then **turn straight to the compulsory questions** in Section A.

Once you've done these questions, move to Section B.

- The question you attempt first really depends on what you are most confident at.

- You then have to select one of the two remaining questions. If you are undecided look at the requirements. It maybe easier to obtain more marks if these are broken down into several smaller parts.

No matter how many times we remind you....

Always, always **allocate your time** according to the marks for the question in total and then according to the parts of the question. And **always, always follow the requirements** exactly. Question 1 part (a), for example, asks you to show the amounts carried forward. You have calculated the figures, you just need to write them down to gain two easy marks. Make sure you get them.

You've got spare time at the end of the exam.....?

If you have allocated your time properly then you **shouldn't have time on your hands** at the end of the exam. But if you find yourself with five or ten minutes to spare, check over your work to make sure that there are no silly arithmetical errors.

Forget about it!

And don't worry if you found the paper difficult. More than likely other candidates will too. If this were the real thing you would need to **forget** the exam the minute you leave the exam hall and **think about the next one**. Or, if it's the last one, **celebrate**!

Question 1

> **Text references.** Chapters 21 and 22 cover the calculation of corporation tax liabilities with losses in Chapter 24. The basic rules for gains are in Chapters 11 and 12 with the implications for groups in Chapter 26. The VAT schemes are in Chapter 29. Chapter 7. Takeovers are covered in Chapter 13. CGT and IHT on gifts are in Chapters 14 and 17 respectively. Ethics are in Chapter 30.
>
> **Top tips.** You do not have to attempt each requirement in order. For example part (d) was a stand alone requirement and could have been attempted first. Do, however, ensure that you put your answer into the correct order when you have finished.
>
> **Easy marks.** You should have found calculating the daughter's additional income tax relatively straightforward.

Marking scheme

				Marks
(a)	Options for loss			
	Current year		1	
	Current year and carry back		1	
	Carry forward		1	
	PCTCT for each year (½ for each)		1½	
	Time limit		1	
	Trading / capital losses carried forward		2	
		Max		6
(b)	Gains group		½	
	One unit for rollover		½	
	Qualifying assets		½	
	Time period		½	
	Used for trading purposes		½	
	Proceeds not reinvested		½	
	Gain rolled over into base cost of asset		½	
	Calculation		1	
	y/e 31.12.07 – 9m 1 day		1	
	Reasons		1	
	y/e 31.12.08 – quarterly instalments		1	
		Max		7
(c)	Scheme is beneficial		1	
	Outline of scheme		1	
	VAT on creditors deferred		1	
	Automatic bad debt relief		1	
		Max		3

(d)   *Takeover of Westplan plc*

Gain on cash	½
No gain on shares	½
Take over old shares' acquisition details	1
Apportion base cost	1
Calculation of gain on cash	1
Base cost of shares	1

	Max	4

Gifts of shares

PETs – no tax during lifetime	½
Chargeable if dies within 3 years	½
BPR @ 100%	1
Annual exemptions	½
Nil band	½
Tax at 40%	½
Deemed disposal at market value	1
Gift relief for unquoted shares	½
Joint election	½
Restriction for non business assets	½
No gift relief for quoted shares	½
Taper relief	1
Annual exemptions	1
Exempt from stamp duty	1

	Max	7

Daughter's tax position

Additional income	1
Gross up dividend	1
Additional tax calculation	1

		3

(e)

Benefit	1
Conflict of interest	1

		2

Format/ presentation   2

                                                    34

(a)   **Trading losses**

There are three options for use of the loss of the year ended 31 December 2005.

(i)   A claim can be made to relieve it in the current year, with the balance carried forward automatically against future trading profits.

(ii)   Claims can be made to relieve it in the current period and then carry the excess back against profits of the preceding 12 months with any balance automatically carried forward.

(iii) No claim is made so the loss is automatically carried forward.

No group relief is available as the two subsidiaries are not acquired until after the loss making period.

Since the company wishes to claim relief as soon as possible this indicates that a carry back claim is needed. Therefore option (ii) above will be most suitable which will require s 393A claims as follows:

•   current year: £79,600 (W)

•   carry back: £161,900 (W) to the six months ended 31 December 2004 and £58,050 (W) to 6 months of the year ended 30 June 2004

The claim must be made within two years of the end of the loss making period, ie by 31 December 2007.

The balance of £60,450 is then carried forward automatically.

Losses carried forward

There are no trading losses unrelieved at 31 December 2006 (W).

The capital loss of £3,000 in the period to 31 December 2006 must be carried forward to set against capital gains in future periods.

Working

Trading losses

	30 June 2004 £	31 Dec 2004 £	31 Dec 2005 £	31 Dec 2006 £
Trading profits	100,000	80,000	–	130,000
Less s393(1) losses b/f	(13,900)	–	–	(60,450)
	86,100	80,000	–	69,550
UK property business profits	30,000	62,000	64,000	66,000
Net chargeable gains (£41,700 – £21,800)	Nil	19,900	15,600	Nil
Total profits	116,100	161,900	79,600	135,550
s393A loss relief (W)				
Current year			(79,600)	
Carry back	(58,050)	(161,900)		
PCTCT	58,050	Nil	Nil	135,550

Loss memo

	£	£
Trading loss b/f under s393(1)		60,450
Utilised in y/e 31 December 2006		(60,450)
Loss in chargeable accounting period	360,000	
s393A		
Current year claim – y/e 31 December 2006	(79,600)	
Carry back claim		
(i) 6 m/e 31 December 2005	(161,900)	
(ii) y/e 30 June 2004		
(restricted to $^6/_{12}$ × £116,100)	(58,050)	
Trading loss c/f under s393(1)	60,450	Nil

(b) **Deferral of gain on disposal of office**

Camel Ltd and Hump Ltd are members of a capital gains group (≥ 75% direct ownership) and are treated as one unit for rollover relief purposes.

Camel Ltd's gain on the disposal of the building can therefore be deferred by a group roll-over relief claim. Camel Ltd's gain is deferred against the base cost of the factory purchased by Hump Ltd.

Rollover relief is available as:

- both assets are qualifying assets (a warehouse and a factory), and
- Hump Ltd reinvests in qualifying assets within three years of the disposal by Camel Ltd.

The deferred gain will be restricted to the extent that the proceeds of sale are not reinvested in the replacement qualifying assets.

The gain that remains chargeable in the year ended 31 December 2007 will be £25,000, being the

Lower of:

(i)	the gain	£64,550 (W)
(ii)	proceeds not reinvested (£425,000 – £400,000)	£25,000

The amount of gain that can be deferred will also be restricted if Camel Ltd has not always used the warehouse for trading purposes until the date of disposal.

259

Working

	£
Sale proceeds (April 2007)	425,000
Less Incidental selling expenses (£9,200 – £1,500) (Note 1)	(7,700)
Net sale proceeds	417,300
Less Acquisition cost (March 1997)	(225,000)
Enhancement expenditure (August 2001) (Note 2)	(56,000)
Unindexed gain	136,300
Less Indexation allowance	
Acquisition cost	(62,000)
Enhancement expenditure	(9,750)
Indexed gain	64,550

Notes

1   Tax adviser's fees are not allowable deductions.
2   Expenditure on repairs is not an allowable deduction.

Corporation tax payments – Camel Ltd

Year ended 31 December 2007

Camel Ltd will be a large company in the year ended 31 December 2008 as its profits are approximately £1.4 million and the upper limit for determining the corporation tax rate is £500,000 (£1,500,000 ÷ 3).

A large company usually pays corporation tax in four quarterly instalments. However, instalments are only due if:

- the company has a tax liability of more than £10,000

- it was not 'large' in the previous period but has 'profits' of over £10 million in this accounting period.

Camel Ltd was not large in the year ended 31 December 2006 and its 'profits' are less than £10 million in the year ended 31 December 2007. It does not need to make instalment payments.

It must therefore pay its CT liability by nine months and one day from the end of the period, ie by 1 October 2008.

Year ended 31 December 2008

Camel Ltd must start paying by instalments in the year ended 31 December 2008. It will need to pay 25% of its estimated CT liability every three months starting 14 July 2008.

(c)   **VAT cash accounting scheme**

Use of the cash accounting scheme, under which VAT is only payable/recoverable when cash is paid to suppliers and received from customers, appears to be favourable for Dromedary Ltd.

As Dromedary Ltd will have an excess of trade debtors over trade creditors, there are two main reasons why the scheme would be beneficial:

(i)   the scheme would allow the payment of output VAT on credit sales to be deferred which would presumably outweigh the delay in recovering input VAT on credit purchases.

(ii)   there will be automatic bad debt relief, as output VAT will not be charged where a customer never pays.

(d) **Report on Harry Lamar's shareholdings**

To: Harry Lamar
From: A Adviser
Date: [date]
Subject: Shareholdings – tax implications

This report covers tax issues relating to:

(i) Takeover of Westplan plc
(ii) Gift of shares to daughter
(iii) Daughter's income tax position

(i) Takeover of Westplan plc

When Eastlane plc took over Westplan plc you received a mixture of cash and shares in exchange for your existing shareholding.

Where this occurs a chargeable gain arises only in respect of the cash consideration received. There is no gain in respect of the shares received; instead the new shares take over the acquisition details of the old shares.

So, a chargeable gain of £40,163 will have arisen in respect of the £75,000 cash received but no gain will have arisen in respect of the 100,000 ordinary shares in Eastlane plc you received. They will have a base cost of £64,750 which you will use when you eventually dispose of the shares (eg when you gift them to your daughter – see below).

See Appendix 1 for calculations of the above figures.

(ii) Gift of shares to daughter

IHT

The proposed gifts of shares to your daughter, Trudy, are potentially exempt transfers (PETs) for inheritance tax purposes. There is no IHT during lifetime but if you were to die within three years of making the gifts they would become chargeable to IHT.

As the Camel Ltd shares are unquoted trading company shares they are business property at the date of gift for Business Property Relief (BPR) purposes. 100% business property relief will be available if the PET becomes chargeable if:

• Trudy still owns the shares at your death, and
• they are still business property at that time.

As Eastlane plc is a quoted company and you do not have a controlling interest the shares are not eligible for BPR.

If the gifts become chargeable, the value of the Eastlane plc shares may be reduced by the annual exemption for 2006/07 and 2005/06, which should both be available as this is your first gift during lifetime.

You will also have your nil rate band to set against the transfer of value of the Eastlane plc shares, which is currently £285,000. Any excess will be taxed at 40%.

> **Top tips.** No credit is available for mentioning the possibility of taper relief on the Eastlane plc shares as the question specifically asked for implications if Charles were to die within the next three years.

CGT

The gifts will also be disposals for CGT purposes. Even though no proceeds will be received from Trudy the gifts will be deemed to take place at the market value at the date of the gifts, as they will not take place at arm's length and you and Trudy are connected persons.

As the Camel Ltd shares are qualifying assets for gift relief purposes (any number of unquoted trading company shares), you and Trudy may make a joint claim to defer the gain arising on those shares.

The gain before taper relief will be rolled over into the base cost of the shares for Trudy. The amount of gain that can be deferred may be restricted by the value of chargeable non business assets held by Camel Ltd if you own at least 5% of the shares in Camel Ltd.

As you do not own at least 5% of the Eastlane plc quoted shares, they are not qualifying assets for gift relief purposes. The base cost for the shares will be the original cost of the Westplan plc shares (see above) and taper relief will run from June 2000. The gain after the annual exemption of £8,800 will be taxable at 40%.

Stamp duty

Transfers of shares usually attract a 0.5% stamp duty charge. There is an exemption for gifts so no stamp duty will be due.

(iii)   Daughter's income tax position

After the gift of the shares, Trudy will change from being a basic rate taxpayer to being a higher rate taxpayer. She will therefore have an additional income tax liability of £1,515 (see Appendix 2).

(e)   Camel Ltd pays for advice given to directors. This is a taxable benefit for the directors, the taxable amount being the cost of the advice to Camel Ltd. Camel Ltd will also have to pay Class 1A NICs.

Where the report commissioned concerns tax issues arising from the directorship or shareholding in Camel Ltd, it is possible that there may be a conflict of interest between the director and the company. It will be necessary to consider whether advice can be given, or whether the conflict is such that it could be necessary to decline the request to prepare a report. If you feel that advice can be given you may still like to suggest that the director should consider obtaining additional independent advice.

Appendix 1 – Takeover of Westplan plc

Gain arising on cash consideration

	£
Cash consideration received (W1)	75,000
Less Deemed cost (W2)	(27,750)
Gain before taper relief	47,250
Gain after taper relief (NBA: 6.00 – 9.05 = 5 years): 85%	40,163
Base cost of shares in Eastlane plc (W2)	£64,750

Workings

(1)   *Consideration received*

	£
Ordinary shares in Eastlane plc (50,000 × 4 ÷ 2=) 100,000 × £1.75	175,000
Cash (50,000 × £3 ÷ 2)	75,000
Total market value	250,000

(2)   *Allocation of original cost*

	£
Total cost of original Westplan plc shares = 50,000 × £1.85	92,500
Ordinary shares in Eastlane plc $\dfrac{£175,000}{£250,000} \times £92,500$	64,750
Cash consideration $\dfrac{£75,000}{£250,000} \times £92,500$	27,750

Appendix 2 – Additional income tax liability

	£	£
Current income level:		
Salary	31,500	
Less: pension contributions (note)	(1,440)	
Employment income		30,060
Bank interest (£800 × $^{100}/_{80}$)		1,000
		31,060
Additional dividend income:		
£12,000 × $^{100}/_{90}$		13,333
Additional tax on £13,333		
£7,275 (£33,300 – [31,060 – 5,035]) @ 10%		
£6,058 @ 25%		1,515

Note. Tax relief is given for pension contributions paid up to the higher of £3,600 and the amount of relevant UK earnings. The full amount is therefore an allowable deduction for income tax purposes.

Question 2

Text references. The income tax computation is in Chapter 1. The EIS scheme is covered in Chapters 2 and 14. Property income is in Chapter 3. The basics of capital gains are in Chapters 11 and 12. The deferral reliefs are in Chapter 14 with leases covered in Chapter 15.

Top tips. It was important in this question to do your calculations first so that you could advise the client sensibly. Make sure that they are in Appendices so that your answer looks as professional as possible.

You were not provided with a structure for this question which made it difficult to know where the marks were allocated. Planning your answer carefully (whether with bullet points or maybe brainstorming with a spider diagram) will help you immensely.

Easy marks. The marks available for stating the conditions for a property to be a furnished holiday letting are easy if you have learnt them.

Marking scheme

		Marks
Gains		
Leasehold property	1	
Warehouse	1	
Performance Plc shares	1	
Peak District house		
FHL	½	
Taper relief position	½	
Delay sale	1	
Treasury stock, car and ISA	1	
Hertfordshire house		
PPR relief	1	
Consider retaining	½	
EIS deferral relief – operation of relief	2	
Amount to invest	1	
Lifetime gifts to brother	1	
Lifetime gifts to charity	1	
Leaving assets on death	1	
Taper relief position for all assets	1	
Annual exemption	½	
CGT due	½	
Due date	½	
Use of two AEs for disposals over two years	½	
Gifts directly to charity	1	
Conclusion	1	
Income tax		
Property business income	1	
Loss on rental to aunt	1	
FHL conditions	1	
Dividends	½	
BSI	½	
Treasury stock interest	½	
Personal allowance	½	
Tax rates and bands	1	
Tax suffered	½	
Tax liability	½	
	Max	24
Format/Presentation		2
		26

[Our address]

[Your address]

[Date]

STRICTLY PRIVATE AND CONFIDENTIAL

Dear Geraldine

Disposal of assets

Thank you for your recent letter.

If you proceed with your plans to sell all of your assets in March 2007, but defer the sale of the Peak District House as suggested below, the total gains after taper relief will be £81,940.

After deducting the capital gains tax (CGT) annual exemption, CGT of £29,256 will be payable (Appendix 1). This is due for payment on 31 January following the year of assessment, ie 31 January 2008.

However, there are reliefs available which could reduce or avoid some of the tax calculated above, and I have considered your reinvestment plan and your assets below.

Reinvestment plan

It appears that your brother's company could be a qualifying company under the Enterprise Investment Scheme (EIS). You should therefore be able to claim CGT deferral relief which will allow you to defer paying tax on your gains. There are other reliefs available for such investments (an income tax reducer and an exemption on the sale of the EIS shares) but these require you to have a holding of less than 30% in the company, so these are not available to you.

The way that the relief works is that the gain on the disposal of your assets is frozen by using the gain to invest in EIS shares and only unfreezes, or crystallises, usually when the shares are sold in the future. When the gain crystallises it will be allowed its original taper relief. An amount equal to the gain must be reinvested in your brother's company to obtain full relief. You may specify a lower amount to take advantage of your annual exemption and taper relief. The investment must take place within the period 12 months before your disposals and 36 months following.

Any lifetime gifts of the shares, perhaps to your brother, would be a deemed disposal at market value and the frozen gain would become chargeable. However you would be able to defer the gain arising on any growth in value of the shares using gift relief so long as you and your brother make a joint election. In that case the gain deferred (before taper relief) would reduce the base cost of the shares for your brother.

Such a gift would also be a potentially exempt transfer for inheritance tax (IHT) purposes. There would be no tax due during your lifetime but a charge could arise for your brother if you were to die within seven years of making the gift.

If you instead gave the shares directly to Cancer Research no CGT or IHT would arise as the transfer would be exempt.

If the shares are retained until your death no CGT will be payable, either on the amount of deferred gains or on any increase in value in the shares themselves, as there is no CGT on death.

Leasehold flat

The sale of the freehold reversion gives rise to a chargeable gain before taper relief of £57,414 but this can be deferred by buying shares in Fred's company (see above).

The only problem I anticipate is finding a buyer for this property at such short notice, but I assume you have already made plans.

Freehold warehouse

The gain arising of £128,000 may be deferred if you buy shares in Fred's company (see above). Full business asset taper relief is available to reduce this gain as it is a business asset held for at least two years.

Shares in Performance plc

The gain of £13,000 can again be deferred by investing in your brother's company.

House in Peak District

If the house is sold in March 2007 a gain of £50,000 will arise, with 50% taper relief available.

However, as the house qualifies as a furnished holiday let (FHL – see below) it is treated as a business asset for taper relief purposes. If you own the property as an FHL for at least 2 years (ie until December 2007), thus delaying the disposal until 2007/08, a further 25% taper relief will be available leaving only 25% of the gain chargeable to CGT.

Treasury stock, car and ISA

No gain will crystallise on these assets as they are not chargeable to CGT. As there is no chargeable gain, deferral relief is not available so there would be no tax benefit of using the proceeds to invest in Marc's company.

House in Hertfordshire

The gain on this house is covered fully by principal private residence relief which exempts the gain. Your absence on the world cruise does not affect this. Again, there is no tax benefit of using the proceeds to invest in your brother's company. You may therefore consider retaining the house for the foreseeable future.

If these suggestions are followed, the capital gains tax consequences are:

2006/07

Crystallise gains on the leasehold property, the warehouse and the shares. Net gains of £123,414 before taper relief (Appendix 3) would arise, if you invest £75,000 in Marc's company. This would lead to CGT payable of £8,821. More of these gains could be deferred if you invested more in Marc's company, but each additional £10,000 invested would reduce taxable gains by £2,500 because of taper relief, and would save CGT of £1,000.

2007/08

Sell the house in the Peak District no earlier than December 2007 and you will obtain a further 25% of business asset taper relief.

By arranging disposals over two tax years there is an added advantage of utilising a second annual exemption. The timing of individual disposals is not so important so long as sufficient gains are crystallised each year to cover the annual exemption.

If you are open to alternative suggestions, assets could be gifted directly to Cancer Research and these gifts would be free of CGT and IHT.

This may cause problems as you would have few assets to generate income on which to live. However, it is possible to avoid or defer CGT under my recommendations above and there would be no tax advantage in making the gifts now.

Income tax liability 2006/07

An income tax liability of £15,717 would be due under self-assessment for 2006/07 (Appendix 4).

The Peak District house is treated as a 'furnished holiday let' as it was available for letting for at least 140 days, was actually let for at least 70 days (16 April 2006 to 30 June 2006) and there were no periods of longer term occupation (ie no single let exceeded 31 days). It is therefore treated as earned income. It is let furnished so a 10% wear and tear allowance is available.

As your aunt was paying a non-commercial, or 'peppercorn' rent during the period she rented the flat from you, the loss arising cannot be used.

Although the advertising costs were incurred when the property was empty, the expense relates wholly and exclusively to the business of letting property and therefore relief is available against the income from the new tenant.

In summary I recommend:

(1)   Delay the sale of the Peak District house until at least December 2007.

(2)   Invest at least £75,000 in Marc's business in 2006/07 and claim EIS deferral relief.

(3)   Possibly retain your main residence as the growth is accruing tax free so long as you remain in occupation of the property.

Please do not hesitate to contact me if you need further assistance.

Yours sincerely

Tax adviser

Appendix 1

Gains on disposal of assets if sold in March 2007

Leasehold flat – sale of long lease

	£	£
Proceeds	67,414	
Cost	(10,000)	
Gain before taper relief	57,414	
Taper relief 7.98 – 3.07 = 8 yrs, non business asset: 70%		40,190

Freehold warehouse

	£	£
Proceeds	280,000	
Indexed cost	(152,000)	
Gain before taper relief	128,000	
Taper relief 4.98 – 3.07 = 8 yrs, business asset: 25%		32,000

Shares in Performance plc

	£	£
Proceeds (10,000 × £2.00)	20,000	
Cost	(7,000)	
Gain before taper relief	13,000	
Taper relief 1.4.99 – 3.07 = 7 yrs, non business asset: 75%		9,750

House in Hertfordshire

	£	£
Proceeds	510,000	
Indexed cost	(172,000)	
Gain before taper relief	338,000	
Less: PPR relief (100%)	(338,000)	
Chargeable gain		Nil
Total gain after taper relief		81,940
Less: Annual exemption		(8,800)
		73,140
CGT @ 40%		£29,256

Appendix 2

Gains on disposal of the Peak District property

2006/07

A gain arises on the disposal of the Peak District property in 2006/07 as follows:

	£
Proceeds	250,000
Cost	(200,000)
Gain before taper relief	50,000
Taper relief 12.05 – 3.07 = 1 yr, business asset: 50%	25,000

2007/08

However, it is recommended that the sale is delayed until at least December 2007 to obtain full business asset taper relief as follows:

	£
Proceeds	250,000
Cost	(200,000)
Gain before taper relief	50,000
Taper relief 12.05 – 3.08 = 2 yrs, business asset: 25%	12,500

This will save at least £5,000 in tax and if your annual exemption for 2007/08 if otherwise unused will save a further £3,520 of tax.

Appendix 3 – recommendation

2006/07

Gain remaining chargeable	25%	70%	75%
	£	£	£
Freehold warehouse	128,000		
Flat - reversionary interest		57,414	
Quoted shares			13,000
House in Peak District – delay to 2007/08			
Less: EIS deferral relief	(4,586)	(57,414)	(13,000)
Gain remaining chargeable before taper relief	123,414	1,143	Nil
Gains after taper relief: 25%/70%	30,853		
Less annual exemption	(8,800)		
Taxable gains	22,053		
CGT @ 40%	8,821		

Therefore if you should invest £75,000 in Marc's business in 2006/07, you will have a tax liability of £8,821.

This must be done within 3 years of the disposals.

Appendix 4 – Income tax computation 2006/07

	Non-savings £	Savings £	Dividends £
Earned income			
Property business income – FHL (W1)	3,608		
Investment income			
Property business income (W2)	41,350		
Dividends received £16,500 × 100/90			18,333
Building society interest £3,600 × 100/80		4,500	
Treasury stock interest received (£25,000 × 9.75%)		2,438	
Less personal allowance	(5,035)		
Taxable income	39,923	6,938	18,333
Tax:			
£2,150 @ 10%	215		
£31,150 @ 22%	6,853		
£(6,623 + 6,938) @ 40%	5,424		
£18,333 @ 32½%	5,958		
	18,450		
Less: tax suffered			
Dividends (£18,333 @ 10%)	(1,833)		
Interest (£4,500 @ 20%)	(900)		
Income tax due	15,717		

Workings

(1) *Property business income – FHL*

	£	£
Rental income (£400 × 11 weeks)		4,400
Less: Expenses		
Council tax	280	
Repairs and maintenance	100	
Wear and tear allowance		
10% × (£4,400 – 280)	412	
		(792)
		3,608

(2) *Property business income (non FHL)*

Flat

	£	£
Rent due: (accruals basis)		
Aunt: £50 × 4	200	
Tenant: 6/12 × £2,500		1,250
Less: expenses:		
7.4.06 Redecoration	(350)	
8.8.06 Advertising		(400)
9.10.06 Electrical repairs		(500)
Loss/ profit	(150)	350

Warehouse

	£
Rent due (4 × £10,250)	41,000
	41,350

Note. HMRC will likely not allow the loss arising in respect of the period when the flat was let to your sister and it has therefore not been set off here

Question 3

Text references. Overseas aspects of CT covered in Chapter 27. Industrial Building allowances dealt with in Chapter 7. Transfer pricing in Chapter 26. Overseas aspects of employment covered in Chapter 10. EU aspects of VAT dealt with in Chapter 29.

Top tips. If you choose a question with several parts such as this, ensure you allocate you time carefully between the parts.

Easy marks. To score well you needed to be able to answer all parts of this question. Do not choose an optional question with several parts such as this one unless you can make a good attempt at all the parts.

Marking scheme

			Marks
(a)	*Liability to corporation tax*		
	Trading within the UK/trading with the UK	1	
	January 2007 to 28 February 2007	2	
	1 March 2007 to 31 July 2007	2	
	Rate of corporation tax	1	
	Accounting periods	2	
	Max		7
(b)	Qualification as an industrial building		
	Camera assembly	1	
	Storage of goods	2	
	Showroom and general offices	1	
	Writing-down allowance	1	
	Max		4
(c)	Not a member of the European Union	1½	
	Member of European Union	1½	
			3
(d)	Substitution of market price in calculating PCTCT	1	
	Market price = arm's length price	1	
			2
(e)	Residence status of director	1	
	Earnings for duties performed in the UK	1	
	Earnings for duties performed in Eyeland	1	
	Investment income arising in Eyeland	1	
			4
			20

(a) (i) Eyetaki Inc will be liable to UK corporation tax if it is trading through a permanent establishment in the UK (trading within the UK). The company will not be liable to UK corporation tax if it is merely trading with the UK.

From 1 January 2007 to 28 February 2007, Eyetaki Inc employed a UK agent, and maintained a stock of cameras in the UK. Provided that contracts for the sale of cameras were concluded in Eyeland, Eyetaki Inc will probably not be liable to UK corporation tax on profits made during this period.

On 1 March 2007, Eyetaki Inc appears to have opened a permanent establishment in the UK by renting an office and showroom, and it is likely that the sales managers will be empowered to conclude contracts in the UK. Eyetaki Inc will therefore be liable to UK tax on the profits made in the UK from 1 March 2007 to the date that the trade is transferred to Uktaki Ltd (presumably 31 July 2007).

Corporation tax will be at the full rate regardless of the level of profits made in the UK, or by Eyetaki Inc, since there is no double taxation treaty between the UK and Eyeland.

(ii) **Uktaki Ltd's accounting periods**

Uktaki Ltd's first chargeable accounting period starts when the company commences trading on 1 August 2007 and ends 12 months later on 31 July 2008. The next period runs from 1 August 2008 to the end of Uktaki Ltd's period of account, 31 December 2008.

(b) Each part of the building must be considered separately.

(i) The part to be used to assemble cameras from components imported from Eyeland will qualify for industrial buildings allowance (IBA) since it is to be used in a trade consisting of a subjection of goods to a process.

(ii) The part used to store goods which are to be subjected to a process, and to store manufactured goods not yet delivered will also qualify for IBAs. Whether the cameras are sold wholesale or retail should not affect the building's classification as an industrial building.

(iii) The showroom and general offices will only qualify for allowances if they represent 25% or less of the total cost of the building. Otherwise, the industrial buildings allowance will be restricted to the other qualifying proportion of the building.

Allowances

A writing-down allowance at the rate of 4% on a straight-line basis will be given, commencing with the accounting period that the building is brought into use.

(c) **Eyeland is not a member of the European Union (EU)**

Uktaki Ltd will have to account for VAT on the value of goods imported from outside the EU at the time of their importation. The value of the goods will include carriage costs, and all taxes, duties and other charges levied on importation. An input VAT deduction will be given on the company's next VAT return.

If Uktaki Ltd arranges for a guarantee to be given, the VAT due on importation can be accounted for on a monthly basis rather than on importation.

Eyeland becomes a member of the European Union

No VAT will have to be paid on importation if goods are purchased from a supplier in another EU state to whom Uktaki Ltd has supplied its VAT registration number. Instead, output VAT will be accounted for in the period which includes the date of acquisition of the goods. The date of acquisition is the earlier of the date of issue of a VAT invoice or the 15th of the month following the removal of the goods. This VAT payable (output tax) is also input VAT which can be deducted in the normal way on that same VAT return.

(d)   As goods are purchased at an over valuation from an overseas holding company, the UK transfer pricing legislation will apply. This means Uktaki Ltd will have to substitute a market price for the transfer price when calculating its profit chargeable to UK corporation tax. The market price will be an 'arm's length' one that would be charged if the parties to the transaction were independent of each other. The exemption for small and medium sized enterprises cannot apply as there is no double tax treaty between the UK and Eyeland.

(e)   The director will come to the UK in order to take up employment for a period in excess of two years, and so will be treated as UK resident for the entire period. The director will only be treated as ordinarily resident in the UK if there is the intention to stay in the UK for three years or more, or if he actually remains for three years.

    (i)   **Earnings for UK duties**

       The director will be subject to UK tax on earnings for duties performed in the UK regardless of his residence status.

    (ii)   **Earnings for duties performed in Eyeland**

       The director will be subject to UK tax on earnings for duties performed in Eyeland if he is both resident and ordinarily resident in the UK. If the director is resident, but not ordinarily resident in the UK, only such earnings remitted to the UK will be taxable in the UK.

    (iii)   **Investment income arising in Eyeland**

       The director is domiciled in Eyeland, and so will only be subject to UK tax on investment income arising in Eyeland if it is remitted to the UK.

Question 4

Text references. The badges of trade are covered in Chapter 6. The income tax computation is in Chapter 1. Capital allowances are in Chapter 7. NICs for the self employed are in Chapter 6. VAT basics are in Chapter 28. The basics of CGT are in Chapter 11. Ethics are in Chapter 30.

Top tips. Look at the mark allocation carefully. Part (d) only received 2 marks so you should not have spent too long on this. As this was an easy two marks to deal with, it may have been worth dealing with this part of the question first. Part (c), by comparison yielded a potential 7 marks, so it would have been important to answer this part reasonably well to achieve a pass mark.

Easy marks. In part (a) you were asked to discuss the badges of trade briefly. If you had learnt them these were easy marks. But were you brief? Do what the requirement asks.

Marking scheme

			Marks
(a)	Subject matter	1	
	Length of ownership	1	
	Frequency	1	
	Work done	1	
	Circumstances responsible for realisation	1	
	Motive	1	
			6
(b)	*Carrying on a trade:*		
	Number of transactions	½	
	Short ownership	½	
	Work done	½	
	Not a forced sale	½	
	Bank loan/equipment/workshop	½	
	Ceasing to restore cars when employment commences	½	
	Action to be taken		
	Tax Return	½	
	Cannot continue to act	½	
	Notify HMRC ceased acting	½	
	Do not need to tell HMRC why ceased acting	½	
	Disclosure	½	
	Money laundering	½	
	Max		5
(c)	Income	½	
	Cost of cars	½	
	Restoration	½	
	Loan interest	½	
	Rent of workshop	½	
	CAs	1	
	PA	½	
	Income tax	1	
	Class 2 NICs	½	
	Class 4 NICs	1½	
	Notify by 30 March	1	
	Registered from 1 March	1	
	Max		7
(d)	Capital assets	1	
	Tax free profit	1	
			2
			20

(a) (i)   *Subject matter of transaction* – where the subject matter is such as would not be sold as an investment (eg 1,000,000 rolls of toilet paper), it is presumed that any profit on the sale is a trading profit. Compare this with an asset with intrinsic value (eg work of art or shares) which is more likely to be held as an investment for enjoyment or income–produced.

(ii)   *Length of ownership* – trading may be inferred where items purchased are sold soon afterwards.

(iii) *Frequency of similar transactions* – transactions which may, in isolation, be of a capital nature will be interpreted as trading transactions where their frequency indicators a carrying on of a trade.

(iv) *Work done on the property* – work done to make an asset more marketable indicates a trading motive.

(v) *Circumstances responsible for the realisation* – a forced sale (eg to raise cash in an emergency) indicates that the transaction is not trading in nature.

(vi) *Motive* – the absence of a profit motive will not necessarily mean that someone is not trading, but its presence is a strong indication that a person is trading.

(b) **Notes for meeting with Sue**

- Vintage cars may be owned for their intrinsic value. However, in this case the number of transactions and short period of ownership indicates trading.

- Sue also carried out substantial work on the cars and it does not seem that there was a forced sale.

- In addition, the fact that Sue took out a bank loan, rented a workshop and acquired equipment indicates that she was trading rather then merely pursuing a hobby.

- If Sue does not continue to restore vintage cars when she starts her new job, it suggests she was trading whilst unemployed.

- If we cannot accept Sue's contention that she was not trading then we would need to prepare her tax return on the basis that a trade was being carried on. If Sue does not agree to this we cannot continue to act for her and we will need to inform HMRC that we are no longer acting.

- We would not need to tell HMRC why we had ceased to act.

- Advise Sue that we may need to make a report under the money laundering regulations. (If Sue genuinely believes she is not trading it is arguable that she is not, in fact, committing a tax irregularity and that a report need not be made. We may need to refer the matter to the ACCA for guidance).

- If Sue's contention is tenable, then we can complete the tax return on the basis that the self employment pages are not required. Since the transactions would not otherwise appear on the tax return, however, it would be worth drawing HMRC's attention to the position by putting brief details in the 'white space' on the return. Only if HMRC are aware of the circumstances is Sue protected from a discovery assessment being made in the future.

(c)

	£	Non-savings/ total income £
Income from sales		200,000
Costs of acquisition £8,000 × 4	32,000	
Restoration costs £12,000 × 4	48,000	
Loan interest £75,000 × 10%	7,500	
Rental of workshop £400 × 12	4,800	
Capital allowances (W)	7,700	(100,000)
Trading income/STI		100,000
Less: personal allowance		(5,035)
Taxable income		94,965

Tax	£
£2,150 × 10%	215
£31,150 × 22%	6,853
£61,665 × 40%	24,666
	31,734

Sue is required to notify chargeability to income tax within six months of the end of the tax year, ie by 5 October 2007, unless she has already received a notice to file a tax return.

Working

Since the trade starts and ends in the same tax year, there is simply the equivalent of a balancing allowance equal to the difference between the sale proceeds and the cost of the equipment.

		£
Proceeds		5,800
Less: cost		(13,500)
BA		7,700

NICs

Class 2	£2.10 × 52	£109

		£
Class 4	£(33,540 – 5,035) × 8%	2,280
	£(100,000 – 33,540) × 1%	665
		2,945

Sue is liable to notify HMRC that she has commenced a trade and so is liable to pay Class 2 NIC. The notification must be made within three months of the end of the month in which trade commenced, ie by 31 July 2006.

VAT

Sue would be liable to notify HMRC of her need to register for VAT by 30 March 2007 (future test – threshold of £61,000 exceeded in next 30 days looking forward from 1 March 2007). She would be registered from 1 March 2007.

(d)   If Sue is not carrying on a trade, the cars would be a capital asset, potentially subject to capital gains tax. However, motor vehicles suitable for private use are exempt assets for CGT purposes, so the profit would be tax-free.

Question 5

Text references. IHT aspects in Chapter 17 and 18. CGT aspects covered in Chapters 11 to 15.

Top tips. Ensure you look at the proposed gifts separately: take it one at a time. Consider both IHT and CGT. At the end compare your results.

Easy marks. Lots of calculations required in this question to support your answer. Make sure your answer is very clear and shows which tax you are considering and which gift/disposal etc. Ideally every calculation should have a heading. This allows the examiner to see clearly what you have done and allocate marks accordingly.

Marking scheme

			Marks
(a)	No IHT at the time of the gifts	½	
	Each gain/loss is by reference to market value	½	
	Shares in BOZ plc		
	Calculation of capital gain	½	
	Non-availability of gift relief with reason	1	
	Non-availability of CGT taper relief	½	
	50% BPR with reason	1	
	Two-year period of ownership	½	
	Excepted assets	½	
	Calculation of PET	1	
	Land in Utopia		
	Calculation of capital loss	½	
	No restriction on use of loss	1	
	APR not available	½	
	BPR not available	½	
	Calculation of PET	½	
	Rolls Royce motor car		
	Exempt asset for CGT	½	
	PET equals market value	½	
	Necklace		
	Calculation of capital gain	1	
	Gift relief not available	½	
	CGT taper relief	1	
	PET equals market value	½	
		Max	10
(b)	The gifts to be made		
	Bruce – the land with reason	1	
	Padma – the necklace with reason	1	
	Calculation showing no taxable gain	1½	
	Inheritance tax due on the two PETs		
	Land	2	
	Necklace	3	
	Inheritance tax on death estate		
	Exclusion of land and necklace	1	
	Reduction in available nil rate band	1	
	Tax saving at 40%	½	
	Overall tax saving	½	
		Max	8
(c)	Delay gifts by one year		
	Identification of issue	1	
	Tax saving	½	
	Use of future annual exemptions		
	Identification of issue	1	
	Tax saving	½	
		Max	2
			20

(a) **Tax implications of the four possible gifts**

All four possible gifts would be potentially exempt transfers (PETs) such that no inheritance tax would be due at the time of the gift.

The capital gain or allowable loss arising on each gift will be computed by reference to the market value of the asset as at the date of the gift.

Gift to Bruce of shares in BOZ plc

Capital gains tax

The gift will result in a capital gain of £32,500 (£77,000 – £44,500).

BOZ plc is Mabel's personal company as she is able to exercise at least 5% of the voting rights. Accordingly, the shares qualify for gift relief. However, gift relief would only be available if Bruce were UK resident or UK ordinarily resident. This is unlikely to be the case as he emigrated to South Africa in January 2003.

Taper relief is not available as Mabel has owned the shares for less than a year.

Note. Luke's period of ownership is not taken into account for the purposes of taper relief as the shares were transferred on death and not via a no gain, no loss transfer.

Inheritance tax

The value transferred will be reduced by business property relief at the rate of 50% because Mabel owns a controlling shareholding in the company. Luke's period of ownership can be taken into account in order to satisfy the two-year period of ownership requirement. The relief is restricted because the company owns excepted assets.

	£
Value transferred	77,000
Less: BPR (£77,000 × 92% × 50%)	(35,420)
Annual exemptions for 2006/07 and 2005/06 (£3,000 × 2)	(6,000)
PET	35,580

> **BPP Tutorial note.** The company owns investment properties that represent 8% of the value of its assets. Hence only 92% of the asset value qualifies for BPR at 50%.

Gift to Bruce of the land in Utopia

Capital gains tax

The gift will result in a capital loss of £24,000 (£99,000 – £75,000). This loss is available for relief against gains made by Mabel in 2006/07 or future years. Mabel and Bruce are not connected persons for the purposes of capital gains tax and therefore, there is no restriction on Mabel's use of the losses.

Inheritance tax

Agricultural property relief is not available because the land is not situated in the UK, the Channel Islands or the Isle of Man. Business property relief is also not available because the farm is an investment and not a business asset.

	£
Value transferred	75,000
Less: Annual exemptions for 2006/07 and 2005/06 (£3,000 × 2)	(6,000)
PET	69,000

Gift to Padma of the Rolls Royce motor car

Capital gains tax

No gain or loss will arise as cars are exempt assets for the purposes of capital gains tax.

Inheritance tax

The PET will equal the market value of the car of £71,000. The annual exemptions have already been used against the gift to Bruce.

Gift to Padma of the necklace

Capital gains tax

The gift will result in the following indexed gain.

	£
Deemed proceeds (market value)	70,000
Less: Cost (probate value when inherited)	(11,500)
Indexation allowance (£11,500 × 84%)	(9,660)
	48,840

Gift relief is not available as the necklace is not a business asset.

For the purposes of taper relief the necklace is a non-business asset owned by Mabel for eight years plus the bonus year. Accordingly, only 65% of the indexed gain will be chargeable to capital gains tax.

Inheritance tax

The value of the PET will equal the market value of the necklace of £70,000. The annual exemptions have already been used against the gift to Bruce.

(b) **The gifts to make**

Mabel's criteria in deciding which assets to give are:

- The gifts must not give rise to any tax liabilities prior to her death.

  The gifts will not give rise to inheritance tax prior to Mabel's death because they are potentially exempt transfers. Accordingly, in satisfying this criterion, it is only necessary to consider capital gains tax.

- If possible, the gifts should reduce the inheritance tax due on her death.

Bruce

A gift of the shares in BOZ plc would result in a capital gain of £32,500. This exceeds Mabel's capital losses and the annual exemption such that a capital gains tax liability would arise. Accordingly, she must give Bruce the land in Utopia. This will result in a capital loss of £24,000.

Padma

There would be no capital gains tax on either of the proposed gifts to Padma. The car is an exempt asset and the capital gain arising on the necklace would be relieved by Mabel's capital losses and the annual exemption as follows:

	£
Capital gain	48,840
Less: Capital loss on the gift to Bruce of the land	(24,000)
Capital losses brought forward	(13,000)
	11,840
Taper relief	× 65%
	7,696
Less Annual exemption (restricted)	(7,696)
	Nil

Accordingly, the gift to be made to Padma should be chosen by reference to the amount of inheritance tax saved. Mabel should give Padma the necklace as its value is expected to increase.

Inheritance tax saved by making the gifts

Inheritance tax will be due on the two PETs if Mabel dies within seven years of the gifts. The gifts will also have an effect on the inheritance tax due on the death estate.

Inheritance tax due on the two PETs

Land in Utopia – 1 February 2007

	£
PET (from (a))	69,000
Nil rate band as at 30 June 2011	285,000
Less Gift in previous seven years (£170,000 − (2 × £3,000))	(164,000)
	121,000

There is no inheritance tax due as the chargeable transfer is less than the available nil rate band.

Necklace – 5 March 2007

	£
Value as at 1 February 2007	70,000
Nil rate band as at 30 June 2011	285,000
Less Gift in previous seven years (£164,000 + £69,000)	(233,000)
	52,000
Inheritance tax (£70,000 − £52,000) × 40%	7,200
Taper relief (4-5 years)	60%
	4,320

Effect on inheritance tax due on death estate

The land and the necklace will be excluded from the estate thus reducing the tax due.

	£
Land in Utopia – value as at 30 June 2011	75,000
Necklace – value as at 30 June 2011	84,000
	159,000
Inheritance tax saved at 40%	63,600

The available nil rate band will also be reduced because the PETs were made within seven years of death thus increasing the tax due.

	£
Reduction in available nil rate band (£69,000 + £70,000)	139,000
Additional inheritance tax at 40%	55,600
Overall saving (£63,600 − £55,600 − £4,320)	3,680

Note. The nil rate band on death is reduced by the whole of the PETs in the seven years prior to death.

BPP Tutorial Note. An alternative answer is as follows:

Inheritance tax if Mabel does not gift to Bruce and Padma

Death Estate on 30 June 2011

	£	£
House and furniture		450,000
Rolls Royce motor car		55,000
Diamond necklace		84,000
Cash and investments		150,000
Boz plc shares	95,000	
Less BPR (£95,000 × 92% × 50%)	(43,700)	
		51,300
Land in Utopia		75,000
Chargeable estate		865,300
IHT liability (865,300 − 285,000) × 40%		232,120

If Mabel gifts land in Utopia to Bruce and Necklace to Padma the inheritance tax liability will be as follows:

Death Tax on lifetime gifts

(i)   February 2007 – PET becomes chargeable

	£	£
Value of gift		69,000
Nil band as at 30 June 2011	285,000	
Less CGT in 7 years before transfer (170,000 – (2 × 3,000)	(164,000)	
		(121,000)
		–

No inheritance tax due as covered by nil band

(ii)

	£	£
March 2007 – PET		70,000
Nil band at 30 June 2011	285,000	
Less CGT in 7 years before transfer (164,000 + 69,000)	(233,000)	
		(52,000)
		18,000

18,000 × 40% = £7,200

Taper relief (4-5 years) 60% × 7,200) =		4,320

(iii)   Estate at 30 June 2011

	£
House and furniture	450,000
Rolls Royce car	55,000
Cash and investments	150,000
Boz shares	51,300
Chargeable estate	706,300
Nil band at date of death	285,000
Less CGT in 7 years before death (69,000 + 70,000)	(139,000)
	146,000
IHT liability (706,300 – 146,000) × 40%	224,120

Tax saving £232,120 – (£4,320 + £224,120) = £3,680

(c)   **Further advice**

Mabel should consider delaying one of the gifts until after 1 May 2007 such that it is made more than seven years after the gift to the discretionary trust. Both PETs would then be covered by the nil rate band resulting in a saving of inheritance tax of £4,320 (from (b)).

Mabel should ensure that she uses her inheritance tax annual exemption of £3,000 every year by, say, making gifts of £1,500 each year to both Bruce and Padma. The effect of this will be to save inheritance tax of £1,200 (£3,000 × 40%) every year.

ACCA Professional Paper P6 – Options Module

Advanced Taxation (UK)

Mock Examination 2

Question Paper	
Time allowed	**Reading and planning: 15 minutes** **Writing: 3 hours**
This paper is divided into two sections	
Section A	**BOTH questions are compulsory questions and MUST be attempted**
Section B	**TWO questions ONLY to be attempted**

During reading and planning time only the question paper may be annotated

DO NOT OPEN THIS PAPER UNTIL YOU ARE READY TO START UNDER EXAMINATION CONDITIONS

Section A: BOTH questions are compulsory and MUST be attempted

Question 1

Gloria Seaford is UK resident and ordinarily resident but is not domiciled in the UK.

Gloria has owned and run a shop selling books, cards and small gifts as a sole trader since June 1992. She purchased her current premises, which were built in 1990, in July 2005 for £267,000. Gloria is registered for value added tax. Gloria will be 56 on 4 January 2007 and, with this in mind, on 1 November 2006 she started looking for a buyer for the business so that she could retire.

Gloria has received an offer of £335,000 for the shop premises from Ned Skillet who intends to convert the building into a restaurant. It can be assumed that the sale will take place on 28 February 2007 and that Gloria will cease to trade on that day.

Gloria estimates that on 28 February 2007 she will be able to sell the shelving and other shop fittings to local businesses for £1,400 (no item will be sold for more than cost). She has agreed to sell all stock on hand on 28 February 2007 to a competitor at cost plus 5%. This is expected to result in sales revenue of £8,300.

The only other business asset is a van that is currently used 85% for business purposes. The van is expected to be worth £4,700 on 28 February 2007 and Gloria will keep it for her private use.

Gloria's tax adjusted trading profit for the year ended 31 October 2006 was £39,245. The forecast tax adjusted trading profit for the period ending 28 February 2007, before taking account of the final sale of the business assets on that date and before deduction of capital allowances, is £11,500. Gloria has overlap profits brought forward of £15,720.

The tax written down value on the capital allowance general pool at 31 October 2006 was £4,050. Gloria purchased equipment for £820 in November 2006. The tax written down value of the van at 31 October 2006 was £4,130.

In 2006/07 Gloria will have property business income of £4,300 and bank interest of £13,500 credited to her bank account.

On 1 November 2004 Gloria inherited the following assets from her aunt.

	Probate value £
Painting	15,200
17,500 shares in All Over plc	11,400

Gloria sold the painting in May 2006 and realised a gain of £7,100. At the end of April 2005 Gloria received notification that All Over plc, a quoted trading company, was in receivership and that there would be a maximum payment of 3 pence per share.

Gloria also intends to transfer shares she owns in Gong plc, with a value of £297,000 and which cost £259,000 two years ago, into a discretionary trust for her nephew Bob on 5 April 2007. Bob is aged 16 and lives with Gloria who has maintained him since the death of his parents in 2001. She will pay any taxes or costs associated with setting up the trust. Gloria previously made a gross chargeable transfer of £125,000 in May 2004.

Gloria is in excellent health and has unused capital losses as at 6 April 2006 of £31,400.

Gloria has been a higher rate taxpayer for many years.

Eric Sloane, a business associate of Gloria, has provided her with the details of a number of investment opportunities including Bubble Inc, an investment company incorporated in the country of Oceania where its share register is maintained. Gloria paid Eric £300 for his advice.

Required

(a) Cessation of Gloria's business

State the VAT implications of Gloria's sale of her business assets and cessation of trade. You may ignore the van in this part of the question. Calculations are not required.

Provide a calculation of Gloria's total income tax and national insurance liabilities for 2006/07. **(11 marks)**

(b) Prepare a report for Gloria concerning the tax implications of her capital transactions during 2006/07 and the taxation issues arising from her investment in the Bubble Inc shares. The report should be in three sections, addressing the three sets of issues set out below, and should, where appropriate include supporting calculations.

(i) 2006/07 capital gains tax liability

Advise Gloria of her CGT liability for 2006/07, providing supporting calculations.

Provide an explanation of the relief available in respect of the fall in value of the shares in All Over plc. You should identify the years in which it can be claimed and state the time limit for submitting the claim. **(6 marks)**

(ii) Discretionary trust for Bob

Discuss the current and potential CGT and IHT implications for Gloria of setting up the discretionary trust for her nephew.

Briefly explain any other circumstances in which the discretionary trust will be subject to IHT.

(11 marks)

(iii) Bubble Inc shares

Explain how Gloria would be taxed in the UK on the dividends paid by Bubble Inc.

Advise on the capital gains tax and inheritance tax implications of a future disposal of the shares.

Clearly state, giving reasons, whether or not the payment made to Eric is allowable for capital gains tax purposes. **(9 marks)**

Appropriateness of the format and presentation of the report and the effectiveness with which its advice is communicated. **(2 marks)**

You may assume that the rates and allowances for the tax year 2006/07 continue to apply for the foreseeable future.

(Total = 39 marks)

Question 2

Your manager has had a meeting with Carl Berman, the new finance director of Discovery Ltd and has sent you a copy of the following memorandum.

To	The files
From	Tax manager
Date	7 May 2007
Subject	Discovery Ltd – review of group companies

Carl Berman (CB) has asked for a review of the activities of the Discovery Ltd group companies.

(1) Discovery Ltd

CB is proposing to sell the current premises from which the company operates to generate much needed funds. The property is standing at an indexed gain of £250,000.

CB has located new premises which are available on a 25 year lease. The company would receive a reverse premium of £54,000 from the landlord to take on the lease.

(2) Screen Ltd

Screen Ltd trades from one hotel and four restaurants. The hotel was previously owned by Discovery Ltd, and was transferred to Screen Ltd on 1 January 2002 on the latter's incorporation. The restaurants are occupied under 20-year leases, each of which has five years remaining. Screen Ltd has substantial trading losses.

CB is proposing to close down the restaurants. This will involve total redundancy payments of £300,000, a loss on scrapping plant and machinery of £20,000, and a payment to the landlord of £50,000 to surrender the four leases.

This expenditure will be funded by Discovery Ltd, who will subsequently write off the intra-group indebtedness due from Screen Ltd which, including monies arising from the above transactions, will total £450,000.

CB intends to sell Screen Ltd to SouthStart plc, an unconnected party, for £1.8 million (the hotel property having an open market value of £1 million).

(3) Joust Ltd

Joust Ltd operates three night clubs, which are highly profitable. Its shares are owned 60% by Discovery Ltd and 20% each by Mr and Mrs Witt, its original proprietors, who established the company in 2000.

It is proposed that Discovery Ltd buys Mr and Mrs Witt's 40% interest. CB has suggested that this could be done by Discovery Ltd acquiring the 40% interest for £600,000, comprising cash of £200,000 and the issue of shares in Discovery Ltd to the value of £400,000. On 1 June 2007 all the shares will be issued to Mr and Mrs Witt and they will receive £50,000 on account. The balance of the cash will be paid to them one year later.

(4) Overrun Ltd

Overrun Ltd runs three health clubs, all of which have made substantial trading losses since they were set up in 2003.

CB intends to transfer the trade from Overrun Ltd to Joust Ltd. The properties that are owned by Overrun Ltd will be revalued and then transferred at this value to Discovery Ltd. The realised surplus thus created will be paid up to Discovery Ltd by way of dividend, and Overrun Ltd will then be put into liquidation.

(5)   Potential acquisitions

CB would like to diversify the group's activities and has in mind acquiring the following:

(a)   The share capital of Lately Ltd, which is presently owned and controlled by a Canadian company. Lately Ltd carries on the trade of retail travel agents from 10 shops in the London area and has been making substantial trading losses to date.

(b)   The business of Brew Ltd, which trades as conference organisers. Discovery Ltd will pay £1 million, comprising £400,000 for goodwill and £600,000 for a short leasehold interest from which the conference organising activities are run.

Tax manager

An extract from an email from your manager is set out below.

Please draft notes in preparation for a meeting with Carl Berman detailing the tax implications of his proposals for all companies and individuals concerned.

I'll leave the structure of the notes up to you. Please ensure that they are logical and easy to follow.

Tax manager

You have extracted the following further information from client files.

- Discovery Ltd is a close investment holding company. Its business comprises its investments in subsidiaries and the ownership of certain freehold properties occupied by itself and other group companies.

- Screen Ltd and Overrun Ltd are wholly owned subsidiaries of Discovery Ltd.

- All group companies are resident in the UK for tax purposes.

- All group companies make up accounts to 30 June.

Required

Prepare the notes requested by your manager.   **(23 marks)**

Appropriateness of the format and presentation of the notes and the effectiveness with which their content is communicated.   **(2 marks)**

You may assume that the rates and allowances for the tax year 2006/07 and financial year 2006 continue to apply for the foreseeable future.

(Total = 25 marks)

Section B: TWO questions ONLY to be attempted

Question 3

Arthur and Cindy Wakefield are married with two children aged four and seven years.

The following information has been extracted from client files and from meetings with Arthur and Cindy.

Cindy:

- Has worked for Picture Perfect Ltd for four years.
- Annual gross employment income is £41,000.
- Only other income comes from assets inherited from her father (see below.)

Arthur:

- Self-employed carpenter.
- Taxable trading profits (after capital allowances) are £26,000 each year.
- Has no other income.

Assets inherited from Cindy's father:

- On 1 November 2006 Cindy inherited UK quoted shares and an investment property in London on the death of her father.

- Probate values of the assets, together with the taxable income generated by them in a full year, are as follows:

	Probate value £	Annual taxable income £
UK quoted shares	305,000	12,300
Investment property in London	320,000	14,100

- Cindy intends to give either the shares or the property to Arthur.

- Objective: to maximise the family's after tax income.

New business:

- Cindy and Arthur plan to start a new business, buying and restoring paintings, on 1 April 2007.
- Will work on the new business in their spare time.
- Cindy will continue to work for Picture Perfect Ltd.
- Arthur will carry on with his carpentry business.

Income and expenditure forecast for new business:

- Income and expenditure forecast, including the cost of equipment, for the first three years to be taken as:

	Year ending		
	31 March 2008 £	31 March 2009 £	31 March 2010 £
Sales	30,000	50,000	60,000
Less Cost of materials and overheads	(18,000)	(24,000)	(25,000)
Purchase of equipment	(56,000)	–	–
Profit/(loss) arising	(44,000)	26,000	35,000

- Figures do not include the cost of annual salaries of £5,100 each.

- May set up a company to run the business.

- Would consider using a partnership, with profits and losses shared equally, if advantageous.

Required

(a) (i) Determine whether Cindy should give Arthur the investment property or the quoted shares in order to achieve her objective. Support your answer with relevant calculations based on a complete tax year.

(6 marks)

(ii) Compute the annual income tax saving from your recommendation in (i) above as compared with the situation where Cindy retains both the property and the shares. Identify any other tax implications arising from your recommendation. Your answer should consider all relevant taxes.   **(3 marks)**

(b) Explain the advantages from a tax point of view of operating the new business as a partnership rather than as a company whilst it is making losses. You should calculate the tax adjusted trading loss for the year ending 31 March 2008 for both situations and indicate the years in which the loss relief will be obtained. You are not required to prepare any other supporting calculations.   **(7 marks)**

(e) Discuss any issues that may arise as a result of acting as a tax adviser for the new business as well as for Andy and Cindy.   **(2 marks)**

You should assume that the income tax rates and allowances for the tax year 2006/07 apply throughout this question.

(Total = 18 marks)

Question 4

You are the tax adviser to Expansion Ltd, a company involved in the computer business. Expansion Ltd wishes to acquire Target Ltd, and has made an offer to the shareholders of that company which it would like to finalise on 1 July 2006.

You should assume that today's date is 15 May 2006.

The following information has been extracted from client files and from meetings with the shareholders.

Expansion Ltd:

- UK resident with no subsidiaries.
- On 1 May 2006 purchased £120,000 of 8% Company Loan Stock.
- Interest is received six monthly in arrears (31 October and 30 April).
- On 31 January 2007 will purchase a new freehold factory for £118,000.

Forecast results for Expansion Ltd and Target Ltd:

- Forecast results for the year ended 31 December 2006 are as follows:

	Expansion Ltd £	Target Ltd £
Adjusted trading profit/(loss)	214,000	(137,700)
Trading losses brought forward	–	(9,200)
Capital gain	–	51,300
Capital losses brought forward	(9,600)	–

Target Ltd:

- UK resident with no subsidiaries.

- Ordinary share capital is owned equally by Arc Ltd, Bend Ltd and Curve Ltd (see below).

- It is not known whether one, two or all three of these companies will accept the offer.

- Capital gain of £51,300 relates to proposed sale of a freehold office building for £140,000 on 15 October 2006. One of the building's four floors has never been used for the purposes of Target Ltd's trade.

Arc Ltd, Bend Ltd and Curve Ltd:

- All UK resident and profitable.
- Not connected to each other or to Expansion Ltd.

Financing the acquisition of Target Ltd:

- Expansion Ltd has sufficient internal funds to finance the acquisition of either one third or two thirds of Target Ltd's share capital.

- If it acquires the entire share capital will have to issue £250,000 of 10% debentures on 1 July 2006.

Debentures potentially issued 1 July 2006:

- Will be issued at a 3% discount to their nominal value.

- Redeemable in five years' time.

- Debenture interest will be paid on 1 July and 1 January.

- Professional fees of £15,250 will be incurred in respect of the issue.

- Expansion Ltd's adjusted trading profit (above) has been calculated *before* taking into account the issue of debentures.

- The company's accounting policy is to write off the cost of finance on a straight-line basis over the period of the loan.

Required

Calculate the corporation tax liability for both Expansion Ltd and Target Ltd for the year ended 31 December 2006 if:

(a)   Expansion Ltd acquires one third of Target Ltd's ordinary share capital from Arc Ltd on 1 July 2006.

(5 marks)

(b)   Expansion Ltd acquires two thirds of Target Ltd's ordinary share capital from Arc Ltd and Bend Ltd on 1 July 2006.   **(3 marks)**

(c)   Expansion Ltd acquires all of Target Ltd's ordinary share capital from Arc Ltd, Bend Ltd and Curve Ltd on 1 July 2006.   **(10 marks)**

Your answer should include an explanation of your treatment of Target Ltd's losses, Target Ltd's capital gain, and Expansion Ltd's issue of debentures. You should assume that reliefs are claimed in the most favourable manner.

(Total = 18 marks)

Question 5

Richard Byte is a computer programmer who started working for Web-Designs Ltd on 6 April 2006.

The following information has been extracted from client files and from meetings with Richard.

Richard:

- Richard received income of £60,000 from Web-Designs Ltd during the 2006/07 tax year.

- Richard is paid a fixed fee for each contract that he works on, and each contract lasts an average of two weeks.

- Works from home.

- Has no other sources of income.

Web-Designs Ltd contracts:

- Richard is under no obligation to accept any of the contracts offered, and carries out the work under his own control.

- He is obliged to do the work personally.

Richard's house:

- Richard never visits the premises of Web-Designs Ltd.
- He uses one room of his five room private residence exclusively for business purposes.
- The total running costs of the house for the year were £4,000.
- He plans to sell the house in five years' time.
- Has always occupied the house throughout his previous ten years of ownership.

Telephone bills:

- Richard's telephone bills are £500 per quarter.
- This is £400 per quarter higher than they were prior to the commencement of his working from home.

Equipment:

- Richard is required to provide all of his own equipment.
- A computer was purchased on 6 April 2006 for £4,480.

Required

(a) List the factors that HMRC will take into account when deciding whether Richard is self-employed or an employee in relation to his work for Web-Designs Ltd, stating whether each factor is likely to indicate that he should be treated as self employed or as an employee. You should confine your answer to the information given in the question. **(4 marks)**

(b) Advise Richard by how much his income tax liability and national insurance contributions for 2006/07 would be likely to increase if he is treated as an employee instead of self employed in respect of his work for Web-Designs Ltd. **(8 marks)**

(c) Indicate briefly whether there is any other way in which Richard could minimize the tax payable on his income from Web-Design Ltd assuming his self-employed status is accepted by HMRC (calculations are not required). **(2 marks)**

(d) Explain to Richard how the use of his house could affect his capital gains tax position when he comes to sell the house in the future. **(4 marks)**

(Total = 18 marks)

Answers

DO NOT TURN THIS PAGE UNTIL YOU HAVE
COMPLETED THE MOCK EXAM

A plan of attack

What's the worst thing you could be doing right now if this was the actual exam paper? Sharpening your pencil? Wondering how to celebrate the end of the exam in about 3 hours? Panicking, flapping and generally getting in a right old state?

Well, they're all pretty bad, so turn back to the paper and let's sort out a **plan of attack**!

First things first

You have 15 minutes reading time. Make sure you spend it wisely, looking through the paper in detail working out which optional questions to do and the order in which to attack the questions. You've then got **two options**. Option 1 is the option recommended by BPP.

Option 1 (if you're thinking 'Help!')

If you're a bit worried about the paper, do the questions in the order of how well you think you can answer them. You may find the questions in Section B less daunting than the compulsory questions in Section A so you may decide to start with Section B. Remember you only need to do two of the three questions in Section B; you may find it easier if you start by deciding which question you will not do and put a line through it.

- **Question 3** is a fairly straight forward question on husband and wife tax planning with some income tax and corporation tax losses. This would be a good warm up question.

- **Question 4** tests your understanding of consortia and groups. If you have a good knowledge of this topic it might be worth starting with this question. You should have been able to gain a high proportion of marks on the question as long as you worked through it methodically.

- **Question 5** compared the tax payable by an employee as opposed to a self-employed trader. There were some easy calculations, so this would be a good question to start with if you like the figure work. You must be careful to state any assumptions you make in doing the sums, and you cannot avoid having to give explanations or advice.

Do not spend more than the allocated time on Section B. When you've spent the allocated time on two of the three questions in Section B turn to the compulsory questions in Section A. Read the questions through thoroughly before you launch into them. Once you start make sure you allocate your time to the parts within the questions according to the marks available and that, where possible, you attempt the easy marks first.

Lastly, what you mustn't forget is that you have to **answer both questions in Section A and two in Section B**. Do not miss out more than one question in Section B and do not waste time answering three questions in Section B or you will seriously affect your chance of passing the exam.

Option 2 (if you're thinking 'It's a doddle')

It never pays to be over confident but if you're not quaking in your shoes about the exam then **turn straight to the compulsory questions** in Section A.

Once you've done these questions, move to Section B.

- The question you attempt first really depends on what you are most confident at.

- You then have to select one of the two remaining questions. If you are undecided look at the requirements. It maybe easier to obtain more marks if these are broken down into several smaller parts.

No matter how many times we remind you....

Always, always **allocate your time** according to the marks for the question in total and then according to the parts of the question. And **always, always follow the requirements** exactly. Question 3 part (a)(ii), for example, asks you to prepare calculations of the tax savings based on a full tax year, so don't waste time preparing a full income tax computation nor on looking at when the assets were acquired.

You've got spare time at the end of the exam.....?

If you have allocated your time properly then you **shouldn't have time on your hands** at the end of the exam. But if you find yourself with five or ten minutes to spare, check over your work to make sure that there are no silly arithmetical errors.

Forget about it!

And don't worry if you found the paper difficult. More than likely other candidates will too. If this were the real thing you would need to **forget** the exam the minute you leave the exam hall and **think about the next one**. Or, if it's the last one, **celebrate**!

Question 1

Text references. VAT is covered in Chapters 28 and 29. The IT computation is in Chapter 1 with NIC for the self employed in Chapter 6. Capital Gains are dealt with in Chapters 11 - 15. Chapter 20 deals with trusts. CGT gift relief is covered in Chapter 14. Overseas aspects of income tax are covered in Chapter 10, with the overseas aspects for CGT in Chapter 15 and for IHT in Chapter 19.

Top tips. Use headings to separate the different parts of question and to show where workings start and end.

Keep answers neat – use lots of paper to spread answers out; this really improves the look and the ease of marking.

Easy marks. Again show all workings and keep all calculations neat, clear and hence easy to mark. Note down any decisions you have made (and why) so all marks can be allocated by the marker.

Marking scheme

				Marks
(a)	Shop premises		1	
	Shelving, shop fittings and stock of cards and gifts		1	
	Stock of books		½	
	Deregistration		1	
	Capital allowances on pool		1	
	Capital allowances on van		1	
	Period ending 28 February 2007		½	
	Profit on sale of books		½	
	Year ended 31 October 2006		½	
	Overlap relief		½	
	Pension		½	
	Bank interest		½	
	Personal allowance		½	
	Tax liability		1	
	Class 2 NIC		1	
	Class 4 NIC		1	
		Max		11
(b)	(i)	Allocation of capital losses	1	
		Gain on shop	½	
		Taper relief	1	
		Annual exemption	½	
		Tax at 40%	½	
		Negligible value claim available with reason	1	
		Calculation of loss	½	
		Must be of negligible value in year claim made	½	
		Time limit for making claim	½	
		Identification of years – past and future	1	
		Max		6

	(ii)	*IHT*		
		IHT on UK assets of non-UK domiciliary	1	
		Net CLT	½	
		Transfer of value	½	
		AEs × 2	½	
		Nil rate band remaining	1	
		Tax @ 20/80 (ie gross up)	1	
		Gross chargeable transfer	½	
		Additional tax if dies within 7 yrs	½	
		Taper relief	½	
		Can reduce tax to nil	½	
		No repayment of tax paid	½	
		Exit charge	1	
		Principal charge	1	
		CGT		
		Deemed disposal at market value	½	
		Gain chargeable at 40%	½	
		Gift relief available as also CLT	½	
		Deferral only	½	
		Reduces base cost for trustees	½	
		Larger gain when they dispose of asset	½	
		Max		11
	(iii)	UK resident taxed on worldwide income	½	
		Remittance basis because non-domicile	½	
		Gross up for foreign tax	½	
		Tax rates	1	
		Double tax relief	1	
		Subject to CGT on worldwide assets if R or OR	1	
		Remittance basis because non-domicile	½	
		Relief for foreign tax	½	
		No relief for loss	½	
		No relief for fee with reason	1	
		Taper relief	½	
		Foreign assets of non domiciliary is excluded property	1	
		Deemed domicile for IHT, 17 out of 20 years	1	
		Resident for at least 15 years	½	
		No business property relief	½	
		Max		9
Format/Presentation				2
				39

(a) **VAT implications of the sale by Gloria of the business assets**

The sale of the premises is an exempt supply for VAT purposes because they are more than three years old. Accordingly, Gloria cannot recover any VAT incurred on any costs relating to the sale.

> **BPP Tutorial Note.** Students might have mentioned that Gloria could make an election to waive exemption over the building as it is commercial property. She would then charge VAT at the standard rate on the sale. Thus VAT incurred on costs relating to the sale could be recovered.

Gloria must charge VAT on the shelving, shop fittings and the stock of cards and small gifts.

The sale of the stock of books will be zero-rated.

Gloria must inform HMRC by 30 March 2007 that she has ceased to trade. Her VAT registration will be cancelled with effect from 28 February 2007.

Note. This is not a transfer of a going concern: the assets are being sold to different purchasers and the building is to be used for a different purpose.

Income tax and national insurance liability for 2006/07

Income tax liability

	£
Trading income (W1)	32,435
Property business income	4,300
Bank interest (£13,500 × 100/80)	16,875
Statutory total income	53,610
Personal allowance	(5,035)
Taxable income	48,575

£	£
2,150 × 10%	215
29,550 × 22%	6,501
1,600 × 20%	320
15,275 × 40%	6,110
Income tax liability	13,146

BPP Tutorial Note. An alternative presentation is:

	Other income	Savings income
	£	£
Trading income	32,435	
Property business income	4,300	
Bank interest		16,875
	36,735	16,875
Less: personal allowance	(5,035)	
	31,700	

Tax due

		£
2,150 @ 10%		215
29,550 @ 22%		6,501
31,700		
1,600 @ 20%		320
33,300		
15,275 @ 40%		6,110
Income Tax liability		13,146

National insurance liability

Class 2

£2.10 per week for the number of weeks she trades in 2006/07

ie 47 × £2.10 = £99.

Class 4

(£32,435 − £5,035) @ 8% = £2,192.

Workings

(1) *Trading income*

	£
Period ending 28 February 2007	11,500
Profit on closing stock (£8,300 × 5/105)	395
Capital allowances (W2)	(2,985)
	8,910
Year ended 31 October 2006	39,245
Less: Overlap profits	(15,720)
	32,435

(2) *Capital allowances*

	Pool	Van	Allowances
	£	£	£
Tax written down value b/f	4,050	4,130	
Addition	820	–	
Less: Disposal proceeds	(1,400)	(4,700)	
	3,470	(570)	
Balancing allowance	(3,470)	–	3,470
Balancing charge × 85%	–	570	(485)
	–	–	2,985

(b) **Report on tax implications of Gloria's 2006/07 capital transactions and the taxation issues arising from her investment in the Bubble Inc shares**

To: Gloria
From: A Adviser
Date: [date]
Subject: Capital transactions for 2006/07 and Bubble Inc shares

This report covers tax issues relating to:

(i) 2006/07 capital gains tax (CGT) liability
(ii) Discretionary trust for Bob
(iii) Bubble Inc shares

(1) **2006/07 CGT liability**

You will have a CGT liability of £5,220 after taking into account your capital losses brought forward from previous years, taper relief and your annual exemption (see Appendix 1).

The shares in All Over plc are worth three pence each so are of negligible value. You can make a claim which will allow you to realise the loss on the shares of £10,875 (Appendix 1) without selling them. This is known as a negligible value claim.

You may claim the loss in any year in which the shares are of negligible value provided you notify HMRC within two years of the end of that year.

Accordingly, you can claim to realise the loss in 2005/06 or even in 2004/05 if you can show that the shares were of negligible value in that year. As you have capital losses brought forward it is unlikely that a claim for either of these years would save tax, unless the losses all arose in 2005/06 and you had taxable gains in 2004/05.

Alternatively, you can claim the loss in 2006/07 which will save tax of £2,175 since the loss will be set against the gain on your shop premises which is eligible for 50% taper relief. A third option would be to claim the loss in a future year if you are then likely to have gains.

(2) **Discretionary trust for Bob**

IHT

A gift to a discretionary trust is a chargeable lifetime transfer. There would therefore be an immediate liability to inheritance tax of £32,750 (see Appendix 2).

The tax shown has been grossed up because you are bearing the tax (rather than the trustees).

The gross chargeable transfer would be £323,750 (£291,000 + £32,750).

If you were to die within seven years, tax at the death rate (40%) would be calculated on this gross chargeable transfer. The tax would be reduced by taper relief (see below) and the tax of £32,750 already paid. Only the balance of tax would be payable. However, none of the tax already paid could be refunded.

Taper relief would apply if you were to die after at least three years of making the gift. For example if you died four years after making the gift taper relief would reduce the tax by 40%.

Discretionary trusts are also subject to the following IHT charges:

(i) An exit charge on the value of property taken out of the trust.

(ii) A principal charge on the capital value of the trust on every tenth anniversary following its creation. The maximum charge is 6%.

CGT

When you make a gift there is a deemed disposal at market value at the date of the gift.

The gain arising on the disposal would therefore be £35,000 (£297,000 – £259,000). The shares would not attract taper relief as they are non business assets held for less than three years.

If the gift is made on 5 April 2007, a CGT liability of £9,140 (£35,000 @ 40% – £24,300 × 50% × 40%) would arise since capital losses previously set against gains eligible for 50% taper relief would now be set against gains with no taper relief.

However, because the transfer is also chargeable to inheritance tax (see above) you can claim gift relief to defer the full gain of £14,000.

The gain deferred would reduce the base cost of the shares for the trustees to £259,000 (£297,000 – £14,000). This will result in a larger gain for the trustees when they dispose of the shares.

(3) **Bubble Inc shares**

Income tax

As you are resident in the UK you are subject to income tax on your worldwide income. However, because you are non-UK domiciled, you will only be taxed on the foreign dividends you remit, or bring into, the UK.

Dividends brought into the UK will be grossed up for any tax paid in Oceania. The gross amount is taxed at 10% if it falls into the starting or basic rate band and at 32½% if it falls into the higher rate band.

Double tax relief will be available so that you do not pay tax twice on the same income. The DTR available will be the lower of the tax suffered in Oceania and the UK tax on the dividend income.

Capital gains tax

Individuals are subject to capital gains tax on worldwide assets if they are resident or ordinarily resident in the UK. However, because you are not domiciled in the UK and the shares are situated abroad, the gain is only taxable to the extent that you remit the sales proceeds to the UK.

Again double tax relief will be available. This will be the lower of the tax suffered in Oceania and the UK CGT.

If, on the other hand, a loss were to arise on the disposal of the shares, this would not be available for relief in the UK.

With regards to the fee paid to Eric, generally when computing a capital gain or allowable loss a deduction is available for the incidental costs of acquisition. However, to be allowable, such costs must be incurred wholly and exclusively for the purposes of acquiring the asset. As the fee paid to Eric related to general investment advice and not to the acquisition of the shares it would not be deductible in computing the gain.

Taper relief will be at non-business asset rates as Bubble Inc is an investment company so long as you hold the shares for at least three years.

IHT

Overseas assets owned by non-UK domiciled individuals are 'excluded property' for IHT purposes and transfers of such property can be ignored.

However, you should be aware that you will be deemed to be UK domiciled (for the purposes of inheritance tax only) if you have been resident in the UK for 17 out of the 20 tax years ending with the year in which the disposal occurs.

It appears from our files that have been resident for at least 15 tax years (1992/93 to 2006/07 inclusive) based on the fact that you have been in the UK running a business since June 1992. If you have been in the UK longer than this, please let me know as soon as possible.

If you are deemed to be UK domiciled the Bubble Inc shares would not be excluded property and would be subject to IHT.

Business property relief would not be available as Bubble Inc is an investment company.

Appendix 1 – 2006/07 CGT liability

CGT liability

	£
Gain on painting	7,100
Less: Capital losses brought forward (Note)	(7,100)
Indexed gain before taper relief	–
Gain on shop (£335,000 – £267,000)	68,000
Less: Remainder of capital losses brought forward	(24,300)
	43,700
Business asset owned for one year	
Gain after taper relief (£43,700 × 50%)	21,850
Less: Annual exemption	(8,800)
	13,050
Capital gains tax at 40%	5,220

Note. The capital losses brought forward are offset against the painting in priority to the shop, as there is no taper relief available in respect of the painting.

Negligible value claim

	£
Value (17,500 × 3p)	525
Cost (probate value)	(11,400)
Capital loss on making the claim	10,875

Appendix 2 – tax implications of setting up the discretionary trust

IHT liability

	£	£
Transfer of value		297,000
Less: Annual exemptions:		
– 2006/07		(3,000)
– 2005/06		(3,000)
Chargeable transfer		291,000
Less: nil rate band	285,000	
Less: gross chargeable transfers in previous 7 years	(125,000)	
		(160,000)
Taxable transfer		131,000
IHT at 20/80		£32,750

Question 2

Text references. Corporation tax for this question is covered in Chapters 21 to 26. Termination payments are in Chapter 5. Capital gains are dealt with in Chapters 11 - 13. Rollover relief is covered in Chapter 14. VAT is in Chapter 28 and 29.

Top tips. It is usual to find some parts of a question difficult. Just make sure that you comment on all information provided in the question – do not miss anything out. If you have a go, stating the basics, you may be surprised at the number of marks you could pick up.

Easy marks. The question did not provide you with the structure for your answer. A plan is essential in these cases as it is up to you to ensure you are methodical and do not miss out on any easy marks. Did you set out your notes in a logical, clear way, using lots of headings and subheadings? This will give you the two presentation marks; you only need a further 10 or so to pass the question!

Marking scheme

			Marks
(1)	Gain	½	
	Reverse premium	½	
	30% CT rate	½	
	Management expense for rent	½	
	Potential for rollover relief	½	
		Max	2

(2) *Closure costs*

Redundancy payments deductible for company	½
Statutory redundancy tax free	½
Contractual payments taxable	½
Ex gratia up to £30,000	½
No deduction for loss on scrapping P&M	½
No balancing allowance in general pool	½
Payment to surrender leases	½
Exempt from VAT	½
Chargeable if option to tax	½
Indebtedness	
Not within loan relationship rules if on behalf of company	½
Trading income if as result of trading transaction	½
Conclusion	½
Sale of Screen Ltd	
Gain on hotel when leaves group	½
Use MV at date of transfer	½
Effect on sale price	½
Gain on sale of shares	½
Availability of substantial shareholding exemption	½
Use of excess management expenses	½
Major change in nature or conduct of trade	½
Cannot use losses	½

10

(3) *Acquisition of 40% interest*

Acquisition of 40% interest	½
Gain in 2007/08	½
Consideration includes deferred consideration	½
No gain on share consideration received (paper for paper)	½
Gain deferred	½
Taper relief continues	½
Additional base cost for Discovery Ltd	½
Companies now in 75% group	½

4

(4) *Transfer of trade*

Transfer of trade	½
No balancing charges	½
No loss of trading losses	½
Conditions	½
No gain/ no loss transfer of properties in gains group	½
Dividend not FII	½
Transfer of going concern outside scope of VAT	½
Otherwise VAT possible	½
Deregistration	½

Max   4

(5) *Potential acquisitions*

Potential acquisitions	½
No rollover for Lately Ltd shares	½
Rollover available for goodwill	½
Rollover available for short lease	½
Depreciating asset implications	½
CT on Lately Ltd profits as trading in UK	½
Losses available for carry forward if no major change	½

Max   3

Format/Presentation   2

25

To: The files
From: A Adviser
Date: 8 May 2007
Subject: Notes for meeting with Carl Berman

Below are the tax implications of the Discovery Ltd proposed group activities.

(1)   Discovery Ltd

Sale of existing premises and lease of new premises

(i)   The capital gain will be taxable as part of profits chargeable to corporation tax (PCTCT).

(ii)   Reverse premium is also taxable on the company as part of PCTCT.

(iii)   Corporation tax rate is 30%, regardless of level of 'profits', as Discovery Ltd is a close investment holding company

(iv)   Rent paid on the lease will be a deductible management expense.

(v)   The group may be able to shelter the capital gain by making a sufficient qualifying re-investment? (see comments regarding potential acquisitions - section (5) below)

(2)   Screen Ltd

(a)   *Treatment of closure costs on restaurants*

(i)   Redundancy payments are deductible trading expenses if paid wholly and exclusively for the purpose of the trade.

(ii)   Statutory redundancy payments made to staff will be exempt from income tax.

(iii)   Additional redundancy payments may also be exempt from income tax if not contractual, ie *ex gratia* compensation payments, up to £30,000 (including statutory amounts received)

(iv)   Payments in excess of £30,000 are taxable in full as specific employment income and are treated as the top slice of income (ie after dividend income where relevant).

(v)   Loss on scrapping plant and machinery is not allowable as a trading expense as it is capital in nature.

(vi)   Assuming that the assets concerned are in the general capital allowances pool, no balancing allowances will arise as trade is not ceasing.

(vii) I believe that the payment of £50,000 to surrender the four leases is a capital sum. Consequently this will not be a deductible trading expense.

(vii) Transactions in connection with leases are generally exempt from VAT.

However, if the company has opted to tax the leases, VAT will be chargeable at the standard rate.

(b)   *Treatment of intra-group indebtedness*

Treatment of the write off of intra-group indebtedness will depend on how the indebtedness arises.

If it represents the advance of monies or payment of debts by Discovery Ltd on behalf of Screen Ltd, then the write off will not be allowed under the loan relationship rules because the companies are connected. No relief will be due to Discovery Ltd but equally no liability will arise in Screen Ltd.

Alternatively, if the debt has arisen as a result of trading transactions (eg sales by Discovery Ltd to Screen Ltd) then the write off will give rise to trading income in the hands of Screen Ltd.

Both the payments (redundancy and to the landlord) are monies paid by Discovery Ltd on behalf of Screen Ltd and therefore fall into the former (non deductible) category.

The loss on scrapping plant is merely a book entry in Screen Ltd's accounting records.

(c) *Sale of Screen Ltd*

(i) As the company is leaving the group within 6 years of an intra-group transfer, a chargeable gain will arise in Screen Ltd in the year in which it leaves the Discovery Ltd group, calculated by reference to the market value of the hotel at the date of the original transfer in 2002.

(ii) This liability is likely to depress substantially the price that SouthStart plc is willing to pay for the share capital of Screen Ltd.

(iii) A capital gain will arise in Discovery Ltd on disposal of its shareholding in Screen Ltd. Although Discovery Ltd is not a trading company, it is likely that the group is a trading group. If so, then the substantial shareholding exemption would apply so that the gain was not chargeable.

(iv) If the exemption is not available excess management expenses brought forward or arising in the same period can be used against the capital gain.

> **BPP Tutorial Note.** Excess management expenses and charges of an investment company may be carried forward and set against total profits of future periods

(v) Screen Ltd's trading losses may not be available after control has passed to SouthStart plc plc if there is a major change in the nature or conduct of Screen Ltd's trade during a three year period which includes the date on which control changed.

(vi) HMRC are likely to argue that the closure of the restaurants amounts to a major change in the conduct of the trade. The sale price to SouthStart plc is therefore unlikely to include an amount for these tax losses if the negotiators acting for the purchasers take the point.

(3) Joust Ltd

Acquisition of 40% interest from Mr and Mrs Witt

(i) The Witts would be subject to capital gains tax in 2007/08 on a gain based on the total consideration to be paid by Discovery Ltd (including the deferred consideration).

(ii) To the extent that the Witts receive share consideration, no gain will arise until the subsequent disposal of these shares (a 'paper for paper' transaction).

(iii) The gain is deferred as the new shares are treated as if they were the old shares (ie take on the acquisition details of the original shares).

(iv) Taper relief will continue to run at the business asset rates.

(v) The £600,000 would be added to the capital gains tax base cost of Discovery Ltd's shareholding in Joust Ltd.

(vi) Discovery Ltd and Joust Ltd will now form a 75% group.

(4) Overrun Ltd

(a) It should be possible to transfer the trade of Overrun Ltd to Joust Ltd without either triggering a tax charge by way of balancing charges on capital assets or forfeiture of the trading losses brought forward in Overrun Ltd by reason of a deemed cessation of trade.

However, Discovery Ltd's shareholding in Joust Ltd must be at least 75% prior to the transfer of Overrun Ltd's trade to Joust Ltd in order for this treatment to apply. The trade should therefore not be transferred from Overrun Ltd to Joust Ltd before Discovery Ltd has acquired the shares of Mr and Mrs Witt (see (3) above).

(b) The properties will be transferred for tax purposes at such value as gives rise to neither gain nor loss in Overrun Ltd's hands, since both companies will be in a 75% capital gains group once the Witts' shares have been acquired by Discovery Ltd.

(c)   The dividend will not be franked investment income in the hands of Discovery Ltd.

(d)   The transfer will be outside the scope of VAT if it can be shown that the trade is a going concern. The properties will also be outside the scope if a group VAT registration exists. If not they will be exempt, if over 3 years old, or standard rated if under 3 years old, or the exemption has been waived. However if Joust Ltd also opts to tax the properties the transfer will be outside the scope of VAT.

(e)   Overrun Ltd will have to deregister within 30 days as it has ceased to make taxable supplies.

(5)   Potential acquisitions

    (a)   *Qualifying investment for rollover relief purposes*

        (1)   Lately Ltd share capital   – no

        (2)   Brew Ltd – goodwill   – no (dealt with under the rules for intangible fixed assets)

                    – short lease   – yes, but a depreciating asset (ie gain will crystallise on earliest of sale of asset, asset ceasing to be used in trade and 10 years' from acquisition).

    (b)   *Lately Ltd tax losses*

    Lately Ltd will have been subject to corporation tax on its profits, even if not UK resident, since it clearly carries on a trade in the UK.

    Its trading losses should be available for carry forward under s 393(1) ICTA 1988 against the future trading profits following the change in ownership provided that there is not a major change in the nature or conduct of the trade.

Question 3

Text references. Husband and wife tax planning is in Chapter 30. Business income tax loss relief is in Chapter 8 and partnerships are in Chapter 9. NIC is covered in Chapters 4 and 6. Corporation Tax is covered in Chapters 21-25. Ethics are in Chapter 30.

Top tips. Make sure you plan this answer especially part (b). This makes you focus on the main points and will help you when you write the answer to mention every thing that is relevant. The examiner has stated that the average mark for answers with plans is generally rather higher than for those without.

Easy marks. Part (a)(i) asks for the calculations (easy marks) as well as a conclusion – ensure you do both. Similarly part (a)(ii) asks you to consider **all** relevant taxes so make sure you look at not only income tax but also the capital taxes (ie CGT, IHT and stamp duties) – as all can apply to a gift.

Marking scheme

					Marks
(a)	(i)	Tax bands		1½	
		Arthur owns investment property	Cindy liability	1	
			Arthur liability	1	
			Total liability	½	
		Arthur owns quoted shares	Cindy liability	½	
			Arthur liability	1½	
			Total liability	½	
		Conclusion		½	
			Max		6
	(ii)	Income tax saved		1	
		Other taxes	Capital gains tax	1	
			Inheritance tax	½	
			Stamp duties	½	
			Max		3
(b)		If company:			
		Tax and NIC on salaries		1	
		If partnership:			
		No taxable income		½	
		Class 2 NIC		½	
		If company:			
		Calculation of loss:	Equipment and CAs	½	
			Salaries	½	
			NIC	½	
		Only option is carry forward		½	
		Fully relieved in two years		½	
		Effective date in respect of cash flow		½	
		Company must make sufficient taxable profits		½	
		If partnership:			
		No salaries or Class 1 NIC		½	
		Calculation		½	
		Loss shared equally		½	
		Each partner can choose relief		½	
		Three possible years		1	
		Year for Arthur		½	
		Year for Cindy		½	
			Max		7
(c)		Client identification process		1	
		Conflict of interest		1	
					2
					18

(a)   **Gift to Arthur**

(i)   **Investment property or quoted shares**

Cindy is a higher rate taxpayer. Arthur is a basic rate taxpayer with taxable income of £20,965 (£26,000 – £5,035). He has £12,335 (£33,300 – £20,965) of the basic rate band remaining.

The family's after tax income will be maximised if the additional income tax on the inherited assets is minimised.

If Arthur owns the investment property:

	Cindy £
Dividend income	12,300
£12,300 at 32½%	3,998
Less: Tax credit at 10%	(1,230)
	2,768

	Arthur £
Property income	14,100
£12,335 at 22%	2,714
£1,765 at 40%	706
	3,420

Total tax payable (£2,768 + £3,420)	6,188

If Arthur owns the quoted shares:

	Cindy £
Property income	14,100
£14,100 at 40%	5,640

	Arthur £
Dividend income	12,300
£12,300 at 10%	1,230
Less: Tax credit at 10%	(1,230)
	Nil

Total tax payable (£5,640 + £nil)	5,640

The family's tax liability will be minimised if Cindy gives the quoted shares to Arthur.

(ii)   **Annual income tax saving and other issues**

Annual income tax saving

If Cindy owns all of the inherited assets the additional income tax is as follows.

	£
Tax on property income (see (i))	5,640
Tax on dividend income (see (i))	2,768
	8,408

The tax saved following the gift of the quoted shares to Arthur is £2,768 (£8,408 – £5,640).

Other issues

Transfers between spouses take place at no gain, no loss for the purposes of capital gains tax. Arthur's base cost in the quoted shares will equal Cindy's base cost of £305,000. He will also take over Cindy's period of ownership for taper relief purposes.

There are no inheritance tax implications due to the exemption for transfers between spouses.

There are no stamp duties on gifts.

(b) **The new business**

There are two tax advantages to operating the business as a partnership.

(i) *Reduction in taxable income*

If the new business is operated as a company, Cindy and Arthur would both be taxed at 40% on their salaries. In addition, employer and employee national insurance contributions would be due on £65 (£5,100 – £5,035) in respect of each of them.

If the new business is operated as a partnership, the partners would have no taxable trading income because the partnership has made a loss; any salaries paid to the partners would be appropriations of the profit or loss of the business and not employment income. Cindy would, however, have to pay Class 2 national insurance contributions of £2.10 each per week. Arthur is already paying Class 2 national insurance contributions because of his self employment as a carpenter

(ii) *Earlier relief for trading losses*

If the new business is operated as a company, its tax adjusted trading loss in the year ending 31 March 2008 would be as follows:

	£
Forecast loss	(44,000)
Purchase of equipment – capital	56,000
Capital allowances (£56,000 × 40%)	(22,400)
Salaries paid to Cindy and Arthur (£5,100 × 2)	(10,200)
Employer's national insurance ((£5,100 – £5,035) × 12.8% × 2)	(17)
	(20,617)

> **BPP Tutorial Note.** First year allowances are available at 40% in the year to 31 March 2008 for small enterprises. However, if students used the 50% rate which applied if one strictly follows the examiner's instructions to use 2006/07 rates and allowances credit would be given.

The loss could not be offset in the current year as the company would have no other income or gains, and therefore, it would have to be carried forward for offset against future trading profits.

The profit for the year ending 31 March 2009, as reduced by the salaries payable to Cindy and Arthur and the capital allowances on the equipment, is expected to be less than the loss available for relief. Accordingly, the trading losses will not be fully relieved until the year ending 31 March 2010. This equates to 1 January 2011 from a cash flow point of view, ie the date on which the corporation tax liability for the year ending 31 March 2010 is payable.

It should also be recognised that the loss will never be relieved if the company ceases to trade before it has made sufficient taxable profits.

If the new business is operated as a partnership, any salaries paid to the partners would not be deductible for the purposes of computing trading profit and would not be subject to Class 1 national insurance contributions. Accordingly, the tax adjusted trading loss in the year ending 31 March 2008 would be as follows:

	£
Forecast loss	(44,000)
Purchase of equipment – capital	56,000
Capital allowances (£56,000 × 40%)	(22,400)
	(10,400)

Arthur and Cindy would share the loss equally and could each choose how to relieve their share in order to obtain relief as early as possible at the highest rate of tax.

The loss could be offset against statutory total income:

- of 2007/08, the year of the loss, or
- of 2006/07, the previous year, or
- of 2004/05, the year three years prior to the year of the loss.

Following the gift of the shares from Cindy, Arthur will be a higher rate taxpayer in 2007/08 but not in the earlier years. Accordingly, he would choose to offset the loss in 2007/08.

Cindy is a higher rate taxpayer in all three years and would therefore, claim to relieve the loss in the earliest possible year, 2004/05.

(c) If you act for the new business you must carry out the appropriate client identification procedures. If the business is a company you will need to see and photocopy documents such as the certificate of incorporation and the memorandum and articles and other documents establishing who are the members and shareholders, and the situation of the registered office. Although these are likely to be Andy and Cindy, who are already clients, it would be good practice to obtain evidence of their identity (one photographic, such as passport and driving licence, and one with address, such as a recent utility bill).

If the business is a partnership, then there may be no formal partnership agreement, and you will need other evidence, such as a copy of a bank statement confirming the name and address. Again, you should obtain evidence for Andy and Cindy.

You will be acting for the new business as well as Andy and Cindy. It is possible that there may be conflicts of interest between the businesses, but it is unlikely that these are currently such that you could not act for all three parties. You must point out the possibility to Andy and Cindy, and you must keep the situation under review so that any threat can be dealt with as soon as it arises.

Question 4

Text references. Groups are looked at in Chapter 26. Rollover relief is in Chapter 14. Loss relief is dealt with in Chapter 24. CT basics are in Chapters 21 and 22.

Top tips. In parts (a) and (b) it was important to spot that Target Ltd would become a consortium company.

Note that under FRS 4 *Capital instruments* the debenture interest, discount and incidental costs should have been written off so as to achieve a constant rate on the outstanding balance in each period. However, the calculations below were those expected from candidates.

Marking scheme

		Marks
One third of ordinary share capital acquired		
Target Ltd	1	
Trading profit/investment income	2	
Consortium relief	2	
Corporation tax	1	
Max		5
Two thirds of ordinary share capital acquired		
Trading profit/investment income	1	
Consortium relief	1	
Corporation tax	1	
		3
All of ordinary share capital acquired		
Election re building	1½	
Rollover relief	2	
Calculation of gain	1½	
Pre-change gain	½	
Issue of debentures	2	
Trading profit	1½	
Group relief	1	
Corporation tax	1	
Max		10
		18

(a) **One third of Target Ltd's ordinary share capital acquired**

Target Ltd	£
Trading profits	nil
Capital gain	51,300
Less s 393A Loss relief (W1)	(51,300)
PCTCT	–

Expansion Ltd	£
Trading profits	214,000
Investment income (£120,000 × 8% × 8/12)	6,400
	220,400
Less: consortium relief (W)	(14,400)
PCTCT	206,000
Corporation tax	
£206,000 × 19%	£39,140

Working

If Expansion Ltd acquires one third of Target it will become a consortium member on 1 July 2006 since Target Ltd is a consortium company. Target Ltd is able to surrender one third of its trading loss to Expansion Ltd. Target Ltd must take into account its own current year profits when calculating the surrender. Only the current year loss can be surrendered, and this is restricted to the corresponding period of 1 July 2006 to 31 December 2006.

BPP
LEARNING MEDIA

	£
Target Ltd's loss	137,700
Utilised itself under S 393A	(51,300)
	86,400
Available to consortium members (one third per member)	28,800

Time apportion £28,800 × 6/12 in order to calculate share of loss for Expansion Ltd in the year to 31.12.06.

Brought forward trading losses can not be surrendered or set against chargeable gains. Trading losses of £9,200 will remain to be carried forward.

(b) **Two thirds of Target Ltd's ordinary share capital acquired**

Target Ltd will become an associated company of Expansion Ltd and the lower and upper limits for corporation tax purposes are therefore £150,000 and £750,000 respectively.

Target Ltd

Target Ltd's corporation tax position will be the same as in part (a) above.

Expansion Ltd	£
Trading profit	214,000
Investment income	6,400
	220,400
Less: Consortium relief (£28,800 × 2 × 6/12)	(28,800)
PCTCT	191,600
Corporation tax at £191,600 × 30%	57,480
Less: marginal relief: £(750,000 − 191,600) × $\dfrac{11}{400}$	(15,356)
CT	42,124

(c) **All of Target Ltd's ordinary share capital acquired**

Target Ltd and Expansion Ltd will be members of the same group relief group and also of the same capital gains group.

Target Ltd

Trading profit	£
Capital gain (W1)	Nil
PCTCT	Nil
	-

Target Ltd's corporation tax position will be the same as in part (a) above.

Expansion Ltd	£
Trading profit (W2)	199,225
Investment income	6,400
Capital gain (W1)	3,225
	208,850
Less group relief (£137,700 × 6/12)	(68,850)
PCTCT	140,000
Corporation tax	
£140,000 × 19%	£26,600

Workings

(1) *Chargeable gains*

Target Ltd and Expansion Ltd should make an election that the office building is treated as if it were being transferred between them immediately before the disposal. The gain of £51,300 will then be treated as made by Expansion Ltd. Election by 31.12.08. £38,475 (£51,300 × ¾) of this gain can be rolled over into the base cost of the new factory to be acquired in January 2007.

	£
Capital gain	51,300
Less rolled over (75% business use)	(38,475)
	12,825
Capital losses b/f	(9,600)
Gain remaining chargeable	3,225

If obtaining relief for Expansion Ltd's capital loss against Target Ltd's gain was one of the main reasons for acquiring the company, then relief could be denied under the anti-avoidance legislation for gains on pre-change assets.

(2) *Trading profit*

The loan relationship legislation does not define 'trading purposes'. If the debenture issue is for trading purposes, then the debenture interest, the 3% discount and the incidental costs of obtaining the finance will be deductible trading profit expenses. Expansion Ltd's trading profit for the year ended 31 December 2006 will be:

	£
Previous trading profit	214,000
Debenture interest (£250,000 at 10% × 6/12)	(12,500)
Discount (£250,000 × 3% = £7,500) × 6/60	(750)
Incidental costs (£15,250 × 6/60)	(1,525)
Revised trading profit	199,225

If the debenture is for non trading purposes the CT computation would be:

	£
Trading profit	214,000
Capital gain	3,225
	217,225
Less loss on loan relationships (6,400 – 12,500 – 750 – 1,525)	(8,375)
	208,850
Less group relief (£137,700 × 6/12)	(68,850)
PCTCT	140,000

> **Top tip.** Either of these approaches would be acceptable. The former is followed in this answer.

Question 5

Text references. Chapter 4 discusses the difference between employment and self employment and also covers national insurance contributions. Chapter 15 deals with principal private residence relief.

Top tips. In part (a), make sure you relate the factors indicating self employment to the facts given in the question.

Easy marks. There were easy marks in part (b) for a reasonably simple income tax computation. Calculation of national insurance contributions is also straightforward.

Marking scheme

			Marks
(a)	Control	½	
	Future work	½	
	Equipment	½	
	Financial risk	½	
	Sound management	½	
	Integral to business	½	
	Short engagements	½	
	Work when chooses	½	
	Must do work personally	½	
	Max		4
(b)	*Self employment*		
	Income	½	
	Office use	1	
	Telephone	1	
	CAs	1	
	Personal allowance	½	
	Income tax	1	
	Class 2 NICs	½	
	Class 4 NICs	1½	
	Employment		
	Expenses	½	
	CAs – employment	½	
	IT liability	1	
	Class 1 NICs	1	
	Additional liability	1	
	Max		8
(c)	Work through company	½	
	IR 35	½	
	Salary	½	
	Dividends	½	
			2
(d)	Apportion for business use	1	
	Last 36 months in full	1	
	2/75th of the gain chargeable	1	
	Taper relief	1	
			4
			18

(a) **Factors indicating self-employment or self employment**

The following factors indicate self employment:

- Web-Designs Ltd does not exercise a great deal of control over Richard.
- Richard is under no obligation to accept further work.
- Richard provides all his own equipment.
- Richard is taking a financial risk by working on a fixed fee basis.
- On the other hand Richard can profit from sound management.
- Richard is not an integral part of Web-Design Ltd eg he never visits the premises of the company.
- All the engagements are for short periods (on average 2 weeks).
- Richard can work when he chooses.

The following factors indicate employment:

- One indicator of employment is the fact that Richard is obliged to do the work personally.

Conclusion

It is likely, looking at the overall situation, that Richard will be treated as self employed.

(b) **Richard Byte income tax and NICs**

Self employed

Income tax

		Non-savings
	£	£
Income		60,000
Less: Use of office 1/5 × £4,000	800	
Telephone £400 × 4	1,600	
Capital allowances		
FYA £4,480 × 50%	2,240	
		(4,640)
Trading income/STI		55,360
Less: Personal allowance		(5,035)
Taxable income		50,325

	£
Tax	
£2,150 × 10%	215
£31,150 × 22%	6,853
£(50,325 − 33,300) = £17,025 × 40%	6,810
Income tax	13,878

National Insurance Contributions

Class 2 NICs £2.10 × 52	£109

Class 4 NICs

	£
£(33,540 − 5,035) = 28,505 × 8%	2,280
£(55,360 − 33,540) = 21,820 × 1%	218
NICs	2,498

Employed

It is likely that HMRC would allow the expenses in respect of the extra telephone as wholly, exclusively and necessarily incurred in the performance of the employment duties. A deduction for use of the house will only be permitted if Richard is required by Web-Designs Ltd to work at home, and does not do so solely through choice. Assuming this is satisfied, only the marginal costs of working from home are allowed, such as additional heat and light. In the absence of additional information it is assumed that taking $\frac{1}{5}$th of the expenses is a reasonable estimate, although it may be lower in practice.

The capital allowances on the computer will also be allowed provided it is necessary for the performance of employment duties.

On this basis, the net employment income would be £55,360 and so the income tax figure will be the same as for self-employment.

However the Class 1 NICs will be based on the salary of £60,000 and will be:

	£
£(33,540 − 5,035) = £28,505 × 11%	3,136
£(60,000 − 33,540) = £21,820 × 1%	265
	3,401

The additional liability if Richard is employed is therefore £903 (£(3,401 − 2,498)).

(c) Richard could supply his services to Web-Designs Ltd through a company.

The IR35 rules would apply since the nature of the contracts is not such that Richard would be treated as an employee.

Richard could draw a small salary from the company to preserve his national insurance contribution record. He could then take additional profits out as dividends. This is likely to save tax and NICs.

A higher salary could be taken if Richard wanted to make pension contributions, or the contributions could be made direct by his company so avoiding NICs.

(d) **Impact on capital gains tax position**

As part of the house will have been used for business purposes for part of the period of ownership the principal private residence relief is restricted. The gain will need to be apportioned between the chargeable and exempt parts in a just and reasonable manner.

As the business part was at some time used as part of the only or main residence, the gain apportioned to that part will qualify for the last 36 months exemption.

In this case it is likely than HMRC will accept that $\frac{2}{75}$th of the gain (ie $\frac{1}{5} \times \frac{2}{15}$) will not attract PPR relief as it relates to the business use, assuming the house is sold in five years time.

Furthermore, the business asset rate of taper relief will apply for the proportion of business use. Although the gain not covered by the PPR relief is attributable to the business use, it is still necessary to split the gain between business and non business use over the last ten years of ownership.

Business use $\quad \frac{5}{10} \times \frac{1}{5} = \frac{1}{10}$

Non-business use $\quad \frac{5}{10} + \frac{5}{10} \times \frac{4}{5} = \frac{9}{10}$

The chargeable gain would then be:

$\frac{2}{75}$ of the gain $\times \frac{1}{10} \times 25\%$

plus $\frac{2}{75}$ of the gain $\times \frac{9}{10} \times 60\%$

Assuming Richard made no other gains, the gain on the sale of his home would have to exceed £½ million before any CGT could be payable.

ACCA Professional Paper P6 – Options Module

Advanced Taxation (UK)

Mock Examination 3 (Pilot Paper)

Question Paper	
Time allowed	**Reading and planning: 15 minutes** **Writing: 3 hours**
This paper is divided into two sections	
Section A	**BOTH questions are compulsory questions and MUST be attempted**
Section B	**TWO questions ONLY to be attempted**

During reading and planning time only the question paper may be annotated

DO NOT OPEN THIS PAPER UNTIL YOU ARE READY TO START UNDER EXAMINATION CONDITIONS

Section A: BOTH questions are compulsory and MUST be attempted

Question 1

Hutt plc has owned the whole of the ordinary share capital of Rainbow Ltd and Coronet Ltd since 1998. All three companies are resident in the UK. Their results for the year ended 31 March 2007 are as follows:

	Hutt plc £	Rainbow Ltd £	Coronet Ltd £
Taxable trading profit/(loss)	(105,000)	800,000	63,000
Capital gain	144,000	–	–
Rental income	65,000	–	–
UK bank interest receivable	2,000	57,000	18,000

Hutt plc's rental income of £65,000 per annum arises in respect of Hutt Tower, an office building acquired on 1 April 2006.

In the year ended 31 March 2006 Hutt plc had a trading profit of £735,000, UK bank interest receivable of £2,000 and a capital loss of £98,000, which was carried forward as at 31 March 2006.

Hutt plc and Coronet Ltd both carry on trades in the UK. Rainbow Ltd conducts both its manufacturing and trading activities wholly in the country of Prismovia. The system of corporation tax in Prismovia is mainly the same as that in the UK although the rate of corporation tax is 28%. There is no double taxation agreement between the UK and Prismovia.

Hutt plc has agreed that it will purchase the whole of the share capital of Lucia Ltd, a UK resident engineering component manufacturing company, on 1 July 2007 for £130,000.

Hutt plc will need to take out a loan to finance the purchase of Lucia Ltd. The company intends to borrow £190,000 from BHC Bank Ltd on 1 July 2007. BHC Bank Ltd will charge Hutt plc a £1,400 loan arrangement fee and interest at 7.25% per annum. Hutt plc only needs £130,000 of the loan to buy the share capital of Lucia Ltd and intends to use the balance of the loan as follows: £45,000 to carry out repairs to Hutt Tower; and the remainder to help fund the company's ongoing working capital requirements.

Lucia Ltd is a UK resident company. The scale of its activities in the last few years has been very small and it has made tax adjusted trading losses. As at 31 March 2007 Lucia Ltd has trading losses carried forward of £186,000. The company's activities from 1 April 2007 to 30 June 2007 are expected to be negligible and any profit or loss in that period can be ignored. Because of the small scale of its activities Lucia Ltd has not been registered for value added tax (VAT) since March 2006. In arriving at the purchase price for the company, the owners of Lucia Ltd have valued the company's trading losses at £35,340 (£186,000 at 19%), as Lucia Ltd has always been a small company.

On the purchase of Lucia Ltd, Hutt plc has plans to return the company to profitability and the budgeted turnover of Lucia Ltd for the nine months ended 31 March 2008 is as set out below. All amounts relate to the sales of engineering components and are stated exclusive of VAT. It can be assumed that all categories of turnover will accrue evenly over the period.

		£
UK customers:	– VAT registered	85,000
	– non-VAT registered	25,000
European Union customers:	– VAT registered	315,000
	– non-VAT registered	70,000
Other non-UK customers		180,000
		675,000

Lucia Ltd will incur input VAT of £7,800 per month from 1 July 2007 in respect of purchases from UK businesses. It will also purchase raw materials from Dabet Gmbh for £17,000 in November 2007. Dabet Gmbh is resident and registered for VAT in Germany.

Lucia Ltd owns a factory that was built in May 1971 at a cost of £210,000. The factory was acquired by Lucia Ltd on 30 June 2003, for £270,000. It can be assumed that the factory's current value of £80,000 will not change in the foreseeable future. On 1 January 2008, Lucia Ltd will sell this factory and take out a short lease on a new, larger one. The indexation allowance applicable to the period June 2003 to January 2008 can be assumed to be £27,000.

It is proposed that an office building owned by Coronet Ltd be sold to Lucia Ltd in May 2008 at its market value. This building will then be sold on by Lucia Ltd, to Vac Ltd, an unconnected third party in June 2008, giving rise to a capital gain of £92,000. The intention is that this gain will be reduced by the capital loss arising on the sale of the factory.

Required

(a) Describe and evaluate the options available in respect of the trading losses of Hutt plc for the year ended 31 March 2007. Your answer should include a recommendation on the most tax efficient use of these losses, together with details of and time limits for any elections or claims that would need to be submitted, assuming that the losses are to be used as soon as possible and are not to be carried forward.   **(13 marks)**

(b) Prepare a report for the management of Hutt plc concerning the acquisition of Lucia Ltd. The report should be in three sections, addressing the three sets of issues set out below, and should, where appropriate, include supporting calculations.

    (i)   The purchase price

        Comment on the valuation placed on Lucia Ltd's trading losses, by the owners of Lucia Ltd.

        Provide an explanation of the tax treatment of the loan arrangement fee and the interest payable on the loan of £190,000, assuming that Hutt plc continues to have bank interest receivable, in the year ended 31 March 2008, of £2,000.   **(9 marks)**

    (ii)   VAT issues

        Provide an explanation of the date by which Lucia Ltd will be required to register for VAT in the UK and any other relevant points in respect of registration.

        Provide a calculation of the VAT payable by, or repayable to, Lucia Ltd in respect of the period from registration to 31 March 2008.

        With reference only to the facts in the question, suggest ONE disadvantage of Lucia Ltd entering into a group VAT registration with Hutt plc.   **(6 marks)**

    (iii) The office building

        Advise on the tax implications of the proposed sale of the office building by Coronet Ltd to Lucia Ltd in May 2008. Your answer should consider all relevant taxes.

        Evaluate the proposed strategy to reduce the capital gain arising on the sale of the office building by offsetting the capital loss on the sale of the factory, on the assumption that both Lucia Ltd and Coronet Ltd will pay corporation tax at the rate of 30%, for the year ended 31 March 2009. **(9 marks)**

Appropriateness of the format and presentation of the report and the effectiveness with which its advice is communicated.   **(2 marks)**

You may assume that the tax rates and allowances for the financial year to 31 March 2007 and for the tax year 2006/07 will continue to apply for the foreseeable future.

(Total = 39 marks)

Question 2

Your manager has had a meeting with Pilar Mareno, a self-employed consultant, and has sent you a copy of the following memorandum.

To   The files
From   Tax manager
Date   31 May 2007
Subject   Pilar Mareno – Business expansion

Pilar Mareno (PM) has been offered a contract with DWM plc, initially for two years, which will result in fees of £80,000 plus VAT per annum.

In order to service this contract, PM would have to take on additional help in the form of either a part-time employee for two days a week, or the services of a self-employed contractor for 100 days per year. She would also have to acquire a van, which would be used wholly for business purposes. PM has decided that she will only enter into the contract if it generates at least an additional £15,000 per annum, on average, for the family after all costs and taxes.

PM's annual profitability and the profit generated by the contract (before taking into account the costs of the part-time employee/contractor and the van) are summarised below.

	Existing business £	New contract £
Sales	210,000	80,000
Less: Materials, wages and overheads	(120,000)	(35,000)
Profit per accounts and taxable profit	90,000	45,000

Supplies made under the contract will be 65% standard rated and 35% exempt for value added tax (VAT) purposes; this is the same as for PM's existing business. £31,500 of the costs incurred in relation to the contract will be subject to VAT at the standard rate. The equivalent figure for PM's existing business is £100,000.

PM has identified Max Wallen (MW) as a possible self-employed contractor. MW would charge £75 per day plus VAT for a contract of 100 days per year, with a rate of £25 per day plus VAT in respect of any days when he is ill (up to a maximum of 8 days per year). PM has a spare copy of the specialist software that MW would need but MW would use his own laptop computer.

Alternatively, PM could employ her husband, Alec (AM), paying him a gross annual salary of £7,600. AM would have to give up his current full time job, but would expect to do other part-time employed work earning a further £10,000 (gross) per annum.

PM estimates that a second hand van will cost £7,800 plus VAT or alternatively, a van could be leased for £300 plus VAT per month. We can assume that if the van is purchased, it will be sold at the end of the two year contract for £2,500 plus VAT.

Tax manager

An extract from an email from your manager is set out below.

Please prepare a memorandum for me, incorporating the following:

1   Calculations to demonstrate whether or not Pilar's desired annual after tax income from the new contract will be achievable depending on:

- whether she leases or buys the van; and
- whether she employs Alec or uses Max Wallen.

You may find it easier to:

(i)   work out the after tax cost of buying or leasing the van. (When calculating the annual cost of the van, assume that the total cost can be averaged over the two years of the contract.)

and then to consider:

(ii)   the after tax income depending on whether Alec is employed or the self-employed contractor, Max, is used.

2   A rationale for the approach you have taken and a summary of your findings.

3   Any other issues we should be considering in respect of Pilar employing Alec, including any alternative to employment.

4   It seems to me that HM Revenue and Customs may be able to successfully contend that Max Wallen would be an employee, rather than a self-employed contractor. Prepare your figures on the basis that he is self-employed but include a list of factors in your memorandum, based on the information we have, that would indicate either employed or self-employed status.

Take some time to think about your approach to this before you start. Also, as always when working on Pilar's affairs, watch out for the VAT as it can get quite tricky. I suspect the VAT will affect the costs incurred so you'll need to address VAT first. Pilar's estimate of the profit on the contract will have ignored these complications.

Tax manager

You have extracted the following further information from Pilar Mareno's client file.

- None of Pilar's VAT inputs is directly attributable to either standard rated or exempt supplies.
- Alec has worked for a UK bank for many years and is currently paid an annual salary of £17,000.
- The couple have no sources of income other than those set out above.

Required

Prepare the memorandum requested by your manager.

Marks are available for the four components of the memorandum as follows:

(1)   Relevant calculations.   **(16 marks)**

(2)   Rationale for the approach taken and summary of findings.   **(2 marks)**

(3)   Other issues in respect of Pilar employing Alec, together with any suggestions as to an alternative to employment.   **(2 marks)**

(4)   The employment status of Max Wallen.   **(3 marks)**

Appropriateness of the format and presentation of the memorandum and the effectiveness with which the information is communicated.   **(2 marks)**

You may assume that the rates and allowances for the tax year 2006/07 will continue to apply for the foreseeable future.

(Total = 25 marks)

Section B: TWO questions ONLY to be attempted

Question 3

Stanley Beech, a self-employed landscape gardener, intends to transfer his business to Landscape Ltd, a company formed for this purpose.

The following information has been extracted from client files and from meetings with Stanley.

Stanley:

- Acquired a storage building for £46,000 on 1 July 1998 and began trading.
- Has no other sources of income.
- Has capital losses brought forward from 2002/03 of £11,400.

The whole of the business is to be transferred to Landscape Ltd on 1 September 2007:

- The market value of the assets to be transferred is £118,000.

- The assets include the storage building and goodwill, valued at £87,000 and £24,000 respectively, and various small pieces of equipment and consumable stores.

- Landscape Ltd will issue 5,000 £1 ordinary shares as consideration for the transfer.

Advice given to Stanley in respect of the sale of the business:

- 'No capital gains tax will arise on the transfer of your business to the company.'

- 'You should take approximately 30% of the payment from Landscape Ltd in shares with the balance left on a loan account payable to you by the company, such that you can receive a cash payment in the future.'

Advice given to Stanley in respect of his annual remuneration from Landscape Ltd:

- 'The payment of a dividend of £21,000 is more tax efficient than paying a salary bonus of £21,000 as you will pay income tax at only 25% on the dividend received, whereas you would pay income tax at 40% on a salary bonus. The dividend also avoids the need to pay national insurance contributions.'

- 'There is no tax in respect of an interest free loan from an employer of less than £5,000.'

- 'The provision of a company car is tax neutral as the cost of providing it is deductible in the corporation tax computation.'

Stanley's proposed remuneration package from Landscape Ltd:

- An annual salary of £40,000 and an annual dividend of approximately £21,000.

- On 1 December 2007 an interest free loan of £3,600, which he intends to repay in two years time.

- A company car with a cost when new of £11,400. The only costs incurred by the company in respect of this car will be lease rentals of £300 per month and business fuel of £100 per month.

- The annual employment income benefit in respect of the car is to be taken as £3,420.

Landscape Ltd:

- Will prepare accounts to 31 March each year.
- Will pay corporation tax at the rate of 19%.

Required

(a) (i) Explain why there would be no capital gains tax liability on the transfer of Stanley's business to Landscape Ltd in exchange for shares. Calculate the maximum loan account balance that Stanley could receive without giving rise to a capital gains tax liability and state the resulting capital gains tax base cost of the shares. **(8 marks)**

     (ii) Explain the benefit to Stanley of taking part of the payment for the sale of his business in the form of a loan account, which is to be paid out in cash at some time in the future. **(1 mark)**

(b) Comment on the accuracy and completeness of the advice received by Stanley in respect of his remuneration package. Supporting calculations are only required in respect of the company car. **(9 marks)**

Ignore value added tax (VAT) in answering this question.

You may assume that the rates and allowances for the financial year to 31 March 2007 and the tax year 2006/07 will continue to apply for the foreseeable future.

(Total = 18 marks)

Question 4

Mahia Ltd is an unquoted, UK resident trading company formed in May 2000. One of its shareholders, Claus Rowen, intends to sell his shares back to Mahia Ltd on 31 July 2007. Another shareholder, Maude Brooke, intends to give some of her shares to her daughter, Tessa.

The following information has been extracted from client files and from meetings with the shareholders.

Mahia Ltd:

- In May 2000 the company issued 40,000 shares at £3.40 per share as follows:

Claus Rowen	16,000
Charlotte Forde	12,000
Olaf Berne	12,000

- Olaf sold his 12,000 shares to Maude Brooke on 1 October 2005 when they were worth £154,000.

Claus and Charlotte:

- Have always lived in the UK.
- Are higher rate taxpayers who use their capital gains tax annual exemption every year.

Maude:

- Was born in the UK, but moved to Canada on 1 April 2003 with her daughter, Tessa.
- Has not visited the UK since leaving for Canada, but will return to the UK permanently in December 2012.
- Is employed in Canada with an annual salary equivalent to £70,000.

Sale of shares by Claus:

- Charlotte and Maude want to expand the company's activities in the UK but Claus does not. The shareholders have been arguing over this matter for almost a year.

- In order to enable the company to prosper, Claus has agreed to sell his shares to the company on 31 July 2007.

Gift of shares by Maude:

- Maude will gift 4,000 shares in Mahia Ltd to her daughter, Tessa, on either 1 August 2007 or 1 June 2008.
- She will delay the gift until 1 June 2008 (Tessa's wedding day) if this reduces the total tax due.
- The tax due in Canada will be the same regardless of the date of the gift.
- She has made no previous transfers of value for UK inheritance tax purposes.
- For the purposes of this gift, you should assume that Maude will die on 31 December 2011.

Market values of shares in Mahia Ltd on all relevant dates are to be taken as:

Size of shareholding	*Market value per share*
%	£
< 25	10.20
25 – 35	14.40
> 35	38.60

Market values of the assets of Mahia Ltd on all relevant dates are to be taken as:

	£
Land and buildings used within the trade	1,400,000
Three machines of equal value used within the trade	15,000
Motor cars used by employees	45,000
Quoted shares	42,000
Inventory, trade receivables and cash	145,000

Required

(a) Advise Claus on the tax treatment of the proceeds he will receive in respect of the sale of his shares to Mahia Ltd. Prepare a calculation of the net (after tax) proceeds from the sale based on your conclusions. **(8 marks)**

(b) Advise Maude on the UK tax consequences of gifting the shares to Tessa and prepare computations to determine on which of the two dates the gift should be made, if the total UK tax due on the gift is to be minimised. Your answer should consider all relevant taxes. **(10 marks)**

You may assume that the rates and allowances for the tax year 2006/07 will continue to apply for the foreseeable future.

(Total = 18 marks)

Question 5

Vikram Bridge has been made redundant by Bart Industries Ltd, a company based in Birmingham. He intends to move to Scotland to start a new job with Dreamz Technology Ltd.

The following information has been extracted from client files and from meetings with Vikram.

Vikram Bridge:

- Is unmarried, but has been living with Alice Tate since 1996. The couple have four young children.

- Receives dividends of approximately £7,800 each year and makes annual capital gains of approximately £1,200 in respect of shares inherited from his mother.

- The couple have no sources of income other than Vikram's employment income and the £7,800 of dividends.

Made redundant by Bart Industries Ltd on 28 February 2007:

- Vikram's employment contract entitled him to two months' notice or two months salary in lieu of notice. On 28 February 2007 the company paid him his salary for the two-month period of £4,700, and asked him to leave immediately.

- On 30 April 2007 the company paid him a further £1,300 in respect of statutory redundancy, together with a non-contractual lump sum of £14,500, as a gesture of goodwill.

Job with Dreamz Technology Ltd:

- Starts on 1 October 2007 with an annual salary of £38,500.

- The company will contribute £9,400 in October 2007 towards Vikram's costs of moving to Scotland.

- In November 2008, the company will issue free shares to all of its employees. Vikram will be issued with 200 shares, expected to be worth approximately £2,750.

Moving house:

- Vikram's house in Birmingham is fairly small; he intends to buy a much larger one in Glasgow.

- The cost of moving to Glasgow, including the stamp duty land tax in respect of the purchase of his new house, will be approximately £12,500.

- To finance the purchase of the house in Glasgow Vikram will sell a house he owns in Wales, in August 2007.

House in Wales:

- Was given to Vikram by his mother on 1 September 1999, when it was worth £145,000.

- Vikram's mother continued to live in the house until her death on 1 May 2007, when she left the whole of her estate to Vikram.

- At the time of her death the house had severe structural problems and was valued at £140,000.

- Vikram has subsequently spent £18,000 improving the property and expects to be able to sell it for £195,000.

- Vikram is keen to reduce the tax payable on the sale of the house and is willing to transfer the house, or part of it, to Alice prior to the sale if that would help.

Required

Prepare explanations, including supporting calculations where appropriate, of the following issues suitable for inclusion in a letter to Vikram.

(a)   The capital gains tax payable on the sale of the house in Wales in August 2007, together with the potential effect of transferring the house, or part of it, to Alice prior to the sale, and any other advice you consider helpful.   **(7 marks)**

(b)   The inheritance tax implications in respect of the house in Wales on the death of Vikram's mother. **(2 marks)**

(c)   The income tax treatment of the receipt by Vikram of the shares in Dreamz Technology Ltd.   **(3 marks)**

(d)   How Vikram's job with Dreamz Technology Ltd will affect the amount and date of payment of the income tax due on his dividend income for 2009/10 and future years.   **(6 marks)**

Ignore national insurance contributions in answering this question.

You may assume that the rates and allowances for the tax year 2006/07 will continue to apply for the foreseeable future.

(Total = 18 marks)

Answers

**DO NOT TURN THIS PAGE UNTIL YOU HAVE
COMPLETED THE MOCK EXAM**

A plan of attack

What's the worst thing you could be doing right now if this was the actual exam paper? Sharpening your pencil? Wondering how to celebrate the end of the exam in about 3 hours time? Panicking, flapping and generally getting in a right old state?

Well, they're all pretty bad, so turn back to the paper and let's sort out a **plan of attack**!

First things first

You have 15 minutes reading time. Make sure you spend it wisely, looking through the paper in detail working out which optional questions to do and the order in which to attack the questions. You've got **two options**. Option 1 is the option recommended by BPP.

Option 1 (if you're thinking 'Help!')

If you're a bit worried about the paper, do the questions in the order of how well you think you can answer them. If you find the questions in Section B less daunting than the compulsory questions in Section A start with Section B. Remember you only need to do two of the three questions in Section B; you may find it easier if you start by deciding which question you will not do and put a line through it.

- **Question 3** is in two parts. Part (a) is about the incorporation of a business. Part (b) concerns giving advice on remuneration packages. Marks were split equally between parts (a) and (b) and it would be important to ensure you could make a good attempt at both parts of this question before choosing it.

- Again, before attempting **question 4** it would have been important to ensure you could make an attempt at both part (a) and part (b). Part (a) covered the purchase of own shares whilst part (b) covered IHT and CGT on a gift.

- The requirements of **question 5** are helpfully broken down and you are told exactly what is required in each part. It is easier to gain marks if you can see where they are allocated so this may well have been a very good question to start with.

Ensure that you do not spend longer than your allocated time on Section B. When you've spent the allocated time on **two** of the three questions in Section B turn to the longer questions in Section A. Read these questions through thoroughly before you launch into them. Once you start make sure you allocate your time to the parts within the questions according to the marks available and that, where possible, you attempt the easy marks first.

Lastly, what you mustn't forget is that you have to **answer both questions in Section A and TWO in Section B**. Do not miss out more than one question in Section B and do not waste time answering three questions in Section B or you will seriously affect your chance of passing the exam.

Option 2 (if you're thinking 'It's a doddle')

It never pays to be over confident but if you're not quaking in your shoes about the exam then **turn straight to the compulsory questions** in Section A.

Once you've done these questions, move to Section B.

- The question you attempt first really depends on what you are most confident at.

- You then have to select one of the two remaining questions. If you are undecided look at the requirements. It maybe easier to obtain more marks if these are broken down into several smaller parts.

No matter how many times we remind you....

Always, always **allocate your time** according to the marks for the question in total and then according to the parts of the question. And **always, always follow the requirements** exactly.

In the compulsory questions there are two marks available for the appropriateness of the format and presentation of the report and the effectiveness with which the advice is communicated. These are easy marks; ensure you get them!

You've got spare time at the end of the exam.....?

If you have allocated your time properly then you **shouldn't have time on your hands** at the end of the exam. But if you find yourself with five or ten minutes to spare, check over your work to make sure that there are no silly arithmetical errors.

Forget about it!

And don't worry if you found the paper difficult. More than likely other candidates will too. If this were the real thing you would need to **forget** the exam the minute you leave the exam hall and **think about the next one**. Or, if it's the last one, **celebrate**!

Question 1

		Marks
(a)	Hutt plc trading losses	
	Within Hutt plc	
	Current year offset	½
	Available profits	1
	Application of the small companies rate limits	1
	Effective rate of tax/relief	1
	No carry back opportunity	½
	Group relief	
	Direct ownership level	½
	Available relief	½
	Coronet Ltd:	
	Available profits	½
	Effective rate of tax	1
	Rainbow Ltd:	
	Effective rate of UK tax	½
	Tax position in Prismovia	1
	Effect of DTR	2
	Recommendation (combination claim)	
	Identify correct objective	1
	Hutt plc – profits at 32¾%	½
	Rainbow Ltd – the balance	½
	Order of elections	1
	Group relief election – both companies/time limit	1
	Current year offset election/time limit	1
	Max	**13**
(b) (i)	The purchase price	
	Trading losses:	
	No current relief in Lucia Ltd	½
	No group relief with reason	1
	No carry forward with reasons	1½
	Conclusion	½
	Loan from BHC Bank	
	Tax deduction per accounts treatment	1
	Total amount allowable in the period	½
	Amount relating to trading purpose	1
	Amount relating to non-trading purpose	2
	Uses of deficit (ie loss)	2
	Recommendation	½
	Max	**9**

(ii)	VAT issues			
	Registration			
	Historic and future limits	1		
	Registration and notification dates	1		
	Calculation			
	Output tax	2½		
	Input tax	1		
	Disadvantage of group VAT registration – either of			
	Lucia Ltd in repayment position;			
	or administrative difficulties	1		
			Max	6
(iii)	The office building			
	Sale from Coronet Ltd to Lucia Ltd			
	Capital gain			
	CGT group	½		
	Consequences	1		
	Election re notional transfer – availability	1		
	Stamp duty land tax	1		
	VAT			
	If group registration	½		
	If no group registration	1½		
	Sale of building to Vac Ltd			
	Pre-entry asset			
	Identify	½		
	Consequences	1		
	Calculation of post-entry loss/tax saving	1		
	Loss on sale – no IA	½		
	Use of market value	½		
	Both companies and time limit	1		
			Max	9
	Format and style			
	Appropriate style and presentation	1		
	Effectiveness of communication	1		
				2
				39

(a)   **Hutt Plc trading losses**

There are three options available to Hutt Plc with regard to its trading losses. It may either (i) use the losses against its own profits, (ii) group relieve the losses, or (iii) use a combination of the two

(i)   **Use within Hutt Plc**

Hutt Plc's profits for the year ended 31 March 2007 are:

	£	£
Trading profits		Nil
Capital Gain	144,000	
Less: losses b/f	(98,000)	
		46,000
Property income		65,000
Interest income		2,000
PCTCT		113,000

Hutt Plc has two associates and therefore the corporation tax (CT) limits must be divided by three to determine the CT rate payable.

Upper limit	1,500,000/3	500,000
Lower limit	300,000/3	100,000

As Hutt Plc's profits are between the two limits it is a marginal relief company and will pay CT at 30% less marginal relief. The marginal rate of tax (ie tax rate on profits above £100,000 and less than £500,000) is 32.75%.

The current year claim is an all or nothing claim and therefore if the losses are to be used in this year, £105,000 must be relieved. This will provide a tax saving of:

	£
£92,000 @ 19%	17,480
£13,000 @ 32.75%	4,258
Tax saved	21,738

It is not possible to make a claim to carry back losses to the previous year, to obtain tax relief in this case at 30% in the year ended 31 March 2006, unless a current year claim has been made. As the losses available are completely used in the current year, a carry back claim cannot be made.

(ii) **Group relief**

As Hutt Plc owns at least 75% of Rainbow Ltd and Coronet Ltd, the three companies are in a group relief group for loss relief purposes. This means that losses may be relieved in the current period to these companies. The choice of which company to relieve the losses to will depend on the tax rate paid by that company.

Coronet Ltd has PCTCT of (£63,000 + 18,000 =) £81,000. This is below the adjusted lower limit of £100,000 and Coronet Ltd therefore pays tax at 19% on its entire profits. There is thus no tax saving in surrendering losses to this company.

Rainbow Ltd has PCTCT of (£800,000 + 57,000 =) £857,000, which means that losses surrendered to it will provide tax relief at 30% ie £105,000 @ 30% = £31,500.

It should be noted that Rainbow Ltd's trading profits will likely also be taxed in Prismovia since their tax system is similar to the UK and it appears that Rainbow Ltd has a permanent establishment in that country. The UK would tax profits of a permanent establishment in another country in the UK (and allow their losses) and we must therefore assume that Prismovia will similarly tax Rainbow Ltd's UK profits in Prismovia.

To ensure that no foreign tax relief is wasted the maximum relief that should be surrendered to Rainbow would be:

	£
UK tax: £857,000 @ 30%	257,100
Overseas tax: £800,000 @ 28%	(224,000)
Maximum tax that can be relieved	33,100
Maximum loss relief claim (÷ 30%)	110,333

As the available loss is less than this amount, the full loss could potentially be set against Rainbow Ltd's profits.

(iii)   Combination claim

Clearly it would be advantageous to be able to obtain relief in Hutt Plc at 32.75% and relief at 30% for the balance in Rainbow Ltd. This would provide relief as follows:

	£
£13,000 @ 32.75%	4,258
£92,000 @ 30%	27,600
Tax saved	31,858

Hutt Plc should therefore make a joint claim with Rainbow Ltd for group relief, surrendering £92,000 to Rainbow Ltd. This must be made within two years of the end of Rainbow Ltd's period of account ie by 31 March 2009.

Hutt Plc should then make a claim for current year relief of £13,000, again within two years of the end of the period in which the loss arose ie by 31 March 2009

(b)   **Report**

To:	Hutt Plc Management
From:	A Adviser
Date:	[date]
Subject:	Purchase of Lucia Ltd

This report covers tax issues relating to:

(i)   The purchase price
(ii)   VAT, and
(iii)   The office building

(i)   **The purchase price**

Valuation of Lucia Ltd's trading losses

Lucia Ltd's (LL) current owners have placed a value of £35,340 on the company's trading losses, which it currently cannot use as it has no other profits to set the losses against.

While it is true that once LL is purchased by Hutt Plc it will be part of the group for loss relief purposes (direct ownership of at least 75%), it will not be possible for Hutt Plc (or any of the other group companies) to claim any of LL's losses that arose in any part of the period prior to the acquisition. Only losses arising once the company joins the group may be group relieved.

In addition, LL will not be able to utilise the losses against its own income once it becomes profitable as HMRC are likely to argue that there has been a major change in the nature and conduct of trade following the change in ownership. As there will no longer be profits from the 'same' trade, LL will not be able to carry forward its losses against these profits and they will be lost.

Consequently there is no real value for the losses in considering the purchase price as they cannot be either group relieved or carried forward in LL.

Loan arrangement fees and interest

Both the loan arrangement fees and the interest due on the loan should be deductible when calculating Hutt Plc's PCTCT, and will broadly follow the accounts treatment (ie accruals basis). Whether the loan has been taken out for trade or non-trade purposes, however, will determine how the tax deduction will be given.

If it is for trade purposes then the deduction will be given directly from trade profits; conversely if the loan is for non-trade purposes it will be deducted according to the rules for non-trade loan relationships.

Of the total proposed loan of £190,000 it appears that only £15,000 (£190,000 – £130,000 – £45,000) will qualify as a trade purpose, as it will be used to fund the company's working capital. The rest of the funds will be treated as used for non trade purposes:

- acquiring shares in another company, even a subsidiary, is treated as an investment purpose; and

- Hutt Tower is let out and is not used in the trade, therefore the repairs will be for investment purposes.

This means that only $\frac{15,000}{190,000}$ × the amount charged in the accounts will be deductible against trade profits; the rest will be deducted from non-trade credits, ie the bank interest receivable.

CHARGED IN THE ACCOUNTS (1.7.07 – 31.3.08):

	£
Fee	1,400
Loan interest	
£190,000 × 7.25% × $^9/_{12}$	10,331
Total	11,731
Trading (× $\frac{15,000}{190,000}$)	926
Non trading (balance)	10,805

As there is only £2,000 of bank interest, this will result in a non trade loan relationship loss (or deficit) of £8,805, which can be utilised as follows:

- set off against Hutt Plc's other current year profits
- carried back one year against non-trade credits (ie bank interest) only
- group relieved in the current period
- carried forward against non-trade profits.

The way in which the loss is used will, as always, depend on marginal tax rates and timing.

(ii)   **VAT issues**

Registration

There are two tests to determine when a business must register for VAT:

(1)   **Historic test**

Taxable supplies over the previous 12 months (looking back from the last day of the month) exceed £61,000. HMRC must be notified within 30 days and registration is required from the first day of the following month.

(2)   **Future test**

Taxable supplies in the next month (looking forward from the first day of the month) exceed £61,000. HMRC must be notified within 30 days and registration is required from the first day of that month.

As the company's turnover for the nine month period to 31 March 2008 will be £675,000 (accruing evenly), this means that the monthly turnover will be £75,000. Therefore, under the future test LL, looking forward from the first day of the nine month period (1 July 2007), will need to notify HMRC by 30 July 2007 and will be registered from 1 July 2007.

VAT CALCULATION (1.7.07 – 31.3.08)

	£	£
All UK customers (Note 1): £110,000 × 17.5%	19,250	
EU customers (Note 2)		
VAT registered @ 0% (zero rated)	–	
non-VAT registered: £70,000 @ 17.5%	12,250	
Other non-UK customers @ 0% (zero rated) (Note 3)	–	
Dabet GmbH (Note 4): £17,000 @17.5%	2,975	
		34,475
UK businesses: £7,800 × 9%	70,200	
Dabet GmbH (Note 4): £17,000 @17.5%	2,975	
		(73,175)
Repayment due from HMRC		(38,700)

Notes

1   It is irrelevant if UK customers are VAT registered – must still charge VAT (the VAT will be a real cost to non-VAT registered customers)

2   If EU customers are registered for VAT, standard rated supplies to them ('despatches') will be zero rated. The EU customer will need to account for the VAT in their home country. Such supplies to non registered EU customers will be charged at 17.5% as normal.

3   Standard rated supplies ('exports') to other non-UK customers (ie those outside the EU) are always zero rated. There is no requirement for the customer to be registered for VAT.

4   EU suppliers charge zero rate on their standard rated supplies to other EU countries. It is necessary for the VAT on acquisitions from the EU to be included on the acquiring business's VAT return both as an input and an output amount in the same period.

Disadvantage of group registration

Where there is a group VAT registration, the representative member makes one VAT return for the whole group. This is usually done for administrative simplification.

However, the disadvantage to LL would mainly be a cash flow issue. Since the majority of LL's supplies are zero rated and it is due a repayment from HMRC it would be entitled to account for VAT on a monthly basis, thus receiving monthly repayments of VAT rather than quarterly. This would not be possible if the company was part of the VAT group.

Keeping a company outside of the group VAT registration would also add a layer of administrative complexity.

(iii)   **The office building**

Tax implications of proposed sale

Corporation Tax

Once LL is acquired by Hutt Plc it will be part of the gains group (at least 75% direct ownership). Consequently any transfer of assets between two gains group companies will take place at no gain no loss, regardless of the amount paid for the asset. The base cost of the asset for the acquiring company is the original base cost plus any indexation up to the date of the intra-group transfer.

Stamp Duty Land Tax (SDLT)

There is an exemption for transfers of land that occur between companies which are under the same 75% ownership. Therefore no SDLT will be due.

VAT

If there is a VAT group, no VAT will need to be charged on the transfer of the asset.

Assuming the building has been owned for more than 3 years (ie it is not a 'new' commercial building), even if there are separate VAT registrations for each company there should be no VAT due as the supply will be exempt. This is the case unless Coronet Ltd had opted to tax the building (ie waived the exemption) in which case VAT would be due at 17.5%.

Capital loss offset

It has been proposed that LL will sell the building transferred by Coronet Ltd and utilise the capital losses arising on the sale of the factory to reduce the gain.

It should be noted that an actual transfer of the building is not required as an election may be made instead, within two years of the end of the period in which the disposal takes place ie by 31 March 2011, to treat the gain as having arisen in the transferee company.

Although this is usually sound tax planning, as LL owned the factory prior to joining the gains group the losses are treated as 'pre-entry' capital losses and their use is restricted.

There are two ways to determine how much of this pre-entry loss may be used.

Market value

A calculation is made as at the date that the company joins the gains group based on the market value at that date. That amount of the loss is 'ringfenced' and cannot be used against the loss arising on assets acquired post-entry.

	£
Proceeds (mv at entry)	80,000
Less: cost	(270,000)
Loss	190,000

Indexation cannot increase this loss. No IBAs have been claimed on the building (as its tax life (25 years) had expired by the time it was acquired by LL) and therefore the full capital loss is allowable.

As it is anticipated that the market value will not increase in the future the whole of this gain is a pre-entry loss and cannot be used.

Time basis

The alternative calculation is to calculate the loss at the date of sale and 'ringfence' the proportion of the loss that arose before the company joined the group based on the length of pre-entry ownership. The factory has been owned since 30 June 2003, the factory will be sold on 1 January 2008 and the company joined the group on 1 July 2007.

Therefore of the total period of ownership of 4.5 years, 4 years relates to the period before LL joined the group.

The pre-entry proportion of the loss that cannot be used is:

$$\frac{4}{4.5} \times £190,000 = £168,889$$

Only the balance of the loss (£190,000 − 168,889 =) £21,111 can be set against the gain on the building, saving tax of (30% × £21,111) £6,333.

It is therefore clearly more beneficial to go with the time basis calculation.

Question 2

Marking scheme

			Marks
(1)	Calculations		
	Employ Alec:		
	Net profit of contract	½	
	Irrecoverable VAT/purchase of van	½	
	Alec's salary and class 1 secondary NIC	1½	
	Tax and NIC saved	½	
	Effect on Alec's income:		
	Identification of issue	1	
	Calculation	1½	
	Offer Max a contract:		
	Fees paid	½	
	Irrecoverable VAT on fees	½	
	Tax and NIC saved	½	
	Supporting calculations		
	Irrecoverable VAT:		
	Identification of issue	1	
	Current partial exemption position	1	
	Application of de minimis	1	
	Irrecoverable amount with new contract	1	
	Purchase of van:		
	Net cost	½	
	Irrecoverable VAT	1	
	Tax and NIC saved	1	
	Cost per year	½	
	Leasing van		
	Rentals	1½	
	Irrecoverable VAT	1	
	Tax and NIC saved	1	
	Max		16
(2)	Rationale and summary		
	Reference to Pilar's family income criterion	1	
	Conclusion re van and implications	1	
	Summary of findings	1	
	Max		2
(3)	Alec's employment		
	Use of partnership	2	
	Secure job, short-term contract	1½	
	Alec would be a separate client from Pilar	1	
	Max		2
(4)	Max's employment status		
	Each valid factor – ½ mark (max 5 factors)	2½	
	Depends on all of the facts	½	
	Max		3
	Appropriate style and presentation	1	
	Effectiveness of communication	1	
			2
			25

MEMORANDUM

To: The files
From: Tax assistant
Date: [date]
Subject: Pilar Mareno – Business expansion

This memorandum covers tax issues relating to Pilar Mareno's (PM's) proposed business expansion.

Rationale

PM will only take on the new contract if it generates at least £15,000 for her and her family. It has therefore been necessary to determine the true cost of the contract and the effect on the whole family.

PM needs to know whether it is more beneficial to employ her husband, Alec, as her assistant or to take on a contractor. In addition she would need to have the use of a van and would like to know whether it would be better from a tax perspective to purchase the van outright or to lease it over a period of, say, two years.

Workings 2 and 3 below show that it is more beneficial to purchase the van outright and therefore this route only has been incorporated into the illustrative calculations in the attached Appendices.

Appendix 1 shows the position if Alec is employed and Appendix 2 shows the position if Max Wallen contracts as PM's assistant.

Other issues regarding employing Alec

As Alec and PM are married, it may be a better decision to enter into a partnership agreement. An appropriate profit share ratio can be decided upon so that Alec receives sufficient income. In addition, they may decide that Alec should receive more than the equivalent of the proposed salary in order to better balance the amount of income taxed in PM's and Alec's hands, as Alec is a basic rate taxpayer.

This would mean that more of the family's income would be taxed at 22% rather than 40%. In addition, Alec's rate of NIC would reduce from 11% (Class 1 primary) to 8% (Class 4). However, the converse of this is that PM's rate of NIC would only be 1% as she is liable at the additional rate.

This would provide more stability for Alec who it is proposed will give up his steady employment for less money and a possible part time position that he has not even found yet.

Alex should take advice about his own personal situation. As Alex and Pilar are spouses there may be a conflict of interest if we offer advice to each. We need to point this out to both clients, but may continue to act if we monitor the situation to ensure that there is not threat to our integrity.

Max Wallen: employed v. self employed

There are a number of factors that HMRC would look at to determine whether Max Wallen is a self employed contractor or an employee.

These include:

- Max provides his own equipment, which indicates he is self employed

- However, he will use PM's own software which could indicate that he an employee

- Max must perform the work himself and cannot send a substitute, which indicates that he is an employee

- He receives sick pay – another indicator that he is an employee

- He is paid by the day with no particular contract tasks – this again would indicate that he is an employee rather than self employed

No one factor is enough in itself to indicate employment or self employment position and therefore HMRC will look at the facts of the individual case to decide Max's status.

> **Summary of findings**
> Whether PM employs Alec or offers a contract position to Max Wallen, both routes will generate over £15,000. It is therefore up to PM to make a decision based on all of the information contained in this memorandum.
>
> Tax assistant

APPENDIX 1 – EMPLOY ALEC AND BUY VAN

	£
Contract profit	45,000
Less:	
irrecoverable VAT (W1)	(8,054)
Alec's salary	(7,600)
Class 1 secondary NIC on Alec's salary £(7,600 – 5,035) @ 12.8%	(328)
Net profit	29,018
Less:	
Income tax: £29,018 @ 40%	(11,607)
NIC: £29,018 @ 1%	(290)
	17,121
Less: Van costs (W2 and W3)	(1,704)
	15,417
Effect on Alec's income (W4) (Note)	402
Total post-tax income	15,819

Note. Pilar has stated that she will enter into the contract if it generates an additional £15,000 for the *family* – Alec's position therefore also needs to be considered.

APPENDIX 2 – OFFER MAX WALLEN A CONTRACT AND BUY VAN

	£
Contract profit	45,000
Less:	
irrecoverable VAT (W1)	(8,054)
Max Wallen's fees: £75 × 100 (No NIC due from Pilar)	(7,500)
irrecoverable VAT on fees:	
£7,500 × 17.5% × 35%	(459)
Net profit	28,987
Less:	
Income tax: £28,987 @ 40%	(11,595)
NIC: £28,987 @ 1%	(290)
	17,102
Less: Van costs (W2 and W3)	(1,704)
Pilar's post-tax income	15,398

Workings

(1) *Irrecoverable VAT*

We are told to deal with VAT first by Tax Manager

EXISTING CONTRACT

Standard rated supplies: £100,000 × 17.5% × 35%	£6,125

This is less than ½ of the total VAT and is below the *de minimis* limit of £(625 × 12 =) 7,500. As a result all of this is recoverable in full.

WITH NEW CONTRACT

	£
Existing contracts (as above)	6,125

New contract: £31,500 × 17.5% × 35%		1,929
Total		8,054

This is less than ½ of the total VAT but exceeds the *de minimis* limit of £(625 × 12 =) 7,500. As a result none of this VAT will be recoverable.

(2)   *After tax cost of buying the van*

	£	£
Cost	7,800	
Less: sale value	(2,500)	5,300
Add: irrecoverable VAT		
£7,800 × 17.5% × 35% (Note 1)		478
Less:		
income tax saved: £(5,300 + 478) × 40%	(2,311)	
NIC saved: £(5,300 + 478) × 1%	(58)	
		(2,369)
Total		3,409
Averaged over 2 years		£1,705

Notes

1   Although the van will be used wholly for business purposes, we are told that exempt supplies will amount to 35% of the contract and therefore this proportion of VAT will not be recoverable.

2   As the van will be sold at a loss, full relief for the expenditure will be allowed through the capital allowances computation and will therefore be fully deductible for income tax purposes.

(3)   *After tax cost of leasing the van*

	£
Lease payments: 12 × £300	3,600
Add: irrecoverable VAT	
£3,600 × 17.5% × 35% (Note)	221
Less:	
income tax saved: £(3,600 + 221) × 40%	(1,528)
NIC saved: £(3,600 + 221) × 1%	(38)
Annual cost	2,255

As the cost of buying the van outright (W1) is cheaper than leasing the van, all calculations in the Appendices have been made on the basis that the van is purchased.

(4)   *Effect on Alec's income*

	£
Original salary	17,000
New income	
working for Pilar	(7,600)
other part time work	(10,000)
Additional income	600
Less:	
additional income tax: £600 @ 22%	(132)
additional NIC: £600 @ 11%	(66)
Net additional income	402

Question 3

				Marks
(a)	(i)	Split of consideration		
		Incorporation relief – conditions	1½	
		Amount of future cash payment:		
		Rationale – gains to equal annual exemption	1	
		Gains on transfer of business	1	
		Gains after incorporation relief:		
		Incorporation relief	1	
		Capital loss and taper relief	1½	
		Calculation of gains after incorporation relief	½	
		Solving to find value of the loan account	1	
		CGT base cost of shares:		
		Value of assets transferred for shares	½	
		Incorporation relief	1	
	(ii)	Benefit of using a loan account		
		Cash flow	1	
		Extract funds with no tax cost	½	
		Max		9
(b)		Advice on remuneration package		
		Dividend		
		Advice is incomplete – reason	1	
		CT position re dividend	½	
		CT position re bonus	½	
		Conclusion with reason	1	
		Interest free loan		
		Advice is incomplete – reason	1	
		Close company	½	
		Loan to a participator and reason	1	
		Tax due /when	1	
		Repayment position	½	
		Company car		
		The advice is incorrect – reason	1	
		Calculation		
		Tax cost	1	
		Tax saving	1	
		Max		9
				18

(a)   (i)   **Transfer of business to Landscape Ltd**

If Stanley transfers his entire business (ie all the assets, excluding cash) to Landscape Ltd (LL) there would be no capital gains tax because of the automatic availability of incorporation relief.

This would allow the gain arising on the transfer of any chargeable assets used in the business to be deferred until such time as Stanley sells the shares in LL. This occurs because the deferred gain (before taper relief) reduces the base cost of the shares received on incorporation.

The full gain may be deferred to the extent that shares are received in exchange for the business. If any other form of consideration is received e.g. cash, loan notes or loan, a gain will arise in direct proportion to the amount of non-share consideration received.

Therefore if Stanley leaves some of the consideration outstanding on loan account a gain will arise in respect of that proportion of consideration.

The maximum loan account balance that Stanley could receive without giving rise to a CGT liability would be £84,597. This is calculated as follows:

GAIN ON BUILDING:

	£
Proceeds (mv)	87,000
Less: cost	(46,000)
Gain before taper relief	41,000

Gain after taper relief: business asset held for > 2 complete years: 25%

GAIN ON GOODWILL:

	£
Proceeds (mv)	24,000
Less: cost	(nil)
Gain before taper relief	24,000

Gain after taper relief: business asset held for > 2 complete years: 25%

Gain on plant & machinery/consumables

Plant & machinery would have had capital allowances claimed on them, and presumably any loss would have been taken through the capital allowances computation. There is therefore no capital loss.

The consumables are not chargeable assets and are therefore exempt from CGT.

The total gains before taper are therefore (£41,000 + £24,000 =) £65,000.

It is easiest to calculate the amount of relief required to ensure no CGT arises by working backwards from the maximum gain:

	£
Taxable gain	Nil
Add: annual exemption	8,800
Gain after taper relief	8,800
Gain before taper relief × 100/25	35,200
Add: losses	11,400
Gain after incorporation relief	46,600
Less: total gains before taper relief	(65,000)
Incorporation relief	18,400

The proportion of consideration that would need to be received in shares to arrive at this amount of incorporation relief would be:

$$\frac{X}{118,000} \times 65,000 = £18,400$$

X = MV of shares = £33,403

Therefore the balance of the consideration (£118,000 − 33,403 =) £84,597 may be left on loan account.

Check:

	£
GBT	65,000
Less: incorporation relief £33,403 × 118,000	(18,400)
Gain	46,600
Less: losses	(11,400)
GBT	35,200
GAT @ 25%	8,800
Less: AE	(8,800)
Taxable gain	Nil

The base cost of the shares would be:

	£
MV	33,403
Less: gain deferred	(18,400)
Cost c/f	15,003

(ii) Benefit of taking payment in form of loan account

The benefit of taking a loan account now is that the company does not have to provide cash up front. Also, it allows the gain to be calculated with no CGT exposure when the loan is eventually repaid.

(b) Remuneration package advice

(i) Dividends v. salary

It is usually more tax efficient to receive dividends rather than a bonus.

However the advice given neglects to mention the fact that Landscape Ltd (LL) will be able to deduct the bonus from its trade profits as salaries and bonuses are treated as being paid wholly and exclusively for the purpose of the trade. This saves tax at 19%.

On the other hand, the dividends paid to Stanley are not tax deductible and therefore are a tax cost to LL at 19%.

Therefore although it is cheaper to pay dividends than salary, the position is not as clear cut as the previous advice suggests.

(ii) Interest free loan

It is true that from an employee's perspective loans under £5,000 are a tax free benefit.

However once again the advice received does not mention the rules applying to close companies. As five or fewer participators control LL, it is therefore a close company. Consequently if the company makes beneficial loans to participators, it will be charged a penalty tax of 25% x the loan.

Therefore LL must pay (25% x £3,600 =) £900 to HMRC in respect of the loan by the usual due date for corporation tax for non-large companies ie 9 months 1 day after the end of the accounting period in which the loan is made (ie 1 January 2009).

This will be repayable by HMRC when Stanley repays the loan. The repayment will be due 9 months 1 day after the end of the accounting period in which the loan is repaid.

(iii) Company car

Whilst it is true that the costs of providing a car are deductible for the company, the advice provided does not consider the difference in amounts taxable and deductible, nor does it consider the different tax rates involved for Stanley and the company.

If we compare the costs involved it will be seen that the advice provided is in fact incorrect.

	£	£
Cost for Stanley:		
Car benefit £3,420 @ 40%	1,368	
Cost for the company		
Class 1A: £3,420 @ 12.8%	438	
		1,806
Less: deductible for the company		
Lease rentals: £300 × 12= £3,600 @ 19%	684	
Business fuel: £100 × 12 = £1,200 @ 19%	228	
Class 1A: £438 @ 19%	83	
		(995)
Tax cost of providing the car		811

Question 4

		Marks
(a)	**Sale of shares by Claus**	
	Purchase of own shares	
	Identify and distinguish between the two possible treatments	1
	CGT treatment applies	1
	Reasons why:	
	Unquoted trading company	½
	Resident and ordinarily resident	½
	Owned for more than 5 years	½
	For benefit of company's trade with reason	1
	Reduction in holding criteria	1
	Not part of a scheme to avoid tax	½
	Availability of advance clearance	1
	Calculation	
	Gain before taper relief	1
	Taper relief	1
	Net of tax proceeds	½
	Max	**8**
(b)	**Gift to Tessa**	
	Stamp duty	
	Not applicable, gift	½
	CGT	
	No CGT due	½
	Reasons why:	
	Not resident or ordinarily resident	½
	Not temporarily non-resident	½
	Asset acquired after becoming resident abroad	½
	IHT	
	IHT applies, UK domiciled & shares are UK property	½
	Gift on 1 August 2007	
	Transfer of value	1
	No BPR with reason	1
	Chargeable transfer (2 × annual exemption)	½
	Taper relief available	½
	Calculation of tax due	½
	Reference to DTR	½
	Gift on 1 June 2008	
	Assumption re Tessa's continued ownership	1
	BPR	1
	Marriage and annual exemptions	1
	Advice	1
	Max	**10**
		18

(a)   **Tax treatment of proceeds**

Claus is selling his shares back to the company that issued them. This is known as a company repurchase of own shares.

The usual treatment for a shareholder when their shares are repurchased in this way is that the excess of proceeds over the amount subscribed for the shares is treated as a net income distribution (ie like a dividend).

	£
Proceeds (16,000/40,000 = 40%) 16,000 × £38.60	617,600
Less: subscription cost: £16,000 @ £3.40	(54,400)
Net distribution	563,200
Gross income to include in tax return x 100/90	625,778
Tax @ 32.5%	203,378
Less: tax credit @ 10%	(62,578)
Income tax liability	140,800
Net cash: £(617,600 – 140,800)	476,800

The above is the case unless the shareholder satisfies a number of conditions which will allow the profit on sale back to the company to be taxed as a capital gain.

The conditions are as follows:

The company

(i)   must be an unquoted trading company
(ii)   the repurchase must be taking place for the purpose of the trade

The shareholder

(i)   must be resident and ordinarily resident in the UK
(ii)   they must have owned the shares for at least five years
(iii)   their holding must be reduced by at least 25%
(iv)   after the repurchase they must own <30%

Generally the repurchase must not be part of a scheme designed to avoid tax. Clearance may be obtained to this effect, in advance of the repurchase, from HMRC.

Based on the facts provided, Claus will satisfy the above conditions and the capital treatment will apply. His net cash following the repurchase will be:

	£
Proceeds (as above)	617,600
Less: cost	(54,400)
Gain before taper relief	563,200
Gain after taper relief: unquoted trading co = business asset > 2 yrs: 25%	140,800
CGT @ 40% (uses AE and is a higher rate taxpayer)	56,320
Net cash £(617,600 – 56,320)	561,280

This is £(561,280 – 476,800 =) 84,480 more than if the income treatment were to apply.

(b)   **Gifting shares**

When an individual makes a gift there are always two main taxes that must be considered. These are CGT and IHT.

There is also one further 'capital' tax that may be considered where assets are being transferred: Stamp Duty or Stamp Duty Land Tax (SDLT) depending on the asset transferred. As the assets here are shares, Stamp Duty may be in question but, as gifts are exempt from Stamp Duty (and SDLT), this tax does not need to be considered further. We therefore focus on CGT and IHT.

CGT

Maude is neither resident nor ordinarily resident in the UK and is therefore not subject to UK CGT under general rules.

She has been outside the UK for more than 5 complete tax years and therefore does not fall within the rules for temporary non-residents. In any case, the shares were acquired after she left the UK and the temporary non-resident CGT rules only apply to assets held pre-emigration.

There are therefore no CGT issues for Maude.

IHT

As Maude appears to have retained her UK domicile she will be subject to IHT on her world wide assets. The shares are UK assets for IHT purposes as they are registered shares in a UK company.

Gifts of assets between individuals are Potentially Exempt Transfers (PETs). There are no tax consequences during the lifetime of the donor. However, if the donor dies within seven years of making the gift the PET will become chargeable and the donee will be required to pay any IHT due.

As we are told to assume that Maude will die on 31 December 2011 and therefore the gift will become chargeable regardless of whether it is made on 1 August 2007 or 1 June 2008.

The value of the gift will be as follows:

	£
Before the gift: 12,000/24,000 = 50% (Note)	
£38.60 × 12,000	463,200
After the gift: 8,000/24,000 = 33.33%	
£14.40 × 8,000	(115,200)
Transfer of value	348,000

Note. After the buy back of Claus's shares there will only be 24,000 shares in issue as the repurchased shares will be cancelled.

GIFT ON 1 AUGUST 2007

	£
Gift	348,000
BPR is not available as shares held < 2 years	
Less: 2 × annual exemptions	(6,000)
PET	342,000
Less: nil band	(285,000)
	57,000
Tax @ 40%	22,800
Less: taper relief (1.8.07 – 31.12.11 = 4-5 years): 40%	(9,120)
IHT due	13,680

Double tax relief should be available if there are any Canadian taxes due in respect of her death.

GIFT ON 1 JUNE 2008

	£
Gift	348,000
BPR @ 100% × £348,000 × $\dfrac{1,605}{1,647}$ (Note)	(339,126)
	8,874
Less: Marriage exemption	(5,000)
Less: – AE 08/09	(3,000)
– AE 07/08	(874)
PET	0

Therefore no IHT is due. This assumes that Maude's daughter retains the shares until her mother's death.

Clearly Maude should wait until June 2008 to make the gift as this produces no IHT charge.

Note. BPR is only available in respect of the underlying business assets of the company

ie $\dfrac{\text{All} - \text{investment \& surplus cash}}{\text{All}}$

The total market value of the company's assets is £1,647,000.

The value of the investments is £42,000 ie the quoted shares. We are not given details of any surplus cash.

BPR is therefore available on. $\dfrac{£1,647,000 \text{ less } £42,000}{£1,647,000}$

Question 5

Marking scheme

			Marks
(a)	Taxable capital gain on the sale of the house		
	Computation of capital gain		
	Untapered gain	½	
	Taper relief	1	
	Annual exemption	½	
	Effect of gift to Alice	1	
	Computation of basic rate band remaining	2	
	Treat ment of payments on redundancy	1	
	Capital gains tax payable	1	
	Advice to delay sale	1	
	Max		7
(b)	Inheritance tax due in respect of the house		
	Gift more than seven years prior to death	½	
	Gift with reservation rules apply	½	
	Consequences	1	
	Max		2
(c)	Shares in Dreamz Technology Ltd		
	Identify two possible treatments	½	
	Treatment if no share incentive plan	1	
	Exemption under share incentive plan	1	
	Withdrawal from plan within three years	½	
	Withdrawal from plan within three to five years	½	
	Max		3
(d)	Amount of income tax on dividend income		
	Tax position whilst working for Bart Industries Ltd		
	No tax payable on dividends	1	
	Computation	1	
	Tax position whilst working for Dreamz Technology Ltd	1½	
	Date of payment of income tax on dividend income		
	Due date with reason	1½	
	Computation	2½	
	Max		6
			18

(a) **CGT on sale of Wales house**

2007/08

	£
Proceeds	195,000
Less: cost 9/99	(145,000)
Less: enhancement	(18,000)
GBT	32,000
GAT: 9.99 – 8.07 = 7yrs: 75%	24,060
Less: AE (£8,800 – £1,200)	(7,600)
Taxable gain	16,400
£9,018 @ 20% (W1)	1,804
£(16,400 – 9,018) = £7,382 @ 40%	2,953
CGT due	4,757

No PPR relief is available, as Vikram Bridge (VB) has never lived in the property as his main residence.

The CGT position would be the same if VB transferred the property to Alice as the disposal would be deemed to take place at market value. The transfer would only be at no gain, no loss if they were married.

One planning point that could help VB would be to delay the disposal one more month in order to obtain one further year of taper relief. A further 5% would be available if the disposal is delayed until September, saving tax of 5% × 32,000 × 40% = £640.

Workings

(1) *VB's income for 2007/08 will have utilised the basic rate band (BRB) as follows:*

	£
B Ltd termination payment – all exempt (W2)	Nil
DT Ltd salary 6/12 × £38,500	19,250
Relocation costs: £9,400 – £8,000 (exempt)	1,400
Dividends: £7,800 × 100/90	8,667
STI	29,317
Less: PA	(5,035)
Taxable income	24,282
Less: BRB	(33,300)
BRB remaining	9,018

(2) *Termination payments*

- The PILON of £4,700 is taxable in 2006/07 as it is a contractual payment.

- Statutory redundancy is exempt from income tax.

- The £14,500 payment is also exempt as it comes within the £30,000 exemption available for ex gratia (ie compensatory) payments.

(b) **IHT on VB's mother's death**

When VB's mother originally made the gift it would have been a PET for IHT purposes. As she survived more than seven years the PET is completely exempt.

However, as his mother continued to live in the property until her death it will be treated as part of her estate for IHT purposes.

Therefore it will be necessary to include £140,000 in her death estate in respect of the property.

(c)   **Income tax treatment of DT Ltd shares**

If an employee received free shares from their employer, under general principles, they will be taxable on the market value of those shares. Therefore VB would include the £2,750 value of the shares in his employment income in 2008/09. There would also be an NIC charge if the shares were readily convertible assets (ie traded on a recognised investment exchange).

However, if the shares are awarded as part of an approved Share Incentive Plan (SIP) there will be no taxable benefit when the shares are awarded so long as the value of the shares is less than £3,000. These 'free' shares are free from income tax (and NIC where applicable) so long as they remain within the SIP for a five year period, at which point they may be removed with no tax consequences.

If the shares are removed from the plan within 3 years there will be an income tax charge on their value when removed. If they are removed within 3 to 5 years, tax will be charged on the lower of the market value when removed and the original value.

(d)   **Taxation of dividend income**

As VB's income will now take him into the higher band of taxation, there will be a tax charge on the dividend income.

Previously, he was a basic rate taxpayer:

	£
Employment income:	
£4,700 × 12/2	28,200
Dividend income (as above)	8,667
Total income	36,867
Less: PA	(5,035)
Taxable income	31,832

The dividends would have been taxed at 10%, but as they come with a 10% tax credit, there was no further liability.

In 2009/10 and following years his position is as follows:

	£
DT Ltd salary	38,500
Dividends	8,667
Total income	47,167
Less: PA	(5,035)
Taxable income	42,132

The whole of the dividend income therefore now falls into the higher rate tax band. It will be taxed at 32.5% and come with the 10% tax credit. The effective tax rate on the net dividend is 25%, which means that (25% × £7,800 =) £1,950 additional higher rate tax will be due on the dividends.

Payment date

The additional tax on the dividends will need to be paid via self assessment by 31 January following the end of the tax year ie by 31 January 2011. The tax due on the DT Ltd salary will be paid via PAYE as normal.

It is also possible that payments on account will need to be made if the tax collected at source on the total income is less than 80% of the total liability, or, conversely the amount not collected at source (on the dividends) exceeds 20% of the total liability.

The total liability will be:

	£
Taxable income (as above)	42,132
£2,150 @ 10%	215
£31,150 @ 22%	6,853
£(33,465 − 33,350) = £165 @ 40%	66
£8,667 @ 32.5%	2,817
Total tax liability	9,951
20% × £9,951	1,990
Tax not collected at source (on dividends) (2,817 − 867)	1,950

Therefore POAs are not required.

BPP
LEARNING MEDIA

Pilot Paper
ACCA model answers

1 (a) Options available in respect of the trading losses of Hutt plc of £105,000

(i) Within Hutt plc

The loss can be offset against the profits chargeable to corporation tax of Hutt plc for the year ended 31 March 2007.

	£
Capital gain	144,000
Less: capital loss brought forward	(98,000)
	46,000
Rental income	65,000
Interest income	2,000
Profits chargeable to corporation tax	113,000

Hutt plc, Rainbow Ltd and Coronet Ltd are associated as Hutt plc controls the other two companies. As a result, the small companies rate lower limit for the purposes of determining the rate of corporation tax is reduced from £300,000 to £100,000. Accordingly, Hutt plc will pay corporation tax at 30% less marginal relief. This means that the first £100,000 of the company's profits will be taxed at 19% and the final £13,000 at the marginal rate of 32¾%.

A current period offset has to be made before losses can be carried back to the previous twelve months. The trading loss for the year ended 31 March 2007 is less than the profits chargeable to corporation tax and therefore a claim to carry back the losses cannot be made.

(ii) Group relief

Hutt plc, Rainbow Ltd and Coronet Ltd are in a group for group relief purposes as Hutt plc controls at least 75% of the other two companies. Any amount of the loss can be surrendered to each of the two subsidiary companies in order to reduce their profits chargeable to corporation tax. The maximum surrender is the profits chargeable to corporation tax of the recipient company.

Coronet Ltd has profits chargeable to corporation tax of £81,000 (£63,000 + £18,000). As stated above, due to the number of associates, the small companies rate lower limit is reduced to £100,000 (£300,000 x □). Accordingly, Coronet Ltd will pay tax at 19%.

The profits chargeable to corporation tax of Rainbow Ltd exceed £500,000 (£1,500,000 x □) and therefore, the company will pay UK corporation tax at the rate of 30%.

However, Rainbow Ltd has a permanent establishment in Prismovia as it manufactures and trades in that country. The profits arising in Prismovia will be taxed in that country at 28%. Double tax relief will be available in the UK in respect of the Prismovian tax suffered, up to a maximum of the UK tax on the Prismovian profits; any surrender to Rainbow Ltd must ensure that relief for the foreign tax suffered is not lost.

The maximum surrender that can be made to Rainbow Ltd whilst preserving relief for the foreign tax is calculated as follows.

	£
Trading profit ((£800,000 x 2%) / 30%)	53,333
Interest income	57,000
	110,333

(iii) Recommendations

In order to maximise the tax saved the losses should be offset against the profits taxed at 32¾% in Hutt plc and the profits taxed at 30% in Rainbow Ltd whilst preserving the relief for the foreign tax suffered.

Accordingly, £13,000 of the losses should be offset against the profits chargeable to corporation tax in Hutt plc with the balance of £92,000 (£105,000 − £13,000) surrendered to Rainbow Ltd. This is less than £110,333, and therefore, preserves relief for all of the foreign tax.

When making a claim to offset a company's trading loss against its total profits, it is not possible to specify the amount to be offset; all of the losses available will be offset subject to the level of taxable profits. Accordingly, in order to achieve the desired result, the two claims must be made in the following order.

1. An election to surrender losses of £92,000 to Rainbow Ltd. This must be made by 31 March 2009, i.e. within one year of the filing date of the claimant company's tax return. Both Rainbow Ltd and Hutt plc must elect.
2. An election to offset the remaining losses (£13,000) against the total profits of Hutt plc should be submitted by the same date, i.e. within two years of the end of the period in which the loss was made.

Tutorial note

The tax computation of Rainbow Ltd for the year ended 31 March 2007 following the group relief claim is set out below. Group relief of £57,000 is offset against the interest income with the balance of £35,000 being offset against the trading profit in order to maximise the double tax relief.

	£
Trading profit (£800,000 – £35,000)	*765,000*
Interest income (£57,000 – £57,000)	*–*
Profits chargeable to corporation tax	*765,000*
Corporation tax @ 30%	*229,500*
Less Double tax relief (£800,000 x 28%)	*(224,000)*
Corporation tax payable	*5,500*

(b) Report to the management of Hutt plc

To	The management of Hutt plc
From	Tax advisers
Date	1 June 2007
Subject	The acquisition of Lucia Ltd

(i) The purchase price

Valuation of the trading losses in Lucia Ltd

Lucia Ltd has no profits in the year ended 31 March 2007 or the previous year against which to offset the losses.

The trading losses arose before Lucia Ltd joined the Hutt plc group, and therefore, they cannot be surrendered to any of the group members.

The losses cannot be carried forward as there will be a change of ownership of Lucia Ltd after its activities have become negligible. Losses arising prior to the change of ownership cannot be offset against profits arising once the trade has been revived.

The losses cannot be used, and therefore, they have no value.

Loan from BHC Bank

Hutt plc is to enter into a loan relationship with BHC Bank. Any amounts charged to the company's profit and loss account in respect of the relationship are allowable deductions for tax purposes. Accordingly, a tax deduction is available for the interest and the loan arrangement fee on the accruals basis.

On the assumption that the loan arrangement fee is charged to the profit and loss account in full in the year ended 31 March 2008, the total amount charged in the accounts will be £11,731 (£1,400 + (£190,000 x 7.25% x 9/12)). The income from which this amount can be deducted in the corporation tax computation depends on the use made of the finance obtained.

	Finance £		Allowable cost £
For the purpose of investments:			
Acquisition of Lucia Ltd	130,000		
Repairs to Hutt Tower	45,000		
	175,000	175/190 x £11,731	10,805
For the purpose of the trade:			
Working capital requirements	15,000	15/190 x £11,731	926
Total finance obtained	190,000		11,731

Where the finance has been used for trading purposes, the cost of £926 is deductible in arriving at Hutt plc's taxable trading income.

Where the finance has been used for non-trading purposes, the cost of £10,805 is deductible from Hutt plc's interest income in respect of loan relationships. This results in a deficit, or loss, of £8,805 (£10,805 – £2,000) in the year ended 31 March 2008.

The deficit can be:
- Offset against other income and gains of Hutt plc of the same accounting period.
- Offset against the previous interest income of Hutt plc of the previous 12 months.
- Surrendered as group relief to companies within the group relief group.
- Carried forward and offset against future non-trading income and gains.

The most tax efficient use of the deficit will depend on the level of profits in Hutt plc and the other group companies in the year ended 31 March 2008.

(ii)   VAT issues

Registration

All the supplies made by Lucia Ltd are taxable supplies for the purposes of VAT. The company must register for VAT:
*   If its taxable supplies in the previous 12 months exceed £61,000; or
*   If its taxable supplies in the next 30 days are expected to exceed £61,000.

It is anticipated that the company's supplies in the nine months ended 31 March 2008 will be £675,000 and that these supplies will accrue evenly over the period. This amounts to supplies of £75,000 per month. Accordingly, Lucia Ltd must register with effect from 1 July 2007 and must notify HMRC by 30 July 2007.

Lucia Ltd intends to make supplies to non-VAT registered customers in the European Union (EU). If Lucia Ltd is responsible for the delivery of the goods it should be aware that once its supplies in any one particular member state exceed that state's 'distance selling' threshold, it may be required to register for VAT in that state.

VAT in respect of the nine months ended 31 March 2008

	£
Output tax	
UK customers – VAT registered (£85,000 x 17½%)	14,875
UK customers – non-VAT registered (£25,000 x 17½%)	4,375
EU customers – VAT registered – zero-rated	–
EU customers – non-VAT registered (£70,000 x 17½%)	12,250
Other non-UK customers – zero-rated	–
Acquisition from Dabet Gmbh (£17,000 x 17½%)	2,975
	34,475
Input tax	
In respect of purchases from UK businesses (9 x £7,800)	70,200
Acquisition from Dabet Gmbh	2,975
	73,175
Repayment of VAT due (£73,175 – £34,475)	38,700

Disadvantage of entering into a group VAT registration

Lucia Ltd makes mainly zero-rated supplies and is in a VAT repayment position. It can improve its cash flow position by accounting for VAT monthly and receiving monthly repayments of VAT. It would not be in a position to do this if it were to register in a VAT group.

Under a group registration, the group's representative member will account for VAT payable to HMRC on behalf of all group companies. It may be some time before Lucia Ltd's accounting system is aligned with that of Hutt plc. The existence of two different systems may create administrative difficulties in preparing a group VAT return.

Note – Only one of the above disadvantages was required

(iii)   The office building

Tax implications of the sale of the office building from Coronet Ltd to Lucia Ltd

Corporation tax

At the time of the transfer, Coronet Ltd and Lucia Ltd will be in a capital gains group as they will both be 75% subsidiaries of Hutt plc. Therefore the transfer of the office building will be deemed to occur at no gain, no loss. Lucia Ltd will have a capital gains tax base cost in the building equal to the cost to Coronet Ltd plus indexation allowance up to the date of the transfer.

Value added tax (VAT)

The transfer will be outside the scope of VAT if the two companies are in a VAT group.

If the two companies are registered separately, the treatment depends on whether or not Coronet Ltd has opted to tax the building. If it has, then the transfer to Lucia Ltd will be standard rated and VAT must be charged. If it has not, the transfer will be an exempt supply.

Stamp duty land tax

There will be no stamp duty land tax on the transfer as both companies are 75% subsidiaries of Hutt plc.

Relief of the gain on the sale of the office building to Vac Ltd

The loss arising on the sale of the factory will be £190,000 (£270,000 - £80,000). Indexation allowance is not available to increase a loss.

Lucia Ltd acquired the factory before it joined the Hutt plc group. Accordingly, the factory is a pre-entry asset and that part of the loss that arose prior to 1 July 2007 is restricted in use. In particular, it cannot be offset against gains arising in other companies in the Hutt plc group or gains on assets transferred from other group members on a no gain no loss basis.

As at 1 January 2008, Lucia Ltd will have owned the factory for four and a half years, of which four years are outside of the Hutt plc group. The pre-entry element of the loss is £168,889 (£190,000 x 4/4.5).

The pre-entry element of the loss could be computed by reference to the market value of the building at the time Hutt plc acquires Lucia Ltd. However this would not be advantageous in this case as the whole of the loss would then be a pre-entry loss.

The balance of the loss of £21,111 can be offset against the gain on the office building. Based on a corporation tax rate of 30%, this will save tax of £6,333.

There is no need to actually transfer the office building to Lucia Ltd in order to relieve the gain in this way. Coronet Ltd and Lucia Ltd can simply elect to treat the gain as if it has been made by Lucia Ltd. The election must be submitted by 31 March 2011, ie within two years of the end of the accounting period in which the disposal of the office building occurs.

2 To   The files
From   Tax assistant
Date   1 June 2007
Subject   Pilar Mareno - Business expansion

This memorandum considers the implications of Pilar Mareno (PM) accepting the DWM plc contract.

Rationale and approach
PM has decided to accept the contract if it generates at least £15,000 per annum on average for the family after all costs and taxes.

PM will either employ her husband, Alec, or use the services of Max Wallen, and will either buy or lease a van. However, it can be seen from workings 3 and 4 that it is cheaper to buy rather than lease the van, and therefore, there are only two options to consider.
* Employ Alec and buy a van – Appendix 1
* Use Max Wallen and buy a van – Appendix 2

Summary of findings
The contract generates sufficient after tax income whether PM buys a van and employs Alec or uses Max Wallen. However, the issues raised below in relation to PM employing Alec should be considered before a decision is made.

Issues in respect of Pilar employing Alec

1. Alec has worked for a UK bank for many years. It is risky to give up an apparently secure job in exchange for a two year contract requiring two days work a week and other, as yet unidentified, part-time work.

    Accordingly, Alec should obtain advice as regards his personal situation. If we are asked to provide this advice we must recognise that Pilar and Alec would be two separate clients. The work would have to be managed in such a way as to ensure that we do not allow the interests of Pilar to adversely affect those of Alec or vice versa.

2. PM and Alec should consider forming a partnership. This would reduce national insurance contributions as Alec would only pay 8% on his share of the profit plus class 2 at £2.10 per week whereas the cost of employer and employee class 1 contributions where Alec is an employee is 12.8% and 11% respectively.

    Alec's profit share could be more than £7,600. This would enable income currently taxed at 40% in PM's hands to be taxed at 22% in Alec's hands. However, this saving in income tax would be offset by increased national insurance costs as the national insurance on PM's marginal income is only 1% whereas Alec would pay 8%.

Employment status of Max Wallen
Max's employment status will be determined by reference to all of the facts surrounding his agreement with PM.

Factors indicating employee status
1. It appears that Max has to do the work himself and cannot use a substitute.
2. Max is to be paid by the day rather than by reference to the performance of particular tasks.
3. Max is to be paid for the days when he is sick.
4. Max is to be provided with the specialist software he needs to do the work.

Factors indicating self-employed status
1. Max provides his own laptop computer.

Tax assistant

Tutorial Note

There is insufficient information provided regarding other factors, such as the level of control over Max's work, to justify their inclusion within the terms of the brief provided.

Appendix 1 – Employ Alec and buy a van

	£
Profit on contract	45,000
Irrecoverable VAT due to partial exemption (W1)	(8,054)
Salary paid to Alec	(7,600)
Class 1 secondary NIC re Alec ((£7,600 – £5,035) x 12.8%)	(328)
	29,018
Income tax and class 4 NIC due (£29,018 x (40% + 1%))	(11,897)
	17,121
Increase in Alec's income (W2)	402
Purchase of van (less than cost of leasing van) (W3 and W4)	(1,704)
Income of family after all taxes	15,819

Tutorial Note:
The salary paid to Alec is a cost as far as Pilar is concerned. The effect of the salary on Alec's income is calculated in working 2, below.

Appendix 2 – Use Max Wallen and buy a van

	£
Profit on contract	45,000
Irrecoverable VAT due to partial exemption (W1)	(8,054)
Fees paid to Max Wallen (100 x £75)	(7,500)
Irrecoverable VAT on fees (£7,500 x 17½% x 35%))	(459)
	28,987
Income tax and class 4 NIC due (£28,987 x (40% + 1%))	(11,885)
	17,102
Purchase of van (less than cost of leasing van) (W3 and W4)	(1,704)
Income of family after all taxes	15,398

Workings

(1) Irrecoverable VAT due to partial exemption

	£
Without the new contract:	
In respect of the existing business (£100,000 x 17½% x 35%)	6,125

This is below the annual de minimis limit of £7,500 (£625 x 12) and is fully recoverable.

	£
With the new contract:	
In respect of the existing business (as above)	6,125
In respect of the costs of the DWM contract (£31,500 x 17½% x 35%)	1,929
	8,054

This exceeds the annual de minimis limit and is irrecoverable.

Tutorial Note
Pilar's taxable turnover is not affected by the sale of the van as it is a capital asset.

(2) Increase in Alec's income

	£
Increase in gross salary ((£7,600 + £10,000) – £17,000)	600
Less income tax and NIC (£600 x (22% + 11%))	(198)
Increase in after tax income	402

Tutorial Note
At the margin, Alec pays income tax at the basic rate of 22% and NIC at 11%.

(3) Cost of purchasing van

	£
Net cost (£7,800 – £2,500) for two year period	5,300
Income tax and class 4 NIC saved (£5,300 x (40% + 1%))	(2,173)
Irrecoverable VAT (£7,800 x 17½% x 35%)	478
Income tax and class 4 NIC saved (£478 x (40% + 1%))	(196)
	3,409
Average cost per year (£3,409 x ½)	1,704

(4) Cost of leasing van (per year)

	£
Lease rentals (£300 x 12)	3,600
Income tax and class 4 NIC saved (£3,600 x (40% + 1%))	(1,476)
Irrecoverable VAT (£3,600 x 17½% x 35%)	220
Income tax and class 4 NIC saved (£220 x (40% + 1%))	(90)
	2,254

3 (a) Use of a loan account

(i) The split of consideration between the shares and loan account

Where all of the assets of Stanley's business are transferred to Landscape Ltd as a going concern wholly in exchange for shares, any capital gains arising are relieved via incorporation relief such that no capital gains tax liability arises.

However, where part of the payment received from the company is in the form of a loan account, Stanley will have chargeable gains as set out below. For Stanley to have no liability to capital gains tax in 2007/08, his chargeable gains must equal the annual exemption of £8,800.

	£
Gain on building (£87,000 − £46,000)	41,000
Gain on goodwill	24,000
	65,000

Gains after incorporation relief:

$$£65,000 \times \frac{\text{Value of the loan account}}{£118,000} \qquad y$$

Less: Capital losses brought forward	(11,400)
	z
Taper relief – business assets owned for at least two years	x 25%
Chargeable gains	8,800

Gains after incorporation relief, y, must equal £46,600 ((£8,800 x 4) + £11,400).

The value of the loan account needs to be £84,597 (£46,600 x £118,000/£65,000) such that the gains after incorporation relief are £46,600 (£65,000 x £84,597/£118,000).

The shares will have a capital gains tax base cost of £15,003 computed as follows.

	£
Market value of assets transferred to Landscape Ltd	118,000
Less Consideration left on loan account	(84,597)
	33,403

Incorporation relief:

$$£65,000 \times \frac{£33,403}{£118,000} \qquad (18,400)$$

	15,003

(ii) The benefit of using a loan account

The loan account crystallises capital gains at the time of incorporation without giving rise to a tax liability due to the availability of capital losses, taper relief and the annual exemption. This reduces the gains deferred against the base cost of the shares in Landscape Ltd from £65,000 to £18,400 such that any future gains on the disposal of the shares will be smaller. Stanley can extract £84,597 from Landscape Ltd in the future with no 'tax cost', by having the loan repaid.

(b) Advice on Stanley's remuneration package

(i) Dividend

The advice in respect of the dividend is accurate but not complete as it ignores the cost to Landscape Ltd. Because Stanley owns Landscape Ltd, he must consider the effect on the company's position as well as his own.

Dividends are not tax deductible. The profits paid out as a dividend to Stanley will have been subject to corporation tax at 19%. On the other hand, Landscape Ltd will obtain a tax deduction at 19% for a salary bonus together with the related national insurance contributions.

There will be an overall tax saving from paying a dividend as opposed to a salary bonus. However the benefit will not be as great as suggested by the advice that Stanley has received due to the different treatment of the two payments in the company.

(ii) **Interest free loan**

The advice in respect of the loan is again accurate but not complete. The loan will not give rise to an employment income benefit as it is for not more than £5,000, but the advice again ignores the position of the company.

As it is controlled by Stanley, Landscape Ltd will be a close company. Accordingly, the loan to Stanley is a loan to a participator in a close company, and as Stanley owns more than 5% of the company's share capital there is no de minimis in this case.

Thus, Landscape Ltd must pay an amount equal to 25% of the loan (£900) to HMRC. The payment will be due on 1 January 2009, i.e. nine months and one day after the end of the accounting period in which the loan is made.

When the loan is repaid by Stanley, Landscape Ltd may reclaim the £900. The repayment by HMRC will be made nine months and one day after the end of the accounting period in which the loan is repaid.

(iii) **Company car**

The advice in respect of the company car is not correct because of the difference in the tax rates applying to the company and to Stanley, and the liability to Class 1A national insurance contributions.

	£
Tax cost of providing car:	
Class 1A national insurance contributions	
£3,420 x 12.8%	438
Income tax on benefit (£3,420 x 40%)	1,368
	1,806
Tax saved:	
Cost of providing car (£400 x 12)	4,800
Class 1A national insurance contributions	438
	5,238
Corporation tax @ 19%	995
Net tax cost (£1,806 – £995)	811

4 (a) Sale of shares in Mahia Ltd

The proceeds received on a purchase by a company of its own shares are subject to either income tax or capital gains tax depending on the circumstances.

The normal assumption on a purchase of own shares by a company is that any payment you receive for the shares, over and above the amount originally subscribed for them, would be an income distribution, and treated in the same way as a payment of a dividend. The net amount received, less the amount originally subscribed, would be grossed up by 100/90 and included in your taxable income.

Alternatively, where the transaction satisfies the conditions set out below, the proceeds are treated as capital proceeds giving rise to a capital gain. Your proposed sale of shares to Mahia Ltd satisfies these conditions and will therefore give rise to a capital gain.
- Mahia Ltd is an unquoted trading company.
- The purchase of shares is for the benefit of the company's trade as the disagreement between you and your sisters is having an adverse effect on the company's trade.
- You are resident and ordinarily resident in the UK.
- You have owned the shares for more than five years.
- You are selling all of your shares such that your holding is reduced by at least 25% and you will own less than 30% of Mahia Ltd following the sale.
- The purchase is not part of a scheme designed to avoid tax.

Advance clearance can be obtained from HM Revenue and Customs, to confirm that the capital treatment applies to a purchase of own shares.

The capital gains tax arising on the sale and the net cash proceeds after tax will be:

	£
Shares sold (40% x 40,000)	16,000
Proceeds (16,000 x £38.60)	617,600
Less: Cost (16,000 x £3.40)	(54,400)
	563,200
Taper relief	
Business asset owned for more than two years – 75% relief	(422,400)
	140,800
Capital gains tax at 40%	56,320
Proceeds after tax (£617,600 – £56,320)	561,280

Tutorial note
Mahia Ltd is a trading company such that its shares are business assets for the purposes of taper relief despite the fact that it owns investments in quoted companies. This is because its non-trading activities are no more than 20% of its overall activities.

(b)   Gift to Tessa

Capital gains tax (CGT)

Maude lives in Canada and is non-UK resident and not-ordinarily resident. In addition, she is not a temporary non-resident for the purposes of capital gains tax as her stay in Canada will be for more than five years.

Accordingly, there will be no UK CGT on the gift of the shares to Tessa.

Even if Maude were a temporary non-resident, there would be no capital gains tax on the gift of the shares as she acquired them after she left the UK.

Inheritance tax (IHT)

As the shares are situated in the UK, UK IHT will be due on any transfers of value concerning them, regardless of the domicile of the transferor. Therefore, we do not need to consider Maude's domicile.

The gift by Maude to Tessa will be a potentially exempt transfer (PET) and no IHT will be payable. In addition, if Maude were to survive seven years from the date of the gift, there would be no IHT to pay on death. However, the question asks us to assume that Maude will die on 31 December 2011. As this date is within seven years of the proposed dates of the gift, there would be a potential liability to IHT on death for each proposed date as follows:

Gift on 1 August 2007

	£
Value of shares before gift (12,000 x £38.60 (50% holding))	463,200
Value of shares after gift (8,000 x £14.40 (33.3% holding))	(115,200)
Fall in value	348,000
No BPR as Maude has not owned the shares for two years	
Annual exemptions for 2007/08 and 2006/07	(6,000)
	342,000
IHT (40% x (£342,000 – £285,000))	22,800
IHT after taper relief (4 to 5 years) (£22,800 x 60%)	13,680

Tutorial Note
On 1 August 2007 Mahia Ltd will have 24,000 issued shares as the shares sold by Claus to the company will have been cancelled.

Double tax relief may be available to reduce this UK liability, in respect of any inheritance taxes payable in Canada.

Gift on 1 June 2008

	£
Fall in value (as above)	348,000
Business property relief (BPR)	
$£348,000 \times \dfrac{£1,605,000 \ (£1,400,000 + £15,000 + £45,000 + £145,000)}{£1,647,000 \ (£1,605,000 + £42,000)}$	(339,126)
	8,874
Marriage exemption	(5,000)
Annual exemptions for 2008/09 and 2007/08 (part only)	(3,874)
	0

Maude should make the gift on 1 June 2008 as this produces a nil IHT liability due to the availability of BPR. This presupposes that Tessa will continue to own the shares or replacement business property up to the date of Maude's death on 31 December 2011, and so preserve the entitlement to BPR.

Stamp duty

As the transfer of shares is made by way of gift, i.e. for no consideration, no stamp duty is payable.

5   (a)   Capital gains tax payable on the sale of the house in Wales

Your taxable capital gain on the sale of the Welsh property will be computed as follows.

	£
Proceeds in August 2007	195,000
Less: Cost (market value as at 1 September 1999)	(145,000)
Enhancement expenditure	(18,000)
	32,000
Taper relief (£32,000 x 75%)	24,000
(non-business asset held for seven years)	
Less: Annual exemption (£8,800 – £1,200)	(7,600)
Taxable capital gain	16,400

Giving the house or part of it to Alice prior to the sale will not reduce the gain as you and Alice are not married. If you make a gift to Alice a capital gain will arise by reference to the market value of the property in exactly the same way as if you had sold the property to an unconnected third party. The gain on such a gift cannot be deferred as the house is not a business asset.

The basic rate band remaining after taxing your income in 2007/08 is as set out below.

When reviewing the computation please note that you do not have any taxable income from Bart Industries Ltd in 2007/08; the payments you received on being made redundant are taxed as follows.
- The payment in lieu of notice of £4,700 is taxed in 2006/07, the year of receipt.
- Statutory redundancy pay is not taxable.
- A non-contractual lump sum up to a maximum of £30,000 is not subject to income tax.

The relocation costs paid by Dreamz Technology Ltd are exempt from income tax up to a maximum of £8,000.

	£
Employment income – Dreamz Technology Ltd	
Salary (£38,500 x 6/12)	19,250
Removal costs (£9,400 – £8,000)	1,400
Dividend income (£7,800 x 10/9)	8,667
	29,317
Less: Personal allowance	(5,035)
Taxable income	24,282
Basic rate band	33,300
Basic rate band remaining	9,018

The computation of your capital gains tax liability is thus:

Capital gains tax:		£
£		
9,018	@ 20%	1,804
7,382	@ 40%	2,953
		4,757

An additional year of taper relief would be available if you were to delay the sale until after 1 September 2007. This would reduce the tax due by £640 (£32,000 x 5% x 40%).

(b)   Inheritance tax due in respect of the house in Wales

Usually, where a gift is made to an individual more than seven years prior to the donor's death, as in the case of your mother's gift of the house to you, there are no inheritance tax (IHT) implications on the death of the donor. However, because your mother continued to live in the house after she gave it to you, the gift will be taxed under the rules applying to 'gifts with reservation of benefit'.

In these circumstances, HM Revenue and Customs will ignore the original gift as, although the asset was gifted, your mother continued to use it as if it were her own. Therefore, the house will be included in your mother's death estate for IHT purposes at its market value at the date of her death, ie £140,000.

(c) Shares in Dreamz Technology Ltd

The income tax treatment of the issue to you of shares in Dreamz Technology Ltd depends on whether the shares are issued via an approved share incentive plan or not.

Where there is no share incentive plan, the market value of the shares received (£2,750) will be taxable as employment income in 2008/09, i.e. the year in which you receive them.

If there is a share incentive plan approved by HM Revenue and Customs then an employer can give shares to its employees, up to a maximum value of £3,000 per employee per year, with no income tax consequences. However, the shares must be kept within the plan for a stipulated period and income tax will be charged if they are withdrawn within five years.

If you withdraw the shares from the plan within three years, income tax will be charged on their value at the time of withdrawal. If you withdraw them more than three years but within five years, income tax will be charged on the lower of their value when you acquired them and their value at the time of withdrawal.

(d) Amount of income tax on dividend income

When you worked for Bart Industries Ltd you were not a higher rate taxpayer as your taxable income was less than £33,300, as set out below. Accordingly, your dividend income was taxed at 10% with a 10% tax credit such that there was no income tax payable.

	£
Employment income (£4,700 x ½ x 12)	28,200
Dividend income (£7,800 x 10/9)	8,667
	36,867
Less Personal allowance	(5,035)
Taxable income	31,832

In 2009/10 your annual salary from Dreamz Technology Ltd less the income tax personal allowance is £33,465 (£38,500 – £5,035). As this exceeds £33,300, all of your dividend income will fall into the higher rate tax band such that it is taxed at 32½% less a 10% tax credit. This gives rise to income tax payable on the dividend income of £1,950 (£8,667 x 22½%).

Date of payment of income tax on dividend income

The tax due in respect of your dividend income must be paid on 31 January after the end of the tax year (i.e. on 31 January 2011 for 2009/10) under self-assessment. You do not have to pay the tax earlier than this by instalments as the amount due is less than 20% of your total annual income tax liability as set out below. The income tax on your employment income from Dreamz Technology Ltd will continue to be collected under the PAYE system.

	£
Taxable employment income (£38,500 – £5,035)	33,465

Income tax:		
£		
2,150	@ 10%	215
31,150	@ 22%	6,853
165	@ 40%	66
Income tax liability on employment income		7,134
Income tax liability on dividend income (£8,667 x 32½%)		2,817
Total annual income tax liability		9,951
Less: PAYE (equal to liability on employment income)		(7,134)
Tax credit on dividend income (£8,667 x 10%)		(867)
Income tax payable via self-assessment		1,950
Threshold for payments by instalments (£9,951 x 20%)		1,990

Tax tables

The following tax rates and allowances are to be used in answering the questions

Income tax

Starting rate	£1 – £2,150	10%
Basic rate	£2,151 – £33,300	22%
Higher rate	£33,301 and above	40%

Personal allowances

	£
Personal allowance	5,035
Personal allowance aged 65 to 74	7,280
Personal allowance aged 75 and over	7,420
Income limit for age-related allowances	20,100

Car benefit percentage

The base level of CO_2 emissions is 140 grams per kilometre.

Car fuel benefit

The base figure for calculating the car fuel benefit is £14,400.

Pension scheme limits

Annual allowance	£215,000
Lifetime allowance	£1,500,000

The maximum contribution that can qualify for tax relief without any earnings is £3,600.

Authorised mileage allowances

All cars:

Up to 10,000 miles	40p
Over 10,000 miles	25p

Capital allowances

	%
Plant and machinery	
Writing down allowance	25
First year allowance – plant and machinery	40
– low emission motor cars (CO_2 emissions of not more than than 120 g/km) (17 April 2002 to 31 March 2008)	100

For small businesses only: the rate of plant and machinery first-year allowance is 50% for the periods from 1 April 2004 to 31 March (6 April 2004 and 5 April 2005 for unincorporated businesses) and 1 April 2006 to 31 March 2007 (6 April 2006 and 5 April 2007 for unincorporated businesses).

Long-life assets

Writing-down allowance	6

Industrial buildings

Industrial buildings Writing-down allowance	4

Corporation tax

Financial year	2004	2005	2006
Starting rate	Nil	Nil	-
Small companies (SC) rate	19%	19%	19%
Full rate	30%	30%	30%
Starting rate lower limit	10,000	10,000	-
Starting rate upper limit	50,000	50,000	-
Lower limit	30,000	300,000	300,000
Upper limit	1,500,000	1,500,000	1,500,000
Marginal relief fraction:			
Starting rate	19/400	19/400	-
Small companies' rate	11/400	11/400	11/400

Marginal relief

$$(M - P) \times I/P \times \text{marginal relief fraction}$$

Value Added Tax

Registration limit	£61,000
Deregistration limit	£59,000

Inheritance tax

First £285,000	Nil
Excess	40%

Capital gains tax: annual exemption

Individuals	£8,800

Capital gains tax: taper relief

The percentage of the gain chargeable is as follows:

Complete years after 5 April 1998 for which asset held	Gains on business assets (%)	Gains on non-business assets (%)
0	100	100
1	50	100
2	25	100
3	25	95
4	25	90
5	25	85
6	25	80
7	25	75
8	25	70
9	25	65
10	25	60

BPP LEARNING MEDIA

National insurance (not contracted-out rates)

		%
Class 1 employee	£1 – £5,035 per year	Nil
	£5,036 – £33,540 per year	11.0
	£33,541 and above per year	1.0
Class 1 employer	£1 – £5,035 per year	Nil
	£5,036 and above per year	12.8
Class 1A		12.8
Class 2	£2.10 per week	
Class 4	£1 – £5,035 per year	Nil
	£5,036 – £33,540 per year	8.0
	£33,541 and above per year	1.0

Rates of Interest

Official rate of interest	5.0%
Rate of interest on underpaid tax	6.5% (assumed)
Rate of interest on overpaid tax	2.25% (assumed)

Stamp Duty and Stamp Duty Land Tax

Ad valorem duty   Rate
Residential property:

£125,000 or less [1]	Nil
£125,001 to £250,000	1%
£250,001 to £500,000	3%
£500,001 or above	4%

[1] for non residential property, the nil rate is extended to £150,000

Shares	0.5%
Fixed duty	£5

Calculations and workings need only be made to the nearest £.

All apportionments may be made to the nearest month.

All workings should be shown.

Review Form & Free Prize Draw – Paper P6 Advanced Taxation (Finance Act 2006) (4/07)

All original review forms from the entire BPP range, completed with genuine comments, will be entered into one of two draws on 31 July 2007 and 31 January 2008. The names on the first four forms picked out on each occasion will be sent a cheque for £50.

Name: _____   Address: _____

_____

_____

How have you used this Kit?
(Tick one box only)

☐ Home study (book only)

☐ On a course: college _____

☐ With 'correspondence' package

☐ Other _____

Why did you decide to purchase this Kit?
(Tick one box only)

☐ Have used the complementary Study text

☐ Have used other BPP products in the past

☐ Recommendation by friend/colleague

☐ Recommendation by a lecturer at college

☐ Saw advertising

☐ Other _____

During the past six months do you recall seeing/receiving any of the following?
(Tick as many boxes as are relevant)

☐ Our advertisement in *Student Accountant*

☐ Our advertisement in *Pass*

☐ Our advertisement in *PQ*

☐ Our brochure with a letter through the post

☐ Our website www.bpp.com

Which (if any) aspects of our advertising do you find useful?
(Tick as many boxes as are relevant)

☐ Prices and publication dates of new editions

☐ Information on product content

☐ Facility to order books off-the-page

☐ None of the above

Which BPP products have you used?

Text	☐	Success CD	☐	Learn Online	☐
Kit	☑	i-Learn	☐	Home Study Package	☐
Passcard	☐	i-Pass	☐	Home Study PLUS	☐

Your ratings, comments and suggestions would be appreciated on the following areas.

	Very useful	Useful	Not useful
Passing ACCA exams	☐	☐	☐
Passing P6	☐	☐	☐
Planning your question practice	☐	☐	☐
Questions	☐	☐	☐
Top Tips etc in answers	☐	☐	☐
Content and structure of answers	☐	☐	☐
'Plan of attack' in mock exams	☐	☐	☐
Mock exam answers			

Overall opinion of this Kit   Excellent ☐   Good ☐   Adequate ☐   Poor ☐

Do you intend to continue using BPP products?   Yes ☐   No ☐

The BPP author of this edition can be e-mailed at: suedexter@bpp.com

Please return this form to: Nick Weller, ACCA Publishing Manager, BPP Learning Media, FREEPOST, London, W12 8BR

Review Form & Free Prize Draw (continued)

TELL US WHAT YOU THINK

Please note any further comments and suggestions/errors below.

Free Prize Draw Rules

1   Closing date for 31 July 2007 draw is 30 June 2007. Closing date for 31 January 2008 draw is 31 December 2007.

2   Restricted to entries with UK and Eire addresses only. BPP employees, their families and business associates are excluded.

3   No purchase necessary. Entry forms are available upon request from BPP Learning Media. No more than one entry per title, per person. Draw restricted to persons aged 16 and over.

4   Winners will be notified by post and receive their cheques not later than 6 weeks after the relevant draw date.

5   The decision of the promoter in all matters is final and binding. No correspondence will be entered into.